THE DESTRUCTIVE POWER OF RELIGION

**Recent Titles in
Contemporary Psychology**

Resilience for Today: Gaining Strength from Adversity
Edith Henderson Grotberg, editor

THE DESTRUCTIVE POWER OF RELIGION

Violence in Judaism, Christianity, and Islam

Volume 2
Religion, Psychology, and Violence

J. Harold Ellens, Editor

Foreword by Martin E. Marty
Ad Testimonium by Archbishop Desmond Tutu

Contemporary Psychology
Chris E. Stout, Series Editor

Westport, Connecticut
London

Library of Congress Cataloging-in-Publication Data

The destructive power of religion : violence in Judaism, Christianity, and Islam / edited by J. Harold Ellens; foreword by Martin E. Marty.

    p. cm.—(Contemporary psychology, ISSN 1546–668X)

  Includes bibliographical references and index.

  ISBN 0–275–97958–X (alk. paper)

  1. Violence—Religious aspects. I. Ellens, J. Harold, 1932– II. Contemporary psychology (Praeger Publishers)

BL65.V55D47 2004

291.1'78—dc21   2003051061

British Library Cataloguing in Publication Data is available.

Library of Congress Catalog Card Number: 2003051061

ISBN: 0–275–97958–X (set)
        0–275–97972–5 (vol. I)
        0–275–97973–3 (vol. II)
        0–275–97974–1 (vol. III)
        0–275–98146–0 (vol. IV)
ISSN: 1546–668X

First published in 2004

Praeger Publishers, 88 Post Road West, Westport, CT 06881
An imprint of Greenwood Publishing Group, Inc.
www.praeger.com

Printed in the United States of America

The paper used in this book complies with the Permanent Paper Standard issued by the National Information Standards Organization (Z39.48–1984).

10   9   8   7   6   5   4   3   2   1

For Debbie, Jackie, Danny, Beckie, Rocky, and Brenda; their quest for faith is heroic; their achievements admirable and profound.

Contents

FOREWORD

"Too bad this set of books is so relevant." That phrase is not a dismissal of, but an advertisement for, this work that will inform and provide perspective for people anywhere who are trying to make sense of the outburst of religiously based violence around the world.

That phrase also echoes the title and theme of the talk, "Too bad we're still relevant!" that I gave at the annual meeting of the American Academy of Arts and Sciences (AARS) in 1996, while closing the books on a six-year, twelve-conference, hundred(s)-scholar, five-volume work, *The Fundamentalism Project*, that the AARS had sponsored between 1988 and 1994.

For more than six years, my associate R. Scott Appleby and I labored with that anxiety, "What if we are irrelevant by the time this is finished?" while we directed the project. My talk included a reminder to the academy that in 1988 they could have chartered all kinds of relevant studies (e.g., U.S.-Soviet Relations in the Twenty-First Century, or Exporting Apartheid from South Africa) that would have been irrelevant by 1996. Since he and I had not asked for the work but had been chosen by the academy, we armed ourselves with yellow highlighters and daily marked the newspaper references that dealt with our subject. We went through many yellow markers, and found the number of references to such hard-line religion increasing.

That report foresaw frustrations and rages of religion-rooted conflict in the new millennium and mentioned that even terrorism would be an instrument of the religiously violent. Still, there were some reasons to hope for a measure of decreased religious conflict, even if it was only to be replaced by other kinds, such as territorial or ethnic conflict, as in Kurdish areas of Turkey or in Rwanda or the former Yugoslavia. Yet all of these conflicts are eclipsed by religious furies and violence.

It is in that context that I help J. Harold Ellens turn this subject over to you who, in libraries, at desks, in classrooms, or at home, are working your way through bafflement over the explosion of violence that grows out of the dark side of religion. "Too bad it's relevant."

Twenty years ago I was blithely teaching American religious history, remarking on the relative tolerance to which we citizens had worn each other down in values and practice. On days off from history, as a former pastor and a theologian-at-the-margins I also found many ways to affirm the healing side of religion. As peers in my generation face the debilitation and death that come with our advanced years, we find ourselves consoling each other with stories about the promises of God the healer. At the same time, many of us have joined forces, professionally, to measure and encourage efforts at employing spiritual means to address issues of health and healing.

We see religion represented through churches, synagogues, and mosques, located cozily next to each other in the alphabets of the Yellow Pages. There are few dead bodies in America as a result of religious conflict. Of course, there were always tensions, bloodless schisms, arguments, and contentions, but the violence related to each has been reasonably held in check.

Then *The Fundamentalism Project* forced me and people with whom I worked to "go global," where we got a very different perspective. Domestically, as we listened to the voice of people who had been victimized or oppressed in the name of religion, we noted how many other words ending in –*press* matched "oppress": repressed, suppressed, and so on, suggesting the negative and destructive roles of religion. We had begun to explore an underside of the presence and power of this force in life and history.

Two days after 9/11 I was scheduled to lecture at the University of Illinois on a theme chosen a year before: "Religion: The Healer that Kills; the Killer that Heals." When the terrorists struck in the name of God in New York, they ensured good crowds for talks like that and gave new impetus for scholars to explore the themes gathered so conveniently in these four books on *The Destructive Power of Religion, Violence in Judaism, Christianity, and Islam.*

I am no newcomer to this field, and I know that most of the authors in these volumes, from biblical scholars to psychoanalysts, have long been at their inquiries. Many of them include just enough autobiography for us to learn that they themselves were often among those who experienced the destructive side of religion. They tell us how they countered it, and some testify to its lasting effects. As I read those chapters, however, I noticed also how often they "kept the faith," pursued the spirit, or stayed with religion, however one wishes to put it, even as they wanted to rein in the destructive forces that issue from it. Professor Ellens himself slips in a word that he thinks characterizes the dimensions of religion that one can affirm: *grace*.

How does one square the study of destruction and the affirmation of construction in this one area of life, religion, as many of the authors undertake to do on these pages? Rousseau once said that readers could expect his thoughts to be consistent with each other, but they could not expect him to express them all at the same time. So here, too, one pictures that when assigned another topic, when placed in the role of the therapist, healer, or pastor, these authors could write essays of note about the constructive side.

But if there is anything consistent in these essays, or, rather, because there is much that is consistent in these essays, it is this coherence that the authors bring to their theme, namely, "it is futile to experience grace or healing so long as":

- People think that all would be peaceful if the whole world turned godless, secular, free of religion.
- Humans live with delusion or illusion about the really destructive aspects of faith and faiths.
- We believe that the dark side of religion is all in the mind, heart, and company of "the other," those people who have the wrong God, the wrong books, the wrong nation in which to live.
- People fail to explore their own scriptures, traditions, and experiences, as they have inherited them from ancestors (e.g., when Christians see *jihad* as the main mark of Islam or when Muslims think *crusades* against infidels are what Christians are all about).
- Humans do not engage in psychological probing of themselves and others, to unearth the tangle of themes and motifs that are destructive when faith or God enters the scene.

The authors of these books are helpful to all who want to effect change in the destructive power of religion. For example, the biblical scholars among them bring to light many destructive stories in scriptures that adherents want to overlook. More and more we learn from these volumes the complex, nether-side of the animating stories of the strangers' faiths. We are compelled here to look at their traditions and sacred scriptures: Qur'an, Torah, New Testament, and more. Too often we read them only in ways that portray an ugliness associated with the other person or company.

Since most writers of these volumes stand in biblical traditions, they take on the stories most would like to overlook: Abraham and Isaac, Jephthah and his daughter, some aspects of God the Father and Jesus the Son relations. They see no way around such texts, and do not offer trivializing pap to give them easy interpretations; but they give us instead tools for interpreting those narratives. These can make us aware and can be liberating.

Psychology plays a very big role in these volumes, in keeping with their auspices and intentions. During the six years of *The Fundamentalism Project*, Dr. Appleby and I, with our board of advisers, jokingly said that we would not let the psychologists in until the third or fourth year. Then we did, and they were very helpful. What we were trying to show the academy and readers around the globe was the fact that there were some irreducibly religious elements in Fundamentalisms.

Of course, religious Fundamentalists think they are *purely* religious; but many scholars in the social sciences "reduced" them: their hard-line views were considered by such scholars to be "nothing but" a reflection of their social class (Marx), or of their relations to their fathers (Freud), or a reflection of their descent from particularly vicious simian strands (Darwin).

In our project we were not able to disprove all that the reducers claimed, and had no motive to do so. *The Fundamentalism Project*, like this one, was to issue new understanding, not new evasion or new apologetic sleights of hand. We simply wanted readers of those books to see, as readers of *The Destructive Power of Religion* should see, the psychological dynamics that are present at the center of all human faith commitments and explanations. One sees much of such connection and illumination in these essays. The introduction of insights from the humanities balances those of social scientists. The religiously committed authors, and those who, at least in their essays, are noncommittal, together with numerous other aspects of these important volumes, help produce a balanced depiction.

What I took away from the chapters, especially, is a sense of the pervasiveness of violence across the spectrum of religions. Not many years ago, celebrated students of myth, or romantic advocates of anything-but-our historic religious traditions, won large enthusiastic audiences for their romantic pictures. *If only* we could get away from Abraham's God, Jesus' Father, and Mother Church's Mary; if only we could move far from Puritan Protestantism with its angry God; if only we left behind Judaism with its Warrior God; if only. . . .

There was great confidence in and propaganda for the notion that we could find refuge in any number of alternatives: gentle, syncretic Hinduism; goddess-rule; mysticism; transcendentalism; animism; Native American thought. However, closer scrutiny showed that only relative distance and the intriguing exoticism of nonconformist alternatives made these other models seem tolerant and gentle. The closer and informed view found violent stories of Hindu-Muslim warfare, tyrannies by what were proposed as the "gentle" human sacrifice, and tribal warfare everywhere. All this is not designed to violate what we are not supposed to violate after reading *The Destructive Power of Religion*, namely, the principle that we are to be self-critical and not irrationally attacking the "other" with finger-pointing. Of course, the "others" *are* in some degree also victims and often perpetrators of the violent and destructive sides of faith.

What goes on, however, as these chapters show, is that there is a dark underside, a nether, shadowed side to every enduring and profound system of symbols and myths, hence to every religion. That may result from deep psychic forces discerned by many of the scholars authoring these volumes. It may result from the realization that the grand myths and stories deal with the wildest and deepest ranges of human aspiration and degradation.

Most of these authors are anything but fatalistic. While there are no utopians here, no idealists who think all will always be well, most of them have a constructive purpose that becomes manifest along the way.

We historians learned from some nineteenth-century giants that we overcome history with history. That is, there is no escape from the world of events and stories and constructions; but we are not doomed to be confined among only violent actions. So with these essays, they make it plain that we are to overcome analysis with analysis, analysis of destruction, which gives insight that can lead to construction. These essays are not preachy: the authors set forth their cases and let readers determine what to do with whatever emerges. I picture a good deal of self-discovery following the discovery of this important work. One hopes that here will be found some glint of discernment that is an expression of—yes, grace!

Martin E. Marty

**Fairfax M. Cone Distinguished Service Professor Emeritus
University of Chicago Divinity School**

Lent 2003

AD TESTIMONIUM

The Destructive Power of Religion is a work of profound research and engaging writing. It is a groundbreaking work with tremendous insight, a set of books that will inform and give perspective to people anywhere trying to make sense of religiously based violence. Professor Ellens has assembled a brilliant stable of insightful and concerned authors to produce four volumes of readable, thoughtful analysis of our present world situation. This contribution will have permanent value for all future research on the crucial matter of religion's destructive power, which has been exercised throughout history, and continues today to give rise to violence in shocking and potentially genocidal dimensions. Future work on this matter will need to begin with this publication. This will become a classic.

Professor Ellens and his team have not produced this important work merely out of theoretical reflection or as viewed from a distant ivory tower. I first met Professor Ellens while he was heavily engaged in psycho-social research in the Republic of South Africa in the 1970s and 1980s, when my country was struggling with some of the worst oppression wreaked upon much of its citizenry by the religiously driven, destructive policies of Apartheid. His comparative studies of educational, health care, and psycho-spiritual resources provided for the black South Africans and the black citizens of the United States were important contributions at a critical time. His orientation is always from the operational perspective, down on the ground where real people live and move and have their being.

In consequence, this massive work is a challenge to those in the professional worlds of psychology, sociology, religion, anthropology, pastoral care, philosophy, biblical studies, and theology. At the same time, it is so highly readable that it will be accessible and downright informative to the layperson or general reader who finds these volumes at the local library. These books are helpful to all who want to effect change in the destructive process in our world, a process too often created or fostered by religious fervor.

It must be noted with equal enthusiasm that the four volumes of *The Destructive Power of Religion* are as urgent in their emphasis upon the positive power—religion's power for healing and redemption of personal and worldwide suffering and perplexity—as they are in boldly setting forth the destructive side. Particularly, the numerous chapters by Professor Ellens, as well as those by Professors Capps, Aden, Wink, Sloat, and others, constantly move us toward the healing perceptions of grace and forgiveness.

Professor Ellens has repeatedly, here and in other works on his long list of publications, called attention to the role redemptive religious power played in the formulation and operation of the Truth and Reconciliation Commission in my country at a time of extreme crisis, thus making possible a thoroughgoing sociopolitical revolution with virtually no bloodshed. He claims, quite correctly, I think, that if it had not been for the pervasive presence of biblical concern and religious fervor in the black, white, and colored populations of our republic at that time, there would have been no way through that sociopolitical thicket without a much greater denigration of the quality of life in our society, and an enormous loss of life itself. I am grateful to him for his insight and his articulation of it for the larger world community. That is typical of the practical approach evident in his work and that of his entire team, which has provided us with this very wise work, *The Destructive Power of Religion*. I commend them unreservedly. I am honored that I have been asked to provide this testimony to the profound importance of these volumes for the world-wide community of those who care.

Archbishop Desmond Tutu
Pentecost 2003

PREFACE

While deeply occupied with the preparation of these volumes, during the Christmas season of 2002, I fell rather inadvertently into a conversation with a young and thoughtful woman, Mollie, who has, consequently, become a genuine friend. Pain prompted our connection; hers, which was more than anyone so young and vital should have to bear, reawakening mine, long, old, deep, soaked in my earliest memories from when I was less than five. Mollie was injured at a tender age and in a manner that made her feel betrayed by God and humankind. My particular personal perplexity started with my mother's frequent illness and absence in my infancy, and was fixed forever in my character and consciousness by the death of my dearest friend on August 3, 1937. Her name was Esther Van Houten, we were both five years old, and we were madly in love. We talked all that summer of starting school together in the fall. We were infinitely joyful. We were gracefully oblivious of the Great Depression in which both our families were caught, and of the lowering clouds of war which would soon take away my older brother and five of hers.

August 3 of that year was a brilliantly sunny day on our remote farmstead southwest of McBain, Michigan. I was standing by the well outside the kitchen window of our farmhouse, vaguely conscious of my mother's image in the window as she prepared my father's mid-morning "lunch." I was thinking of Esther and expected any moment to run across the country road and up the driveway to her yard to while away the morning with her. I heard the screen door of her home slam shut.

My heart leaped, and I looked up anticipating seeing her with her long blond hair and bright blue eyes—like my mother's eyes. There she stood, at the top of the driveway, completely on fire, and she burned to death right there. I helplessly called for my mother, but there was nothing one could do out in that remote place on August 3, in 1937. A sheet of darkness came down on me and did not begin to rise again until I was seven. During those two years, my brother Gordon died, my sister, my dear grandfather, and two neighbor children. Death seemed everywhere. The darkness has never completely gone away.

What connected me with Mollie is our common "case regarding God." It is our common case in that we discovered that we hold it in common and that is how we found each other; but it is also a common case because the longer I live and the more I learn the clearer it is that this is the case every thinking and feeling person has regarding God. It is common among humans to live with this perplexity. The ancient Israelites who gave us their Bible, and with it the heritage Jews, Christians, and Muslims hold in common, formulated the perplexity in the question, "How is God in history, particularly our usually troubled and often wretched history of wickedness, destruction, and death?" How can God promise so much prosperity and security through the prophets and deliver so little safety for faithful, vulnerable, hopeful humans? How can God entice a fourteen-year-old girl into the quest for faith and in that very context fail to protect her from injury and betrayal? God seems perfectly capable of engineering a majestic creation and strategizing its evolution through eons of productive time, but he cannot keep a five-year-old girl from death by fire? I spent my entire life, from age seven on, devoted to a single course toward, into, and in the ministry of theology and psychology, confidently trying to recover the trust that God, in a prosperous providence, would embrace my children and carefully shepherd them into health, wisdom, safety, and success; in the faith, in fruitful marriages, in joyful parenting, and in the fulfillments of love. I entrusted my children to God's care while I was busy "doing the work of God's Kingdom." I did my side of the "bargain" very well. God did not do as well on his side of the equation.

All this has caused me to work very hard to rethink my entire notion of God, and especially my theology of sacred scriptures. I do not see how any honest and honorable person can get through an entire lifetime without being forced to do this very same thing, forced by what has always been the ordinary horror and daily trauma of life, personal and universal. Unless one is able to see the unsacred in sacred scriptures, what can the sacred mean? Unless one has a comprehensive way to come to terms with the horror of life, how can celebration of the gracious be anything but psycho-spiritual denial? There can be no question that the God of the Hebrew Bible, and the God who is reported to have killed Jesus because, after getting ticked off at the human race, he could not get his head screwed on right again unless he killed us or somebody else, is abusive in the extreme. To salvage a God of grace out of that requires some reworking of the traditional Judaic, Christian, and Muslim theologies of sacred scripture. The difficulty that prevents us from writing God off completely and permanently is the fact that both the Old Testament and the New Testament, as well as the Qur'an, have woven through the center of their literary stream a more central message as well. The notion, unique in all human religions, that Abraham seems to have discovered, which is so redemptive in these sacred scriptures, is the claim that the real God is a God of unconditional grace—the only thing that works in life, for God or for humans. The human heartache is universal. The perplexity pervades everything in life. The question is, "Is there any warrant that the claims for grace do too?"

I do not feel like the Lone Ranger in this matter. Of course, there is Mollie's case, but everyone who has been around for a while knows a long list of the Mollies in this world. I have sat in my psychotherapist and pastoral counselor chairs for 40 years and have noticed that this is the "case regarding God" that perplexes most thoughtful and informed people; and most have been afraid to say it aloud, or have had no good opportunity to do so. Mollie said it aloud to me and immediately I recognized the sound of it. It is our common human story. It has ever been so, since reflective humans first opened wondering eyes upon this planet. Many years ago Barbara Mertz wrote a telling book about ancient Egypt. She called it, *Red Land, Black Land.*[1] She noted that we cannot speak of those mysterious days and people of so long ago without being awed by their way of dying and their funerals. They recorded them grandly in their even grander tombs. It is a simple story, the same as ours; a story in Mertz's sensitive words, "of our common human terror and our common hope."

The Destructive Power of Religion, Violence in Judaism, Christianity, and Islam, is a work in four volumes about our common human terror and our common hope. I hope you will find it stirring, disturbing, and hopeful.

J. Harold Ellens
Epiphany 2003

Note

1. New York: Dell Publishing, 1966, 367.

ACKNOWLEDGMENTS

Dr. Chris Stout invited me to write a chapter in his earlier, remarkably important four-volume set, *The Psychology of Terrorism*. I was pleased to do so, and we published my chapter there under the title "Psychological Legitimization of Violence by Religious Archetypes." Debbie Carvalko, acquisitions editor at Greenwood Press, found the chapter valuable and asked me to expand it by editing a work, which I have titled *The Destructive Power of Religion*. Thus, these four volumes were thoughtfully conceived and wisely midwifed. The birth is timely, since it seems everywhere evident that the world needs these reflections just now, more than ever. I wish, therefore, to acknowledge with honor and gratitude, Debbie's kind proficiency and Chris' professional esteem. I wish, as well, to thank the 30 authors who joined me in creating this work. I wish to express my gratitude to Beverley Adams for her meticulous work in reading the proofs of these volumes, while I was too ill to do so.

CHAPTER 1

Introduction: The Interface of Religion, Psychology, and Violence

J. Harold Ellens

Introduction

Religion is serviced directly by two scientific disciplines: theology and psychology. The former, whether Biblical Theology or Philosophical Theology, serves religion by explaining the written documents of its sacred scriptures. Psychology serves religion by explaining the nature and function of "living human documents" (Gerkin, 1984). Therefore, the relationship between the disciplines of Psychology and Theology is crucial. I have spent my professional lifetime on the exploration of the interface between psychology and theology with the purpose of discerning the manner in which they illumine each other and help us understand the nature of persons, culture, and religion.

Psychology and Theology, as discreet disciplines, are, in an equivalent sense, both sciences through which it is possible and necessary to discern the world of reality. They are windows through which to see and understand the nature and warrants of religion, as well as to perceive its subterfuges and destructive forces. Both are essential scientific lenses through which the world of divine and human reality may be discovered. Therefore, no one can claim to be serious about his or her scientific endeavors in these two fields without illumining psychological models and perspectives with the scientific insights of theology, and illumining theological models and perspectives with the scientific information of psychology. Any

Celebration of the Psychological Department of Clark University in 1909 (Jung, William James, Freud, etc.). Library of Congress.

assessment of the nature and function of religion in human affairs that does not take seriously both of these disciplines, as scientific lenses through which "to read God's thoughts after him," is not a serious endeavor.

For Judaism, Christianity, and Islam, the scientific underpinnings of theology, such as sacred text interpretation, namely, text analysis, linguistic studies, cultural data, literary-historical evaluations, archaeological investigations, and philosophical reflections, are crucial to understanding the roots of these religions. Such analysis and interpretation of the roots and grounds of religion are an enterprise upon which all the tools of human inquiry must be brought to bear in order to distill from sacred texts and their history the full range of the cognitive and affective import that the texts offer the inquirer.

Exposition

A half century ago the Christian Association for Psychological Studies (CAPS) was established with the intent that the Christian community should explore in a systematic way the relationship between religion and our personal and communal state of health. The assumption behind that concern was the conviction that the interface between our psychological states and our religious posture has much to do with the well-being of persons and society. Moreover, it became clear from the kinds of papers that were read at CAPS convocations that frequently the nature of our personal religion or spirituality, and the theological constructions it produces, creates or expands psychopathology and social dysfunction.

There was a corollary implication at the center of this quest for understanding the interface of psychology and religion. It was the notion that if we could understand how religious faith interfaces with human health, religion with psychology, we would also see, conversely, how the psychological insights we have about the dynamics of human health and illness might illumine the messages in sacred scriptures, and contribute to shaping responsible religion. That was a fruitful set of objectives that has become the focus of inquiry for a wide world of scholarship today. A similar professional endeavor was initiated by Wayne Rollins about twelve years ago, in the form of a Psychology and Biblical Studies Seminar, to be held annually as part of the convocation of the Society of Biblical Literature (SBL). It was the quest, represented by these two professional scientific enterprises that has occupied my entire professional career.

The work of William James provided a useful framework for the kind of science we were seeking to do. Whether one worked in his light or countered his notions, he was the unavoidable rock to which one anchored or on which one was honed to a finer edge. Religion is a psycho-spiritual practice that has a cultural character and cultic expression. It is a sociological process as well as an expression of a worldview. Both psychology and religion are the proper objects of scientific research. Each has its own universe of discourse, paradigms, arena of inquiry, database, and objectives within the framework of scientific inquiry. Each has its own forming and informing history. What we have sought in this scientific quest to understand the relationship between psychology and religion is their mutual illumination of each other.

Unfortunately, there is today in Judaism, Christianity, and Islam a large and growing community of "true believers" who would split the world of scientific inquiry from the world of religious faith and practice. Such believers are Fundamentalist in theology, literalist in interpretation of their sacred scriptures, and traditionalist in their application of this rigid and aggressive form of religious practice to the operations of daily life. They split the inquiry into the nature of this material world from the inquiry into the nature of the transcendental or spiritual world. They hold the notion that the revelation regarding the nature of God evident in creation is different in value from that of their sacred scriptures. They also tend to claim that what we see through religion and what we see through psychology are two radically different realms of reality, namely the world of the natural and of the supernatural, which cannot be made to illumine each other.

Religion and psychology stand legitimately on their own foundations, and read carefully are two equivalent sources of illumining truth. Speaking religiously, they are two equivalent sources of God's self-revelation in nature and in sacred scriptures. Conversely, speaking psychologically, they are two equivalent subjects of scientific study, assessment, and description. This is true in Judaism, Christianity, and Islam. Psychology and Theology are not alien in any inherent sense. When they seem at odds, paradoxical, disparate in some way, it must always be because of a dysfunction on one of two counts. Either we have failed to do the scientific inquiry well enough to really understand the religion or the psychology, or we have drawn erroneous conclusions and not allowed each of the disciplines to illumine the other adequately.

Wherever truth is found it is truth, having equal warrant with all other truth. Some truth may have greater weight than other truth in a specific situation, but there is no difference in its warrant or valence as *truth* (Ellens, 1982, 24). If you have just been hit by a car and are bleeding from the jugular, the truth about blood pressure and arterial closure may be significantly more important at that moment than any religious truth. There are undoubtedly other circumstances in which religious truth may be more important than the truth about blood pressure. In any case, truth is truth, regardless who finds it, where, how, or in what form.

The criterion of effectiveness in the mutual illumination of psychology and religion is not the effectiveness with which our psychological insights fit in with our theological worldview or our theological insights fit in with our psychological worldview. Rather, it has to do with whether psychology and religion make discernible claims upon each other that force a modification of one by the other or make them more understandable. It has to do with the way in which religion resolves problems in the internal coherence of psychology; or how psychological data and insights illumine a sacred scripture. The Natural and Social Sciences must inquire, finally, of religion, and religion must listen and commune with the Natural and Social Sciences in order to make sense of itself.

This is particularly true as the world moves further past the tragedy of September 11, 2001, and into the recognition of how directly Fundamentalist religion, and its ethical and theological structures, is tied to the monstrous human potential for violence. Not only are al Qaeda driven by that kind of wretched religion, but so are the adherents of those forms of Christianity that promote violent Zionism as a strategy for precipitating a world cataclysm, purportedly to bring history to its consummation and force the onset of a messianic world order. Similar religion-driven violence characterizes such Christian movements as those that violently ravage abortion clinics and kill those who work there, though I agree with the concern to question the appropriateness of abortion, in any case. Jewish supporters of preemptive defense and Palestinian suicide bombers are equivalent examples of the intimate connection between certain forms of religion, possessed of a pathological Fundamentalist psychology, and violence.

When psychology and religion are split off from each other they cannot illumine each other with their crucial health-affording insights. Then sick religion shapes pathological psychology and wreaks violent havoc upon the social order. Little argument is required these days to carry this case. The reality of it is everywhere thrust upon us. This present volume of *The Destructive Power of Religion*, which we have titled *Religion, Psychology, and Violence*, addresses in detail how destructive the forces of pathological psychology and sick religion can become. Fifteen seasoned scholars from continental Europe, Latin America, and the United States have joined forces to present this multifaceted but carefully focused volume.

A continuing struggle to understand and employ the potentials of healthy psychology and religion for mutual illumination is imperative for at least two concrete reasons. First, it is becoming increasingly clear, clinically, that a very large portion of the destructive forces humans set in motion against each other, at the individual and societal or national level, derive from genetic or biochemical sources. That correlates with the recent evidence of very high percentages of prison inmates falling into the category of borderline psychotics. When that factor is combined with the government statistics on the relative ineffectiveness of its costly prison rehabilitation programs and attempts to train the so-called hard-core unemployed, one is forced to ask to what extent these latter conditions are driven by the former. Moreover, there seems to be a significant correlation between the psychological patterns in Fundamentalist religion and the attraction of psychopathological persons to it.

As we are faced with the significant correlation between biochemically based psychopathology and the limits of such persons' potential for rehabilitation or social function, on the one hand, and the inclination for such pathological persons to congregate around Fundamentalist religious systems, on the other, we are faced with an enormous religious and psychological problem. The religious problem is the classical problem of determinism, namely, the extent to which such pathological persons are unable to exercise the personal freedom to choose sane courses of action. The ethical problem is that of whether the state or some external entity such as the medical profession can or should take responsibility for compelling medication of such pathological persons so as to render them amenable to rehabilitation and social function, for their own good and that of society. Thus, it is clear that religion and psychology are thrown inextricably together in these applied operations.

It is possible today to bring the insights and models of psychology to bear upon sacred scriptures and upon the persons who wrote them and the characters presented in them, assessing the nature and function of the author, of the intended audience, of the real audiences in the history of the sacred texts, together with their interpretations, and thus assess the reasons, healthy or pathological, for the constructs that were expressed in the sacred texts and in subsequent uses made of them. That is to say, in addition to all the other text-critical tools mentioned early in this chapter, which are legitimately applied to the texts of sacred scriptures, surely we must apply the paradigms for understanding how humans function, what they tend to say, why they say what they say, the way they say it, and what these messages mean as seen through standardized psychological paradigms. Scholarship in the sacred scriptures of Judaism and Christianity has gone much further along this road than the scholarship addressing the sacred scriptures of Islam. Considering the nature of the human mind and personality, it is imperative to recognize that the mutual illumination of all scientific disciplines is essential to a full-orbed and honest achievement in any of them (Jaki, 1984; Schuurman, 1980).

Finally, it is imperative to note that violence is bred in our Western societies, not only by the bizarre theological and ethical constructs of specific Fundamentalist groups in the Western religious worlds of Judaism, Christianity, and Islam. As I indicated in the introductory chapter to the first volume of this series, violence is endemic throughout all aspects of the Western and Near Eastern world because of the long-standing and pervasive influence of the essential religious metaphor of cosmic conflict, present for the last three millennia in these religions and cultures, shaped as they were by ancient Israelite religion. Even the rather thoroughly secularized world of Europe and America, which has long since lost its conscious memory of Judeo-Christian roots, is still shaped by the unconscious psychological archetypes produced by the ancient Israelite religious metaphor. Both the religious and secular communities of the Western and Near Eastern worlds operate with the internal model that history is the battleground of a cosmic war between God and the Devil, good and evil. This warfare is waged in the sociopolitical arena and on the battlefield of the human heart. It is expected to continue until some final solution is found. It remains to be seen, according to this worldview, whether good or evil will triumph in human history. In any case, an unconscious longing to have done with this soul-wearying and world-wasting conflict increasingly drives a death wish for some kind of cosmic cataclysm, the relief and release of the final Armageddon.

Such unconscious ideation readily becomes a self-fulfilling prophecy, as in the lives of the terrorists of September 11, 2001, suicide bombers, and designers of preemptive defense. However, the problem is infinitely more extensive. If you remember the very popular *Rocky* series of Hollywood productions, or the *Rambo* series, you will recall that a highly individualized form of this cosmic conflict shaped the plot and story line of each movie. More recently, the almost addictive social attraction to *The Lord of the Rings, Harry Potter*, and similar lesser features, in literature and film, plays out the same metaphoric psychological process: the quest for final cataclysmic solutions in a world that is caught in a transcendental cosmic conflict.

Moreover, one need only stop for a half hour in any game machine arcade in the Americas or Europe, Japan or Australia, South Africa or any other culture influenced by Western social values, to notice the glassy-eyed addiction of young people to acting out symbolic murder scenes and extermination of entire groups of persons, as well as massive property structures, in the most extreme forms of violence in the virtual reality of those machines. One can see and hear the offensive animalist gestures and sounds of glee and satisfaction expressed by these young people as they create, in that virtual world, the abuse, destruction, conflagrations, and termination of people and things for which some dark archetype in their infected souls longs.

Conclusion

Harold Kushner was infinitely closer to divine and human reality when he wrote his illuminating book *When Bad Things Happen to Good People*. The implication of his thesis is the grace-filled suggestion that this world is not an arena of cosmic evil and good, but a rather flat-footed pilgrimage of human quest for growth, fulfillment, and goodness. The presence of God in this world of human experience is, as intimated by the bright side of the biblical narrative, a congenial and forgiving presence. The problem of human suffering in a world with a good God and no cosmic evil force can be accounted for readily by two facts. The first is that God put us in charge of this world, as the ancient Hebrew writer perceived when he or she penned the cultural mandate in the first creation story. Genesis 1:28 describes God as saying, "You be fruitful and multiply and replenish the earth, and have dominion over it. . . ." By this act of delegating both responsibility and authority to us, God ties his own hands. If you delegate these prerogatives to your subordinates or children, you cannot continue to thrust in your hand daily or weekly to straighten things out or micromanage.

Second, it is Kushner's view that God created this world as an arena of freedom, from the subatomic-particle level to the cell level to the mammal level to the level of the human will. Within that arena of freedom, God so thoroughly respects the cause-and-effect dynamics of history and the developmental dynamics of human personality that he will not violate our choices and their consequences. If we do not resolve the problems of life and history, God cannot do so. We are his agents. It is a divine-size task and we have only human resources, so there will be bad choices, inadequate efforts, limited effectiveness, and the pain of growth, change, and loss. We can imagine a perfect world but we can only create an imperfect one, so we experience the grief-loss of that disparity. We call the shortfall evil, but that is too heavy a word for it. It is human error, but as Martin Luther is said to have remarked, "Sin boldly," for we live in a matrix of divine forgiving grace.

However, this perspective of grace has been eclipsed for 3,000 years by the metaphor of cosmic conflict, with the divine violence that metaphor models and the human violence that metaphor induces. If that metaphor had any reality in it, there would be some justification for this monstrous misdirection of religion and culture during these three millennia. However, there is no evidence for a force of cosmic evil. There is no place for that notion in a world of a God of radical, unconditional, and universal grace. There is no empirical data to suggest such a mischievous metaphor or worldview. There is no hypothesis that could function more poorly in accounting for the problem of pain than this immensely destructive psycho-spiritual subterfuge. Instead of the worldview of grace and growth through which religious metaphors would create subconscious psychological archetypes of decency, gentleness, and mutuality, we have a worldview of paranoia, conflict, violence, and alienation. Everywhere in the societies of the Western and Near Eastern world this is evident; in every nook and cranny of our social process and psychological states, this mindset reigns. This volume of fourteen learned and articulate chapters explores that tragic state of affairs.

References

Aden, L., Benner, D. G., & Ellens, J. H. (Eds.) (1992). *Christian perspectives on human development.* Grand Rapids: Baker.

Aden, L., & Ellens, J. H. (Eds.) (1998). *The Church and pastoral care.* Grand Rapids: Baker.

Cobb, J. B., Jr. (1969). *God and the world.* Philadelphia: Westminster.

Cobb, J. B., Jr. (1982). *Process theology as political theology.* Manchester: Manchester University Press.

Cobb, J. B., Jr., & Gamwell, F. I. (1984). *Existence and actuality, conversations with Charles Hartshorne.* Chicago: University of Chicago Press.

Cobb, J. B., Jr., & Griffin, D. R. (1976). *Process theology, an introductory exposition.* Philadelphia: Westminster.

Ellens, J. H. (1987). Biblical themes in psychological theory and practice. In D. G. Benner (Ed.), *Christian counseling and psychotherapy.* Grand Rapids: Baker.

Ellens, J. H. (1989). A psychospiritual view of sin and sickness: The nature of human failure. In L. Aden & D. G. Benner (Eds.), *Counseling and the human predicament, a study of sin, guilt, and forgiveness.* Grand Rapids: Baker.

Ellens, J. H. (1982). *God's grace and human health.* Nashville: Abingdon.

Gerkin, C. V. (1984). *The living human document.* Nashville: Abingdon.

Jackson, S. M., & Gilmore, G. W. (Eds.). (1950). *The new Schaff-Herzog encyclopedia of religious knowledge* (Vol. II). Grand Rapids: Baker.

Jaki, S. L. (1978). *The road of science and the ways of God.* Chicago: University of Chicago Press.

Jaki, S. L. (1984). *Cosmos and creator.* Chicago: University of Chicago Press.

Kushner, H. (1981). *When bad things happen to good people.* New York: Schoken Books.

Miles, J. (1995). *God, a biography.* New York: Knopf.

Schuurman, E. (1980). *Reflections of the technological society.* Toronto: Wedge.

Schuurman, E. (1980). *Technology and the future: A philosophical challenge.* New York: Radix.

Tracy, D., & Cobb, J. B., Jr. (1983). *Talking about God, doing theology in the context of modern pluralism.* New York: Seabury.

Wolterstorff, N. (1976). *Religion within the bounds of reason.* Grand Rapids: Eerdmans.

CHAPTER 2

VIOLENT RELIGION: RENÉ GIRARD'S THEORY OF CULTURE

Mack C. Stirling

Introduction

René Girard (1923–), a recently retired professor of French language and civilization at Stanford University, has developed a wide-ranging theory of human culture. Girard derived his ideas from intensive study of the major texts of the Western cultural tradition, especially in the fields of literature, anthropology, psychology, and biblical studies. His theory addresses the nature of human desire and the relationship of desire to violence. Girard postulates that human culture, including archaic religion, originated in communal or collective violence. Archaic religion with ritual sacrifice functioned to perpetuate and maintain culture. Archaic religion therefore arises from *originary* communal violence and, in turn, uses carefully controlled collective violence (ritual sacrifice) to vent hostility and prevent widespread individual violence, with its potential to destroy the community. Although formal religious ritual sacrifice plays an extremely minimal role in modern culture, the ideation, language, and social structures of our violent origins are still very much with us, though commonly unrecognized. Humans are disposed toward self-justifying and self-differentiating violence, often done in the name of God.

Much of Girard's work has been dedicated to elucidating the relationship between his model of culture and biblical revelation, including the role of Christ. Girard maintains that the Bible both confirms his insights and facilitates extension of their implications. Girardian theory thus has implications for biblical hermeneutics as well as for a broad range of human studies. Detractors have objected that Girard's theory is too simple to be useful, too ambitious to be valid, too "Christian" to be academically respectable, or too demeaning of humankind to be acceptable. Advocates see it as the basis for a potentially unifying science of human culture, much as Darwin's theory of evolution unified the field of biology.

Exposition

The purpose of this chapter is to describe and illustrate the cultural theory of René Girard. I will do this in three parts. First, I will present Girard's theory of human relations; second, his theory of cultural origins; and third, Girard's perspective on biblical revelation. I will use the books of René Girard, himself, and several of his major interpreters. Criticism and defense of Girard's model are largely beyond the scope of this introduction, as are substantive descriptions of Girard's relationship to other important theories of the past 150 years.

Theory of Human Relations

Mimetic Desire

Fundamental to the thought of Girard is his concept of mimetic desire. Indeed, his theory is sometimes called the *mimetic theory* (Girard, 1996b, 7).

Girard proposes that all humans learn their desires from other people in the culture around them by imitation or copying. Furthermore, this imitated desire is accompanied by an acquisitive drive to possess what the *other* has. The imitated (learned) desire coupled with the acquisitive drive is what Girard terms *mimetic desire.* He developed this concept of desire from study of the novels of Cervantes, Stendhal, Flaubert, Proust, and Dostoyevsky. The development of this insight is detailed in *Deceit, Desire and the Novel* (Girard, 1996a). Mimetic desire is well illustrated in Cervantes's novel, *Don Quixote.* Don Quixote conceives his passion to set out on a quest from his reading about the legendary exploits of Amadis the Gaul, which he subsequently imitates.

Humans desire things because others have them. In other words, they desire objects because of the influence of others. It is the pos-

Don Quixote and other characters from Cervantes' story, engravings by Michael van der Gucht. Library of Congress.

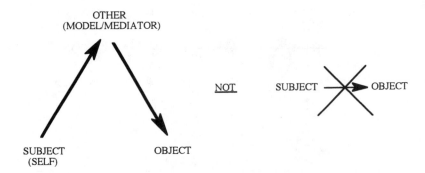

Figure 2.1 The Triangular Structure of Desire

session of an object by the other that creates its perceived value and sets the stage for impassioned desire of the object by the desiring subject. Thus, the fundamental structure of desire is triangular (see Figure 2.1). The subject copies or imitates the desire of the other (*model* or *mediator*) for an object. This is sharply contrasted with a linear concept of desire wherein the subject directly and spontaneously desires an object for its own sake. Rather, other humans mediate our desires:

> ... desire, is not directed towards an original or privileged object. This is a primary and fundamental difference from Freud. Desire chooses its objects through the mediation of a model. It is a desire modeled on the other, yet identical with the intense yearning to reduce everything to oneself.... The model designates the desirable object by desiring it himself. Desire is always mimetic of another desire ... (Girard as cited in Schwager, 1987, 9)

Mimetic desire results from and reflects a general human mimetic capacity, namely, the ability to learn. We learn virtually everything, including language, from others. This powerful ability to learn from others is, of course, one of the fundamental differences between humans and animals. Mimetic capacity is a necessary prerequisite for *hominization*. Mimetic capacity and its *sequelum*, mimetic desire, are inherently morally neutral but defining properties of all humans. Without mimetic capacity, we could learn nothing, either good or evil.

Girard does distinguish between physiological needs and mimetic desire. Every person needs water, food, and shelter from the elements. Sex drive appears to have a physiological basis. Mimetic desire does not generate these basic needs. It is rather in the fulfillment of these needs that mimetic desire comes to play a major role. What type of clothing? Which sexual partner? Which kind of house? In answering these questions, we take our lead from the culture around us, learning to desire things because their possession by others gives them value in our eyes. This is the fundamental premise of advertising and marketing. Mimesis generates passionately experienced *perceived* needs.

Gil Bailie (1995, 116–118) illustrates mimetic desire with the example of the childhood nursery. He asks us to imagine a nursery replete with a selection of toys. One child enters and exhibits only a casual interest in the nearest toy. A second enters the nursery. Eventually a time comes when the second child chooses a toy. It is then, and only then, that the first child suddenly realizes that the toy chosen by the second child was the very one he really wanted all along! The selection of a toy by the second child informs and inflames the desire of the first.

The structure of mimetic desire is clearly evident in the Garden of Eden story from Genesis 2–3 (Bailie, 1995, 137–138). God commands Adam and Eve not to eat of the fruit of the tree of knowledge of good and evil, lest they die. They do not, until the serpent appears and tempts Eve. The serpent leads Eve to the issue of the forbidden fruit and contradicts God's warning about death. He then says, "For God knows that when you eat of it your eyes will be opened, and you will be like God" (Gen. 3:5 NIV). The serpent thus insinuates that God is a rival of man. Only then, imitating the serpent's own rivalry of God, does Eve see "that the fruit of the tree [is] good for food and pleasing to the eye, and also desirable for gaining wisdom" (Gen. 3:6). She partakes of the fruit. Thus, the serpent mediates for Eve his rivalry with God, which Eve then learns to desire.

Romantic love also illustrates triangular mimetic desire (Girard, 1996a, 96–112). Classically, there are two overlapping triangles involved, one with the boy as subject and one with the girl as subject. I will consider the boy as subject. The object is the girl's body. The social group at large mediates what kind of girl is desirable. The girl (model) reflects this, as she values her own body. The subject's (boy's) indicated desire for the girl's body increases its value still more in her (model's) eyes as she absorbs the boy's desire for her. She then reflects this to the subject, making herself still more desirable to him. And so it goes in an increasing crescendo of mimetic desire. She is on the way to becoming a "goddess" in the boy's eyes and in her own. If the girl is also involved as subject with the same boy as model/mediator, sparks will truly fly. No wonder lovers see each other as god and goddess until the romantic bubble bursts!

Girard's concept of desire contrasts significantly with that of Freud. For Freud, desire is primarily sexual and linear. Freud's idea is epitomized by the Oedipus complex. Here, the son has a primary spontaneous sexual desire for the mother and then secondarily comes in conflict with the father. For Girard, desire is not primarily sexual, nor is the Oedipal complex fundamental to human interaction. This is not to say that the Oedipal syndrome does not occur, but rather that it results from the son imitating the father's sexual desire for his mother.

The Self and the Other

As a logical corollary to his concept of mimetic desire, Girard (1987a, 284–430) maintains that we construct our very identities through the eyes of others. We become what we choose to take into ourselves from our mimesis of other humans. In other words, the human self, or psyche, exists only in, and because of, relationships. Girard terms this way of looking at human psychology *interdividual psychology*.

Although Girard affirms that humans possess a desire for being, he clearly rejects the Romantic idea of a purely autonomous self with independently conceived desire:

> Once his basic needs are satisfied (indeed, sometimes even before), man is subject to intense desires, though he may not know precisely for what. The reason is that he desires being, something he himself lacks and which some other person seems to possess. The subject thus looks to that other person to inform him of what he should desire in order to acquire that being. If the model, who is apparently already endowed with superior being, desires some object, that object must surely be capable of conferring an even greater plenitude of being. (Girard, 1977, 146)

We imitate those whom we perceive to possess a greater aspect of being than ourselves. We become whom we imitate. A person who claims to be independent and autonomous is deluded. Even a person who consciously rejects the mores and mindset of his culture or social group is reacting against the group and therefore dependent on it. Instead of becoming a positive image of the other, such a person becomes a negative image of the other.

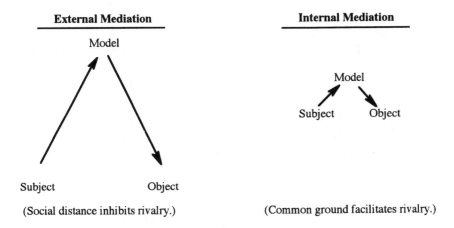

Figure 2.2 External versus Internal Mediation

With respect to the models we imitate, Girard (1996a, 9) distinguishes between what he terms *external mediation* and *internal mediation*. External mediation exists when the subject and model are distant from one another in a sociocultural or economic perspective. The very distance between the two precludes or inhibits rivalry. Don Quixote, for example, could not enter into meaningful rivalry with the fictional Amadis. Likewise, there is never a hint of rivalry between Don Quixote and his loyal servant, Sancho Panza. Similarly, in the Middle Ages a king would have been an external mediator for a peasant, given the immense social distance between them.

Internal mediation, on the other hand, is present when the subject and model are close socioculturally (see Figure 2.2) Consider an assistant professor of cardiothoracic surgery and a resident in training under him. The only things separating them are social convention and a few years, or surgical cases, of experience. The resident (subject) is in a very real sense in the process of becoming the attending (model). As the surgical skills of the resident approach or threaten to exceed those of the attending resident, the potential for rivalrous conflict becomes acute.

Mimetic Rivalry

After a subject has learned to desire an object from a model/mediator, conflict can easily result. Conflict requires only that the desired object(s) be limited and that the subject and model occupy common ground (internal mediation). The model who possesses the desired object, thus giving it its value, is at first admired, even idolized, by the subject for his apparent possession of greater being. However, the model often desires the very adulation which the subject has for him. This adulation by the subject, after all, imbues the model with a greater sense of being. He, therefore, quite naturally acts in some way to impede the subject's acquisition of the object. This obstruction has several effects. It serves to increase the value of the object in the eyes of the desiring subject. This, in turn, increases the value of the object for the possessing model. The crescendo of mutually inflamed desire results.

This process puts the subject into a *mimetic double bind*. On the one hand, the model seems to say, "desire this object." On the other hand, he says, "you can't have this object." This double bind in the mind of the subject leads to resentment of the admired model. The friend is becoming an enemy. The subject blames and resents the resisting model for the diminished sense of being he experiences as a result of seeing himself through the model's eyes. The model, who has shown him what he lacks, prevents him from obtaining it. Since we all imitate models, mimetic rivalry is a nearly ubiquitous feature of human relations.

Schwager (1987) perceptively describes the thoughts and passions of two protagonists trapped in mimetic rivalry and demonstrates the fundamental connection between violence and desire:

> Since rivalry originates in the good and the apparently praiseworthy imitation of a model, the first resistance of the model is always surprising and painful for the disciple. Not recognizing the nascent rivalry, the disciple is hurt and does not understand the admired idol's behavior. The model considers the aspirations of the disciple uncontrolled and ungrateful. If the excitement increases, it renders the two protagonists quite blind towards their own action. Each thinks the other has lost his or her head. Both feel not only hurt but also compelled to take counteractions. Since human behavior is always complex and ambiguous, the passion-clouded look at the past behavior of the model or disciple who has now become the enemy will, with instinctive certainty, find actions to prove that the other has had bad intentions right from the beginning. The impression of injustice suffered takes deep root within one, and the conviction grows that counteractions are justified, even necessary. (17)

A critical feature of mimetic rivalry is that each protagonist blames the other for the conflict.

The pattern of perceived justified action and counteraction, so well described by Schwager, seems to account for the seemingly universal human fixation on reciprocity or retribution. We constantly act and think in terms of what we perceive to be a fair exchange. At the same time, agreement on what constitutes a fair exchange is virtually impossible given the impassioned partisan thinking resulting from mimetic rivalry. There is a strong tendency to overreact. Each person tends to see the anger, offense, and overreaction of the other and not of himself. Reciprocal violence arises from this distorted concept of retribution for wrongs the other seems to have committed against oneself.

Mimetic rivalry thus naturally escalates. Trivial causes or conflicts are magnified by ever more passionate interchanges between model and subject into huge problems. As this happens, desire, which at first only imitated another's desire for an object or status or perceived good, progressively loses sight of the original object and becomes fixed on the other person. Desire becomes inextricably linked to the *necessary* different other. The original desired object is lost. Instead of the object being rendered precious by the other's desire, the other's desire has become the precious entity (Schwager, 1987, 12). Desire has then lost any moorings it had in reality and has become transformed, fixating itself on distorted perceptions and imaginations of the other. Girard (1996a, 83–95) calls this transformed desire *metaphysical desire*. One object is easily exchanged for another at this point in the quest for metaphysical competition. Metaphysical desire stands at the threshold of psychopathology (Girard, 1987a, 296–297).

As the subject becomes chained to the model by desire in conflictual mimesis, the rivalry becomes consuming. Time and energy better spent in a constructive fashion become invested in the rivalry, spent in metaphysical projections and retaliations. This advanced state of unresolved mimetic rivalry captures the subject to the extent that he structures his life around the rivalry. Girard terms this state *scandal* (Girard, 1987a, 416; Hamerton-Kelly, 1994, 95–96). The subject is obsessed with equaling or surpassing the model. Paradoxically, at the same time, the subject needs the model, which he will lose if he surpasses him. Thus, the subject becomes possessed by irreconcilable contradictions, which cause him to "stumble" over the model. The model is both attacked and supported, both loved and hated, both admired and resented. The model has become both the subject's idolatrous god and his devil. Scandal is inherently unstable because of its intensity. It is ripe for resolution by violence or the outbreak of psychopathology.

Two rivals locked into intense mimetic conflict imitate each other's words, gestures, and actions. As a result, they come to resemble each other more and more, becoming *doubles* of each other (Girard, 2001). All angry humans resemble one another. As James Williams (1992) notes, "The doubles are alike but they mistakenly see a great difference between them[selves]" (Williams as cited in Girard, 2001, 22, n. 2). *Violence erases difference* and makes people more alike.

Girard (1977, 44–45) illustrates doubling by referring to the duel between Eteocles and Polynices in Euripides's *Phoenician Women*. The two brothers contend for the throne of Thebes. The clash is characterized by exact symmetry. Each brother matches the other betrayal for betrayal, blow for blow, weapon for weapon, and wound for wound until both lie dead in the dust. The brothers are exact doubles, although each sees the other as a betraying monster who deserves to die. The scandalous rivalry precludes either brother from enjoying his heritage.

Intense mimetic rivalry leading to scandal, doubling, and eventually violence is very dangerous for society as a whole, not just for the immediate participants. The reason is man's mimetic nature. As observers acquisitively imitate the original combatants, scandal and violence can rapidly spread from one person to another like a contagion. This can readily degenerate into unremitting violence with the potential to destroy society. In the *Phoenician Women*, the struggle between Eteocles and Polynices claims many lives and nearly destroys Thebes.

As previously mentioned, Girard sees metaphysical desire with advanced scandal or doubling as the threshold of psychopathology. Mimetic crises can precipitate psychopathology. For example, in the increasing crescendo of conflictual mimesis, desire and violence become linked. This can provide substrata for sadism or masochism. In the ever-oscillating conflict with the rival, one is prone to irrational delusions of victory (mania) or defeat (depression). The more tightly one is chained to the other in conflictual mimesis, the more likely one is to feel possessed by the other, to feel that the other is inside oneself.

The love/hate relationship with a rival can magnify to the level of hallucination, as explained by Girard (1987a):

> When mimetic rivalry has "undifferentiated" all relationships, not the double but difference is a hallucination. The hallucinatory reading of doubles is the last trick desire plays in order not to recognize . . . that

the mimetic partners are identical . . . If the madman sees double, it is because he is too close to the truth. (302)

As mimetic rivalry leads to doubling, the recognition of loss of difference is often intolerable. This amounts to the loss of the necessary different other, the rival around which one has structured one's life. One solution to this problem is to engender the hallucination of a demonic, monstrous, or, alternatively, divine other. The other is now imaginary, but derived from real human rivalry. Such a person "chooses, in short, to sacrifice his experience and his reason in preference to abandoning his desire" (Girard, 1987a, 303).

Mimetic Crisis and Violent Resolution

Mimetic desire leads almost invariably to mimetic rivalry. As a result, virtually all people participate in many relationships characterized by mimetic conflict. These conflicts are often relatively mild or are held in check by common sense or societal norms and pressures. If this were not so, culture as we know it could not exist. Nonetheless, individual escalation of mimetic rivalry to the level of scandal is not uncommon. In this situation, intense passions of hate, anger, and resentment are experienced as overwhelming. An attempt at violent resolution often follows. The violence can be directed in three possible directions: (a) toward the model (murder); (b) toward the subject (suicide, insanity, or submission); or (c) toward a relatively arbitrary third entity (scapegoat). The first two targets are easily understood; the third, perhaps less so. Although anger originates in specific relationships, it is relatively blind and easily shifted from one person to another. Hostility is a burden looking for an outlet. All of us are familiar with the phenomenon of taking out one's frustrations from work at home or vice versa. Family members are, in fact, sometimes killed by one another because of high levels of frustration outside the home. These arbitrary third parties (scapegoats) are surrogate victims substituted for the original rival.

The story of Saul and David in the Bible is an excellent illustration of advanced mimetic rivalry. David bursts on the scene to popular acclaim during Saul's reign over Israel. He immediately becomes a scandal for Saul. Saul brings David into his court (1 Sam. 6:14–21; 17:55–18:11), denoting David's status as inferior. However, David proves to be too popular (1 Sam. 18:5–16). Saul thereafter oscillates between trying to murder David (1 Sam. 19:11; 20:32–33; 23:1–14) and submitting to him (1 Sam. 25:16–22; 26:17–25). Meanwhile, Saul blames (scapegoats) his son Jonathan for his support of David (1 Sam. 20:28–32). He massacres the priests at Nob as surrogate victims for David because of their unwitting support for him (1 Sam. 22:11–19). All this fails to give Saul the supremacy he so earnestly desires. Saul then prepares for a great and final battle with the Philistines. He obtains a pre-battle consultation with the medium at Endor, during which he sees the spirit of the prophet Samuel. This can be understood as a lapse into insanity (1 Sam. 28). Subsequently, the great battle lost, Saul falls on his sword to commit suicide (1 Sam. 31:1–6). Saul's life thus demonstrates every possible response to a scandalous rivalry.

Saul's experiences may seem far removed from the everyday life of most people, but this is not true. All people coexist with some tension from a number of mimetic rivalries; and, likewise, virtually all act to diffuse the tension by some form of scapegoating. Consider, for example, two thoracic surgeons, both vying to be recognized as the superior surgeon in a hospital. They may find a measure of unanimity by unitedly demeaning a partner or employee or vilifying a competitor. The unanimity against a third person lowers the interpersonal tension between them. Such behavior seems to occur naturally and almost unconsciously, often not noticed or understood by the participants. The Bible provides another instance. Herod and Pilate became friends as a result of their collusive involvement against Jesus, having formerly been enemies (Luke 23:1–12). Is it not the case that much of human agreement is agreement *against* someone or something? Think of the power of war to unify a nation, particularly if it is perceived by the majority as a just war. On a smaller scale, who has never participated with colleagues in the demeaning of another at school, home, work, or church? No one. All humans have participated in scapegoating behavior and are scapegoaters.

We have seen that man's mimetic capacity/mimetic desire is a good thing, enabling him to participate in human culture. On the other hand, we have seen that mimetic desire leads almost invariably to rivalrous conflict which, if not controlled, could easily lead to culture-destroying violence. This raises the question of how human culture is possible. How did it arise in the first place? How is it maintained? Why are we all seemingly natural scapegoaters? What is the connection of violence and scapegoating to religion? It is to these questions we now turn.

Theory of Cultural Origins

Girard (1987a, 84–104) refers to *hominization* as the process of transition from animal to man. Hominization first requires evolution or production of the anatomical and neurological capacity for detailed symbolic communication. Girard does not substantially address this biological issue, content to accept the findings and conceptual model (evolutionary theory) of modern biology. The second requirement for hominization is the creation of a symbolic system of communication, which enables societal differentiation (culture). It is here that Girard has developed some of his most profound insights.

Three factors are of paramount importance in Girard's development of his theory of the origin of human culture. The first is his concept of mimetic desire, described previously. Human beings everywhere and at all times are the same, enmeshed in mimetic rivalry, possessed of latent or overt hostility, and prone to violence. The second factor is the ubiquitous finding of ritual human sacrifice wherever one peers into the distant past of human societies. The third is the large number of myths from many cultures which speak of the killing of a god that benefited society (Leeming, 1994, 58–61). As Schwager (1987) says, "Indeed, virtually all peoples have stories to tell how a cult hero was killed and how he rose to new life and brought blessing to the community" (24). Integrating these factors, Girard postulates that human culture originated in the violent murder of a human being, *the scapegoat.*

This is not limited to one event; rather, human culture has been established or reestablished in many different times and places, but always by the structuring mechanism of the scapegoat. Ritual human sacrifice is a representation of the *originary* murder. Myths are stories that conceal, fully or partially, the founding murder. Myths therefore obscure the reality of human violence.

Girard first developed these ideas in *Violence and the Sacred* (1972/1977), being heavily influenced by his study of Greek drama. He later extended them in *Things Hidden Since the Foundation of the World* (1978/1987) and *The Scapegoat* (1982/1986). Clearly, Girard's thesis of hominization and cultural origins is not historically verifiable in the sense of having an eyewitness report. It is best judged on its ability to explain and synthesize a vast amount of information from the human sciences and the humanities. James Williams (1992) aptly summarizes the issues:

... I am not proposing that Girard's theory be judged on the basis of whether in a strict sense it is factually accurate concerning original "hominization" ... Nor do I think the question is whether it accounts for all the basics of human culture in every detail ... The question is whether the model has great analytic power in the interpretation of the data. Will it make sense in response to certain questions about religion and culture in a way that other models do not? (14)

General readers may be surprised at the assertion made earlier of the pervasiveness of human sacrifice in archaic cultures. Many seem to have the idea that human sacrifice was exotic and relatively rare, being limited to groups whose thirst for sacrificial victims is well known, like the Aztecs. This is not the case. For example, human sacrifice appears to have been prevalent among the ancient Greeks, the esteemed forebears of much of Western culture. In Athens and other cities a marginal person, called the *pharmakos*, was kept at public expense. During the yearly festival of Apollo, or additionally during times of perceived stress like plague or famine, the *pharmakos* was paraded through the city and beaten by the crowd. He was then either expelled or killed by stoning or being thrown from a cliff (Girard, 1977, 94–98; Hornblower & Spawforth, 1996).

The Scapegoat

Girardian theory posits that we imagine a group of humans in *mimetic crisis*. Many mimetic rivalries have advanced to a point of extreme intensity. By imitation, the contagion of hostility and rivalry diffuses itself through the group. All are doubles. Opponents are seen as enemies who must be destroyed. There are sporadic outbursts of violence. It is a war of all against all. Bonds holding the group together are in the process of dissolution. The world is experienced as fragile and disintegrating. Panic sets in.

The scenario just outlined can be descriptive of human groups at many times and places. It can apply, for example, to an ancient city, or even a modern one, threatened by famine or plague. External stress exacerbates mimetic conflict, which precipitates a mimetic crisis. As violence, both verbal and physical, progressively increases, the previously established cultural differentiation is progressively effaced. Differences disappear and the community descends into chaos.

A similar scene can be imagined for a group of biological humans with highly developed mimetic capacity prior to hominization. Behavior is instinctual and mimetic. In the competition for scarce resources (food, shelter, mates) mimetic rivalry increases precipitously, leading to a mimetic crisis. Every human is against the other, cooperation is not possible, and the group is faced with self-destruction.

As was described earlier, mimetic conflict is generally rooted in more than one person (relationship) and the prime focus of the anger is relatively easily shifted from one person to the next. Now, let us return to the mimetic crisis with passions of envy, resentment, anger, and hate at the boiling point. Let us suppose that one person locked in serious mimetic conflict transfers his primary hostility from his original rival to another person. If the rival imitates him in this shift, or if the direction of the hostility now corresponds to that of yet a third person, two or three people will suddenly find themselves in unanimity in the midst of a sea of chaos. Imitation by still a few more will then fuel rapid polarization of the entire group against a single person. A "snowball" effect ensues. The intense passions of advanced mimetic crisis, previously dispersed throughout the group, now become concentrated on one person. He suddenly appears or seems *different* to the crowd. All of the blame, focused before on one's rival, is now attributed to one person. He is seen as guilty for the sins of the entire group and therefore responsible for whatever ills beset the group (mimetic crisis). He is perceived to be the embodiment of evil, the ultimate demonic, monstrous rival of all. Suddenly and unconsciously the crowd, now a lynch mob, moves on the *one* and kills him. He is the *scapegoat*.

The choice of scapegoat is relatively arbitrary. However, people who possess unusual features which make them stand out from the group as a whole are more likely to become the focus of collective violence. Examples include those with illness or physical deformity, the extremely poor or rich, foreigners or outsiders, twins (natural doubles), and beggars or rulers (Girard, 1986, 17–21). Nonetheless, any person is capable of serving as a scapegoat, given the right circumstances, as the occasional selection of victims by lots indicates (Josh. 7; Jon. 1). Closely related to the relative arbitrariness of the victim is the victim's *innocence*. This does not necessarily mean the human victim has never done anything wrong. It means, instead, that he is not guilty of the collective guilt and blame the community projects upon him.

The crowd, formerly at odds, has now acted unanimously in concert. The sins and the evil of the crowd, along with impassioned resentment and hate, have been psychologically projected onto or transferred to the scapegoat. Hostility has been vented; unity and peace prevail. This *catharsis* is so powerful and effective that it simply seems beyond human capacity and is therefore assumed to be of divine origin. A miracle has occurred. Transcendence apparently beyond anything humanly possible is experienced. The *sacred* has been created. The participants are unaware that they have created the sacred by their own mental projections around the scapegoat/victim, who was created by their unanimous violence. Human violence has created the sacred but misrecognized it as an experience with "god." Thus, "Violence is the heart and secret soul of the sacred" (Girard, 1977, 31). Subsequently, other things which seem utterly beyond human control or comprehension are connected to the transcendence of the violent sacred. These include the universe, weather, plague, floods, earthquakes, and the like.

Paradoxically, the overwhelming peace and unity experienced by the community now cause it to see the scapegoat/victim in a different and more positive light. Goodness, peace, stability, and order seem to flow back from the scapegoat, from the sacred, to the community. The scapegoat is perceived to be a powerful god, capable of bringing blessing. The scapegoat/god is therefore both bad and good, capable of causing disorder and bringing order. He is therefore *bivalent* (Girard, 1977, 136; Hamerton-Kelly, 1994, 11–12). The powerful bivalent god seems now to have caused the disorder in the first place, required a victim for its resolution, and brought resolution with the death of the victim. Hence comes the idea of the dying and reviving god who blesses society.

It is helpful to reiterate that the bivalent god of the violent sacred is created by the mental projections of the crowd around the scapegoat/victim. The projection occurs in two movements, both characterized by illusion and misrecognition (see Figure 2.3). The first is to project guilt and hate upon the victim. The second is to perceive unity, guiltlessness, and love coming from the victim. The Girardian term for this process is the *double transference* (Girard, 1987a, 37; Hamerton-Kelly, 1994, 141–142). Thus, the double transference mentally transfers blame and guilt for the individual sins of the group, to the victim. In addition, blame for the victim's death, the collective action of the group is transferred to the victim. The death is perceived as the will of god, the work of god, or not even as a death at all. The victim is not dead, but alive in "the sacred." As a result, *the unanimous voice and will of the crowd are perceived to be the voice and will of God.* These fundamental misperceptions constitute the primal lie, which stands between the scapegoat/victim and the cultural order,

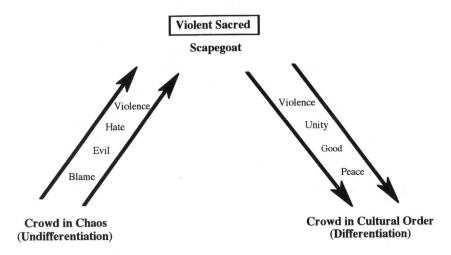

Figure 2.3 Violent Sacred Created by the Double Transference

namely, *vox populi vox deo est.* The self-deception of the crowd veils its ability to see its own violence. The scapegoat is hidden. Violence has covered its own tracks.

The crowd has passed from a mimetic crisis caused by super-heated mimetic rivalry to a peaceful order caused by mimetic polarization on the scapegoat. Mimesis causes the problem but is also the cure. Similarly, the "bad" violence of the mimetic crisis has been terminated by the "good" violence against the scapegoat. Thus, the poison is also the antidote, which is the double and paradoxical meaning of *pharmakon* in Classical Greek (Girard, 1977, 95). Using a small dose of the disease to effect a cure seems to be a deeply ingrained human reflex. It accounts for Moses raising a bronze snake on a pole to cure his people of snakebite (Num. 21:4–9) and for the Philistines making models of tumors (buboes) and rats in response to an apparent outbreak of the plague (1 Sam. 5–6). It is also the basis for modern medical vaccinations for immunization.

The spectacle of a crowd rushing upon a victim to annihilate it is far removed from the experience of most people in today's world. Nonetheless, both literature and the historical record document its significance in the past. Euripides's tragedy, *The Bacchae*, is a profound example (Girard, 1977, 126–139). *The Bacchae* culminates with the tearing to pieces of Pentheus, King of Thebes, by a band of women led by his own mother, Agave. In Dionysiac intoxication these women lose dif-

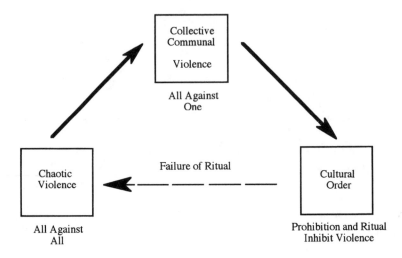

Figure 2.4 The Cycle of Human Culture = Eternal Return of Mythology

ferentiation and roam as a pack of wild animals. They do not recognize Pentheus as human and are unable to hear or comprehend his urgent appeal to their sanity just before they dismember him.

Consider also the stoning of Stephen in Acts of the Apostles 7. Stephen accused his audience of persecuting the prophets and of betraying and murdering Jesus, the Righteous One. The story then moves rapidly to its dramatic conclusion:

> When they heard this, they were furious and gnashed their teeth at him. But Stephen, full of the Holy Spirit, looked up to heaven and saw the glory of God, and Jesus standing at the right hand of God. "Look," he said, "I see heaven open and the Son of Man standing at the right hand of God." At this they covered their ears and, yelling at the top of their voices, they all rushed at him, dragged him out of the city and began to stone him. (Acts 7:54–58)

The precipitous, unanimous, unthinking violence of the polarized crowd that no longer wishes to hear is transparent, indeed.

Girard maintains that it is on such victims that human culture was created and has been maintained (see Figure 2.4). Near the beginning of *Violence and the Sacred* he comments, "If the surrogate victim [scapegoat] can interrupt the destructuring process [loss of differentiation in mimetic crisis], it must be at the origin of [cultural] structure" (Girard, 1977, 93). Near the end of the same book Girard concludes:

All religious rituals spring from the surrogate victim, and all the great institutions of mankind, both secular and religious, spring from ritual. Such is the case, as we have seen, with political power, legal institutions, medicine, the theater, philosophy, and anthropology itself. It could hardly be otherwise, for the working basis of human thought, the process of "symbolization," is rooted in the surrogate victim. (306)

We will now investigate how the scapegoat generates human culture.

The Scapegoat Generates Culture

There are several critical and interrelated concepts that are essential to understanding how the scapegoat generates/maintains culture. First, the violent energy that the undifferentiated crowd projects to the scapegoat is reflected back from the scapegoat as the power which generates difference (cultural order). Compulsion by violence is therefore inherent in the system of cultural order. Diffuse violence is focused on the scapegoat by the crowd and returns to the crowd as the differentiating violence of culture. As difference is established, external mediation comes to predominate over internal mediation, thereby diminishing rivalrous conflict. Second, the first social differentiation is the difference between the scapegoat and the crowd. All other differentiations (ranks, social prestige, and the like) flow from this originary differentiation. Third, religion is the fundamental institution of culture, originating in the false transcendence of the violent sacred and functioning to maintain the cultural order. Religion, and therefore culture, consists primarily of ritual, prohibition, and myth (Girard, 1977, 89–118). Fourth, the difference between the scapegoat and the crowd is the basis for symbolic thought or language. In all this it is obvious that Girard categorically rejects Rousseau's idea of the social contract where men of understanding and goodwill voluntarily organize human society.

Language

Modern structuralist linguistics sees language as a system of signs. Each *sign* consists of two parts: (a) *signifier*, which is the visual or sound element and (b) *signified*, which is the meaning associated with the visual or sound element. Each signifier gains its meaning only in contrast to (in differential relation to) the other signifiers (Saussure, 1959). Girard accepts this but proposes that we see the (real) scapegoat/victim as the original sign: "The signifier is the victim. The signified constitutes all actual and potential meaning the community confers on to the victim and, through its intermediacy, on to all things" (Girard, 1987a, 103). The victim gains its differential meaning in the process of exclusion from the group:

> This is the model of the exception that is still in the process of emerging, the single trait that stands out against a confused mass. . . . It is the model of drawing lots, of the short straw, or, of the bean in the Epiphany cake. Only the piece that contains the bean is truly distinguished; only the shortest straw, or the longest, is meaningful. The rest remain indeterminate. This is the simplest symbolic system. . . . (Girard, 1987a, 100–101)

Girard thus goes beyond structuralism to postulate the scapegoat phenomenon as the historical genesis of the structure of language itself. Mimesis produces the victim, which generates language. Therefore, both mimesis and victimization are *prior* to symbolic representation (language).

Girard (1987a, 103) goes on to postulate that the original victim would at first be signified by new victims of ritual sacrifice, with verbal language arising later in the ritual context. Other significations would flow from the original signification associated with the victim, in relation to the original sign of the victim. Since human language is formed by the generative scapegoat mechanism, it is the *logos of violence.* This renders it exceedingly difficult for humans to think in other than sacrificial terms.

Ritual

Ritual sacrifice originated in the fear of archaic communities of returning to the original mimetic crisis, or, in other words, in the terror of the violent sacred (Girard, 1987a, 103). Ritual sacrifice is the first cultural act, the first cultural institution. All other rituals and all other cultural institutions have their origin in ritual sacrifice. Our culture therefore descends from the violent sacred. Readers who are interested in other theories of the origin of sacrifice should refer to Eliade (1987) and Williams (1992, 14–20).

The crowd's instinctive fear of the diffuse earth-shaking violence of the previous mimetic crisis is easy to understand. Schwager (1987, 20) compares it to a child who, once burned, instinctively stays away from the fire. The crowd, in the aftermath of the spontaneous murder, must imagine how to re-experience the salvation the murder brought. Ritual develops as an organized, controlled series of actions designed to model or recapitulate the original mimetic crisis and its resolution. Rites commonly begin with actions that arouse violent

War dance of the Sauks. Library of Congress.

mimetic passions and decrease differentiation, but in a relatively controlled setting. Examples include dancing, singing, shouting, war
games, games of chance, violation of regular social norms, wearing of
masks, and the like. Mardi Gras is a modern model of the mimetic crisis of undifferentiation with chaotic behavior, violation of societal
norms, and doubling (masks).

The preliminary rites bring the crowd together in a state of
excited expectation. The aroused passions are then transferred to a
sacrificial victim, human or animal, which is killed or expelled. This
re-presentation of the founding murder vents hostility and resentment outside the group. Reconciliation between people is effected and
the fabric of society is repaired or reinforced. Peace and order result.
Ritual sacrifice has brought *the blessing of god*. The ritual of bull-
fighting is an example of modern animal sacrifice.

Girard thus sees the primordial murder as historically antecedent
to human sacrifice, which in turn precedes the development of animal
sacrifice. Later derivations include gifts at the altar and then institutions of economic exchange. Human societies tend to evolve toward
less costly sacrifice. However, in times of crisis, there is a tendency to
retrogress in the opposite direction to ritual human sacrifice or even
spontaneous collective murder, riot, or war.

Paradoxically, some sacrificial rituals involve scrupulous attention to super-order, rather than disorder, prior to killing or expelling the sacrificial victim. For example, in the Day of Atonement ritual (Lev. 16) both people and priests make extensive ritual preparations to *increase* differentiation prior to killing and expelling the two goats. Modern military parades similarly function to increase differentiation. Rituals of undifferentiation and super-differentiation are two sides of the same coin, stemming from the bivalent nature of the scapegoat. Disorder and undifferentiation correspond to the scapegoat before it is killed; order and differentiation, after.

Prohibitions

Prohibitions are a set of rules which evolve to prevent a return to the mimetic crisis. In this respect, they have the same function as ritual. Prohibitions are sacred just like the social order they uphold. Rules against murder, theft, adultery, incest, and the like, evolve to address the areas in which mimetic rivalry is likely to occur. These are all crimes typically attributed to the original scapegoat/victim. Thus, the essence of prohibition is not to behave in the "wicked" ways the scapegoat did to "cause" the original mimetic crisis. Rules that maintain the social hierarchy are similarly based on fear of approaching too closely the scapegoat/victim or the violent sacred. Just as it is dangerous to get too close to the violent sacred, it is also dangerous to get too close to members of the social hierarchy. In this way prohibitions facilitate external mediation and inhibit conflict. Prohibitions therefore help retain the "blessing from god." As the prohibitions are observed, the community experiences peace and has the time and energy to participate in fruitful economic endeavors. Life is good. God is pleased.

On the other hand, as prohibitions are violated the community may descend into a mimetic (*sacrificial*) crisis. Ritual sacrifice, when effective, will restore order. More serious crises may require either a more prestigious victim or a greater number of victims for ritual sacrifice to be effective. The mimetic or sacrificial crisis is experienced as the wrath of god. The scapegoat/victim/god has returned to punish the community for its evil. If ritual sacrifice is not effective in resolving the crisis, the community has reached the point at which only the uncontrolled spontaneous unanimity of a re-founding murder stands between the community and dissolution.

These principles are well illustrated by the story of Phinehas in Numbers 25. Israel has transgressed the prohibitions against adul-

tery and idolatry by consorting with the Midianites. The wrath of the
Lord brings a plague against Israel. The Lord commands ritual sacrifice of the *leaders* of the people. Moses proposes instead a judicial
killing of only the men who participated in the idolatry. The community, however, remains paralyzed while an Israelite man brings a
Midianite woman right into the middle of Israel's camp. Phinehas,
before the "eyes of the whole assembly," drives a spear through the
guilty Israelite and his consort. This spontaneous murder turns away
the wrath of the Lord, and cultural order is reestablished as Phinehas
and his descendants are given an eternal priesthood.

Myth

Myth is the narrative which corresponds to ritual and prohibition
(Hamerton-Kelly, 1994, 149). Myth, as a manifestation of language,
necessarily follows the killing of a victim. Myths are created by participants in collective victimage and reflect their distorted illusions
around the victim in the violent sacred. As Girard (1977) says,
"Myths are the retrospective transfiguration of sacrificial crises, the
reinterpretation of these crises in the light of the cultural order that
has arisen from them" (64). Myths are stories that derive from the
actual killing of a victim by a group, but which reflect the lies of the
double transference. The awful reality of human violence is at least
partially concealed, and often totally effaced, by the corresponding
myth. Thus, Saddam Hussein can speak of the World Trade Center
disaster as a redemptive event. It is the sacrificial crisis that should
settle a score and make community more possible. Remember that
Hussein remembers what most of us have forgotten, namely, that he
was in a brother-brother role with the United States while we were
supporting the Mujahadeen against the Soviet Union in Afghanistan
less than two decades ago. He perceives himself betrayed by "the
brother" and so, unconsciously, supports al Qaeda actions against the
United States as the sacrificial crisis which will restore community.
In any case, Hussein and al Qaeda will see these kinds of events in
terms of the myth that they are the will of God enacted by these
heroic servants of God, the terrorists. That sounds uncommonly
ignorant but it makes a certain sense within the dynamics of Girard's
model.

Mythology is a human response to the false transcendence of the
violent sacred. The process transforms the bivalent human
model/rival into the bivalent good/evil scapegoat victim and then
into the bivalent benevolent/malevolent idolatrous deity. The gods of

archaic religion, of mythology, are simply divinized human scape-goats. Human culture is steeped in the false gods of its own creation, steeped in idolatry.

Myths serve to maintain the border between the sacred and the profane created by the scapegoat mechanism. As described earlier, humans have a natural tendency to want to believe they are right and good while their rival is wrong and evil. Mythology correspondingly transforms the violence we do to others and the violence we project onto others (scapegoating) into holiness. Instead of facing our own evil, myths allow us to think that the other (scapegoat) is evil and we are good. The other (scapegoat) is the cause of all our troubles. Now that the evil other (scapegoat) is gone, our society is clean and pure and worthy of the blessing of god. I have placed scapegoat in paren-thesis to emphasize that it is not recognized as such by the mythical mind. Myths hide the truth of the victim. Myths allow sacrificers to think they are doing God a favor instead of seeing their own violence.

In mythology, the themes of monsters (demonized or hallucinated doubles) and generation or creation from violence are common. In the Babylonian creation myth Marduk slays Tiamat to create heaven and earth and then forms humans from the bones and blood of Tiamat's lover, the monster Kingu (Leeming, 1994, 25). Girard asks us to see human victims behind these dead and living gods.

Girard (1987a, 119) sees the key elements of myth (variously pres-ent) as (a) the theme of violent undifferentiation, (b) exaggerated accusations, (c) representation of collective violence, (d) founding of culture or creation, and (e) the absolute certainty of the hero's guilt. For example, Oedipus is categorically assumed to be guilty of patri-cide and incest and therefore the cause of the plague in Sophocles's tragedy *Oedipus the King*. It is precisely this all-pervasive assumption of the hero's guilt that enables myth to hide the scapegoat mecha-nism. Thus, myths are structured by (result from) the scapegoat mechanism, but conceal it.

Other Cultural Institutions and Social Hierarchy

Religion (ritual, prohibition, myth) is thus the product of the vio-lent sacred. All other cultural institutions descend from religion, although the descent may be masked by a series of mythological sub-stitutions (see Figure 2.5). The connection of the legal system to rit-ual sacrifice and prohibition is quite readily seen (Girard, 1977, 22). Vengeance is reciprocal, or mimetic, violence which, if unchecked by societal mechanisms, can easily spiral out of control and destroy soci-

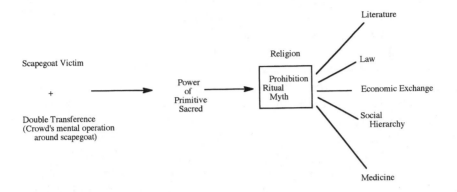

Figure 2.5 The Scapegoat Generates Culture

ety. Ritual sacrifice is the reflection of retaliatory violence onto a surrogate victim who cannot strike back. Sacrifice is designed to prevent uncontrolled vengeance by using carefully directed "good" violence to conduct "bad" violence out of the group. Our modern legal system appears more rational since it represents a reasoned attempt to punish the guilty. It is rationalized vengeance. Nonetheless, it clearly preserves the mimetic reciprocity of violence and, like sacrifice, uses carefully calculated "good" violence to control "bad" violence. Justice is not obtained with ritual sacrifice. It is often not obtained with modern legal systems either. Our legal system is very inadept at proportioning shared responsibility for crimes and nearly completely unable to assess community responsibility.

Social hierarchy is generated in relation to the scapegoat/victim. Priesthood, as illustrated by Phinehas, arises as individuals become sacred executioners, charged with channeling the violent power of the group onto the sacrificial victim (Hamerton-Kelly, 1994, 146). This is a dangerous occupation, indeed. The violent power involved can easily turn priests into victims of the crowd, either for failure to control violence or for perceived violation of sacred prohibitions. This is almost certainly illustrated by the story of Nadab and Abihu (Lev. 10), who were killed by "fire from the Lord" because they offered "unauthorized fire" before the Lord.

Girard (1987a, 51–57) proposes that kingship arose as a consequence of a waiting period between the identification of a victim and the completion of the sacrifice. During the interval, the aura of sacred violence becomes attached to the pending victim, and he finds a way to exploit this power to gain control of the group. Kings are never very far from becoming sacrificial victims, as the bloody European revolutions of the last 400 years demonstrate. A god is a dead king. A king is a living god (Hamerton-Kelly, 1994, 147).

Literature either conceals or reveals the victimage mechanism, always bearing some relationship to the power of mimesis and the primitive sacred. Economic exchange derives from the exchange between group and victim. Medicine (use of therapeutic drugs) and surgery are both based on the principle of carefully directed good violence to cure or prevent bad violence (disease or death).

In summary, we are constituted psychosocially by the violent surrogate victimage mechanism. Man is in a mimetic predicament, imprisoned by the mythology of the violent sacred. This understanding provides a unique perspective on the biblical revelation, to which we now turn.

Perspective on the Biblical Revelation

Readers who have absorbed the Girardian theory to this point may well be wondering what special significance Girard sees in the Bible. Is not the deity of the Bible just another bivalent god, punishing and blessing, saving and destroying, alternately violent and loving? Is not Jesus just another mythological dying and reviving god, another murdered mortal deified after his death by the lie of double transference? Not so, says Girard (1984), "The Bible is not a myth."

The Bible, in fact, is the very opposite of myth. It represents a force of revelation from God whose purpose is to bring an end to all mythology (Girard, 1986, 100–101). The Bible functions to desacralize myth, ritual, and even prohibition, thus emptying the violent sacred of its power. This disclosure involves revelation of the violent scapegoat victimage mechanism on which man has erected his culture. The lie of the double transference is penetrated, and the innocent victims hidden by mythology since the foundation of the world are unveiled. In the process, true transcendence is disclosed in a nonviolent, loving deity. The Bible allows man to see both the innocent victims he has killed and the true God, who is passionate for the innocent victims; the God who said to Cain, the murderer, "What have you done? Your brother's blood cries up to me from the ground" (Girard, 1987a, 154–155).

Revelation is required because human language, our manner of thinking, and indeed our psychosocial constitution are formed by, *and thereby entrapped by*, the scapegoating mechanism that generates culture. As Girard (1987a) states:

> You cannot become aware of the truth unless you act in opposition to the laws of violence, and you cannot act in opposition to those laws unless you already grasp the truth. All mankind is caught within this vicious circle. (218)

Without revelation humankind would be unable to see outside its violently determined cultural system. Revelation from outside the system or structure of our culture allows us to penetrate both the veil our mythology has placed over the victim and the veil of our human ignorance of the true nature of God. God's challenge in the process of revelation is to speak to us according to our language, in order to deconstruct the scapegoat mechanism which has formed our language.

Revelation involves God taking the side of the victim, demonstrating a God of victims who does not want sacrificial victims of any kind (Williams, 1992, 12). This *non-sacrificial* understanding of God stands in opposition to the *sacrificial* understanding of God (gods) inherent in mythology:

> ... far from being a gratuitous invention, myth is a text that has been falsified by the belief of the executioners in the guiltiness of their victim ... in other words ... myths incorporate the point of view of the community that has been reconciled to itself by the collective murder and is unanimously convinced that this event was a legitimate and sacred action, desired by God himself, which could not conceivably be repudiated, criticized, or analysed. (Girard, 1987a, 148)

Mythology sanctifies the social order generated by the victimage mechanism. In contrast, the true God takes the side of the victim against the social order.

The Bible provides the earliest and most sustained revelation of the victimage mechanism in human history. The process of revelation begins with ancient Israel. Here, presentation of the relationship of God to violence is ambiguous. Sometimes God is portrayed as perpetrating violence himself or as commanding human violence; sometimes as nonviolent. This is because the Hebrew Bible is written sometimes from the perspective of the victimizers (mythology) and sometimes from the perspective of the victims (revelation). The process of revelation begun in the Hebrew Bible is brought to its culmination in the New Testament Gospels. The teaching, suffering, and resurrection of Christ completely reveal the victimage mechanism of human culture. In addition, the loving and nonviolent nature of God is fully revealed in Jesus (Girard, 1987a, 211–213).

In summary, four basic principles can be inferred behind a Girardian perspective on the Bible. First, the Bible reflects and results from God's revelation to a people, though they were not always able to receive it fully. Second, God is nonviolent and loving. Third, our human mimetic nature inevitably results in mimetic conflict, with human culture being founded by collective violence against a surrogate victim, which generates the violent sacred. Fourth, when God is portrayed in a biblical text as violent, it results from human violence being projected onto God by writers still in the grip of the violent sacred (mythology).

The Hebrew Bible

In the Bible, our mimetic nature, mimetic rivalry, and surrogate victimage are all revealed, as a number of the previous examples have shown. In contrast to myths, the Hebrew Bible often succeeds in appropriately placing responsibility for violence on the human perpetrators. A good example is the story of Cain in Genesis 4. Cain's jealousy of his brother, Abel, escalates to a mimetic crisis and Cain kills Abel. Cain then goes on to found a city. Thus, the first murderer is responsible for building the first city. The myth of the founding of Rome is similar. Romulus kills Remus and then builds Rome. Both stories perceptively delineate the connection between murder and human culture. In the Bible, however, Cain's murder of Abel is denounced as a great sin, whereas, in the Roman myth, the killing of Remus is justified because Remus did not respect the proper boundaries of the city. Girard (1987a) explains:

> The motive for the killing is at once insignificant—since the city does not yet exist—and crucial, literally fundamental. In order for the city to exist, no one can be allowed to flout with impunity the rules it prescribes. So Romulus is justified. (146)

In myth the sacred social order is always justified; in the Bible it is progressively overturned.

Exodus relates the story of the Israelites leaving bondage in Egypt and entering the Sinai wilderness to be constituted as a covenant people of the Lord. The Israelites leave (or are expelled) at the end of a series of ten plagues, presented as the work of the Lord mediated by Moses. The plagues are a series of entomological, meteorological, and epidemiological disasters culminating in the death of all Egyptian firstborn. The Israelites are protected from the plagues and, in particular, are saved from the death of their firstborn by ritual animal sacrifice (Passover lamb). They leave Egypt under the protection of the Lord, pass through the Sea of Reeds, and go on to enter formally into a covenant relationship with the Lord at Mount Sinai. In Exodus 14, the Lord is presented as gaining glory for himself by totally destroying the pursuing Egyptian army in the Sea of Reeds.

A Girardian perspective on the Exodus story would see the attribution of the plagues and other violence to the Lord as mythological. Rather, the plagues indicate a severe mimetic crisis in Egyptian society. Spontaneous violence breaks out and possibly ritual human sacrifice. The Israelites largely escape spontaneous violence by uniting together and offering effective ritual animal sacrifice. The Israelites are scapegoated by the Egyptians as the cause of the mimetic crisis. They flee, pursued by the Egyptians. In a Girardian analysis, the Lord is not revealed in the catastrophic violence, but rather in taking the side of the victimized Israelites and calling them to a new kind of society in a covenant relationship with himself. The history of ancient Israel thereafter is the history of a long struggle to achieve and retain this special relationship with the Lord. It is a story of progress and relapse. Periods of order maintained by covenant law and ritual animal sacrifice alternate with periods of chaos and reversion to human sacrifice or virtual societal dissolution. Along the way, profound revelatory insights are interspersed with mythological stupor.

The story of Joseph illustrates profound understanding of the innocent victim as well as the means of nonviolent, nonrivalrous reconciliation (Gen. 37–50; Girard, 1987a, 149–153; Williams, 1992, 54–60). Joseph is the favorite of the eleven sons of Jacob. The favoritism shown to Joseph induces intense mimetic rivalry among the brothers, and they decide to get rid of him. The brothers debate killing Joseph, but decide to sell him into slavery in Egypt. This occurs unbeknownst to Jacob. After becoming a trusted servant, Joseph is cast into prison because of *false* charges of adultery with his master's wife. Then the course of Joseph's life turns. He is abruptly released from prison for helping Pharaoh predict and plan for a coming famine. The brothers come to Egypt seeking food and unknowingly encounter Joseph as Pharaoh's vizier. Joseph frames his brothers for theft and then demands Benjamin, Jacob's twelfth and now favorite son, as ransom. The brothers are horror stricken, assuming that this catastrophe is just punishment for their long-ago sacrifice of Joseph. Furthermore, the brothers now cannot bear the thought of Jacob losing Benjamin as he once lost Joseph. One of the brothers, Judah, offers his own life as sacrifice in return for Benjamin. Joseph then reveals himself to his brothers, forgives them, and provides food to save his family.

Myth is subverted at many levels in the Joseph story. Mimetic rivalry is revealed, but the innocence of the excluded victim, Joseph, is steadfastly maintained. Furthermore, reconciliation is not brought by exclusion of the victim. Rather, it is the brothers' contrition over what they did to Joseph, combined with Joseph's forgiveness, that heals the family. Finally, Joseph brings salvation as a living person and not as a dead deified victim.

The story of the killing of Saul's sons during the reign of King David is quite different (2 Sam. 21:1–14). David's people experience three years of famine. The Lord is consulted and informs them that the crisis has been caused by bloodguilt on the land caused by *Saul's* wanton slaughter of the Gibeonites. David consults the Gibeonites, who suggest that seven of the descendants of Saul "be killed and exposed before the Lord" (2 Sam. 21:6). This amounts to human sacrifice, and it is carried out on seven of Saul's grandsons. After their ritual killing ("exposure before the Lord"), the rains come, bringing an end to the famine. This text is impregnated with the language and thought of myth. The Lord is presented as a violent and capricious deity who is punishing Israel during the time of David for unassuaged bloodguilt from the time of Saul. The Lord then relents only when offered sufficient sacrificial victims. Human motives in the selection of the victims and human responsibility for the killings are both totally obscured.

Girard's model of culture is priceless in helping us to understand how such contradictory texts can reside together in the same book. In addition, Girard shows us how to use both kinds of texts in a meaningful way to learn about the nature of God and the nature of man.

Even when a biblical text is deeply mired in the mythological sacrificial perspective, it often leaves clues which enable us to criticize it (Bailie, 1995, 135). These clues allow us to see the human violence and surrogate victimage mechanism, which the text significantly obscures. For example, the killing of seven of Saul's grandsons for a putative offense of Saul two generations earlier flatly contradicts the law of Deuteronomy that states that children are not to be put to death for the sins of their parents (Deut. 24:16). The spectacular killing by Phinehas of an idolatrous/adulterous couple, which brought an end to a plague on Israel in the wilderness, was also previously mentioned. Phinehas's reward of an eternal priesthood is totally consistent with the workings of the violent sacred and myth. However, the text specifically goes out of its way to record the names of both the man and the woman Phinehas killed. This is indicative of the revelatory pressure behind the biblical text, which forces us to see the real human victims of our violence, thus preventing the retrospective mythological deification of our victims.

The dialogues between Job and his "friends" in the Book of Job present a clash between two opposing concepts of God. The friends represent a sacrificial concept of God. This is a God of violent retribution who appropriately punishes his enemies (sinners). Job is suffering; the friends assume he has sinned. Girard perceptively sees the friends as emblematic of a persecuting crowd that is striving to push Job into death in order to preserve the integrity of their community (Girard, 1987b, 3–8). The God of the friends is the God of the violent sacred, of the sacred social order. Job begins with a concept of God essentially identical to that of the friends, a just God who appropriately punishes sin. This causes terrible tension inside Job. He is torn between conviction of his own innocence and his belief that God is behind his misfortune.

In the darkness of his distress, Job attains a new understanding of God by virtue of four great revelatory insights (Job 14:13–17; 16:18–21; 19:25–27; 23:3–7, 10; Girard, 1987b, 138–146). Job ultimately grasps that God is not persecuting him. Job comes to apprehend God as one who would cover his sins and be his ultimate advocate, taking the side of the victim against the sacred social order. This God has the power to restore Job's life and bring him forth refined as "gold." The truth of Job's insights versus the sacrificial theology of the friends is confirmed in the epilogue where the Lord states to the friends, " . . . you have not spoken of me what is right, as my servant Job has" (Job 42:7).

Girard (1987a) perceives in the Hebrew Bible " . . . an increasing subversion of the three great pillars of primitive religion: first, mythology, then the sacrificial cult [ritual] (explicitly rejected by the Prophets before the Exile), finally the primitive conception of the law [prohibitions] as a form of obsessive differentiation . . . " (154). This subversion reflects " . . . a work of exegesis . . . operating in precisely the opposite direction to the usual dynamics of mythology and culture" (Girard, 1987a, 157). As we have seen, mythological concepts, although found in the biblical text, are subverted by revelation of the innocent victim and the God of victims. The law as a compulsive system of differentiation (prohibitions) is simplified and transformed (subverted) by statements like "love your neighbor as yourself" (Lev. 19:18).

In the writings of the great pre-Exilic prophets the sacrificial rites of ancient Israel are also subjected to substantial criticism. This prophetic critique of sacrifice includes Amos 5:21–25, Hosea 5:6 and 6:6, Micah 6:6–8, Isaiah 1:11–14, and Jeremiah 7:21–23. Two examples serve to illustrate the issue:

> For I desire mercy, not sacrifice, and acknowledgement of God rather than burnt offerings. (Hos. 6:6)

> For in the day that I brought them out of the land of Egypt, I did not speak to your fathers or command them concerning burnt offerings and sacrifices. But this command I gave them, "Obey my voice and I will be your God, and you shall be my people; and walk in all the way that I command you, that it may be well with you." (Jer. 7:22–23, RSV)

From a Girardian perspective, these texts are reflective of a revelatory pressure attempting to move ancient Israel out of a sacrificial religion and into a covenant community constituted by contrition, forgiveness, and love.

It is perhaps in the fourth "servant song" of Isaiah that the founding mechanism of human culture is most clearly revealed (Isa. 52:13–53:12; Girard, 1987a, 155–157). This describes a man who was despised, rejected by his community, and eventually killed. He is explicitly acknowledged as being righteous and without deceit or violence. The community reflects on the man's persecution and death with transcendent insight:

> Surely he took up our infirmities and carried our sorrows, yet we considered him stricken by God, smitten by him, and afflicted. But he was pierced for our transgressions, he was crushed by our iniquities; the punishment that brought us peace was upon him, and by his wounds we are healed. (Isa. 53:4–5).

Here we have an innocent victim who is killed for the sins of the community and whose killing brings healing to the group. Most significantly, these truths are finally understood by the persecutors themselves.

However, even in this text at the summit of inspiration in the Hebrew Bible, Girard finds a remnant of the violent sacred: "Yet it was the Lord's will to crush him and cause him to suffer . . . " (Isa.

53:10). Girard (1987a) concludes that in the Hebrew Bible " ... we never arrive at a conception of the deity that is entirely foreign to violence ... only the texts of the Gospels manage to achieve what the Old Testament leaves incomplete" (158).

New Testament Gospels

The culmination of biblical revelation is found in the New Testament Gospels. In the teachings, life, and death of Jesus Christ, there is complete, unambiguous disclosure of human violence and divine nonviolence.

A penetrating revelation of the murder and self-deception at the heart of human culture is found in the New Testament texts often called the "woes against the Pharisees" (Matt. 23; Luke 11:37–53; Girard, 1987a, 158–167). Jesus, speaking to the Pharisees, declares:

> Therefore I am sending you prophets and wise men and teachers. Some of them you will kill and crucify; others you will flog in your synagogues and pursue from town to town. And so upon you will come all the righteous blood that has been shed on earth, from the blood of the righteous Abel to the blood of Zechariah, son of Berekiah, whom you murdered between the temple and the altar. I tell you the truth, all this will come upon this generation. (Matt. 23:34–36)

Although this text is directed against the Pharisees, Girard rightfully insists that Jesus has all of humanity in mind. This is denoted by Jesus's reference to "all the righteous blood that has been shed on earth." Abel's murder is the first in the biblical tradition, occurring well before the formation of ancient Israel. Jesus is therefore referring to all of human history. Girard (1987a) adds that there was " ... nothing on earth ... superior to the Jewish religion and the sect of the Pharisees" (175). To criticize the best is to criticize everything that is lesser. Jesus' criticism of the Pharisees is therefore applicable to all people. The Pharisees represent the Jews, who, in turn, represent all humanity. The Gospel message will put all people into the position here occupied by the Pharisees.

Jesus predicts that the Pharisees will turn to violence and pursue victims. This is the age-old attempt to secure peace by the scapegoat mechanism. However, this will not bring the stability and unity they pursue. Their violence will not disappear with the disappearance of their victims. Instead, their violence will rebound onto the persecutors themselves. Jesus attributes none of this violence to God. It will be the unavoidable consequence of their own actions.

Previously, Jesus had unmasked the fundamental lie at the root of human culture; the lie of the double transference and mythology:

> And you say, "If we had lived in the days of our forefathers, we would not have taken part with them in shedding the blood of the prophets." So you testify against yourselves that you are the descendants of those who murdered the prophets. (Matt. 23:30–31)

The critical element to avoid participating in the murder of innocent victims, of prophets, is to understand and admit one's culpability in violence. The first step to becoming a murderer is to misrecognize one's own capacity for violence. All people have participated in the violent scapegoating mechanism of human culture and are, to some extent, the spiritual descendants of those who killed the prophets. Nonetheless, most people are resistant to receiving this information.

Jesus exposes the deeply ingrained human reflex to misrecognize one's own violence and project it onto someone else. He compares the Pharisees to the whitewashed tombs they have built for the prophets killed by their fathers:

> Woe to you teachers of the law and Pharisees, you hypocrites! You are like whitewashed tombs, which look beautiful on the outside but on the inside are full of dead men's bones and everything unclean. In the same way, on the outside you appear to people as righteous but on the inside you are full of hypocrisy and wickedness. Woe to you teachers of the law and Pharisees, you hypocrites! You build tombs for the prophets and decorate the graves of the righteous. (Matt. 23:27–29)

As noted, the Pharisees represent all humanity. Girard (1987a, 163) perceptively sees the whitewashed tomb as a metaphor for human culture. Just as the tomb covers a rotting corpse, so does mythology cover over the founding murder. Furthermore, sacrificial ritual and then post-ritual institutions, such as the law and political systems, progressively obscure their origin in the founding murder.

Revelation of the scapegoat mechanism is almost unbearable. It confronts us with our guilt, which is uncomfortable at best. Furthermore, it threatens to destabilize society by robbing the scapegoat mechanism of efficacy as more and more people side with the victim. The temptation is almost overwhelming to eradicate the revelation by continuing to kill, " . . . strange as it may seem, in order not to know that they [we] are killing" (Girard, 1987a, 163). Girard asks in reference to the stoning of Stephen, "How can we miss the point that they kill in order to cast off an intolerable knowledge and that this knowledge is, strangely enough, the knowledge of the murder itself?" (172)

Luke concludes his account of the woes against the Pharisees with the observation that " . . . the Pharisees and the teachers of the law began to oppose him fiercely and to besiege him with questions, waiting to catch him in something he might say" (Luke 11:53–54). By disclosing that "religion is organized around a more or less violent disavowal of human violence" (Girard, 1987a, 166), Jesus violated the supreme prohibition of human culture. His death was then inevitable unless he compromised with violence, which he consistently refused to do.

The Gospel accounts of Jesus's death recapitulate the essential features of culture-founding violence (Girard, 1987a, 167–170; 1986, 100–124). Jewish society is in crisis, wracked by internal dissension and hatred for the Roman oppression. Near the end of his public ministry, Jesus enters Jerusalem to great public acclaim. Within a week there is rapid polarization against him. Jewish religious authorities are jealous and threatened. The Jewish public is disillusioned because Jesus does not provide the deliverance they expect. Charges of sin, sedition, and blasphemy are brought against Jesus. Roman authorities are coerced by the crowd to see Jesus as undesirable. Even the closest disciples temporarily melt into the crowd, betraying Jesus, denying him, or not speaking in his defense. All are against one. Jesus stands in the place of all victims since the foundation of the world. Jesus is crucified. He forgives his crucifiers because "they know not what they do."

But the Gospels are not written from the perspective of the persecuting crowd, as is myth. They are produced retrospectively by witnesses to Jesus' resurrection who have grasped the truth of the victim and the lie of the crowd. Jesus is declared to be sinless. The passionate mimetic violence of the crowd is exposed, including its power to seduce even the strongest of the apostles, Peter (Girard, 1986, 149–164). Meaningful reconciliation between the Jewish factions and the Roman occupiers does not occur. Even the disciples are left in a paralyzed stupor by the death of Jesus. The death of the victim does not revitalize culture in any way.

Furthermore, the resurrection of Jesus leaves his tomb open and empty. It cannot be closed over to be whitewashed and used in the distortions of myth making. Gathering will not occur around the dead victim killed by unanimous violence and deified by the false transcendence of the double transference. The crowd will no longer be unified effectively by victims. Instead, gathering will occur around the living (resurrected) victim, who was already God before he came. This gathering will take place by individual repentance of violence and imitation of the love of Christ. Humankind is called from the *logos of violence* to a *new logos of love* (Girard, 1987a, 263–280).

Girard (1987a, 180–223) objects strongly to conceptions of Jesus' death as a ritual sacrifice required or engineered by the Father in order to satisfy offense given God by human sin. This represents a capitulation to the false (sacrificial) mythological concept of a deity who requires sacrificial victims in order to bless mankind. Such a sacrificial understanding of God will only enhance our natural propensity for self-justification through "sacred" violence. The death of Jesus was not a ritual sacrifice required by God. It was a collective murder performed by human beings. We, having participated in the scapegoating violence of human culture, are responsible for the death of Jesus, not the Father.

Girard does agree that the death of Jesus can be seen as a sacrifice in a different sense. Sacrifice in this sense is a voluntary giving of oneself for the other (Girard, 1996b, 69, 117, 272). Ritual sacrifice is ultimately the killing of one's mimetic rival. Jesus' sacrifice is the renunciation of mimetic rivalry and commitment to the betterment of the other. Jesus died because he could not do otherwise and still remain true to his message of nonviolence and nonrivalry. Jesus died to culminate the revelation of the violent victimage mechanism of human culture, which we, blinded by the mimetic predicament, could not otherwise see. Jesus suffered himself to become "scapegoat for the world" in order to get us to renounce all scapegoating (Schwager 1987, 137–214). Jesus died because we needed it, not because the Father did.

The two opposing kinds of sacrifice are illustrated by the judgment of Solomon between two prostitutes (1 Kings 3:16–28; Girard, 1987a, 237–243). Two harlots have sons. One son suddenly dies at night. Both women contend for the remaining son and appeal to Solomon. Solomon proposes to bring a sword, cut the child in two, and give half to each mother. The false mother agrees to this proposal. She represents the sacrificial killing of a victim to effect reconciliation between rivals. The true mother begs Solomon not to kill the child and offers to give him up to the other mother. This mother represents the sacrificial giving of oneself for the good of the other. The behavior of the true mother prefigures that of Christ.

The teachings, life, death, and resurrection of Jesus bring into the world the ultimate and complete revelation of our mimetic violence, the scapegoat mechanism of human culture, and the transcendent love and nonviolence of God. Girard (1987a) reasons:

This unprecedented task of revealing the truth about violence requires a man who is not obliged to violence for anything and does not think in terms of violence; someone who is capable of talking back to violence while remaining entirely untouched by it. It is impossible for such a human to arise in a world completely ruled by violence and the myths based on violence. (218)

Girard thus concludes that Jesus is divine. He states, "To recognize Christ as God is to recognize him as the only being capable of rising above the violence that had, up to that point, absolutely transcended mankind" (Girard, 1987a, 219). Girard also says, "Jesus is the only person to achieve humanity in its perfect form, and so to be one with the deity" (216). Jesus is both God and human and therefore able to reveal God to humankind.

In a profound summary of the necessity of Jesus' death in order for us to receive the ultimate revelation, Girard (1987a) states, "A non-violent deity can only signal his existence to mankind by having himself driven out by violence; by demonstrating that he is not able to establish himself in the 'Kingdom of Violence'" (219). Jesus speaks, in the process of being driven out, by means of witnesses he has influenced enough to grasp the significance of his life and message. In this way, Jesus vanquishes violence without violently resisting it. To conquer violence with violence would be no victory at all.

Jesus' entire life is a model of mimesis of the Father: "I tell you the truth, the Son can do nothing by himself; he can do only what he sees his Father doing, because whatever the Father does the Son also does" (John 5:19). However, Jesus's mimesis of the Father is nonrivalrous, performed in the spirit of humble obedience (Matt. 26:39). Jesus calls us to this same good mimesis of God. Jesus mediates the Father to us, thereby serving as a bridge between the kingdom of violence and the kingdom of God (Girard, 1987a, 216). Jesus calls us to construct ourselves in relation to the Father (true worship) instead of in relation to the victimizing crowd (idolatry). Mimesis of God need not involve rivalry since God possesses an infinity of being and an infinity of goodness to share. God is not a rival of humanity. This is in clear contrast to the serpent in the Garden of Eden, which tried to convince Eve of God's jealousy (Gen. 3; Schwager, 1987, 177). The serpent represents Satan, who, like Jesus, imitates God but who, unlike Jesus, does so rivalrously (Girard, 1996b, 197).

Satan means "adversary"; Devil, "accuser." These names evoke the concepts of mimetic rivalry and victimage. Setting aside the question of the "real" existence of Satan, Girard (1996b, 194) sees Satan as the principle both of disorder and of order in human culture. As we have seen, both disorder and order result from mimetic conflict and violence. Girard thus brings an intriguing perspective to Jesus' paradoxical question: "How can Satan drive out Satan?" (Mark 3:23). Here, Girard sees Jesus referring to the mimetic chaos of all against all that is resolved (driven out) by mimetic polarization of all against one victim. Satan thus has two aspects or faces: (a) every man against his brother (disorder), and (b) every man against a scapegoat victim (order).

The Gospel revelation defeats that face of Satan that brings order to human society at the expense of victims. The defeat occurs because the death of Christ on the cross completely and openly reveals scapegoat victimage. This robs the scapegoat mechanism of its effectiveness since it can function effectively only to the extent that the participants do not understand what they are doing. The Cross brings understanding and engenders concern for victims. This destabilizes human culture generated by scapegoat victimage (see Figure 2.6), which brings us to the other face of Satan. Girard (1996b) explains:

> The Satan who is defeated by the Cross is the prince of this world, Satan as a principle of order. We must remember that Satan is also the prince of disorder and this other Satan is still intact, and . . . [is] "unleashed" . . . by the greater and greater loss of scapegoat effectiveness that characterizes our world more and more with the passing of time. (209)

As the surrogate victimage mechanism fails, overall violence paradoxically increases. Since the face of Satan that brings order is disarmed, the other face, disorder, reigns. This Satan, chaos from unvented mimetic hostility, can be defeated only by individual repentance and love.

Christianity has been associated with much violence in the past 2000 years. Jesus himself warned: "Do not suppose that I have come to bring peace to the earth. I did not come to bring peace, but a sword" (Matt. 10:34). Girard makes it possible for us to understand this difficult statement from the Prince of Peace. First, as surrogate victimage fails to bring peace to a group, the quantity of violence

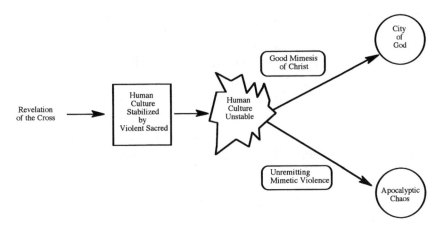

Figure 2.6 The Gospel Destabilizes Human Culture

increases as many individuals come into conflict. Second, as the power of the victimage mechanism wanes, there is a reflex to revivify it by increasing the number of victims or the status of the victims. Thus we have the regicides of the European revolutions of the last 400 years and the genocides of the twentieth century. Third, Christians have frequently misperceived the message of Christ, holding to a sacrificial concept of God and doing much violence in his name.

Christians have persecuted Jews and heretics in the Inquisition and persecuted Muslims and other Christians in the Crusades. They have, in effect, said, "If we had lived in the days of our Jewish fathers, we would not have taken part with them in shedding the blood of Jesus" (Girard, 1987a, 175). They have spoken wrongly, not understanding the Cross. Would we not have done the same in their place?

How will we now speak in the freedom and responsibility of the Cross? The revelation of God, culminating in the Cross, has set us free from the endlessly repeating cycle of mythology: chaos, surrogate victimage, order (Girard, 1996b, 205). The Cross has set us free from prohibitions not subsumed in the injunction to love. The Cross has set us free from ignorant scapegoating of innocent victims. The Cross has revealed us to ourselves; we now "know what we do." We must choose between mimesis of Christ or descent into apocalyptic violence. Girard (1986) says it best:

> In [the] future, all violence will reveal what Christ's Passion revealed,
> the foolish genesis of bloodstained idols and the false gods of religion,

politics, and ideologies. The murderers remain convinced of the wor-
thiness of their sacrifices. They, too, know not [yet] what they do and
we must forgive them. The time has come for us to forgive one another.
If we wait any longer there will not be time enough. (212)

References

Bailie, G. (1995). *Violence unveiled*. New York: Crossroads.

Eliade, M. (1987). Sacrifice. In *The encyclopedia of religion* (Vol. 12, 544–557).
New York: MacMillan.

Girard, R. (1977). *Violence and the sacred* (P. Gregory, Trans.). Baltimore:
Johns Hopkins University Press. (Original work published 1972.)

Girard, R. (1984). *The Bible is not a myth*. In R. Fox, S. C. Walker, & C. Visick
(Eds.), *Brigham Young University Forum on Literature and Belief: Vol. 4.
Literature and belief* (7–15). Provo: Brigham Young University Press.

Girard, R. (1986). *The scapegoat* (Y. Freccero, Trans.). Baltimore: Johns
Hopkins University Press. (Original work published 1982.)

Girard, R. (1987a). *Things hidden since the foundation of the world* (S. Bann &
M. Metteer, Trans.). Stanford: Stanford University Press. (Original work
published 1978.)

Girard, R. (1987b). *Job: The victim of his people* (Y. Freccero, Trans.).
Stanford: Stanford University Press. (Original work published 1985.)

Girard, R. (1996a). *Deceit, desire and the novel* (Y. Freccero, Trans.).
Baltimore: Johns Hopkins University Press. (Original work published
1961.)

Girard, R. (1996b). *The Girard reader* (J. G. Williams, Ed.). New York:
Crossroads.

Girard, R. (2001). *I see Satan fall like lightning* (J. G. Williams, Trans.).
Maryknoll: Orbis. (Original work published 1999.)

Hamerton-Kelly, R. G. (1994). *The gospel and the sacred*. Minneapolis:
Fortress.

Hornblower, S., & Spawforth, A. (Eds.). (1996). *The Oxford classical dictionary* (3rd ed.). Oxford: Oxford University Press.

Lemming, D. (with Lemming, M.). (1994). *A dictionary of creation myths*.
Santa Barbara: ABC-CLIO.

Saussure, F. de. (1959). *Course in general linguistics* (W. Baskin, Trans.). New
York: The Philosophical Library.

Schwager, R. (1987). *Must there be scapegoats?* (M. L. Assad, Trans.). San
Francisco: Harper & Row. (Original work published 1978.)

Wallace, M. I., & Smith, T. H. (Eds.). (1994). *Curing violence*. Sonoma:
Polebridge.

Williams, J. G. (1992). *The Bible, violence, and the sacred*. Valley Forge: Trinity
Press International.

CHAPTER 3

Judaism, Christianity, and Girard: The Violent Messiahs

Cheryl McGuire

Introduction

The purpose of this chapter is to open an inquiry into the nature of a special type of messianic belief of the Middle Judaism period: 300 B.C.E. to 200 C.E. Specifically, I will discuss the influence of Numbers 25, the story of Phinehas's[1] zeal, in light of later priestly messianic expectations. This story records a zealous murder that turned back the wrath of God and "stayed the plague" in Israel. I will suggest that even in Davidic kingly definitions of the anointed one, the Messiah, the priestly function of the violent, purging, and expiating high priest is never very distant. I believe the expectation that the messiah would act with *zeal* became imbedded in the culture of messiah expectation.

However, it is not my purpose or desire to force a false consistency upon the complex movements and structures of the Middle Judaism period. I hope, instead, to introduce some new ideas, and to bring together some old ones, in this discussion of Middle Judaism and messianism.

After introducing my interest in this subject, I will discuss the messiah as a priest-figure, and suggest a modern model for examining the Priest-Messiah. After laying this foundation, I will examine the text of Numbers 25, defining its important terms and main points, and then look at Middle Judaism texts that refer, directly or indirectly, to this scriptural episode. I will then draw some conclusions about messiahs and priestly violence, and will devote a section to arguments for and against messianic violence in the Gospels. I will suggest that eschatological ideas of the period along with post–Middle Judaism messianic thought continued to be influenced by the zeal of righteous priestly behavior, with unhappy results. Finally I will draw some overall conclusions about the importance of the messianic model I have developed.

Statement of Personal Interest and Purpose

As a child growing up in a conservative Christian environment, I learned early what and who the Messiah was. I knew he was born at Christmastime, that he was a good, handsome man who loved children, that bad people killed him in a bad way, but that he rose again and lived on invisibly to hear my nighttime prayers. I also understood that he was *our* Messiah, and that people who were too stupid or too stubborn to "believe in him" and thus become one of us were all in very big trouble. But the ones in trouble seemed far away, and in my self-centered world I knew that as long as I believed in him, the Messiah would reward me by protecting me from all evil.

It was a child's belief: an easy, wide-eyed acceptance of a lovely, comforting fable, at least for those of us who were "us," and not "them," not unlike believing in Santa Claus and the tooth fairy. Eventually, as my perceived world became more real and thus more problematic, I had to put aside the story, and seek a more adult understanding[2] of first causes and less than final answers, of evil stronger than promised invisible protections. I heard sermons of an angry, vengeful God who would eventually destroy all the wicked of the earth, even while I was watching scenes of the horrors of World War II death camps, aired several years after the fact, on our television screen. We lived in the South, and as I grew older I understood that people were beaten and killed by the same group who professed a belief in my childhood Messiah. In school we studied wars fought in the name of the Messiah, of whole peoples obliterated under the sanctioned violence of easy religion. I came to understand that the Prince of Peace Messiah belief had a dark side. Worst of all, for me, that darkness became familiar and intimate as I experienced repeated domestic violence, justified on a daily basis by the various names of Messiah.

Why does a religion that promises peace deliver so much violence? What is there about the human condition that sanctions violence and even elevates it to a sacred, sacrificial position? These are basic questions, which some have indeed attempted to answer, and that I will attempt to discuss below.

Exposition

Through the twenty centuries of the Common Era no concept has remained so constant or held out so much hope for Christians as the idea and image of a bloodied, mutilated, abandoned, pacific, and sacrificial Messiah, single and unique, who has come and who will come again. Rabbinic Judaism rejected the messianic ideal after the devastation of the failed Bar Kochba revolt of the early second century (135 C.E.). That failure, combined with the Christian ownership of Jesus as Messiah, would keep Judaism from embracing messianism openly until Saadia Gaon (882–942 C.E.) formally institutionalized Jewish messianism in his post-Talmudic masterpiece *The Book of Beliefs and Opinions* (Alexander, 1998, 456). Interestingly, another of the "revealed" religions, Islam, also developed within its evolving Shiite traditions the idea of a last and great *messianic* prophet (Friedlaender, 1992, 113–161).

The body of confessional literature, propagandistic apologetics, and scholarly study regarding messianic belief in all three of these religions is staggering. Messiah belief is at the center of conflict of the twin religions Judaism and Christianity,[3] and the idea of who owns the Messiah has its roots in first-century Judaism. On the other hand, there are many beautiful and hopeful ideas surrounding Messiah beliefs. Much has been written about them, expressing peace, celebrating the birth of a baby who would bring healing and truth to all mankind. It is a lovely image. We must look beyond that image, however, and inspect the dark underbelly of Messiah ideology and development: the avenging, purifying Priest/Messiah: Phinehas and his zeal.

Messiah as Priest

Messiah means anointed. Joseph Fitzmyer says that in the Hebrew Bible, the term *mashiah* occurs 39 times in the Old Testament. Four of those occurrences are in Leviticus, and refer to priests. Once *mashiah* refers to Saul's shield. Twice the term refers to Israel, or its reigning king, as a metonym. Still, *mashiah* refers most often to a king, often in the contemporary past. Interestingly, however, there is no reference in the Pentateuch to a king as Messiah, or to a king of

Israel as such in any of the major prophets' writings. King Zedekiah is the sole instance in Lamentations 4:20. References to David as *mashiah* are not messianic in the full-blown sense (Fitzmyer, 2000, 77).

John Day, in "The Canaanite Inheritance of the Israelite Monarchy" refers to the early melding of priest/king functions in the figure of Melchezidek (Day, 1998, 73). Gerbern Oegema notes that priests, as well as kings, were ritually anointed, though for different purposes (Oegema, 1998, 50). Given these historical observations, combined with the Phinehas episode discussed below, it is not surprising that messianic priestly expectation existed during the Middle Judaism period, as several sources attest. For instance, James Dunn, in a section on messianic ideas available in current usage at the time of Jesus, writes:

> "Messiah" is also used of a hoped-for *priest* figure. This is explicit in the same "messiahs of Aaron and Israel" references from Qumran . . . A further element which should be reckoned within the total picture is the promise of a "covenant of perpetual priesthood" made to Phinehas, which evidently fascinated and influenced more than one branch of early Judaism, not the least the Zealots. (Dunn, 1992, 367–368)

J. M. Roberts also agrees with the inclusion of priestly messiahs, noting that two of the priest-promise texts "make the bestowal of the priesthood a reward for the priest's violent actions of killing on behalf of Yahweh." Roberts goes on to note "their similarity in this regard raises the possibility that all these traditions may be variants of a single original" (Roberts, 1992, 48).

Solomon Zeitlin describes *who* is anointed in the Old Testament (king, priest, prophet), but denies the validity of Christian messianic interpretation. He points out that the first anointed was Aaron, the first priest. Samuel anointed the first king, Saul, and in doing so said, "Is it not that Yahweh hath anointed thee to be a *nagid* over His inheritance?"[4] Saul thus became divine and thus became a *mashiah* of Yahweh.[5] The same thing happened to David, with God promising "David that the kingship would be an inheritance of his family and *would last forever*"[6] (Zeitlin, 1974, 396). This language will be duplicated in the Phinehas story, with the promise from God being directed at the priest.

Zeitlin gives his own commentary regarding *mashiah:* "There is no indication anywhere in the Bible of the coming of a personal Messiah, natural or supernatural. The word *mashiah* appears in the Bible several times. It has the connotation of anointed and refers to the high priest or the king of the family of David." Zietlin believes that Psalm 84:10: "look upon the face of thine *Mashiah*," refers to the anointed high priest. Psalm 105:15, "Touch not my *mashiah* and do my prophets no harm," again refers to the anointed high priest, according to Zeitlin. Zeitlin also interprets the use of *mashiah* in Daniel 9:25 as a reference to the high priest who, "during the Second Commonwealth, was the spiritual as well as the secular ruler of the people" (Zeitlin, 1974, 397).

It is well known that certain Qumran documents describe a priestly Messiah. Harris Lenowitz writes: "There had already existed a two-messiah doctrine—involving a holy priest and a holy king, a pairing that had actually functioned in a couple of cases" (Lenowitz, 1998, 31). Lenowitz goes on to describe the roles of king, prophet, and priest as combining into one figure:

> Gradually, these three different roles are transformed and at last combined in a single figure by the postexilic period who would be capable of performing all three functions. He would be the victorious king of a unified nation; he would critique social conduct and prophesy a specific date for the reign of the nation's God over the whole earth; he would exemplify the pure, holy attributes that are required of an officiating priest. As the combination is melded and transformed, the lines that differentiate the functions are erased. The act of anointing itself disappears altogether by the time of the destruction of the Second Temple in the first century C.E. (Lenowitz, 1998, 9)

Additionally:

> Under the impact of what actually happened to kings, prophets, and priests in the face of crises, these multiple ways of understanding or explaining the role of the messiah established a broad range of expectations, almost any of which, met in some way or another, might satisfy a following. . . . The supernatural attribute of eternal life and the shape-changing capacity of the messiah figure as prophet-*cum*-king-*cum*-priest are trans-human qualities that are possessed by the messiah as sociopolitical emblems. (Lenowitz, 1998, 12–13)

Others who wrote similarly of the link between priest and king in messianic expectation included William Horbury in his discussion of I Maccabees 2:49–70 (Horbury, 1998, 57). Fitzmyer speaks of the expiating (priestly) function of the Messiah (90–91), and points out that the Teacher of Righteousness in the Qumran scrolls is a priest (Fitzmyer, 2000, 103).

Phinehas the Violent Messiah Priest

One significant factor of the Phinehas narrative in Numbers 25 and related passages of the Hebrew Bible is the identification of the priest Phinehas with Elijah. S.G.F Brandon writes: "There is evidence that in certain Jewish circles during this period Phinehas was identified or equated with Elijah. This connection was of considerable conse-quence, as we shall see, because Phinehas acquired thereby the Messianic or eschatological significance accorded to Elijah in Mal. iv.5" (Brandon, 1967, 45).

Brandon also points out that "The Gospels provide evidence of such current belief (regarding Elijah/Phinehas): Herod Antipas thought that Jesus was John the Baptist *redivivus*, and the return of Elijah, to 'restore all things,' was commonly expected—this latter belief being transformed among the Zealots into an expectation of a Phinehas *redivivus*, as we have noted" (Brandon, 1967, 181).

Raphael Patai, in *The Messiah Texts*, expounded further on this link-ing of Phinehas with Elijah:

> In the Bible, Elijah is depicted as a zealous prophet of God who waged a ruthless war against Canaanite idolatry in Israel, defeated the prophets of Baal on Mount Carmel in a great rainmaking contest in which he proved the power of God, retraced the footsteps of Moses to Mount Horeb (traditionally identified with Mount Sinai), and ascended to heaven in a chariot of fire (1 Kings 18, 19; 2 Kings 2). (Patai, 1979, 131)

Patai then quotes from an old *piyyut*, sung at the Havdala ceremony at the outgoing of the Jewish Sabbath:

> Elijah the prophet, Elijah the Tishbite, Elijah the Gileadite,
> Quickly let him come to us with Messiah ben David,
> The man who was zealous for the name of God
> The man to whom the tidings of peace were given by Yekutiel,[7]
> The man who approached and atoned for all the Children of Israel.[8]

Patai explained the verse, referring to Elijah the peacemaker:

> R. Shim{on ben Laqish said: "Pinhas is Elijah. The Holy One, blessed be He, said to him: 'You established peace between Israel and Me in This World, even so in the Future to Come you will be the one who will establish peace between Me and My children. . . .'" R. Elizer said: "The Holy One, blessed be He, changed the name of Pinhas to Elijah of blessed memory from among the inhabitants of Gilead. [This] teaches [us] that he made Israel repent on the Mount of Gilead. . . ." (Yalqut Shim: oni, par. 771). (Patai, 1979, 131)

Zeron, in "The Martyrdom of Phineas-Elijah," traces the identification of Phinehas with Elijah in works of Pseudo-Philo, in the gospel of Mark (the transfiguration), Origen, Midrash, and Malachi. Zeron then presents the tradition that Phinehas/Elijah became a kind of heavenly gatekeeper (Zeron, 1979, 99–100).

To summarize, while the use of *mashiah* refers most often to kings, it also refers to priests. Additionally, the *idea* of a priest being anointed carries over to later messianic expectation. One of the most important priestly examples is that of Phinehas, and he became a paradigm for future priestly behavior. He is thought of so highly that his name and identity were fused with Elijah, who is called the peacemaker, he is thought to have been translated, and his return is still looked forward to today. Last, I suggest that even when the messianic roles blended into one (king, prophet, priest), the priestly purifying role of Phinehas was still alive and well in the surviving messianic figure.

René Girard and Religious Violence

While it may seem intrusive to overlay a twentieth-century postmodern, and still evolving, philosophical school upon the ancient records and behaviors as we know them, several scholars have done just that (Seland,[9] Boccaccini [*Middle Judaism*, 1991, 3] and Horsley & Hanson [*Bandits, Prophets, and Messiahs*, 1985, xviii]). Additionally, it is my personal belief that all history is interpretive, all knowledge cumulative. That is, we do not change history or modify ancient behaviors simply because we attempt to understand or interpret that history and those behaviors. While we cannot apply current cultural standards to a people so removed from us in time and space that even their very ideas may constitute the equivalent of a foreign language, it is our task to understand the records that come down to us in the light of everything else that we also know. Or perhaps more humbly, it is our task to test what we think we know against the historical record.

The interpretive model that I will use for this paper is based on the work of René Girard. Girardian thought presents a model of culture with important implications for religion.[10] The nature of humankind, according to my reading of Girard, is neither good nor bad, but mimetic. We learn everything from others, and want what others have. This desire is triangular, involving a subject (a) who desires an object (b), through the eyes and example of a mediator (c). This triangular desire inevitably leads to acts of violence, which Girard calls the *violent sacred*. Human culture derives from and originates in the violent sacred, created by the substitution of one for all. The violence of the murder is transformed by the lie of the double transference into the sanction of the social order. "Good" violence creates differentiation (Stirling, 1999, 4).

In the current instance, according to the text of Numbers 25, Phinehas, through a violent, murderous act, stopped the plague in Israel. Again, according to the text, Phinehas was rewarded, via a direct communication from God, with an eternal priesthood. According to Girardian theory, if you were an Israelite, and you too wanted the reward of God, just like Phinehas received, you would mimic the act of Phinehas to get it. In terms of Girard, you are the subject (the one desiring), the object is the reward given by God, and Phinehas is the mediator, having replaced God in this role by demonstrating and justifying acts of violent zeal that need to be performed before the reward is given.

This idea became extremely important during the time of the Maccabees, and was also used by Philo in justifying acts of mob retribution (or Phinehas-like zeal) in order to achieve self-redress at the time of Jesus. I believe the idea of a violent priesthood became imbedded in Middle Judaism thought, and lives on today.

Even though development of messiah-thought and ideology in the Second Temple Period depended upon a combination of Davidic promises of real-time political and eschatological kingship, and evolving mystical and revelational concepts of a being coming from heaven, the importance of a violent, purging, atoning priesthood cannot be separated from these ideas, even when that priesthood is not specifically mentioned. Rather, the role of the avenging priest, when not specifically stated, was merely subsumed into the definition of another, whether king or heavenly messenger, who will also be acting in the role of priest as well as king or angel. Traditions became mingled,[11] and the violent mediator, whether his name was changed or otherwise hidden, remained within the messiah ideology until the present day.

Presenting a viewpoint alternative to that of violent avenger, Lenowitz writes:

> The Jewish community and the larger society are partners in the ritual dance of destruction; they come together to destroy the messiah, then move apart to resume their old positions in the status quo. In the context of the ritual, the messiah does not actually ignite the flames of the

apocalypse; rather, his immolation sheds light on what a society must do in order to go on. (Lenowitz, 1998, 5)

However, the two positions, messiah/priest as violent mediator, and messiah as violent victim, are merely two sides to the same coin. In each instance, society is saved and purified because of the act of the messiah. Girard writes in *Violence and the Sacred*: "The sacrificial process prevents the spread of violence by keeping vengeance in check. Violence and the sacred are inseparable" (Girard, 1972, 18–19).

Put yet another way, Phinehas is much like Caiaphus the New Testament High Priest. Caiaphus said: "You know nothing at all! You do not understand that it is better for you to have one man die for the people than to have the whole nation destroyed."[12] Or perhaps it is Caiaphus who was like Phinehas. Both priests acknowledged, and performed, the salvific violent act, which the texts bring to us as purifying and necessary. In the record of Phinehas, the plague was stayed and peace was restored. In the New Testament account, the death of Jesus did bring temporary peace to the Jewish officials. Even in Lenowitz's view, the ritual of messianism is ongoing because the ritual is necessary for the order of society. Yet, Lenowitz writes: All the Jewish messiahs are dead (Lenowitz, 1998, 4). How can society go on without its messiahs, which give order and meaning?

Thankfully, in the current instance, we are not without a messiah. We have Phinehas, and it is time to look at his text, below.

Numbers 25:1–18, RSV: Phinehas's Story

1   While Israel dwelt in Shittim the people began to play the harlot with the daughters of Moab.
2   These invited the people to the sacrifices of their gods, and the people ate, and bowed down to their gods.
3   So Israel yoked himself to Ba'al of Pe'or. And the anger of the LORD was kindled against Israel;
4   and the LORD said to Moses, "Take all the chiefs of the people, and hang them in the sun before the LORD, that the fierce anger of the LORD may turn away from Israel."
5   And Moses said to the judges of Israel, "Every one of you slay his men who have yoked themselves to Ba'al of Pe'or."
6   And behold, one of the people of Israel came and brought a Mid'ianite woman to his family, in the sight of Moses and in the sight of the whole congregation of the people of Israel, while they were weeping at the door of the tent of meeting.

7   When Phin'ehas the son of Elea'zar, son of Aaron the priest, saw
    it, he rose and left the congregation, and took a spear in his hand

8   and went after the man of Israel into the inner room, and pierced
    both of them, the man of Israel and the woman, through her
    body. Thus the plague was stayed from the people of Israel.

9   Nevertheless those that died by the plague were twenty-four
    thousand.

10 And the LORD said to Moses,

11 "Phin'ehas the son of Elea'zar, son of Aaron the priest, has
    turned back my wrath from the people of Israel, in that he was
    jealous with my jealousy among them, so that I did not consume
    the people of Israel in my jealousy.

12 Therefore say, 'Behold, I give to him my covenant of peace;

13 and it shall be to him, and to his descendants after him, the
    covenant of a perpetual priesthood, because he was jealous for his
    God, and made atonement for the people of Israel.'"

14 The name of the slain man of Israel, who was slain with the
    Mid'ianite woman, was Zimri the son of Salu, head of a fathers'
    house belonging to the Simeonites.

15 And the name of the Mid'ianite woman who was slain was Cozbi
    the daughter of Zur, who was the head of the people of a fathers'
    house in Mid'ian.

16 And the LORD said to Moses,

17 "Harass the Mid'ianites, and smite them;

18 for they have harassed you with their wiles, with which they
    beguiled you in the matter of Pe'or, and in the matter of Cozbi,
    the daughter of the prince of Mid'ian, their sister, who was slain
    on the day of the plague on account of Pe'or."

In the first verses, the problem is stated: Israel is not keeping herself separate and pure, and, in Girardian terms, differentiation is
being dangerously lost. On a Girardian model, the people of Israel
are beginning to construct themselves in relationship with the
Moabites; they are being mediated *by* the Moabites. The text tells us
that God, being jealous, became very angry at this turn of affairs, and
instructed Moses to take the chiefs of the people and make a public
example of them by killing them and hanging them in the sun before
the people. Note that these chiefs were not necessarily the guilty parties, and Moses in fact did not do what God commanded, but instead
told the judges to slay the guilty. The text does not tell us whether
this action was carried out or not, but things did not get better. "One
of the people" brought a Midianite woman to his family, in full view
of everyone. S. C. Reif lends the interpretation that the woman was a

diviner, and she was brought with her tent and shrine into the camp (Reif, 1971, 206). Phinehas then took matters into his own hands, and with a spear, killed both the man and the woman. Thus "the plague was stayed from the people of Israel."[13]

One of the unavoidable lessons of the Phinehas story is, when faced with a plague, the best thing to do is find a scapegoat. The plague in literature and myth represents undifferentiation, social disorder, a kind of group insanity. "This sacrificial element can be limited to the assertion that all the death and suffering from the plague [are] not in vain, that the ordeal is necessary to purify and rejuvenate the society" (Girard, 1978, 136 ff.).

For this act of purification, Phinehas is rewarded through God's mediator Moses. Through Moses, God says that Phinehas had God's jealousy (zeal), and thus kept God from consuming his people. Therefore, Phinehas is rewarded with a *covenant of peace*, because he was the one who had made an atonement—as interesting a euphemism for murder as can be found. Seland suggests "In later traditions, perhaps already in the Old Testament traditions and texts, this reward served as a legitimation for his descendents to the priesthood. Later it even served as legitimation for the High-priesthood (cf. Sirach 45:23–24)" (Seland, 1995, 47).

As for the surviving Israelites, not only is the plague stayed, but they are also granted permission to unite (differentiate) against a common enemy, the Midianites, who have "harassed" them.

The Phinehas episode is not pretty, and not for those who want their Bible revelation inspired and inerrant. Yet what it does reveal is so deeply profound as to strike at the very heart of human culture. What Phinehas did, in a moment of zeal, was substitute "good" or "sacred" violence for the "bad" violence of disorder. I suggest that this became the role of the Priestly Messiah ideology of Middle Judaism.[14]

Some Middle Judaism Texts That Relate to the Phinehas Story, and Their Historical Context Within the Rise of Messianic Thought

It probably goes without saying that there is a difference between the way the Christian world understands messianic thought today and the way it was understood in Middle Judaism. There was very little of what can be called pure messianism between 500–200 B.C.E., and scholars disagree on whether certain texts were messianic or not. Interestingly, Fitzmyer reminds us that the *Encyclopedia Judaica* does not begin dating messianic ideas until about 65 C.E. (Fitzmyer, 2000, 81). While it must be remembered that Rabbinic Judaism reacted against Christian messiah beliefs and the disaster of Bar Kochba, this claim of late messianic development helps us to remember that which has been accepted by the Christian tradition as purely Christological may not be so, and the appearance of messiah literature did not spring spontaneously clear and pure from nothing.

Shaye Cohen agrees that the Old Testament texts were not originally messianic, and he states that "all eschatological doctrines," end time or ultimate future, are innovations of second temple Judaism (Cohen, 1987, 23). Thus, part of our task is to understand how the Old Testament texts and the history of the time gave birth to these eschatological doctrines.

The most important Old Testament text in which the Phinehas episode receives comment is Psalm 106:28–31, which, Torrey Seland believes, with H. J. Kraus, stems from exilic or post-exilic times (Seland, 1995, 47). Similarities in the Psalm and the Numbers text include the fact that Israel bound herself to Baal-Peor, the mention of sacrifices to another god, and the plague that was ended by the action of Phineas (Ibid.).

But there are also differences. In the Psalm, the story undergoes revision. The sacrifices mentioned are, in Psalm 106:28, "sacrifices offered to the dead," and adultery (if indeed that is what it is; again see Reif: "What Enraged Phinehas?") is not mentioned. The killing of Zimri and Cozbi is not explicitly stated. The action by Phinehas is mentioned, but circumscribed by the verb *pll*. Still Seland (Seland, 1995, 47–48) suggests that in both the Numbers account and the Psalm, Phinehas is performing an intercessory act, not an act of judgment. In the Psalm, the act was "reckoned to him for righteousness," a statement reminiscent of Genesis 15:6 (Abraham).[15] Seland argues that this concept was very influential in certain Middle Judaism texts including 1 Maccabees 2:52; Romans 4:3, 22; Galations 3:6; and James 2:23 (48).

The Maccabees

Jonathan Goldstein provides excellent commentary on 1 Maccabees, where the author of that book describes the actions of Mattathias as patterned after and justified by the zeal of Phinehas. According to I Maccabees, Mattathias was justified in taking over both the priesthood and the function of ruler by doing the deeds of Phinehas.

Goldstein explains that on his deathbed, old Mattathias is portrayed as charging his sons to carry on tasks comparable to those of Phineas, Joshua, and David, as if they, too, could earn the rewards received by those ancient heroes (Goldstein, 1976, 6). It is not insignificant to see Phinehas, the priest, linked with Joshua, the prophet, and David, the king. In all instances the heroes mentioned performed violent acts in the name of their God, and all would be transformed into foundational messianic figures.

The time of the Maccabean revolt was considered to be the "Age of Wrath" (Goldstein, 1976, 7), and especially during this time, faithfulness like that of Phinehas would preserve the sons of Mattathias. From Goldstein:

> The author [of 1 Maccabees] says that the story of Mattathias follows the model of the story of Phineas. Both words and content follow the model. Both narratives take place at a time of God's wrath against Israel. Just as Phineas in Num. 25:7 "saw" that nothing was being done about the mixed marriage that had angered God and "rose and left the congregation," so Mattathias "saw" the apostasy in Judah and Jerusalem and "rose and left" Jerusalem for Modein. Just as Phineas showed "zeal" and acted on behalf of the "anger" of the Lord and stabbed the sinful couple in their illicit bedchamber, the place of their sin, so Mattathias was "filled with zeal and anger" and slew the idolater on the altar, the place of his sin. . . . the author lets his Jewish reader draw the inference: as Phineas was rewarded by being made the founder of the high priestly line, so will Mattathias be rewarded. (Goldstein, 1976, 6–7)

Goldstein draws further parallels from the Maccabean text, including the fact that Mattathias, like Abraham, has been ready to sacrifice his own offspring (1 Macc.1:50, 2:17–21). Such righteousness will preserve the parents in the "Age of Wrath" (Goldstein, 1976, 7). Finally, Phinehas (and Mattathias) are linked with Elijah, who also did deeds of zeal in an age of wrath. Therefore, Mattathias's family may look forward to rewards like Elijah's, perhaps the gift of prophecy, if not assumption into heaven. This is no messianic text, however. For the author of 1 Maccabees, purification and the *de facto* end of the persecution can come about only as a result of military victories (8). Those victories alone were "sufficient signs" of divine approval (75).

The military victories, resulting as they did from zealous acts, were to be fixed in public memory forever through the dedication of the new altar and yearly celebrations of that dedication with the annual festival of Hanukkah, the Feast of Dedication (Goldstein, 1976, 9). Even though later official memory would change the historical reality of the Maccabees into something else, the linking of the zeal of Phinehas with other major players of biblical text and with divinely sanctioned violence could not help but live on in the continuing development of Middle Judaism ideas.

Gerbern Oegema sees Messianic ideas already developing previous to, or simultaneously with, the Maccabees: "In the period to the Maccabees, approximately 164 B.C.E., or roughly from the beginning of the third century B.C.E. until the first third of the second century B.C.E., important 'messianic' expectations can be found in the Septuagint, Ben Sira, the Apocalypse of Daniel and 1 Enoch 83–90" (Oegema, 1998, 39).

Explaining the process, Oegema discusses the transmission of older texts into a new messianic idea that included a strong priestly messianic figure, often the second of a pair of two messiahs (Oegema, 1998, 40–41). Indeed, the priestly idea sometimes included the idea of a "restoration" of priesthood (43). Relying on Lust, Oegema concludes that the Septuagint version of Ezekiel 21.3–32, for instance, can be interpreted as "a priestly messianic expectation directly opposed to a royal Davidic messianic expectation" (46, fn. 33).

Oegema sees a clear link to Phinehas in another text of the period, Ben Sira. While Oegema does not claim messianic expectations or messiah concepts for the book of Ben Sira, he does state that:

> Even when for Ben Sira Joshua and Simon are not comparable or have nothing in common (although both stories follow after each other without any intermission) in cp. 50 he affirms without doubt the religious authority of the high priest of his days at the beginning of the second century B.C.E. The Temple is of central importance for him. Simon is compared with the sun, the moon and the morning star, when he fulfils in full high priestly robes the service of the Temple on the day of Yom Kippur. The closing verse (50.24) is used to express the hope that God will keep his covenant with Phinehas and preserve it for Simon and for his seed "for ever." (Oegema, 1998, 53–54)

Oegema claims that while messianic expectations can be found in earlier times, namely, mainly in the Hebrew Bible, in Zechariah, in the Septuagint, and in some of the Psalms as well as in Ben Sira, the messianic interpretations and the conceptualization of eschatological liberation figures reach a first climax in the Daniel Apocalypse and in its later additions (Oegema, 1998, 70). The Apocalypse of Daniel, in its conceptualization of latter-day figures, clearly marks the end of the biblically oriented period up to the time of the Maccabees. At the same time, the Apocalypse of Daniel stands at the beginning of a new period, which in the time of the Maccabees is characterized by a totally new view on history and thus of a new messiah concept (Ibid.).

This new view of history involved periodization, enabling the delineation of time into past, present, and future. Future events were given a time (period), and end-time events could also be articulated. Promises made in the past could be reinterpreted, allowing for future fulfillment. This future-time ideology and growth of messianic expectation would continue to find its roots in the past, especially the past of the Torah: of actions performed by and covenants made with mythologized figures such as Abraham, David, Elijah, and Phinehas.

The Dead Sea Scrolls

In Daniel, the future figure is "one like a man," neither kingly nor priestly (Oegema, 1998, 56–57), but other sources later than Daniel begin to define the role of the coming one in kingly and priestly terms. For instance, *The Testament of Levi*, not surprisingly, looks for a coming high priest with royal attributes (79). In the *Sibylline Oracles*, we "do not find expressions 'Messiah' or 'Anointed'." Nevertheless, latter-day expectations have been formulated here, in syncrestic fashion, and an important part of that formulation is the new priest.

Robert Eisenman interprets certain writings from Qumran as referring to a priestly Messiah. While this interpretation is not unusual—perhaps even obvious, Eisenman also developed the theme of the violent priesthood, and he also seems to be making the argument that the Qumran community was overwhelmingly Zaddokite in nature. He suggests that in almost all of the Qumran sources, arguments for a priestly Messiah can be made, and in some the priestly idea, incorporating the Phinehas history, is paramount. For instance, "Ecclesiastics is patently a 'priestly' book as the amount of space spent praising Aaron and Phineas, to say nothing of Simeon—more than for Jacob, Moses, David, and others put together—attests" (Eisenman, 1983, 10).

> Finally, if there is substance to any of these extensions and identifications, "The priesthood after the order of Melchizedek" must be related

to what we have called "the Zealot." based on the "the zeal of Phineas" and invoked on behalf of Simeon the Righteous, Mattathias, and Onias in the Hebrew version of Ecclesiasticus, 1 Maccabees, and 2 Maccabees respectively. (Eisenman, 1983, 6)

Other authors write more of the dualism of the Middle Judaism period. In several places in *Beyond the Essene Hypothesis*, Boccaccini writes of the cosmic dualism that developed during this time. Cohen says that: "Some of these [Middle Judaism] schemes are so dualistic that we can debate whether or not they should be called monotheistic. The God of second temple Judaism was much more "transcendent" than the God of pre-exilic Israel. God needed intermediaries to run the world, and humanity needed intermediaries to reach God" (Cohen, 1987, 23).

I suggest that during the Middle Judaism period, certain historical ideas regarding the violent priestly messiah, based on the language of the Phinehas story, became incorporated into this idea of a necessary intermediary. For instance, Daniel and Enoch act as mediators with divine wisdom granted from God (Boccaccini, 1998, 136). Yet within these traditions is an underlying realization that even the divine mediator must be able to either act or support the zeal of God. Daniel, for instance, mediates what could easily be called the zealous punishment of Nebuchadnezzar and King Belshazzar (142). Like Zimri and Cozbi (accepting Reif's explanation), both kings are guilty of claiming power for themselves, and refusing to recognize the sovereignty of God. Boccaccini writes that the king's power "originates and is limited by a 'jealous' God" (143). Thus the king's power remains legitimate unless the king denies God's sovereignty. Then the mediator can act, like Phinehas, as the instrument of God's jealousy. By doing so, the mediator has absorbed the priestly role of punishment and purification.

Other texts show a clearly defined priestly figure. While the king-messiah may be a warrior king (Cohen, 1987, 90), liberating his people, a king is not often called on to make expiation. This is the duty of a priest, or priests, as stated in the opening words of the Congregational Rule of Qumran: 1Qsa (1Q28a):

This is the Rule for all the congregation of Israel in the last days, when they shall join [the Community to wa]lk according to the law of the sons of Zadok the Priests and of the men of their Covenant who have turned aside (from the) way of the people, the men of His Council who keep His covenant in the midst of iniquity, offering expiation (for the Land).[16]

While priests are offering expiation (a term used for Phinehas's act in Numbers), the royal Messiah of 1QSb (1Q28b) is being blessed to "ravage the earth with your scepter (Numbers 24:17); may you bring death to the (Isaiah 11:4) ungodly with the breath of your lips!"[17] In another Qumran text we read of a "Messiah from Israel and Warrior-Priest, Messiah from Aaron and Teacher of Righteousness."[18] Other scrolls refer to a high priest as leader of the Qumran community. For instance, the *Pesher* on *Habakkuk* (1HpHab) equates the Teacher of Righteousness with the historical leader of the Qumran community with the Priest who interprets the words of the prophets and makes ultimate judgment (Cohen, 1987, 108). The War Scroll speaks of a "Warrior High Priest" whose work of "commanding the destruction of the Kittim" is equal in importance to the "Prince of the Congregation" (114).

Many more examples could be given from the Qumran texts. The point is that the development of the messiah figure, so often characterized as Davidic, almost always involves a priestly figure either directly or indirectly. The role of the priest is to purify, by violent means, the people, land, or temple so that the people in general can experience peace, and the foundational document for this idea is the Phinehas story.

Philo Judaeus

Taking another perspective, Torrey Seland has studied the works of Philo, especially as Philo interpreted Numbers 25 as justification for acts of zealous self-redress (lynch-law) in first century Alexandria.[19] Some of Seland's most valuable work involves his understanding of the meaning of the Phinehas text as Philo applied it in the Middle Judaism period. For instance, Seland suggests that Philo's understanding of being a holy people derived from the Phinehas story: "The holy was experienced as a power, and not as something in repose; it was rather something urgent, and in every case incalculable" (Seland, 1995, 101).

Within this urgency was the need to be pure. Purity laws were boundaries, maps, putting things in order (Seland, 1995, 101). In order to maintain purity, every Israelite should be willing to be a punishing agent, to act with zeal. Even the mild-mannered can have this zeal (129), especially when certain crimes are committed that require immediate redress. Quoting Philo:

And it is well that all who have a zeal for virtue should be permitted to exact the penalties offhand and with no delay, without bringing the offender before jury or council or any kind of magistrate at all, and give full scope to the feelings which possess them, that hatred of evil and love of God which urges them to inflict punishment without mercy on the impious. They should think that the occasion has made them councilors, jurymen, high sheriffs, members of assembly, accusers, witnesses, laws, people, everything in fact, so that without fear or hindrance they may champion religion in full security (Laws).

Seland continues: "This statement is followed by a reference that there is recorded in the Laws the example of one who acted with this admirable courage; and the Phinehas episode from Numbers 25 is recorded" (Seland, 1995, 37).

While the idea of the priestly messiah, based on the Phinehas text, is being developed elsewhere in Middle Judaism, here in Philo's Alexandria the same text is used to encourage acts of zeal when certain crimes against the Torah are committed. In both cases, Phinehas has been the justification for a violent, purging, expiating priestly mentality.

Outside of Philo, Seland defines the zeal of Phinehas as being equal to the zeal of God. Zeal is wrath and judgment, but also a rescue. "The zeal of God, according to the OT, is an aspect of God's holiness, of his nature" (Seland, 1995, 43).

To sum up so far, I have shown that the zeal of Phinehas is an integral part of the messianic development of Middle Judaism. Goldstein, Oegema, Eisenman, and Cohen have all referred to Phinehas as foundational for the messianic priestly figure. Goldstein, Brandon, Patai, and Cohen demonstrated the link between Phinehas and Elijah, a link which elevates Phinehas even more. Seland demonstrated the importance of the Phinehas episode in the sanction of violent self-redress in the works of Philo.

Phineas and the Zeal of God in the New Testament: Jesus as Violent Messiah

Seland's main point in *Establishment Violence in Philo and Luke* is that violent self-redress did occur in New Testament times, and the stoning of Stephen, the attempted stoning of the woman in John 8, and the numerous mentions of violence directed against Paul were likely to have been real occurrences. Seland believes the justification for these acts lay in the understanding and interpretation of the Phinehas text, current to the time of Middle Judaism. He suggests that this zeal was performed not by a distinct party of zealots, but by any who felt they were defending the honor of God (Seland, 1995, 2). Seland presents an interesting study regarding Paul's use of "the works of the law" in Romans 3:28, tracing the phrase through Qumran texts to Psalm 106:30 to Numbers 25 (29–30).

Historically, we know that this was a period of messiahs, and these messiahs were militant, filled with zeal. This phenomenon has been well studied. Horsley suggests the messiahs had two overall goals: achieve liberation and reestablish an egalitarian social structure (Horsley, 1992, 101). Smith traced resistance of Rome to the Maccabeans' admiration of zeal:

> From at least Maccabean times many Jews fostered the admiration of zeal, and individuals undertook, or were thought, to be zealots on the models of Phineas and Elijah. This admiration and these models were presumably influential in shaping resistance to direct Roman government, in which resistance the first prominent figure was Judas of Galilee.[20]

It is not surprising then that some scholars would take a new look at the most important historical messiah figure: Jesus. For centuries the messiah I described as my childhood messiah was the messiah of pope and peasant alike; but recently, others have had a different idea. Horsley, for instance, suggests that Jesus came out of the same peasant movement that produced other militant messiahs of the period (Horsley, 1992, 84). He points out that popular Israelite kingship has three principal characteristics: it was constituted by popular election or anointing; it was conditional on the king's maintenance of a certain social policy; and the anointing of a new king, by the people, was clearly a revolutionary act (88–89). Along this line, Lenowitz suggests "The relocation of Jesus to Judaea in the birth narrative, and from there back to the Galilee, and then from there back to Jerusalem might reflect the ambivalent attitudes of his movement (as well as of the Davidic ideology) toward a policy of violence, associated with the Galilee, that was conducted in Judaea" (Lenowitz, 1998, 281, fn. 13).

This, and other studies also,[21] increases the likelihood that Christ was not as pacific as the Gospels portray him, especially in the beginning of his ministry, and maybe even at the end. After devoting a chapter to the Gospels' portrait of a "pacific Christ," Brandon concludes with this reminder: "However, it is well to remember that Christian tradition has preserved, in the Apocalypse of John, the memory of another, and doubtless more primitive, conception of

Christ—of the terrible Rider on the White Horse, whose 'eyes are like a flame of fire, . . . He is clad in a robe dipped in blood, and the name by which he is called is The Word of God . . . From his mouth issues a sharp sword [of Phinehas]?[22] with which to smite the nations, and he will rule them with a rod of iron; he will tread the wine press of the fury of the wrath of God the Almighty. On his robe and on his thigh he has a name inscribed, King of kings and Lord of lords (Rev. xix.12 ff.)" (Brandon, 1967, 320).

Oegema also points out New Testament texts that reveal a Jesus described in the eschatological and messianic beliefs of the time, including:

> 1 Thessalonians 1:10: And to wait for his Son from heaven, whom he raised from the dead, even, Jesus, which delivered us from the wrath to come. (Oegema,1998, 169)
>
> 2 Thessalonians 2:8: And then shall the Wicked be revealed, whom the Lord (Jesus) shall consume with the spirit of his mouth, and shall destroy with the brightness of his coming. (Oegema, 1998, 171)

Oegema concludes that Jewish apocalypticism is the hidden "mother of Christian theology," because "without seeing Pauline theology within the context of Jewish apocalypticism it is almost unintelligible, and on the other hand that with him Christian theology has removed itself from its Jewish roots and has become independent of it in such a degree that one has to speak already in Paul's theology of a 'parting between mother and son'" (Oegema, 1998, 184).

Additionally, Brandon links Jesus more directly with Phinehas. He argues that the fact Jesus had to be taken at night after a betrayal suggests that Jesus had "no intention of surrendering himself voluntarily, as a kind of sacrificial victim, to his enemies" (Brandon, 1967, 351). In a footnote, Brandon writes, "It is legitimate to wonder whether the bystanders mistaking of Jesus' cry of Eloi, Eloi[23] for an invocation of Elijah, if authentic, might indicate that they regarded him as a Zealot, invoking the aid of the Zealot Messiah, i.e., Elijah-Phinehas, according to the Zealot conception" (351, fn. 9).

Eisenman has also seen Jesus act zealously:

> Chief among these claims is the requirement of "zeal for the Law" as a prerequisite for service at the Temple altar. . . . Jesus himself displays some of these attitudes in the Gospel portrayal of the Temple-cleansing affair where "Zealot" language is explicitly attributed to him.[24] Similar "zeal" for the Temple is attributed to his brother James in the portraits of his "Piety" (*Hesed*) and Righteousness in early Church literature.

Not only does James 2:10 stress his "zeal for the Law." but all accounts dwell on how the flesh on his knees resembled "camel's hide" from all the importuning of God he did in the context of what appears to have been a Yom Kippur atonement. Similar "zeal" (as well as "Rock," "Fortress," "Shield," and "Protection" imagery) is also referred to in the Qumran Hymns usually attributed to the personal composition of the Righteous teacher himself. (Eisenman, 1983, 10)

Elsewhere Seland, referencing C. K. Barrett, says, "the Phinehas episode may be a part of the background of John 16:2, where it is stated the "the hour is coming when whoever kills you will think he is offering service to God" (Seland, 1995, 59). In discussing the zealotic influence on Jesus, Brandon challenges: "If theological considerations make it necessary to prejudge the historical situation and to decide that Jesus could not have involved himself in a contemporary political issue, the judgment must accordingly be seen for what it is. In making it, the criteria are theological, not historical (Brandon, 1967, 25). The harmful impact of these theological considerations cannot be minimized.

The Doubling (Rivalry) of Christian and Jewish Messianic Ideas, and the Continued Influence of Priestly Zeal in Messianic Development

Lenowitz points out that the Gospels were completed around the time of the Bar Kosiba revolt (132 C.E.), and thus developed together, with their texts placing the two messiahs in opposition to each other. These opposing texts become "a foundation for the realities and texts of all later Jewish messiahs" (Lenowitz, 1998, 32). Earlier, Lenowitz spoke of the mimetic doubling of Christian and Jewish messianic ideas: "Christian influence on [Jewish] messiah doctrine can also be detected in the loving attention paid, measure for measure, to the sufferings of this doomed messiah and his citizenry" (31).

In "Ancient Judaism and Christianity,"[25] David Flusser argues that the hostile opposition that developed between Jews and Christians was necessary for the development of Christianity. Flusser demonstrates that Christians either could not, or would not, see pro-Jewish themes in the Gospels, and concludes: "It should be recognized that Christian anti-Judaism was not a coincidental lapse. Anti-Judaism stood godfather to the formation of Christianity."

However, from a Girardian perspective, this hostile opposition was necessary for the development of *both* Rabbinic Judaism and

Christianity. While both traditions mimicked each other in terms of the "sufferings of the doomed messiah and his citizenry," these sufferings were not without well-known outbreaks of divine zeal.

Twelfth-century Maimonides, perhaps inadvertently, opened the door to this zeal while insisting on a messianic pacific position. Lenowitz explains that Maimonides feared the violent anti-Jewish outbreaks that occurred when Jews heeded the calls of messiahs, and thus it is not "worth the risk of heeding their calls" (Lenowitz, 1998, 66). One of the attributes of a true messiah, according to Maimonides, is to achieve and urge all Jews to strict obedience to written and oral Torah, and to *"fight the battles of God"* (67). As during the time of Phinehas, God needs an intermediary to fight battles based on Torah obedience.[26]

Additionally, the messianic and eschatological ideas of punishment of the wicked before the peace of the righteous, which developed during the Middle Judaism period, continued to impact Judaic and Christian thought. For instance, speaking of Daniel 9:24, Boccaccini writes: "As in Dream Visions, the exile will end only by the intervention of God and the inauguration of the eschatological era, which it was hoped would follow the events of the Maccabean period. After the *divine punishment* there is no more history; God's forgiveness marks the end of history" (*Beyond the Essene Hypothesis*, 85). Just as the belief in divine punishment existed in many forms in Middle Judaism, it continued through the development of Christian ideologies to the present time. This divine punishment, which will *finish* transgression, *put an end* to sin, and *atone* for iniquity, and thus bring an *everlasting* righteousness,[27] is strangely reminiscent of the language of the Phinehas episode. Thus over time the twin developments of Middle Judaism, Christianity, and Rabbinic Judaism, have assimilated this and other texts into their historical and—in the case of Christianity—messianic perspectives without ever realizing that what has also been absorbed is the imagery of the violent, purifying, purging act of the intermediary priest. This violent purging is nothing other than a sacrificial offering that must be accomplished before peace can come.

The apocalyptic vision, complete with violent purging, is certainly alive and well today. James Williams writes:

> A sacrificial reading of the biblical tradition stays within the boundaries of the centrality of sacrifice and regeneration through violence. In Christianity, for example, those who hold to a doctrine of salvation through the sacrifice of Christ that satisfies a just—and justly angry— God (even if this sacrifice was once and for all), read biblical texts in terms

of this central sacrifice. Likewise, Christians as well as Jews who envision a final apocalypse as the destruction of the wicked by a triumphant God or Messiah, tend to see the world and read the Bible sacrificially.

From the standpoint of a sacrificial reading the Bible recounts the revelation of a God who seeks to redeem the world through individuals and a people whom he chooses but who must be tried and purged so that they may be holy and righteous bearers of the divine revelation. (Williams, 1994, 73)

That many do read the Bible in exactly this way is attested to by Robert Bater, who writes,

Finally, we note the embarrassing enthusiasm of a large segment of fundamentalist preachers for the preaching of Armageddon. . . . Millenarianism is that particular brand of Christian apocalyptic, pessimistic [writing] about any amelioration of the world's misery before the return of Christ, which became the majority Adventist view in the nineteenth century, and again now in the last half of the twentieth. (Bater, 1994, 296)

Current Jewish commentaries include those of Jacob Milgrom, who states, "The rabbis were uncomfortable with Phinehas's act." Still, the act was never repudiated, because "the Holy Spirit testified that his zeal for God was genuine" (Milgrom, 1990, 215), and the expiation prevented God's wrath (217). J. H. Hertz, an older and more conservative commentator, explains that: "The act of Phinehas was accepted by God as a national atonement . . . " (Hertz, 1964, 686).

Messianism, in its varied Middle Judaism forms, has always included an overarching violent component, most easily defined through the relationship of messianic ideology to the priestly, divinely sanctioned violence of the Phinehas story. Many scholars, research, and several authors, including some not specifically quoted herein,[28] have mentioned the high price, in death and suffering, that has been paid for messianic belief. Whether the suffering is that of a righteous people awaiting rescue (one result of which is the impetus of hastening . . . i.e., causing one's own people to suffer in a frenzy of antinomianism[29]) or the death and suffering inflicted by God and his anointed on sinners, the result is the same.

According to our texts and according to popular understanding in any time period, should a messiah come to relieve the suffering of his people, he would do so either violently or accompanied by violence. Beliefs in a warrior-messiah, informed by ancient traditions regarding king, prophet, and especially priest, continue. Violence is an inseparable, if hidden, part of messianic ideology.

Conclusion

The huge impact of the Phinehas story in the development of messianic thought in Middle Judaism is shown by the numerous Phinehas texts and references of the period. The Numbers 25 text still impacts the children of the period, namely, Christianity and Rabbinic Judaism. Further, Girardian theory suggests the Phinehas story contains all the elements of the "violent sacred," which orders society and keeps overwhelming violence at bay. These elements include the apostasy (not recognizing the authority of God), the outbreak of the plague, the act of Phinehas, the plague ending, and the reward of Phinehas (Seland, 63 ff.). Girardian theory suggests these are the elements that give the story such power, and I suggest that these elements carry through the story and later developments, to the present day. The result is sanctioned violence: for the Christian, in the name of the Prince of Peace, and for the Jew, in the name of the God who approved of Phinehas's zeal.

My childhood Messiah is being celebrated in song and ritual around the world. I suggest that this Messiah is, at least in part, the result of a story that contains within its hidden past the Phinehas desire to find peace through zealous violence.

Addendum

Since the initial writing of this chapter during the fall of 2000, world events, including the destruction of the World Trade Center on September 11, 2001, and its aftermath, have demonstrated even more powerfully the horrific consequences of religiously sanctioned violence. A Girardian interpretation of the Phinehas story helps to explain the ongoing motivation for religiously driven murderous zeal currently being practiced by radical extremists, not only among Muslims, but certainly among Christians and Jews as well. While the world is brought to the brink of the extreme mimetic crisis called war, those who study peace would do well to turn, quite deliberately, from the zeal of Phinehas and instead focus on the greater Girardian message: that peace also has its foundational story, found in the Gospels, of a High Priest who illuminated the way out of humanity's self-destructive demand for the murder of sacrificial scapegoats.

Notes

1. Throughout this chapter, a variety of spellings of Phinehas's name (Phinehas, Phineas, Pinkas, Pinhas) will reflect the various transliterations of the Hebrew text used by different authors.

2. As Paul also stated, in 1 Corinthians 13:11.

3. Boccaccini discussing Judaism and Christianity as being twin sons of the same mother in *Middle Judaism*, 14.

4. 1 Samuel 10:1.

5. Ibid., 26:11.

6. Ibid., 7:8–16.

7. One of the names of Moses, according to Patai.

8. According to Patai: Reference to Pinhas son of Eleazar son of Aaron, who was jealous for his God and made atonement for the Children of Israel (Num. 25:13), and whom the Aggada identifies with Elijah.

9. Seland writes: "What we consider as 'historical facts' are by themselves meaningless. They become meaningful only in a frame of reference. In order to understand we have to interpret."

10. Stirling, 1. I am indebted to Dr. Stirling for much of my Girardian presentation, and, additionally, I have included several Girardian texts in the bibliography.

11. Cf. Boccaccini: *Beyond the Essene Hypothesis*, 89.

12. John 11:49–50, NRSV.

13. Interestingly, Milgrom adds that later tradition [Josephus], interpreting the "plague" as slaughter, claims that Phinehas's example was followed by his loyal supporters, and it was they who slew the twenty-four thousand Israelites.

14. It is important to remember that only one side of the story is being told; we have no idea of the guilt or innocence of the victims, because their voice has been completely silenced.

15. I am interested in Carol Delaney's treatment of the Abrahamic legacy as one that sanctions, at least in the popular mind, the righteousness of one who is willing to sacrifice his own child.

16. Translation by Vermes, *Scrolls*, 100, quoted in Cohen: *The Anointed and His People* (92).

17. Translation by Vermes, *Scrolls*, 237. References to biblical passages by Cohen: *The Anointed and His People* (93).

18. Cohen, *The Anointed and His People*, relying on Kippenberg, *Religion*, 106–117 (101).

19. Seland, *Establishment Violence in Philo and Luke*.

20. Ibid., quoting in fn. 184 on page 70: M. Smith, "Zealots and Sicarii" (9).

21. For instance, Brandon, in fn. 3, 352, referring to H. W. Montefiore's "Revolt in the Desert?," N.T.S. VIII (1961–62), states that (136) the phrase "sheep without a shepherd" means, according to Old Testament usage, "an army without a general," and then discusses the possibility, at least, that

Jesus was considering a military/political messiahship, which he later could have rejected.

22. My question.

23. Mark 15:34.

24. Elsewhere in his book, Eisenman takes issue with Brandon and others who claim the Zealots constituted a specific, separate *revolutionary* movement within Judaism. See particularly fn. 50 on 48.

25. In Flusser: *Judaism and the Origins of Christianity,* 575–587.

26. I am not sure Maimonides himself would say that God needs an intermediary, even though his text infers exactly that.

27. Daniel 9:24 (NSRV) reads: Seventy weeks are decreed for your people and your holy city: to finish the transgression, to put an end to sin, and to atone for iniquity, to bring in everlasting righteousness, to seal both vision and prophet, and to anoint a most holy place.

28. Specifically Biale and Taubes, but others, like Lenowitz, also.

29. Mentioned in several texts, including Lenowitz and Biale.

References

Alexander, P. S. (1998). "The King Messiah in Rabbinic Judaism." In J. Day (Ed.), *King and messiah in Israel and the Ancient Near East: Proceedings of the Oxford Old Testament Seminar* (456–473). Sheffield: Sheffield Academic Press.

An analytic approach to the Mishnah, the Gemara, and the Midrashim produced in the rabbinic Yeshivot. Most interesting was the idea that messianism was embedded in the rabbinic liturgy, keeping it from disappearing, and giving credibility to its official reentry in the work of Saadia Gaon.

Bater, B. R. (1994). Apocalyptic religion in Christian Fundamentalism. In M. I. Wallace & T. H. Smith (Eds.), *Curing violence* (287–304). Sonomo: Polebridge Press.

This article specifically deals with current-day apocalyptic fundamentalisms, based on modern readings—or misreadings—of ancient texts.

Biale, D. (1992). Gershom Scholem on Jewish messianism. In M. Saperstein (Ed.), *Essential papers on Messianic movements and personalities in Jewish history* (521–550). New York University Press.

This article provided a clear overview of Gershom Scholem's writings about, and struggles with, Jewish messianism.

Boccaccini, G. (1998). *Beyond the Essene hypothesis.* Grand Rapids: Eerdmans.

This book is recommended reading for anyone wishing to understand cutting-edge scholarship in the field of Middle Judaism sectarian divisions. Both this book and *Middle Judaism* are incredibly exciting reads. Boccaccini makes his academic scholarship accessible and deeply moving as he untangles historical myth and misconceptions with an easy, almost deceptive, clarity.

Boccaccini, G. (1991). *Middle Judaism.* Minneapolis: Fortress.

Boccaccini presents an invaluable bibliography of centuries (Josephus to 1990) of writing concerning the Middle Judaism period. His history and "cross-section" of second century B.C.E. thought is the best summary/analysis of this material that I have read to date. In fact, Boccaccini's ability to summarize/analyze complex documents and histories is nothing short of awe-inspiring, as is his obvious commitment to both ancient materials and present-day peoples impacted by the ancient literature.

Brandon, S. G. F. (1967). *Jesus and the Zealots.* Manchester: Manchester University Press.

I found this book fabulously interesting. Brandon does not claim that Jesus was a Zealot so much as he makes the case that Jesus could not have avoided being influenced by Zealots. This scenario, of course, depends on one's acceptance of the Zealots as a separate, well-defined sect in Middle Temple Judaism, and it is easy to criticize some of Brandon's conclusions in the light of the most recent sectarian scholarship. Brandon's argument, however, that Jesus chose a Zealot for a disciple and never condemns the Zealots (327) is one of compelling interest for me.

Burkert, W., Girard, R., & Smith, J. Z. (1987). *Violent origins: Ritual killing and cultural formation* (R. G. Hamerton-Kelly, Ed.). Stanford: Stanford University Press.

This book was useful in providing additional background for Girardian theory as I presented it in my paper.

Cohen, S. J. D. (1987). *From the Maccabees to the Mishnah.* Philadelphia: Westminster.

Cohen states at the onset that he is trying to present a work useful for scholar and layperson alike, and I think he succeeds admirably. Material this complex is not easy to present simply; Cohen does a fine job.

Day, J. (1998). The Canaanite inheritance of the Israelite monarchy. In J. Day (Ed.), *King and messiah in Israel and the Ancient Near East: Proceedings of the Oxford Old Testament Seminar.* (72–90). Sheffield: Sheffield Academic Press.

This article was useful specifically in its subtopic: "King as Priest after the Order of Melchizedek."

Delaney, C. (1988). *Abraham on trial: The social legacy of Biblical myth.* Princeton: Princeton University Press.

I used this book as a kind of comparative background, measuring my own treatment of Phinehas against Delaney's brilliant and moving questions of a faith that has made a virtue out of the willingness to sacrifice a child. In the same way, I have tried to question a tradition that has made a virtue out of a violently murderous "zeal," calling it righteousness, and sanctioning the blood spilled in its name.

Dunn, J.D.G. (1992). Messianic ideas and their influence on the Jesus of history. In J. H. Charlesworth (Ed.), *The Messiah* (365–381). Minneapolis: Fortress.

Since, in the interest of time, I was seeking out articles that dealt with the idea of priestly messiah ideas, it will come as no surprise that Dunn discusses both the Phinehas episode and priestly-messiah traditions in this article.

Eisenman, R. H. (1983). *Maccabees, Zadokites, Christians and Qumran: A new hypothesis of Qumran origins.* Leiden: E. J. Brill.

This book, with its 38 pages of small-print text and 58 pages of smaller-print notes, helped me understand further the theories which I had read elsewhere concerning Jesus and the Zealots. Also, Eisenman's thoughts on priesthood/ Phinehas/righteousness corresponded to many of my own, and I used him in my paper. However, Eisenman's "new hypothesis" of the Qumran community being mostly Zadokite in nature is one not supported in other literature. I am not expert enough to pass judgment on Eisenman's research, which seemed to me prodigious, but I also am uncomfortable in accepting his conclusions without further study. My intuition says that there is much in Eisenman's work to save and build from, but I am wary of his final conclusions.

Fitzmyer, J. A. (2000). *The Dead Sea Scrolls and Christian origins.* Grand Rapids: Eerdmans.

This is mainly a compilation of some of Fitzmyer's articles and lectures. Fitzmyer has an intimate knowledge of Dead Sea documents, and his easy access to ideas within the scrolls themselves was very helpful to me.

Flusser, D. (1988). *Judaism and the origins of Christianity.* Jerusalem: Magnes Press, Hebrew University.

I would have liked to have more thoroughly read this text. I chose a small portion only, owing to time constraints: "The Crucified One and the Jews," 575–587, which I quoted in my paper. The entire work represents a portion of Flusser's English writings, which often appear in footnotes and bibliographies of other authors. Even so it is 650 pages, excluding bibliography.

Forster, W. (1964). *From the exile to Christ* (G. E. Harris, Trans.). Philadelphia: Fortress. First ed. 1959.

This is an early look at the "parties" within Judaism, utilizing information from the Qumran Scrolls. Harris is openly Christian, and ultimately elevates a confessional belief in Jesus above all other considerations, ending with a specifically Christian (and it could be argued, anti-Jewish) polemic. While this weakens the book, I found Forster interesting specifically for this reason: he has valuable things to say and represents a specific stage in the fascinating development of Middle Judaism scholarship.

Friedlaender, I. (1992). Shiitic influences in Jewish sectarianism. In M. Saperstein (Ed.), *Essential papers on Messianic movements and personalities in Jewish history* (113–161). New York: New York University Press.

A very thorough treatment of messianic development in a later period, both in Judaism and Islam. I used this information in a small part of my paper showing how the violent priestly messiah has moved on to modern times.

Girard, R. (1986). *The scapegoat* (Y. Freccero, Trans.). Baltimore: Johns Hopkins University Press.

One of my favorite Girard texts, this book contained invaluable discussion of certain New Testament ideas, including the Passion and the Caiaphus rationale: *it is better that one should die* ...

Girard, R. (1978). *To double business bound.* Baltimore: Johns Hopkins University Press.

A collection of essays that were very tough to read the first time I attempted them, some years ago, but which are worth the effort of a second and third time through. The title refers to Girard's theory of the conflict with the mimetic double, a conflict which, if left unchecked, will invariably end in subjugation and/or murder.

Girard, R. (1972). *Violence and the sacred* (P. Gregory, Trans.). Baltimore: Johns Hopkins University Press.

A study of human evil, further developing Girard's theory of scapegoating and mimetic behavior.

Goldstein, J. (1976). *I Maccabees.* Anchor Bible 41. New York: Doubleday.

Besides translation, Goldstein provides excellent commentary on the use of Phinehas as a Maccabean model. See especially introduction pages 5–8 for Goldstein's analysis of this comparative framework.

Hamerton-Kelly, R. G. (1994). *The Gospel and the sacred: Poetics of violence in Mark.* Minneapolis: Fortress.

This book contains an explanation of Girardian theory, which Hamerton-Kelly names the generative mimetic scapegoating mechanism. For further notes on this text, see comments on the author's article, below.

Hamerton-Kelly, R. G. (1992). Sacred violence and the Messiah: The Markan passian narrative as a redefinition of messianology. In J. H. Charlesworth (Ed.), *The Messiah.* (461–493). Minneapolis: Fortress.

This article became a longer book, noted above. Hamerton-Kelly is a Girardian thinker, and in this piece he presents the idea that the violence in Mark shows Jesus as the one who turns the tables on violent scapegoating, showing a different, clearer way. In other words, this article represents the gospel text as demonstrating an attack on the sacrificial system, instead of succumbing to it.

Hertz, J. H. (1964). *Soncino edition of the Pentateuch and Haftorahs.* London: Soncino Press.

   I used the Numbers 25 commentary from Dr. Hertz to demonstrate how this text is interpreted today. Even though Dr. Hertz is dead, this commentary still commands respect, and is thus still alive in the current culture.

Horbury, W. (1998). Messianism in the Old Testament Apocrypha and Pseudepigrapha. In J. Day (Ed.), *King and messiah in Israel and the Ancient Near East: Proceedings of the Oxford Old Testament Seminar* (402–433). Sheffield: Sheffield Academic Press.

   Horbury argues that messianic hope was more pervasive in the years from Haggai to Bar Kochba than is usually allowed. He suggests that the so-called "messianic vacuum" has been overstated.

Horsley, R. A. (1992). Popular Messianic movements around the time of Jesus. In M. Saperstein (Ed.), *Essential papers on messianic movements and personalities in Jewish history* (83–112). New York: New York University Press.

   For comments, see below.

Horsley, R. A., & Hanson, J. S. (1985). *Bandits, prophets, and messiahs: Popular movements in the time of Jesus.* Minneapolis: Winston Press.

   This represents a broader explanation of many of the ideas expressed in Horsley's paper cited above. Emphasis is placed on the role of the peasantry in creating and supporting popular uprisings, and the underlying foundations for that role. Popular memory and egalitarian desires, as well as a well-thought-out historical framework for discussing these movements within Second Temple Judaism, help make this a useful book.

Hoskins, R. K. (1997). *Vigilantes of Christendom: The story of the Phineas priesthood.* Lynchburg: Virginia Publishing Co.

   This book is a good starting place for anyone interested in knowing more about supremacists who call themselves the Phineas Priesthood.

Lasine, S. (1994). Levite violence, fratricide, and sacrifice in the Bible and later revolutionary rhetoric. In M. I. Wallace & T. H. Smith (Eds.), *Curing violence.* (204–229). Sonomo: Polebridge Press.

   This article represents an attempt to understand the subject in light of Girardian theory.

Lenowitz, H. (1998). *The Jewish messiahs: From the Galilee to Crown Heights.* New York: Oxford University Press.

   Lenowitz takes an unflinching and sometimes shocking look at messiahs: "At this point, we can say without equivocation that all Jewish messiahs are dead (4)." This is an excellent source for historical messiah identification, and for an attempt at a reasoned explanation of the messiah phenomenon.

Mason, R. (1998). The Messiah in the postexilic Old Testament literature. In J. Day (Ed.), *King and messiah in Israel and the Ancient Near East: Proceedings of the Oxford Old Testament Seminar* (338–364). Sheffield: Sheffield Academic Press.

In contrast to Horbury, above, Mason believes post-exilic Old Testament literature is practically bereft of messianic expectation, specifically the renewal of the Davidic line. Mason does, however, give emphasis to the importance of the priestly line in what Messianic expectation he does see (347).

Milgrom, J. (1990). *The JPS Torah commentary: Numbers*. Philadelphia: Jewish Publication Society.

Milgrom emphasizes Rabbinical discomfort with Phinehas's self-redress, stating that only God could have saved Phinehas from excommunication for murder, and that what stayed the plague was really Phinehas's *prayer*, not his violence. Other citations are included in my paper.

Myers, J. M. (1974). *I and II Esdras*. Anchor Bible 42. New York: Doubleday.

This was my primary source for I and II Esdras translation.

Oegema, G. S. (1998). *The anointed and his people: Messianic expectations from the Maccabees to Bar Kochba*. Sheffield: Sheffield Academic Press.

A very systematic and thorough look at the period and the beliefs in question. Certainly Oegema addresses the idea of the priestly messiah. From his very organized presentation, I could educe more clearly than from other texts which sources related to my topic of Phinehas/priestly messiah traditions. In the end, Oegema concludes that the "idea" of messianism in Judaism may be an elusive modern overlay. *"We can only locate its historical realizations, but not the idea itself . . ."* (306).

Patai, R. (1979). *The messiah texts*. Detroit: Wayne State University.

Patai was useful in his categorizations (see his chapter headings). The material from this book relates specifically to "legends," and as such provides a fascinating look at Talmudic, Midrashic, and Kabbalistic texts dealing with messiah belief. Patai's linking of Elijah with Phinehas was very useful to my study.

Peters, J. *Numbers 25:1–15*. http://www.alltel.net/'jpeters/pe38.html.

As with my other Internet source, I used this quickly found commentary to illustrate current colloquial use of the Phinehas story.

Reif, S. C. (1971, June). What enraged Phinehas?—A study of Numbers 25:8. *Journal of Biblical Literature, 90*(2), 200–206.

I found this article because Torrey Seland leaned on it so heavily. Reif concludes that it was not the sexual activity between Zimri and Cozbi per se which was so terrible, but the act of bringing Cozbi and her shrine, for the purposes of divination, into the camp.

Roberts, J.J.M. (1992). The Old Testament's contribution to messianic expectations. In J. H. Charlesworth (Ed.), *The Messiah* (39–51). Minneapolis: Fortress.

Roberts explores roots of different messiah traditions, including priestly messiah traditions.

Rooke, D. W. (1998). Kingship as priesthood: The relationship between the high priesthood and the monarchy. In J. Day (Ed.), *King and messiah in Israel and the Ancient Near East: Proceedings of the Oxford Old Testament Seminar* (187–208). Sheffield: Sheffield Academic Press.

Rooke believes that these two institutions, priesthood and kingship, are inexorably related. When the two functions are separate, they stand in tension with each other. When the functions meld into one person, that person is supposed to fully act the roles of both king and priest.

Ruffner, R. L. *Heroes of the Bible.* Power—December 1993. http://www.southavencoc.org/Power/p1993/Heroes.htm.

I used this source to illustrate current use of the Phinehas story. I don't know anything about Ruffner except for this Internet claim: "Roelf Ruffner preaches the truth in Marlin, Texas."

Saperstein, M. (Ed.). (1992). *Essential papers on messianic movements and personalities in Jewish history.* New York: New York University Press.

Much of this collection covered later time periods than my current study. However, the relevant articles—listed separately in this bibliography—were excellent, and the book itself attests to the enduring Messianic idea specifically throughout Jewish history to the present day.

Schiffman, L. H. (1991). *From text to tradition: A history of Second Temple and Rabbinic Judaism.* Hoboken: Ktav Publishing House.

Schiffman is an excellent conservative Jewish scholar. We used this text and the one following in Boccaccini's undergraduate classes at the University of Michigan.

Schiffman, L. H. (1998). *Texts and traditions: A source reader for the study of Second Temple and Rabbinic Judaism.* Hoboken: Ktav Publishing House.

Schweid, E. (1992). Jewish messianism: Metamorphoses of an idea. In M. Saperstein (Ed.), *Essential papers on messianic movements and personalities in Jewish history* (53–72). New York University Press.

An excellent summary of the history of Jewish messianism, emphasizing kingship and violent redemption yet allowing for additional messianic ideas, in this case, judges as messiahs.

Seland, T. (1995). *Establishment violence in Philo and Luke: A study of nonconformity to the Torah and Jewish vigilante reactions.* Leiden: E. J. Brill.

This was the text that first convinced me, through Seland's sources and footnotes, as well as his emphasis on Phinehas/zeal/righteousness in violent self-redress of the period, that there would be enough material on my topic of Phinehas and messianism to warrant a paper. If Phinehas had provided a model for vigilante action, my thought was he probably had provided a model for other kinds of violent salvific activity. This very thorough study, including much discussion about the earlier work of E. R. Goodenough, had its origin in Seland's Ph.D. thesis.

Smith, M. (1992). Messiahs: Robbers, jurists, prophets, and magicians. In M. Saperstein (Ed.), *Essential papers on messianic movements and personalities in Jewish history* (73–82). New York: New York University Press.

A provocative article on different Messiah figures at the time of Jesus. Especially interesting to me was the linking of magic with messianism (an idea I wanted to develop as it relates to the Phinehas episode, but I simply ran out of time). Smith also mentions Elijah—who, as I demonstrated in my paper, can and sometimes is a Phinehas synonym—as both prophet and magician.

Stirling, M. (1999, July). *Introduction to Girardian thought.* Stirling's unpublished lecture notes in author's possession.

I was fortunate to be present when Dr. Stirling gave this very clear analysis of Girardian theory; he remains for me one of the true unsung experts in this field, waiting publication and discovery.

Taubes, J. (1992). The price of messianism. In M. Saperstein (Ed.), *Essential papers on messianic movements and personalities in Jewish history* (551–558). New York: New York University Press.

This article gave me more than I expected. Taubes sees the political and spiritual danger of messianism, but seemed unable to articulate just what the danger is or how it occurs. The article was reacting to Gershom Sholem.

Werblowsky, R. J. Z. (1992). Messianism in Jewish history. In M. Saperstein (Ed.), *Essential papers on messianic movements and personalities in Jewish history* (35–52). New York: New York University Press.

This article offered no support for my thinking on the priestly messiah. It did, however, emphasize the terrorizing violence that precedes the messiah's coming.

Williams, J. G. (1994). Steadfast love and not sacrifice. In M. I. Wallace & T. H. Smith (Eds.), *Curing violence* (71–99). Sonoma: Polebridge Press.

Williams argues against reading the Gospels as having a sacrifice that satisfies a just (and justly angry) God at their center. Williams also argues against final apocalyptical (destruction of the wicked) thinking. Williams has translated several of Girard's works.

Zeitlin, S. (1974). *Studies in the early history of Judaism* (Vol. 2). New York: Ktav Publishing House.

Zeitlin writes from a distinctly Jewish perspective, and thus provided a valuable perspective for me. Especially interesting was Zeitlin's view of the early Church fathers' interpretations of Messiah in Hebrew Bible texts (396 ff.).

Zeron, A. (1979). The martyrdom of Phinehas-Elijah. *Journal of Biblical Literature, 98*(1), 99–100.

This short article explores the identification of Phinehas with Elijah in New Testament and Middle Judaism texts.

CHAPTER 4

The Dynamics of Prejudice

J. Harold Ellens

Introduction

Prejudice has a bad reputation. It should have. It is everywhere and always destructive. Prejudice prevents an objective and sympathetic view of or address to anything. It is uniformly and consistently uncongenial with the best interests and quality of human life. Most human beings, I am quite sure, find prejudice reprehensible, but all of us are afflicted by it. We disapprove it, but we do it nonetheless. Pogo was right, "We have met the enemy and it is us!"

Prejudice afflicts us in two ways. We are all prejudiced about something and that obstructs our ability to deal with that specific matter, or the persons to which it applies, in the best possible way. Moreover, we are all recipients of the damage other persons' prejudices inflict upon us. I am 70 years old. It was a shock to me to notice that as I passed the age of about 60, at which time I suffered some heart trouble and aged rather more quickly than I had before then, the young clerks in the drugstore or hardware store clearly distanced themselves from me. Whereas the former attendants had been rather congenial, the new and younger ones now treated me as an object. Of course, they had no way of knowing that I was a retired U.S. Army colonel, an internationally known scholar, a noted lecturer, and a rather nice guy. They could only see that I was an old man who had not had the good sense to die and stop cluttering up their lives. At least that is my perception, perhaps my prejudice.

I notice that whether it is a matter of courtesy in driving on the highway, caring for my interests at a department store, or responding to my requests at a restaurant, airline counter, or other service setting, I am no longer seen by young adults as a *person;* unless they know me, need something from me, or are under my authority as in the case of my students, for example. Instead of being a person I am now an object, often made to feel that I am an inconvenience to those folks. I notice that I am not alone. I watch this happening as well to my friends and colleagues. It always makes me chuckle to see the reaction when I am with one of my elderly friends and we are treated like objects until I introduce him as the federal judge, or the U.S. senator whom they may not have recognized, or a general officer from my army days. Suddenly the prejudice that we are simply a couple of old guys who are a drag upon the U.S. economy evaporates and for a little while we are seen as persons.

I am certain that if one asked these young folks whether they were prejudiced against old people, they would stand aghast at the suggestion. I am sure they are not at all aware of their internal image of gray-haired and wrinkled persons as irrelevant, burdensome, and undesirable. That is the nature of prejudice, theirs and mine. It usually operates quite destructively at the unconscious level, and for that very reason is so abusive and does so much damage to the personhood and circumstances of real live human beings. Moreover, young folk have no special mortgage on prejudice or a special predilection toward it. As I write these paragraphs I am very much aware of my need to reflect upon my own temptation to paint all young adults with this same tar brush, when in fact my own adult children and young people I work with everyday are ample evidence that most young adults are sensitive and generous, perhaps less dogmatic and judgmental than I.

The sensitivity of a senior scholar and old soldier and the insensitivity toward an old man by young people are painful, of course, but they are relatively trivial forms of prejudice, if one compares them with the biases which have wreaked upon humanity the destruction of racism, genocide, exploitive warfare, economic manipulation, or class and caste distinctions and elitism. These forms of institutionalized prejudice have formed the underpinnings of the abuses of power and have written the subtext of human history from its earliest recording until now. Moreover, the tragedy of it is in the fact that the pain and abuse of prejudicial behavior fall upon real live and lively human persons of flesh and blood and mind and spirit. This violence is tangible, not theoretical; palpable, not abstract. "If you prick us, do we not bleed? If you tickle us, do we not laugh? If you poison us, do we not die?" (Shakespeare, *The Merchant of Venice*, III, 1).

Exposition

Recently, my friend federal Judge John Feikens sent me a note with a fine piece attached from the *New York Review of Books* (October 18, 2001). It was Henry Hardy's column, "Notes on Prejudice," in which he presented a direct transcript of a manuscript of Isaiah Berlin. Hardy quoted at length Isaiah Berlin's "hurried notes ... for a friend,"[1] explaining that Berlin's inner soul "is vividly expressed" in those notes. The friend, who was planning a lecture on prejudice, had asked Berlin for some suggestions. Since Berlin was going abroad that day, he quickly penned his answer.

Hardy described Berlin's intense observations there as "somewhat breathless and telegraphic" and conveying "with great immediacy Berlin's opposition to intolerance and prejudice, especially ... stereotypes, and aggressive nationalism." The wisdom of Hardy's selection of this material for *New York Review of Books* is obvious when we note that its date is just one month after the World Trade Center tragedy. There venomous religious and cultural prejudice wreaked havoc on our entire nation—indeed upon the entire world. One might summarize Berlin's passionate expression in one sentence. "Few things have done more harm than the belief on the part of individuals or groups (or tribes or states or nations or churches) that he or she or they are in the *sole* possession of the truth: especially about how to live, what to be and do—and that those who differ from them are not merely mistaken, but wicked or mad: and need restraining or suppressing. It is a terrible and dangerous arrogance to believe that you alone are right: have a magical eye which sees the truth: and that others cannot be right if they disagree."

In 1996 Elizabeth Young-Bruehl published a superb analysis of this affliction of human psychology and society. She called it *Anatomy of Prejudices*.[2] Her superior work has not been superseded. Her focus is mainly upon anti-Semitism, racism, sexism, and homophobia. However, her general assessment of the psychodynamics of this psychosocial malady leads us to an appreciation of the similarities all forms of prejudice manifest, the distinctive characteristics of each type, and the subtle and blatant forms of their social expression. From the slightest slur to the stupid joke to the violent act, even war, prejudice functions like the sophisticated computer virus which adapts its own structure as it goes along eating up all the resources available, and using the wholesome qualities and energies by turning them on their heads and redirecting their trajectories to create evil. What were growth-inducing insights are turned into malevolent analyses and defensive-aggressive reactions, filled with and generating paranoia and hate.

Young-Bruehl observes upon the great difficulty we have in stepping outside our own prejudices, even in our endeavor to speak or write wisely about prejudice. She wonders why, " . . . on this topic of prejudices, so much has been written on such shaky foundations, with such a recycling of clichés and unfounded conclusions. I became convinced that the way we have learned to speak in . . . America about prejudices is a very large part of our prejudice problem, a part of which we are, daily, unaware" (2). She points out that when Gordon Allport wrote his valuable treatise, *The Nature of Prejudice*, and surveyed the total scope of the subject in mid-twentieth-century America, he announced his objective as seeking out the root of prejudice so as to understand its nature.[3] While the course Allport set for the investigation of prejudice was a worthy one, his model was limited by the implied assumption that "prejudice is something singular with one nature and one root" (Young-Bruehl, 16). However, Allport actually is at some pains to declare that, "It is a serious error to ascribe prejudice and discrimination to any single taproot, reaching into economic exploitation, social structure, the mores, fear, aggression, sex conflict, or any other favored soil. Prejudice and discrimination . . . may draw nourishment from all these conditions, and many others" (Allport, xii). Allport wishes to teach plural causation, but he acknowledges that he is by professional habit disposed to emphasize the role of learning, cognitive processes, and personality formation. "It is true that I believe," says he, "it is only within the nexus of the personality that we find the effective operation of historical, cultural, and economic factors . . . for it is only *individuals* who can feel antagonism and practice discrimination . . . I place a heavy and convergent emphasis upon psychological factors" (xii–xiii).

Allport drew out these psychodynamics of prejudice in a surprisingly creative way for a scholar working on this issue so early in our cultural awareness of the need to study it systematically. He put his finger on the central dynamic of prejudice. His words seem as wise and applicable a half century later as they must have seemed forward-

A visitor to the Henry Ford Museum looks inside the actual bus on which civil rights pioneer Rosa Parks refused to give up her seat to a white man in Montgomery, Alabama, during the early days of the American civil rights movement. AP/Wide World Photos.

looking and wise when he published them a decade after the close of World War II.

> At the time when the world as a whole suffers from panic induced by the rival ideologies of east and west, each corner of the earth has its own special burdens of animosity. Moslems distrust non-Moslems. Jews who escaped extermination in Central Europe find themselves in the new State of Israel surrounded by antisemitism. Refugees roam in inhospitable lands. (ix)

Allport points out that black people particularly suffer indignities from whites and fanciful racist doctrines are invented to justify it. He believes, undoubtedly correctly, that this constitutes a kind of condescension. Moreover, he is especially indignant about the pervasive prejudices in the United States and thinks them the most intricate and endlessly antagonistic of all, based upon no good foundation in reality, but rather in uninformed imagination. "Imaginary fears can cause real suffering." The rivalries and hatreds are as old as sin, but the technology for inflicting damage upon one another is more lethal because it brings us so much closer to each other.

Allport did not develop his psychological perceptions very extensively because his approach was, in the end, primarily sociological. However, one experiences throughout his work that he kept his eye open to the inner psychodynamics of the individual. He would, I think, have agreed with the perception that prejudice is primarily a defensive aggressive psychological phenomenon, that it is rooted in ignorance or bad information about the person or community against which the prejudice is directed, that it is generated by the primal human urge to survival combined with the paranoia which lack of accurate information produces, and that it expresses itself as an intention to devalue, disarm, and extinguish the relevance of the object of the prejudice. This psychological process may take the form of slights and verbal disrespect, intimidations and social degrading, physical deprivations and assaults, catastrophic violence and war, or extermination of the object of the discrimination and hatred.

In their superb chapters in this volume, Stirling and McGuire explicate the model of René Girard for explaining how specific persons or groups become identified in or by a society as the object of prejudice and its social consequences. They develop Girard's essentially psychoanalytic understanding of these forms of isolation, alienation, devaluation, and extermination, pointing out particularly his metaphor of the scapegoat. This is, of course, an old metaphor, already prominent in ancient Israelite religion and in the Hebrew Bible, which that religion produced. It is carried over in formative ways into the Christian Scriptures of the New Testament and into Islam's sacred scriptures, the Qur'an.

Girard's point comes down to the psychoanalytic insight that the scapegoat, whether it is an individual or another society, becomes a projection of the shadow side of the source or enactor of the prejudice. Prejudice always generates and is generated by an "us versus them" mindset. The circumstances of life often produce realistic situations in which there arise a real-life us and them. My family and I live in North America. There are many other humans who do not, including a number of my relatives for whom I have great affection. They live in Germany. Whether we discuss the geography of Greenland or the current perspectives on American policy toward the Near Eastern nations and cultures, it is inevitable that their perspective will be that of those who must look westward toward Greenland

and ours that of those who must look eastward. That may seem irrelevant, but psychoanalytic psychologists know that the simple difference makes a discernible psychological difference in the way we and they think of Greenland.

On the infinitely more complex and serious matter of Near East policy, the differences in perspective will inevitably be much more remarkable. We may even have the same basic facts and principles in mind, but we will see the implications of them differently if our primary unconscious interest is American and theirs is German. With some significant conscious and rational thoughtfulness we may be able to place ourselves in each other's shoes and gain more global views that might be almost identical, but even then certain flavors and tastes, so to speak, will still make our feelings about the matter distinctive to each of us.

We can, of course, have important differences without resorting to prejudice. We may take a gracious, thoughtful attitude which empowers us to understand a wide range of views on a matter without feeling less passionate about the one we support. We may be able to allow the others to have their point of view as a legitimate alternative way of looking at things. Or we may feel strongly that the facts are such that they really have no moral right or rational justification to hold to such an ill-informed outlook. However, even then, it is not necessary for us to resort to prejudice, which is a need to devalue or damage the other person or community because of the positions they take, the attitudes they evince, or the behaviors they act out.

Prejudice is the irrational, unconscious, devaluation of another for no other reason than that the "other" is different. Prejudice increases with ignorance and the paranoia it generates. Prejudice identifies, isolates, and alienates its object. The further this process progresses the easier it is to project upon that "other" those things we hate in ourselves. We always hate most in others what we cannot stand in ourselves. Our own flaws, distortions, iniquities, self-defeating habits, and failures we see readily in others, or believe we do, and unconsciously we attack those in them that we know we should extinguish from ourselves. Therefore, those things that we cannot face in ourselves, for which we cannot forgive ourselves, we make into the reasons for devaluing or destroying them.

If those dysfunctions in ourselves which we cannot stand, cannot deal with, cannot correct, or cannot forgive, happen to be religiously and morally laden with some kind of divine censure, in our perception, we will see our attack upon those very things in others as divinely sanctioned, justified by God, even the imperatives of his own will and mandate for us. We may feel called by God, in such instances, to wreak havoc upon those others who are the "legitimate" objects of our prejudice. This surely was the motive and mindset of the terrorists of the 9/11 tragedy. It is the outlook of Christian pro-lifers, whose disgust with abortion on demand may be appropriate, but who are intent upon killing doctors and nurses who service abortion clinics. It seems to have been clearly the case of the ancient biblical Israelites who confused their own acquisitive prejudices with the divine will when it came to extermination of the Canaanites "because the cup of their iniquity was filled." Few readers notice that the cup was filled with exactly the idolatrous and abusive behavior to which the Israelites were forever inclined themselves, given half a chance to diverge from the "call of Yahweh" to be a distinctive people of grace. It is surely the disposition and dynamics of the modern Palestinians and Israelis who seem forever ready to destroy their own world to save it.

Allport had an interesting way of getting at the underpinnings of these psychological dynamics of prejudice. He thought that our negative prejudices are the obverse of those things that we love and cherish, and that the most important categories we have in terms of which to think and feel about things are our personal values. We live by and for them, without consciously needing to think about them or evaluate them. We defend them in terms of the intensity of our feelings about them, and we compel our reason and assessment of evidence to fit in with them. "As partisans for our own way of life we cannot help thinking in a partisan manner. Only a small portion of our reasoning is ... 'directed thinking' ... controlled exclusively by outer evidence and focused upon the solution of objective problems.... Such partisan thinking is entirely natural, for our job in this world is to live in an integrated way as value-seekers. Prejudgments stemming from these values enable us to do so" (24).

Unfortunately, prejudgments can easily slide into prejudice. Allport was aware of the fact that affirming our way of life may lead to the "brink of prejudice." He cites Spinoza's notion of "love-prejudice," namely, having more love feelings for someone or something than is appropriate to that object. We "overgeneralize" the virtues of such objects, whether a lover, a doctrine, a church, a nation, or a cause.

> ... This love-prejudice is far more basic to human life than is its opposite, hate-prejudice (which Spinoza says "consists in feeling about anyone

through hate less than is right"). One must first overestimate the things one loves before one can underestimate their contraries.... Positive attachments are essential to life.... Why is it that we hear so little about love-prejudice—the tendency to overgeneralize our categories of attachment and affection? (24–26)

Allport answers his own question by pointing out that love-prejudices create no social problems. Hate-prejudice, however, is a narcissism in which my interests are asserted at the expense of other people. This social danger gives rise to conflict because of the overvaluing of my own mode of life and the underprizing of that of the others. This produces a sense of threat in both directions. Freud asserted that it is in these undisguised "antipathies and aversions" that the destructive self-love of narcissism can be discerned, inciting social violence.

Particularly relevant to our present moment in history and the international circumstances in the Western world is Allport's next paragraph.

The process is especially clear in time of war. When an enemy threatens all or nearly all of our positive values we stiffen our resistance and exaggerate the merits of our cause. We feel—and this is an instance of overgeneralization—that we are wholly right. (If we did not believe this we could not marshal all our energies for our defense.) (26)

The implication of this is that if we are completely correct in our view the enemy must be completely in the wrong and should be exterminated. War exemplifies clearly how our primal love-prejudice is our primary motivation and our hate-prejudice is the derivative underside of it.

Isaiah Berlin thought that under these circumstances of significant conflict of values we tend to operate from the certainty that there is only one worthy goal for one's self, church, nation, or humanity; "only one true answer to the central questions which have agonized mankind"; and that it is worth risking all for that final solution, no matter how costly. We tend to be particularly willing to accept exorbitant costs in loss and suffering, particularly if it is mainly the enemy's loss and suffering. He cited Robespierre as saying, "through an ocean of blood to the Kingdom of Love."[4]

Berlin grieved that if we have not learned from history the foolishness and self-defeat in this outlook, "we are incurable." That may be so. It is almost certainly so if we cannot rid ourselves of the West's endemic tendency to assume that human conflicts, like God's conflicts in the Hebrew Bible, are ultimately best resolved by precipitating catastrophe. This leads us to delay earlier, safer, and saner resolutions of misunderstandings and collision courses of policy or ambition, trusting that if all else fails, which it surely will in such an irresponsible model, we can always resort to the ultimate violence. We are inherently addicted to cataclysm, so we do not fear our prejudices as much as we fear the loss of what we "love more than is right."

During the last decade of the twentieth century Robert M. Baird and Stuart E. Rosenbaum edited a series of psychosocial studies entitled *Contemporary Issues.* These amounted to a series of handbooks on various topics related mainly to legal and ethical issues in social management. One useful monograph in the series was entitled *Bigotry, Prejudice and Hatred, Definitions, Causes and Solutions.*[5] Two chapters in this volume proved to be particularly helpful. Chapter 10 by Elliot Aronson investigated "Causes of Prejudice." Pierre L. van den Berghe wrote the following chapter on "The Biology of Nepotism." Both of these relate directly to this particular phase of our discussion here, in that they address the underside of our love-prejudice and paint a picture of a Girardian take on our hate-prejudice. Aronson led off with the following paragraph,

> . . . one determinant of prejudice in a person is a need for self-justification . . . if we have done something cruel to a person or a group of people, we derogate that person or group in order to justify our cruelty. If we can convince ourselves that a group is unworthy, subhuman, stupid, or immoral, it helps us to keep from feeling immoral if we enslave members of that group, deprive them of a decent education, or murder them. We can then continue to go to church (or Synagogue or Mosque, I would add) and feel . . . good . . . because it isn't a fellow human we've hurt. Indeed, if we're skillful enough, we can even convince ourselves that the barbaric slaying of old men, women, and children is a . . . virtue—as the crusaders did when, on their way to the holy land, they butchered European Jews in the name of the Prince of Peace. . . . this form of self-justification serves to intensify subsequent brutality. (111)

Sociological studies tend to suggest that the more the security of one's status and power is jeopardized, the more prejudiced one tends to be and behave. Van den Berghe, who published *The Ethnic Phenomenon* with Greenwood Press in 1987, makes a cogent argument for finding the roots of prejudice in nepotism. His basic argument is that "ethnic and racial sentiments are extensions of kinship sentiments. Ethnocentrism and racism are thus extended forms of nepotism—the propensity to favor kin over nonkin. There exists a general behavioral predisposition, in our species as in many others, to react favorably toward other organisms to the extent that these organisms are biologically related to the actor. The closer the relationship is, the stronger the preferential behavior" (125). Blood is still thicker than water, apparently.

It is interesting, of course, that humans are seldom cannibals, and if they are it is generally with great revulsion and in extremity. Most humans are willing to consume other mammals, birds, and creatures lower on the evolutionary tree, such as fish. Even many of those who argue for being vegetarian on the grounds that one ought not to eat "meat" will, nonetheless, eat chicken and fish. The former is presumably from the dinosaur line and the latter from the reptilian line, both a long way from our human branch of the tree. Those vegetarians who also avoid chicken, fish, and dairy, vegans, who wish only a strictly vegetarian diet, are usually mystified when I ask them how they can possibly tolerate killing these living things they eat, the poor lettuce leaf, celery stalks, beautiful carrots, and the like. They tend to respond that these are short-lived forms of life anyway, are planted for harvesting, and have no consciousness or feelings.

Of course there is a significant debate about whether the last claim is true. There seems to be adequate evidence that plants respond to what seems comparable to our central nervous system stimulation. However, when all is said and done, the argument boils down to the fact that plants are so far down the evolutionary tree as to be not worth considering as a life-form in the sense that humans are life-forms. Van den Berghe's claim is vindicated by this rather simple human proclivity to argue for the privilege of those most like us and against the privileged status of those most unlike us. Thus blacks can more easily feel and act out prejudice against whites than against other blacks, and whites have demonstrated the same thing on their side of the equation, in monstrous ways, throughout history.

However, Young-Bruehl is less certain than van den Berghe that the familial connections in the dynamics of prejudice are biological or grounded in kinship issues. She wonders, with Erich Fromm, whether the familial influence is not rather psychosocial, particularly the sociological side of it. She investigated (Young-Bruehl, 1996, 64–65) the extent to which it is the family power structure and the values related to it that set the course for prejudicial patterns and dispositions. Adorno and Horkheimer were sure that the patriarchal family is the nexus of prejudice by reason of its authoritarian socialization of the family members.[6] This is basically the "frustration-aggression" model for explaining prejudice as rage displaced upon a scapegoat and forming the foundation for such models as that of Girard.

In the end, Young-Bruehl concludes that the sources and dynamics of prejudice are so complex that one must avoid above all the temptation to generalizations, normally the objective of all science. Instead, she urges, we must address the operational issues of prejudicial behavior in specific situations: specific categories such as racism, sexism, homophobia, anti-Semitism; and specific incidences such as this lynching, that genocide, this caste system, that slavery, this riot, that family feud. I agree, but it is clear that there are generalizing similarities at work in the tragedies of prejudice. They include the following list of factors. First, the difficulty humans have in living with the unknown and the very different. Second, the human tendency to make dogmatic claims that differences of values and styles mean the moral inferiority of the other. Third, the human inclination to fear the unknown or different and react to or act out that fear in defensive aggressive strategies. Fourth, the human need to justify those feelings and that behavior by demonizing the object of the prejudice. Fifth, the corollary behavior of isolating, alienating, devaluing, degrading, disempowering, and if necessary exterminating that object, whether a person or a community. Sixth, the human inclination to believe there is a single and final solution to the impasse of difference and conflict. Seventh, the willingness to pay any price for the ultimate cataclysm which will resolve the tension, stress, and burden of that impasse, particularly if that cost is mainly at the expense of the object of the prejudice, the enemy.

Conclusion

It is clear that prejudice is a devastating force in our political and social order, and that it arises in a very sick psychology at the center of our souls and imposes a large toll upon our spirituality. It is the shadow side of our inherent need to survive, grow, develop, and achieve freedom and stasis. It may be considered to have a positive side, in Spinoza's sense of "love-prejudice." Humans are capable of imagining a virtually perfect world and are able to create only a flawed one. The distance that our real world falls short of our idealized imagination we identify as failure and pain. We internalize that pain as guilt rather than simply being able to accept it as a function of our limited humanness. That guilt prompts us to self-justification and defensive aggressive behavior, setting in motion the strategies of prejudice discussed above.

The general claim of this chapter and of these volumes is that our ancient religious metaphors create that kind of negative psychological archetypes at our centers. These inflame our prejudices and the psychodynamics behind them. At the center this is a spiritual problem, and there is no fixing it except with a spiritual renewal, which is framed and shaped and driven by a theology of grace, a religion of grace, a sociology of grace, and a self-psychology of grace. Divine grace! Human grace. Grace is unconditional positive regard for the other. Judaism hatched this idea of unconditional grace as the redemptive dynamic of true religion and healthy psychology. As I argued previously, all three major Western religions, Judaism, Christianity, and Islam, have, as their mainstream, this notion of grace inherited from the precursors of Judaism, namely, ancient Israelite religion, the religion of the Hebrew Bible.

For 3,000 years, however, this mainstream has been muddied, distorted, and obscured by a completely erroneous religious metaphor: the notion that this world is the arena of an apocalyptic cosmic conflict between good and evil. This useless and psychotic metaphor seems to justify our worst prejudices and our most destructive behavior. Yet it has no ground under it. There is no evidence for ontic evil. However, in all three of these major religions, our sacred scriptures lock us into this notion. It defines us. Unless we radically revise our theology of sacred scriptures in all three religions, we cannot escape this prison house of prejudice. We cannot transcend the built-in bigotry. We cannot become fully human.

Notes

1. The *New York Review of Books*, October 18, 2001.

2. Young-Bruehl, Elizabeth. *Anatomy of Prejudices*. Cambridge: Harvard University Press, 1996.

3. Allport, Gordon. *The Nature of Prejudice*. Garden City: Doubleday Anchor, 1958.

4. Hardy thinks this may be a reference Berlin makes "off the top of his head," so to speak, to Robespierre's sentences, *"en scellant notre ouvrage de notre sang, nous puissons voir au moins briller l'aurore de la felicite universelle"* ("by sealing our work with our blood, we may see at least the bright dawn

of universal happiness"), in *Rapport sur les principes de morale politique que doivent guider la Convention nationale dans l'administration interieure de la Republique*, Paris, 1794, 4.

5. Baird, Robert M., and Stuart E. Rosenbaum (Eds.). *Bigotry, Prejudice and Hatred, Definitions, Causes and Solutions.* Part of the series *Contemporary Issues.* New York: Prometheus Books, 1992.

6. Adorno, Theodor, and Max Horkheimer. *The Authoritarian Personality.* New York: Harper, 1950.

CHAPTER 5

VIOLENCE, PREJUDICE, AND RELIGION: A REFLECTION ON THE ANCIENT NEAR EAST

Edmund S. Meltzer

It is obvious even to the most casual reader, museum-goer, or tourist that images of warfare and violence permeate the artistic, iconographic, and textual record of the religions of the ancient Near East. (In the present discussion I shall focus on Egypt, because it is my primary area of study, but I shall not entirely confine my comments to it.) It would plainly be special pleading and revisionist nonsense to claim that ancient Egypt and its neighbors had religions of sweetness and light, peace and love. At the very dawn of recorded history, if not before, the emergent Pharaonic state is defined by the motif of the king—the divine king—smiting his defeated enemies,[1] while nearly ubiquitous in the New Kingdom and later are scenes in which the deity hands the sword to the ruler.[2] And these are, if more than the tip of the iceberg, certainly much less than the total roster of visual testimonies to victorious war in the art of Egypt—let alone of the entire ancient Near East, where one has *inter alia* the magnificent, panoramic military scenes in Assyrian art. Scholars have attempted to analyze these motifs on a profound level[3] and have debated whether, or to what extent, the smiting scene is an ideological archetype or a representation of a unique historical event, a metaphor or a depiction of an actual ceremonial execution.[4] Early claims by some scholars that the great pyramid age of the Old Kingdom was largely pacific have long been abandoned,[5] and the attempt to identify pacifism in the reigns of Queen Hatshepsut and the "heretic" king

Akhenaten have likewise lost credibility.[6] At least in the case of the
Egyptians, the ideal of a world without war or conflict was thought
to pertain to the afterlife rather than the here and now,[7] though of
course Egypt itself was supposed to be free of civil strife. What, then,
if anything, does the ancient Near East have to teach us about the
problem of religion and violence, other than giving us more examples
of what to avoid? I contend that we can indeed learn something positive from those great cradles of civilization, something other than an
excuse to indulge in unjustified feelings of superiority.

The violence memorialized and given permanent, ideal form in the
textual and visual record had an indisputable religious dimension.
A category of the civil or secular state apart from the sovereignty of
the deity or deities did not exist; war was waged under the auspices
of the deity, and in Egypt it was a deity incarnate who personally led
the troops into battle. In the religious dynamics of the ancient Near
East, it was commonplace for war to be perceived as, on one level,
combat between the national or state deities of the opponents. The
victor would often take the principal cult image from the sanctuary
of the defeated people's deity and carry it off to the fane of the victorious god or goddess.[8] If the defeated people could win a subsequent
war, they would reclaim their image and also carry off that of their
rivals. There was, however, a line that they apparently did not cross,
and that was the delegitimization of the opponents' deity/ies and religion and the persecution of their opponents, or of other peoples in
general, because of their religion. This is, of course, a step, which
seems to have become a norm in far too much modern religious discourse, which then becomes intertwined in the discourse of politics,
oppression, exploitation, and terrorism. If the Assyrians defeated the
Egyptians, they considered that the god Ashur was victorious over
and hence stronger than the god Amen-Re. They did not, however,
deny the existence of the Egyptian deities, condemn Egyptian religion as error, attempt to convert the Egyptians to the Assyrian faith,
or persecute, discriminate against, or massacre Egyptians on religious grounds. In their worldview, this would simply have made no
sense. (They could and did, of course, selectively massacre Egyptians
for disloyalty or political insurrection.) By and large, the tendency
was to expand the boundaries of the pantheon by accepting the
deities of other civilizations, both by honoring the deities of foreign
regions when one traveled and by adopting the deities of newcomers
(even captives or invaders, or people with whom one often fought). As
time went on, deities could be identified with one another across cul-

tural/linguistic lines: Amen-Re with Zeus, Thoth with Hermes, and so on. A Persian-Jewish writer named Artapanus went so far as to equate Thoth-Hermes-Mercury with Moses.[9] An important precedent in Pharaonic times was the identification or syncretism of the Egyptian Set with the Syro-Canaanite-Phoenician storm-god Baal.

Very good illustrations of some of the types of religious dynamics to which I refer can be found in the Hebrew Bible. The Assyrian defeat of the northern kingdom of Israel did not mean to the Assyrians that the God of Israel did not exist or that the Israelites practiced a "false" religion. When the Assyrians settled the first foreign deportees in the conquered land of Israel, some of the newly settled people were killed by lions, whereupon:

> They said to the king of Assyria: "The nations which you deported and resettled in the towns of Samaria do not know the rules of the God of the land . . ."
>
> The king of Assyria gave an order: "Send there one of the priests whom you have deported; let him go and dwell there, and let him teach them the practices of the God of the land." (II Kings 17:26–27)[10]

Also, to the strong condemnation of the Chronicler,

> After Amaziah returned from defeating the Edomites, he had the gods of the men of Seir brought, and installed them as his gods; he prostrated himself before them, and to them he made sacrifice. (II Chronicles 25:14)[11]

It is also most notable that in the Book of Jonah, God accepts the repentance of the Assyrians without requiring them to change their religion! Yet another extremely striking instance of religious interaction narrated in Tanakh is the encounter between the pious king Josiah of Judah and the Egyptian monarch Necho II in 609 B.C.E., when it was the Egyptian monarch, not the Judahite reformer, through whom God spoke:

> "What have I to do with you, king of Judah? I do not march against you this day but against the kingdom that wars with me, and it is God's will that I hurry. Refrain, then, from interfering with God who is with me, that he not destroy you." But Josiah would not let him alone; instead, he donned [his armor] to fight him, heedless of Necho's words from the mouth of God; and he came to fight in the plain of Megiddo. (II Chronicles 35:21–22)[12]

It would be incorrect to maintain that among the ancient Near Eastern civilizations, no deities were ever "purged" and no religious movements proscribed. In the Second Dynasty of Egypt, there seems to have been a struggle between Horus and Set, perhaps related to political frictions, which ended in a reconciliation.[13] Much later, in the first millennium B.C.E., Set (whose reputation had always been somewhat precarious because of his mythological role as the murderer of Osiris) fell into extreme disfavor and attempts were made to expunge him.[14] The most celebrated instance of the purging of deities in ancient Egypt is certainly the exclusivist movement of Akhenaten, under whom—some years into his reign—divinities other than the Aten, or sun-disk (and, it has been argued, he himself and his consort, Nefertiti), were proscribed.[15] His short-lived movement was in its turn declared anathema, and he was the victim of a *damnatio memoriae*. Also, in the Neo-Babylonian dynasty, the enthusiastic promotion of moon-worship by the scholarly king Nabonidus was regarded as aberrant by some of his compatriots.[16] On the whole, however, it remains a fair generalization that ancient Near Eastern religions did not delegitimize one another or persecute one another's followers.

Relevant to the eventual crossing of this line, or slide down this slope, is the gap between King Amaziah's action quoted above and the Chronicler's attitude, which illustrates a fundamental point of which everyone is aware: that Israelite religion parted company with what one might call the "normative" ancient Near Eastern religions. One of the most powerful manifestations of this parting of the ways is the prophetic polemic against idolatry, which is a misrepresentation of the deities of the other civilizations (and apparently of many Israelites) and the significance of icons in their worship, as discussed very lucidly by Michael B. Dick.[17] Either the biblical characterization is a hostile caricature, or it shows that the Israelites were so removed from the religious consciousness of their neighbors—and ancestors—that they no longer comprehended the nature of the deities and divine images of other nations. The great Israeli scholar Yechezkel Kaufmann thought the latter, and ascribed the "revolutionary" idea of monotheism to an intuition in the mind of Moses[18]—an explanation that seems like a secularized version of revelation. This would also seem similar to Henri Frankfort's perception, since the great scholar of the "Chicago School" held that polytheism could not give rise to monotheism, as they represent fundamentally different mindsets.[19]

Another interrelated focus of the growing exclusivism of Israelite religion was the rivalry between YHWH and Baal, the dominant deity of the Syro-Canaanite religion, with a major culmination in the account of the showdown between Elijah and the prophets of Baal on

Baal, god of the thunderstorm, gilded bronze idol from
Minet-el-Beida, the port of ancient Ugarit (Syria). Erich
Lessing/Art Resource, New York.

Mt. Carmel in I Kings 18,[20] apparently precipitated by Ahab's marriage with the Phoenician Jezebel and their promulgation of Baal-
worship. Paradoxically, on one level, the narrative can be interpreted
as indicating how similar major aspects of the worship of Baal and
YHWH were at the time, and indeed the resemblance of the Baal-
theophanies in Ugaritic literature to biblical psalmody is sometimes
so striking as to be uncanny,[21] as is the Psalm-like nature of some
Egyptian hymns.[22] But the description in I Kings 18 gives no hint of
this kinship or fraternal dimension. Reading the account, one is

struck forcibly by the uncompromising ferocity of the struggle on both sides: Queen Jezebel's campaign to exterminate the prophets of YHWH and the retaliation of YHWH and his mediator Elijah. YHWH burns up the sacrifice and everything around it, apparently desolating the top of the mountain, whereupon at Elijah's bidding the people seize all the prophets of Baal and Elijah kills them. To the present-day critical reader, it looks like what we would call a "grudge match" or "cycle of violence." If indeed texts have power, especially sacred texts—and the ancient peoples certainly thought so—then such a text is not only, or even primarily, a narrative of something that may have happened, but a model of divine will and both divine and human action that exerts a continuing influence, setting in motion a dynamic with which all of the "Abrahamic" traditions have had to wrestle.[23]

Two rather provocative observations seem difficult if not impossible to avoid concerning the disadvantages or pitfalls of strict monotheism and of a rigid scriptural canon. For the strict monotheist, all divine volition must have one source, and this entails the attribution of violent and vengeful actions to one and the same deity and makes them an indelible part of the divine persona. Those traditions that we label "polytheistic" have the flexibility of compartmentalizing the divine sufficiently to place responsibility for many (though certainly not all) repugnant actions on certain deities, and thus to marginalize them to a greater extent.[24] Likewise, if a text is part of a rigid scriptural canon regarded as the word of the deity, it cannot be ignored or avoided (although attempts can be made to interpret it more innocuously, a tactic often employed by Rabbinic Judaism), and it must retain some defining role for a deity's nature and a tradition's identity. If, however, there is a looser accumulation of traditional sacred texts or classics without canonical force, this also provides greater flexibility, making it easier to ignore or marginalize a "toxic" text. As a concomitant of these reflections, those scholars who take a critical stance outside the monotheistic traditions have a crucial role to play in forcing us to question widespread assumptions of the moral superiority of those traditions.[25]

In a development fraught with paradoxes and ironies, the growing exclusivist tendencies of Israelite religion (some of which developed or were further exacerbated in a type of milieu and social dynamic described below) were ultimately even further intensified by the fellow "Abrahamic" religions of Christianity and Islam. Upon examination, the situation was multifaceted and the hardening of attitudes was not limited to the Israelite tradition and its offshoots.

So, what changed? In this brief article I cannot pretend to propose any sort of comprehensive explanation, which would necessarily be facile and superficial. I can, however, register my impression that in the course of the later Iron Age, the Persian and Classical periods, the Near Eastern/Mediterranean world appears to become more "modern" in some ways that give one a disconcerting sense of déjà vu, and I can suggest some of the dynamics that appear to be operating. Prejudice and ethnocentrism had apparently always existed, but they take on something that more closely resembles their modern garb as one approaches the turn of the era. The world becomes increasingly crowded, and increasingly, for a variety of reasons, groups of people are living outside the countries of their origin or heritage. Some are traders, some are mercenaries, others are refugees and deportees. As a result, many different cultural groups find themselves having to coexist in close proximity within the same country or the same city, and sometimes one seems to perceive another's customs as intrusions or as incompatible with one's own.[26] The outbreak of anti-Semitism culminating in the destruction of the Jewish temple at Elephantine during the Persian period seems to have had as a contributing factor the objections of the priesthood of the god Khnum to the sacrifice of lambs, the sacred animal of Khnum being the ram.[27] Groups in proximity likewise found themselves at odds over each other's purity requirements. It is in this light that we should understand Genesis 43:32:

> They served him by himself, and them by themselves, and the Egyptians who ate with them by themselves; for the Egyptians could not dine with the Hebrews, since that would be abhorrent to the Egyptians.[28]

In accordance with the approach of my teacher, Prof. Donald Redford, I think it is instructive to take this description as belonging to a Late Period milieu.[29]

In Egypt, the degree of ritual purity maintained by the Libyan dynasts who controlled the country was unacceptable to the invading Kushite king Piye (formerly read Piankhy), who was of course not an Egyptian himself,[30] and who exemplified a type of holier-than-thou piety to which one is not accustomed among the Egyptians themselves.

Historical/cultural one-upmanship also reared its head as an expression of group rivalries, as reflected for instance in the controversy between Apion and Josephus, and what seems to have been the Egyptian response to the Exodus tradition.[31] The Baal-YHWH conflict in the pre-Diaspora period, which we have noted above, seems to belong to this type of cultural antagonism. Such rivalries were also partly prompted, or at least exacerbated, by a nativist apocalypticism on the part of conquered and occupied peoples.[32] Despite all of these frictions, however, one gets the impression that much of the cultural interaction that went on was constructive and healthy, characterized by much cultural cross-fertilization and enrichment.[33]

If we are correct in suggesting that in at least one important respect the world's politically entangled religious communities have slid further down a slippery slope than their predecessors in the ancient Near East, how do we in the present day climb back up, hopefully to reach the greater height, which has so far eluded us? Perhaps the humility of that very realization is a necessary step.

Notes

1. The Narmer Palette is probably the most famous example. Cf. A. R. Schulman, *Ceremonial Execution and Public Rewards: Some Historical Scenes on New Kingdom Private Stelae* (Freiburg: Universitätsverlag; Göttingen: Vandenhoeck and Ruprecht, 1988); E. S. Hall, *The Pharaoh Smites His Enemies* (Munich: Deutscher Kunstverlag, 1986).

2. A. R. Schulman, "Take for Yourself the Sword," in B. M. Bryan & D. Lorton, eds., *Essays in Egyptology in Honor of Hans Goedicke* (San Antonio: Van Siclen Books, 1994), 265–295.

3. W. M. Davis, *Masking the Blow: The Scene of Representation in Late Prehistoric Egyptian Art* (Berkeley: University of California Press, 1992).

4. Schulman, both works cited; E. Hornung, "History as Celebration," in idem, *Idea into Image*, E. Bredeck, trans. (New York: Timken Publishers, 1992), 147–164; and D. B. Redford, *Pharaonic King-Lists, Annals and Day-Books* (Mississauga: Benben, 1986), xvii–xxi, 133f.

5. D. B. Redford, *Egypt, Canaan, and Israel in Ancient Times* (Princeton: Princeton University Press, 1992), Ch. 2.

6. For Hatshepsut, see Redford, *Egypt, Canaan, and Israel,* 149 with n. 97; for Akhenaten, see Schulman, "Hittites, Helmets and Amarna: Akhenaten's First Hittite War," in Redford et al., *The Akhenaten Temple Project, Vol. 2* (Toronto: Akhenaten Temple Project/University of Toronto Press, 1988), 53–79.

7. J. L. Foster, *Hymns, Prayers, and Songs: An Anthology of Ancient Egyptian Lyric Poetry* (Atlanta: Scholars Press, 1995), 157f.

8. A. K. Grayson, "Mesopotamia, History of," in D. N. Freedman, ed., *Anchor Bible Dictionary* (New York: Doubleday, 1992), Vol. 4, 761–763, 766. Several Ptolemaic texts refer to the repatriation of Egyptian divine images that had been carried off by the Persians; my former student Ma Xiaohua refers to these accounts and suggests that they are attributing propagandistically to the Persians' destruction really inflicted by the Assyrians: *Persian Ruling Policies in Late Egypt and Egyptian Reactions* (M.A. thesis, Northeast Normal University, Changchun, China, 1995), 6f with notes 8–13.

9. G. Mussies, "The Interpretatio Judaica of Thot-Hermes," in M. Heerma van Voss et al., ed., *Studies in Egyptian Religion Dedicated to Professor Jan Zandee* (Leiden: E. J. Brill, 1982), 89–120.

10. *Tanakh: A New Translation of the Holy Scriptures According to the Traditional Hebrew Text* (Philadelphia: Jewish Publication Society, 1985), 596.

11. *Tanakh*, 1605.

12. *Tanakh*, 1622; cf. Redford, *Egypt, Canaan, and Israel*, 448f.

13. E. S. Meltzer, "Horus," in D. B. Redford, ed., *Oxford Encyclopedia of Ancient Egypt* (New York: Oxford University, 2001), Vol. 2, 119–122.

14. H. Te Velde, "Seth," in *Oxford Encyclopedia*, Vol. 3, 269–271.

15. The most balanced and up-to-date treatment of this extremely controversial subject is E. Hornung, *Akhenaten and the Religion of Light*, D. Lorton, trans. (Ithaca: Cornell University Press, 1999).

16. M. Roaf, *A Cultural Atlas of Mesopotamia and the Ancient Near East* (New York: Facts on File, 1990), 201; Grayson, "Mesopotamia, History of," 766.

17. M. B. Dick, "Worshiping Idols: What Isaiah Didn't Know," *Bible Review* 18/2 (April 2002): 30–37; see also the present writer's letter to the editor, "Egypt, Too," *Bible Review* 18/4 (August 2002): 6.

18. Y. Kaufmann, "The Bible and Mythological Polytheism," *Journal of Biblical Literature* 70 (1951): 179–197.

19. H. Frankfort in idem et al., *The Intellectual Adventure of Ancient Man* (Chicago: University of Chicago Press, 1946) (abridged edition: *Before Philosophy* [Harmondsworth: Penguin Books, 1949]).

20. *Tanakh*, 552–555; J. Day, "Baal," in *Anchor Bible Dictionary*, Vol. 1, 545–549.

21. J. Day, "Baal."

22. M. Lichtheim, *Ancient Egyptian Literature*, Vol. 2 (Berkeley: University of California Press, 1976), 104–114; J. L. Foster, *Echoes of Egyptian Voices* (Norman: University of Oklahoma Press, 1992), 63–79.

23. Analogously, at a major interfaith dialogue in the Twin Cities in 1982, Rabbi Irving Greenberg stated that there is "a shrine to hate in the Gospels."

24. We do not wish to oversimplify the complex concept of "polytheism," which is a topic for a study at least as substantial as this. With regard to

Egyptian religion, a very felicitously expressed, judicious, brief summation is provided by J. L. Foster in the Introduction to his *Hymns, Prayers, and Songs: An Anthology of Ancient Egyptian Lyric Poetry* (Atlanta: Scholars Press, 1995). For an understanding of divine beings in ancient Egypt as an open-ended collectivity, see my article "A Reflection on the Category *Ntr* in Ancient Egyptian Religion," *NAOS: Notes and Materials for the Linguistic Study of the Sacred* 12/1–3 (1996): 2–4.

25. The most eloquent and erudite exponent of that perspective known to me is Terence DuQuesne, who has written prolifically on Egyptian and comparative religion, e.g., *Black and Gold God: Colour Symbolism of the God Anubis* (London: Dath Scholarly Services/Darengo Publications, 1996); cf. my review article " 'Who Knows the Color of God?' " in *Journal of Ancient Civilizations* 11 (1996): 123–129.

26. A. B. Lloyd, "The Late Period," in B. G. Trigger et al., *Ancient Egypt: A Social History* (Cambridge: Cambridge University Press, 1983), 316–318.

27. Lloyd, "The Late Period," 317. Worthwhile comments on this episode and its context are made by Ma Xiaohua, *Persian Ruling Policies in Late Egypt and Egyptian Reactions*, 41–42, and my former student Yan Haiying, *The Famine Stela on Sehel Island: Translation, Commentary and Historical-Comparative Analysis* (Ph.D. dissertation, Northeast Normal University, 1994), 50–54.

28. *Tanakh*, 71.

29. Redford, *Egypt, Canaan, and Israel*, 422–429; and idem, *A Study of the Biblical Story of Joseph* (Leiden: E. J. Brill, 1970).

30. For a good translation of the account of Piye's Crusade, or perhaps one could equally say *jihad*, see M. Lichtheim, *Ancient Egyptian Literature*, Vol. 3 (Berkeley: University of Califronia Press, 1980), 66–84. A personal aside: In the energetic and wide-ranging conversations that took place when I was a graduate student at the University of Toronto—often involving Geoff Freeman, Don Redford, Terry Miosi, Ron Leprohon, and myself—comparisons were made between the Sudanese Mahdist movement of the nineteenth century and the Kushite invasion under Piye (Mahdism being, to my mind, one of the earliest and most striking manifestations of radical "Islamist" movements impacting the Western powers). While there are certainly strong differences between the movements—Piye's was not a grass-roots revolutionary uprising—there are interesting parallels as well. In addition to Piye's preoccupation with holy places and incessant piety, his campaign against the Libyan dynasts then ruling Egypt and their impurity resonates with the Mahdi's targeting of the Turks (though they were fellow Muslims) and the British. A most interesting eyewitness account of the Mahdist conflict (albeit one with axes to grind) is R. C. Slatin (Pasha) and F. R. Wingate, *Fire and Sword in the Sudan*, rev. ed. (London: Edward Arnold, 1930). Rudolf Slatin was a British-appointed Governor-General of

the Sudan who publicly converted to Islam to bolster the loyalty of his Egyptian troops, and who spent years as a prisoner of the Khalifa.

31. D. B. Redford, *King-Lists*, 276–296; P. W. van der Horst, "The Way of Life of the Egyptian Priests According to Chaeremon," in M. Heerma van Voss et al., ed., *Studies in Egyptian Religion Dedicated to Professor Jan Zandee* (Leiden: E. J. Brill, 1982), 61–71.

32. Redford, *King-Lists*, 276–296; idem, *Egypt, Canaan, and Israel*, 471 (though I cannot agree with Redford's deprecatory dismissal of the literature or the movements in question); A. K. Bowman, *Egypt After the Pharaohs: 332 BC–AD 642* (Berkeley: University of California, 1986), 30f; Ma Xiaohua, *Persian Ruling Policies*, 34–40.

33. Lloyd, "The Late Period," 317f; for interaction between Egyptians and Greeks, see especially R. S. Bagnall, "Greeks and Egyptians: Ethnicity, Status, and Culture," in R. S. Bianchi, ed., *Cleopatra's Egypt: Age of the Ptolemies* (Brooklyn: Brooklyn Museum, 1988), 21–27; D. R. McBride, "The Development of Coptic: Late-Pagan Language of Synthesis in Egypt," *Journal of the Society for the Study of Egyptian Antiquities* 19 (1989): 89–111; idem, "Gnostic and Traditional Egyptian Religious Affinities in the Magical Papyri," *Journal of the Society for the Study of Egyptian Antiquities* 27 (1997 [2000]): 42–59. This claim of religious affinity prevails despite the earlier aversion described by Herodotus (Lloyd, "The Late Period," 316).

The writer thanks Dr. J. Harold Ellens for his encouragement and helpful suggestions in the writing of this chapter.

CHAPTER 6

THE HISTORICAL JESUS AS A JUSTIFICATION FOR TERROR

Charles T. Davis III

Introduction

New modes of consciousness explode from the unconscious depths of the psyche, motivating unanticipated, radical changes in social life that cannot be explained solely on the basis of historical antecedents. The French Revolution is the product of such an upheaval. The men of the Revolution understood this and declared that with their actions a new creation was appearing. As a part of this new creation, there arose a new critical biblical scholarship based upon the hermeneutics that developed in the German universities during the nineteenth century. The focal point of the German New Testament scholarship was the Quest for the Historical Jesus (Quest) spawned by the Revolution. The Quest ultimately failed as a scientific, historical search for Jesus the man. In 1906 Albert Schweitzer demonstrated that it is impossible scientifically to reconstruct the life of Jesus, because there are no adequate sources of evidence. Were the Quest simply a rational inquiry it should have ended, but it did not.

Why does the Quest continue in the absence of rational justification? Clearly, unconscious, archetypal, forces drive this quixotic search for Jesus. The shift from the descriptive title given his book by Schweitzer—*Von Reimarus zu Wrede*—to the archetypally powerful title given via the English translation—*The Quest for the Historical Jesus*—suggests the presence of an unconscious force mediated by the myth of the Quest for the Holy Grail. Since any "quest" is an "expression of the urge to discover what 'holds the world together at its inner core' (Goethe, *Faust*)" for the purpose of establishing "an order and meaning for our place in the cosmos" (Whitmont, 1997, 152), we must at the very least take the Quest to be more than a simple academic exercise.

The Quest originates in an environment where archetypal forces were at work. An examination of how mythic figures of Jesus were used both to oppose and support the Terror reveals the presence of an archetypal component that passes largely unrecognized into modern biblical scholarship.

Images of Jesus Invoked in the Rhetoric of the Revolution

The role of the unconscious in the Revolution is very strong. Even the historian J. McManners (1970) notes that as we delve into the Revolution, we enter a region where we may "identify and explain certain broad tendencies in the pattern of events" and also discover that "the explanation of the peculiar actions of individuals within these broad tendencies leads into obscure byways running off over the edge of the map of rationality" (85). It is a region in which the opponents of the Revolution, and of Modern Science, are written into the revolutionary past as barbarians who are completely "other" and thus are appropriate targets for violence and abuse—an issue explored by B. T. Cooper (1995) in her article "Rewriting the Revolutionary Past in *Les Prussiens en Lorraine*" (127). It is in this region, where things run off the map of rationality and legitimate history, that we discover the historical Jesus challenging the mythical Christ.

The King as the Deputy of God and Christ

The French monarchy was founded upon the theory of Divine Right. In *The Religious Origins of the French Revolution*, D. K. Van Kley (1996) describes a royal religion that "while assimilating aspects of Catholicism, endowed the French monarchy with reliquary sanctity, thaumaturgical prowess, and immortal as well as mortal body" (11). Van Kley documents the demise of this theory during the Jansenist controversy as a key factor in the development of the Revolution along with the anti-Christian spirit of the French *philosophes* who undermined the Christian foundations of French identity (3). The "divine king" was secularized through the efforts of both the philoso-

Louis XVI being led to the guillotine at the time of his execution. Library of Congress.

phers and the theologians. This was the prelude to the secularization of religion itself.

Documents collected by P. H. Beik (1970) in *The Documentary History of Western Civilization: The French Revolution* provide examples of Van Kley's (1996) contention that the French king was regarded as living a life transcending that of ordinary mortals. M. de Lamoignon, Keeper of the Seals of France, argued on behalf of Louis XVI before Parliament on November 19, 1787, that the king is accountable only to God for his exercise of power (Beik, 1970, 2.). This position was reaffirmed by Louis XVIII when he issued his "Declaration of Verona" from exile in 1795 (Beik, 1970, 327–328). He attributes the evils of revolutionary France to the departure of the nation from traditional wisdom, and he depicts Louis XVI as a martyr living in imitation of God in Christ (Beik, 1970, 329). Louis XVIII appears to be guided by the conservative pull of the Father archetype when he ignores the rational evidence for the Terror as a monumental upheaval in French social life. The medieval Christian view of Jesus as Pantocrater is still operative in his royal viewpoint, although by 1795 almost everyone recognized that a revolution had occurred. For example, the moderate royalist Mallet du Pan wrote in 1795 to his friend Saladin-Egerton of the need to establish a monarchy appropriate to the post-revolutionary climate rather than simply attempting to reinstate the Ancient Regime (Beik, 1970, 340–341). Du Pan

argued that a new monarchy would have to be built upon a "conse-
cration of some of the results of the revolution" (Beik, 1970, 341). It
appears that an astute royalist like du Pan could see by 1795 that the
person of the king was no longer regarded as holy. The medieval
worldview had been overturned.

Examination of the unconscious dimension of the rejection of the
French King and the Christ reveals how radical the Revolution really
was. Carl Jung (1959) argues in *Aion* that "every king carries the
symbol of the self" (198). The king is the archetypal *Anthropos*, the
original man "who not only begets, but himself is, the world" (198).
The same can be said of the Christ "since Christ as the 'Word' is
indeed . . . the symbol of the inner 'complete' man, the self" (Jung,
1959, 200). From a psychological perspective, we see that the
Revolution was a rejection of both the Christ and his representative
the King of France as symbols of the Self. The key question is "What
replaces the Christ and the King as images of the *Anthropos*, the Self,
as a result of the Revolution?" Is the Quest simply destructive of the
old order, or is it subconsciously a search for a new symbol of Self?

Kant, Reimarus, and the Humanistic Jesus

Modern biblical criticism has its roots in the scientific revolution.
Immanuel Kant published the *Critique of Pure Reason* in 1781 as a
defense of the scientific method against the skepticism of Hume. This
event heralded an impending intellectual revolution. William Barrett
(1987) in *Death of the Soul* quotes the poet Heinrich Heine as comparing Kant "to Robespierre . . . who brought in the Reign of Terror and
destroyed the *ancien régime*" because "Kant laid waste the traditional
arguments for God and undermined theology" (51–52). Clearly, intellectual and revolutionary political forces converged in the late eigh-
teenth century to explode the traditional worldview using the new
critical methods rooted in Science. The Quest began as a product of
the new criticism as practiced by Hermann Samuel Reimarus.

Lessing published the work of Reimarus posthumously between
1774 and 1778. The seventh excerpt of Reimarus's work was entitled "Concerning the Purpose of Jesus and His Disciples . . . "
(Jeremias, 1964, 4). It drew a careful distinction between the aim of
Jesus, which came to a tragic end with his cry of dereliction and
death on the cross, and the aim of the disciples who fabricated the
resurrection and founded the Church upon a lie (Jeremias, 1964, 4).
The resurrection is a fraud perpetrated by Jesus' power-hungry dis-

ciples; consequently, the Church is an evil institution bent on enslavement through deception.

The new critical scholarship energized the propaganda of the Revolution. Henri Daniel-Rops (1965) argues in *The Church in an Age of Revolution, 1789–1870,* that the "theories of Reimarus" were "adopted by Voltaire . . . as well as by "a whole army of pamphleteers" (308). He also notes that during the French Revolution, Charles Dupuis's *Origine de Tous les Cultes* assured its readers that "men would soon come to regard Jesus as on a level with Heracles, Osiris and Bacchus" even as "Volney's *Ruines* seriously maintained that the life of Christ was nothing more than an exact representation of the sun's course through the signs of the Zodiac" (308). Criticism was very useful to the Revolution. It supported the claim that a lying Church needed to be removed by revolutionary action.

As Jeremias (1964) notes, the study of the life of Jesus initiated by Reimarus became the preoccupation "in which the Enlightenment now engaged" (5). The personality of the historical Jesus replaced the traditional interest in Christology. There was a revolt against Christian doctrine in favor of the religion of Jesus. What Jeremias fails to perceive is that this movement was much more than an activity "inspired by liberal theology" (5). The academic quest was deeply rooted in the political milieu of the Revolution. Theology was following in the footsteps of political change in an attempt to remain relevant in the new Modern Age.

D. F. Strauss republished Reimarus and popularized Voltaire in Germany. In *Das Leben Jesu Kritsch Bearbeitet,* published in 1835, Strauss helped achieve the goal of Charles Dupuis that men should regard Jesus as a mythological figure and God as "merely the human race" (Daniel-Rops, 1965, 309). Daniel-Rops notes that Strauss "took his place among the originators of atheistic humanism, whose most outstanding protagonists were Hegel, Feuerbach, Karl Marx, and Comte" (309). There is a direct genealogical link between the radical elements of the Revolution and Life of Jesus scholarship.

Albert Schweitzer (1961) argues in *The Quest for the Historical Jesus* that Reimarus is revolutionary because "before Reimarus, no one had attempted to form a [critical] historical conception of the life of Jesus" (13). What Schweitzer fails to note is that this new phenomenon is rooted in the revolutionary climate of Europe. Jesus scholarship was never politically neutral. Reimarus, Voltaire, Lessing, and the philosophers of Enlightenment helped to produce the "new order," "the new creation," spoken of by the political leaders of the Revolution. Thought both preceded and complemented political action. Reimarus is certainly the first of a new breed. The historian is no longer a theologian; the critic no longer a churchman.

Vincent Harding (1983) notes in *There Is a River* that the black man's first encounter with the Western Christ came as he was loaded "on the good ship *Jesus*" (3). The white European, Harding notes, was experiencing

> religious, civil, and commercial revolutions [that] were creating new men and women, new institutions, new hungers for the riches of other people's lands which could only lead to harsh conflicts . . . *Popes, bishops, and professors* provided the blessing and the rationale for their incursions into the lives and histories of other civilizations. (5–6, emphasis added)

Harding correctly places academic scholarship within its political context. Scholarship may be politically unconscious but never politically neutral. The "historical Jesus" is not an ivory tower fiction but a creation of the professors, wittingly or unwittingly, striving to justify the revolutionary violence of the French Revolution. Ralph Waldo Emerson rejected the tendency to justify the Revolution. He declared: "All attempts to contrive a system are as cold as the new worship introduced by the French to the goddess Reason—today, pasteboard and fillogree, and ending tomorrow in madness and murder" (Ahlstrom, 1967, 315). Without Reimarus's historical Jesus to justify the Terror as a revolt against "lying priests," "the projected others," in the name of Justice and Humanity, the Revolution might well stand as a rootless act, an insane act, splitting the Modern Age from all previous human generations.

Scientific criticism and the new historical image of the "Christian Church as a hoax created by power-hungry priests" came together in the rhetoric of the radical elements of the Revolution, but it was the older Protestant image of Jesus that dominated the initial efforts to reform the French economy. The use of a mimetic hermeneutic to justify violence is made clear in these events.

The Restoration of the Primitive Model Established by Jesus Christ

Martin Luther championed a mimetic hermeneutic that is supported in the unconscious mind by the Myth of the Golden Age of Origins. M. Eliade (1964) notes in *Myth and Reality* that "the idea implicit in this belief is *that it is the first manifestation of a thing that is significant and valid,* not its successive epiphanies" (34). For Protestants, the paradisiacal, or pristine, moment was the primitive Church through the first five general councils. E. Rosenstock-Huessy (1969) observes in *Out of Revolution* that

> the German Reformation ventured to declare that between 600 and 1500 *"densissimae tenebrae"* had obscured the earth. The Pope had governed as the Anti-Christ, and had poisoned the real Christian gospel. A "new learning" was begun by Luther and Melanchthon to restore the pure Pauline faith. (363)

By means of the metaphor of the "dark age," Luther unwittingly laid the archetypal foundation for Protestant violence against Catholics.

The "dark age" is also a metaphor with roots in the Enlightenment. Historian Peter Gay (1966) comments in *The Enlightenment: An Interpretation, the Rise of Modern Paganism,* on the humanistic origins of this metaphor:

> When Petrarch removed the label "Dark Ages" from classical, pre-Christian times and fastened it instead on the Christian Era, he made a tentative beginning toward the periodical scheme that would come to dominate the Enlightenment. (74)

A genuine revolution began as a new time was revealed to Reason (Mommsen, 1959, 129). In 1342/1343, Petrarch abandoned the old model of periodization centering upon Creation, declaring that he would write only of Rome from Romulus "through the first hundred years of the Empire" (Mommsen, 1959, 111). For the Enlightenment, the Golden Age is ancient Greece and Republican Rome. Petrarch provided the archetypal justification for a new paganism as well as for violence against Christians, the proponents of ignorance—themes that would later dominate the Revolution.

The reform of the Church's ownership of properties was an early goal of the Revolution. The first enlightened efforts to reform the Church envisioned that

> the excessive wealth of the Church would be siphoned off... the Church would be reformed and the aristocratic monopoly on high ecclesiastical promotion would be ended. (McManners, 1970, 25)

The National Assembly did not anticipate the revolutionary course of events that it would unleash by this enlightened reform.

These early efforts at reform of the Church were energized by the Protestant hermeneutic of a return to the primitive Church as interpreted by the Jansenist theological movement—hyper Augustinianism—within the Church. McManners (1970) observes that the lower clergy's "demand for economic justice more and more became tied up with a movement of theological opinion known as 'Richerism'" (16–17) that had its roots in Jansenism. Edmond Richer argued the case for the lower clergy by reference to Jesus' division of the disciples into the Twelve and the Seventy, according to the Gospel of Luke. The bishops descend from the apostles but are not entitled to despotic power. The lower clergy has the right to meet in a synod to share in the government of the Church. Richer envisions the restoration of an ancient pristine order as the path to reform.

The mimetic hermeneutic was soon united with concrete political action. On October 10, 1789, Talleyrand, Bishop of Autun, proposed the seizure of Church property in the name of restoring this wealth to the purposes intended by the original contributors (Ferrero, 1968, 42–43). This bold move, approved on November 2, stripped the Church of its economic power by the transfer of its properties to the State. The next move was to attack the rights of the clergy. On May 29, 1790, the archbishop of Aix, during the debate on the Civil Constitution of the Clergy, argued that the French Church be recalled "to the priority of the primitive Church" (Beik, 1970, 136). Jean Baptiste Treilhard argued during the session of May 30 that the New Testament model was for the people to elect pastors and proposed the question "How can the old order of things which created the splendor of the Church be re-established?" (Beik, 1970, 139). Clergy were forced, by action of the Constituent Assembly on November 27, 1790, to swear an oath to the Civil Constitution of the Clergy, an event that McManners (1970) views as marking "the end of national unity, and the beginning of civil war" (38).

Ironically, the destruction of the Catholic clergy was accomplished in the name of a return to the primitive example of Jesus Christ in a country that persecuted Protestants. The archetypal image of the Golden Age does not observe dogmatic boundaries.

De-Christianization: The Worship of Reason, Nature, and the Supreme Being

The Revolution was not a reform but a true revolution. The Force of Nature rather than the Christian God was regarded as sacred and as the locus of all meaningful human action. The Christian model had to fall before this new experience of Nature. Nevertheless, biblical images could still be employed even by radicals. In 1785 Francois N. Babeuf, the communist revolutionary, interpreted the Revolution as a new Exodus from Egypt as he called upon the nation to "let everything return to chaos and from the chaos come forth a new and regenerated world" (Beik, 1970, 358). In the same vein, Robespierre spoke eloquently of "the new order of things" in his speech on suffrage delivered in April 1791 (Beik, 1970, 154).

Two months after the Terror, a revolutionary calendar was introduced. "In it," says McManners (1970), "the world began anew, not with the birth of Jesus, but with the proclamation of a republic in France" (99) on September 22, 1792. Jesus was not, however, excluded. S. E. Aulard (1966) notes that the founders of the new religion and authors of the Terror, the Voltairian Hébertists, "took pleasure in extoling that 'fine sansculotte Jesus'" (111; also, Ferrero, 1968, 157). An aristocratic Christ, not a peasant Jesus, was the enemy of the Revolution.

The Cult of Reason, rooted in natural science, was instituted to replace Christianity, rooted in revealed science. On November 10, 1793, the Cathedral of Notre Dame was rededicated as the Temple of Reason with the call that the nation accept "no more priests, no other gods than those Nature offers us!" (Beik, 1970, 270–271). The altar was a mountain. Borne by four citizens, the goddess Liberty, wearing the Phrygian bonnet and holding a pike, bowed to Reason (Beik, 1970, 269; Schama, 1990, 778). The congregation sang the words composed by Chenier:

> Thou, holy Liberty, come dwell in this temple; be the goddess of the French . . . Warrior liberators, powerful, brave race, armed with a human sword, sanctify terror. (Beik, 1970, 271)

The Virgin Mary is replaced by the goddess Liberty, who sends forth her warriors to make terror a holy instrument of political change! This grounding of Reason in the archetype of the Great Mother Goddess has chilling implications. It legitimized Terror in the name of Reason as an instrument of political change—a kind of philosophical equivalent of Jihad—that cannot be challenged by rational argument since it is driven by unconscious forces.

In the ritual for the rededication of Notre Dame, we find other indications of the archetype guiding the Festival of Reason. Mithra, the hero, emerged from a rock wearing a Phrygian cap, having a knife, and carrying a torch. He went forth to conquer the Sun and to kill the Bull of the Great Mother. In the new Temple of Reason, there is a marriage between the warrior goddess Liberty, the feminine counter-part of Mithra (Baring & Cashford, 1993, 409; Cumont, 1956, 179) and philosophical Reason. Apparently sensing this archetypal con-nection, sculptor Frederic Auguste Bartholdi cast Lady Liberty in the image of Mithra as Sol Invictus, "the governer of the world" (Cumont, 1956, 186). As Christianity was displaced, a new mythol-ogy was introduced by the Revolution: the mythology of the Great Mother Goddess, Mother Nature, who was celebrated as the source of life and fertility. Under her auspices life renews itself but is also destroyed. This archetypal root undergirds both the Revolution's commitment to violence as the catalyst needed for a new creation and its search for a "natural" Jesus as the alternative to the biblical Christ.

The liturgy for the rededication of Notre Dame would be only of historical interest were it not for the presence of the Goddess myth in contemporary life. In *Return of the Goddess*, Whitmont (1997) doc-uments the power of this new mythology over the contemporary psy-che and questions how we might "channel and safely direct the reemergence of the Goddess and of her Dionysiac son and consort" (149) away from its more violent expressions.

The Cult of Reason also has links to a patriarchal god. It appropri-ated the term *Supreme Being*, a prevalent philosophical and Roman Catholic term for God, thus giving itself a link to Christianity (Thompson, 1976, 112). In the festival of Reason celebrated in the Cathedral of Saint-Jean three weeks after the rededication of Notre Dame, Reason was praised as the Supreme Being (Schama, 1990, 779). This is archetypally consistent since the Terrible Father is a counterpart of the Great Mother (Neumann, 1973, 186).

Robespierre was deeply concerned that morality keep pace with the new political order, but he could not accept the implicit atheism of the Cult of Reason. He proposed an alternative cult of the Supreme Being that succeeded the cult of Reason by legal decree on May 7, 1794. This became the revolutionary alternative to the Catholic Church and its "lying priests" (Thompson, 1976, 112, 115). The roots of the new cult in the Great Goddess mythology is evident. The true priest of the Supreme Being is Nature; the universe is his temple, and his wor-ship is the practice of natural virtue (115).

Jesus was incorporated into the new religion. McManners (1970) notes: "Virtuous men were praised and, in some festivals [of Liberty], reverence was paid to an unecclesiastical Jesus, whose only possessions were his virtues, and whose only crown was of thorns" (102). Morality and social action were the new focal points of religion. Jesus was depicted as the great teacher of natural morality wherever the impact of the Revolution was strong.

Revolutionary morality was grounded in Petrarch's humanistic vision of republican Rome as the Golden Age. Jacques-Louis David, the artist and pageant master of the Revolution, was able to impart Petrarch's vision to the population of Paris and to use it as a force for revolution. For example, D. L. Dowd (1948) writes in *Pageantmaster of the Republic* of David's *The Lictors Bring Back to Brutus the Bodies of His Sons* that this painting had a

> triple appeal to the public: it was inspired by the classical spirit so alien to the medievalism they were destroying; it glorified the simple moral virtues of a republican hero; and it faithfully displayed the picturesque externals of antiquity which enjoyed the popular fancy. (19)

The vision of Christendom that had civilized Europe was to perish by the hands of the citizens of a new but imaginary Roman republic. Rousseau (1953) declares in *The Confessions:*

> Unceasingly occupied with thoughts of Rome and Athens, living as it were amongst their great men, myself by birth the citizen of a Republic and the son of a father whose patriotism was his strongest passion, I was fired by his example, *I believed myself a Greek or a Roman.* (7, emphasis added)

The influence of the myth of the Golden Age upon Rousseau's thinking is evident. His glorification of Nature is beyond dispute.

The Revolution inspired a new hermeneutic driven by the myth of the Golden Age. Rosenstock-Huessy (1969) notes that "the French invented the period of the 'Renaissance,' beginning about 1450 and ending in 1498 or 1500 or 1517" (699). One of the darkest centuries in Western history, a period of atrocities, "was turned into the Golden Age of the Renaissance after 1815" (700). The French Revolution of 1789 required this new period in order to make events fit "into the Jacobin scheme of progress and self made manhood" (699). It also inspired a new historical schema.

Wilhelm von Humboldt, writing in Paris in 1796, created the new historical schema. Following Petrarch's lead, he dealt with antiquity no longer as the Old Testament but as Greece and Rome. The Church has no part in the new schema. The Middle Ages were now only "the era from the decline of taste and scientific culture [in antiquity] until their steady and full regeneration" in the Renaissance (Rosenstock-Huessy, 1969, 701–702). Hegel created a periodization of world history into four eras: "the Oriental Empire, the Greek Empire, the

Roman Empire, *the Germanic Empire*" (Collingwood, 1956, 57, note 2, emphasis added). It is in light of this addition of the Germanic Empire that we should, perhaps, understand the opening lines of Albert Schweitzer's (1961) *Quest for the Historical Jesus:*

> [W]hen, at some future day, our period of civilization shall lie, closed and completed, before the eyes of later generations, German theology will stand out as a great, a unique phenomenon in the mental and spiritual life of our time. (1)

However derived, Schweitzer's nationalistic perspective obscures the roots of the problem of the historical Jesus in the Revolution. While it is true that the first Life of Jesus scholars are German, it was the French Revolution and the Enlightenment that made the Quest so imperative.

The Completion of the Religious Revolution

Regrettably, Schweitzer (1961) abolishes our memory of the Revolution by claiming the Jesus of the French Revolution as the great achievement of Germanic theology (1); consequently, he views Ernest Renan as articulating "German thought in a novel and piquant form" (191)—a sentiment also promulgated by the French Catholic opponents of Renan (Gaigalas, 1972, 33–60). Were Schweitzer entirely correct in his judgment, it would be hard to explain why Renan was buried in the Pantheon in 1892 along with other heroes of the Revolution (Schweitzer, 1961, 180), including Rousseau and Voltaire. R. M. Chadbourne (1968) acknowledges Renan's dependence upon German scholarship but argues that his work is creative in transcending his sources (60; Gaigalas, 1972, 129). Renan is original in that he gave France its finest example of the historical Jesus portrayed as the ideal sansculotte revolutionary—an interpretation obliquely reflected in Father Victor Delaporte's comment that the State honored Renan because he was "the enemy of Christ" (Gaigalas, 1972, 128).

In his *Vie de Jésus* (1863), Renan took the Quest in a new direction. He introduced the sociological positivism of Comte, according to which science replaces belief in supernatural beings, into biblical criticism (Dansette, 1961, I, 311). Renan employed criticism to strip away the legend and the myth associated with Jesus in the interest of revealing the historical person. Renan reconstructed an idealized sansculotte Jesus, who is a model for all who seek authentic humanity. Jesus is portrayed by Renan (1936) as a sensuous and imaginative natural man who realized the biblical dream of a "universal religion of the spirit" (Chadbourne, 1968, 66). With Jesus, Renan (1936) states effusively, "an absolutely new idea, the idea of worship founded on purity of heart, and on human brotherhood . . . entered the world" (98–9). Jesus was the first to declare the "doctrine of the liberty of the soul" from political and ecclesiastical oppression (115). The French Revolution was no innovation; it was the rekindling of the revolution begun by Jesus (74, 225; see Chadbourne, 1968, 81). The Revolution is not an act of madness but of consummate sanity.

Renan (1936) boasts that Jesus' actions were driven by faith rather than reason. To his contemporaries he, like the Revolutionaries, appeared to be a fanatic, one possessed (220). The excesses of the Terror that appalled the merely reasonable man who lacked the revolutionary faith and enthusiasm of Jesus and the Revolution (225) are accepted by Renan as a human and historical necessity:

> [N]o revolution is effected without some harshness. If Luther, or the actors in the French Revolution, had been compelled to observe the rules of politeness neither the Reformation nor the Revolution would have taken place. (220)

Thus, Renan justifies the violence of the new Revolutionary hermeneutic.

The new secular religion of humanity as God, supported by Renan (Chadbourne, 1968, 50) and the Revolution, is no innovation. In this view, it was Jesus who first established "a pure religion, without forms, without temple, and without priests" that was "the moral judgment of the world, delegated to the conscience of the just man," who would be the "arm of the people" (Renan, 1936, 201–202). This pure gospel of Jesus was opposed by the feudal church, royalty, and religious orders (203). Renan (1936) observes that it is a tribute to the deceiving powers of the priests that they could convince "the most selfish, proud, hard and worldly of all human beings, a Louis XIII, that he was 'in spite of the Gospel . . . a Christian'" (218).

Anti-royalists, terrorists, pamphleteers, de-Christianizers, sansculottes, and the Enlightenment philosophers are given a new value by Renan (1936); they are branches on the tree of which the Kingdom of God is root and stem (203). Renan is not, however, an uncritical supporter of the Revolution (Chadbourne, 1968, 90). Renan (1936) foresees that the Revolution will remain fruitless until it takes as its "rule the true spirit of Jesus" and renounces the world as the way to possess it truly (203). He hopes for a renewed and humanistic Christian

Church that will return to the core message of its founder: the religion of love.

Retrospectively, Renan (1936) gave the Revolution historical and humanitarian roots. His sansculotte Jesus is the truly human Jesus, who championed the "despised classes" against priests and doctors of the law (105). This Jesus ensures the new order and will prevent any return to the past. Jesus marks the shift of the ages. He belongs both to antiquity and to the new world of the Revolution. There is no need for guilt in the aftermath of the Terror.

Equally important, Renan's work links the royal and ecclesiastical establishments to the aristocratic Jewish leadership of antiquity, the enemies of Jesus (105, 225). This in effect justified violence against religious Jews, clerical leaders, and the royalists. Jesus "proclaimed the rights of man, not the rights of the Jew . . . the religion of humanity, established not upon blood, but upon the heart" (170).

The Challenge to Our Values

The historical Jesus revealed by scholarship and implemented politically by the Revolution is the embodiment of the values of Enlightenment humanism. He is most often imagined as a teacher of a natural morality and virtue, a harbinger of democracy and communism, and above all a fallible human being whose tragic life suggests mental disturbance. In his analysis of the Western rebellion against the sacred, Albert Camus (1956), in *The Rebel*, argues that the freethinkers, by denying the divinity of Christ, appropriated him as a prime example of the innocent man tormented by God (34). Camus correctly detects a deeply ingrained strain of animosity as the affect driving the historical-critical investigation of Jesus and its tendency to revise history in the name of Reason:

> During the two centuries which prepare the way for the upheavals, both revolutionary and sacrilegious, of the eighteenth century, *all the efforts of the freethinkers are bent on making Christ an innocent, or a simpleton, so as to annex Him to the world of man*, endowed with all the noble or derisory qualities of man. Thus the ground will be prepared for the great offensive against a hostile heaven. (34–35, emphasis added)

The archetypal pattern of the scapegoat is operative with a new twist; it is God rather than mankind who loads His guilt upon the man Jesus. This god must be rejected in the name of humanity as Jesus is reclaimed.

From Reimarus to the present, this image of a "Christ created by lying priests" is a shadow projection of the science of biblical scholarship, whose task it is to restore the historical Jesus, or to demythologize the text of the New Testament. This task requires at least a tacit acceptance of atheism. Although the Quest begins with a natural science that affirms a transcendent moral power, or Supreme Being, whose signature is evident in the natural order, it ends with a science that declares there are no gods and never were. The Divine is regarded by science as an outmoded hypothesis that continues only as a symptom of neurosis (Freud).

As a churchman and a scholar, Walter Wink (1973) confronted this abrasive truth in *The Bible in Human Transformation:* "Historical criticism is bankrupt" (1). Wink argues that the method

> had a vested interest in undermining the Bible's authority, that it operated as a background ideology for the demystification of religious tradition, that *it required functional atheism for its practice.* (4, emphasis added)

The growing sterility of Western scholarship is a problem evident to those who are marginalized by relegation to a pejorative "Third World" envisioned by scholars.

Aleksandr Solzhenitsyn (1980) clearly delineates the problem in his Harvard commencement address, "A World Split Apart." He observes that in spite of its technological achievement, the West finds itself in "a present state of weakness" that "means that [a] mistake must be at the roots, as the very basis of human thinking in the past centuries" (5). Solzhenitsyn identifies the mistake as the Renaissance-Enlightenment view of rationalistic humanism that proclaims and enforces "the autonomy of man from any higher force above him" (5). This view places mankind in the center of the cosmos at the expense of losing the Spirit. Modern man, the man of the French Revolution, all too eagerly embraces "all that is material with excessive and unwarranted zeal" (5).

The one billion–strong Muslim segment of the Third World is acutely aware of the trend noted by Wink and Solzhenitsyn. M. Qutb (1964) deplores the "deification of science" both for its denunciation of revealed religion and for its creation of a world "devoid of all meaning and purpose with no higher order or power to guide it" (22). This Western development is viewed by Qutb with alarm all the more since, as he perceives world events, "science with all its dreadful weapons is employed for the extermination of the human-race" (24).

A. A. Maududi (1971) shares this view. He particularly deplores the fact that "the idea that religion has no right to interfere in politics, economics, public morality, law, learning and knowledge, or any other section of social life, became an essential part of the fundamental principles of the new [Enlightenment] civilization: Religion is an individual, personal affair" (4–5)—a condition confirmed to be present in America by Will Herberg (1960) in *Protestant, Catholic, Jew.*

Given this view of Western Enlightenment civilization expressed by scholars like Qutb and Maududi, it is understandable that many in Islam feel threatened by the incursion of the West into their cultures. It is against such a background that the call to Jihad is being made and answered by many today. In the context of contemporary political reality, where both religion and science can supply an ideology for Terror, we can ill afford to ignore Third World criticism of Western hermeneutics and the questions it poses. Is Western thinking truly unable to relate to "any deeply rooted autonomous culture" as a result of the assumption that our Enlightenment hermeneutic is superior and will ultimately be convincing to the Third World, as Solzhenitsyn (1980) claims (1)? Is the secular world truly secure, or are we witnessing an Islamic Revolution to counter the anti-religious French and Russian Revolutions, as proposed by Maududi (1971)? Is there a dark, unconscious side of our scholarship to which we are consistently blind, owing to our scientifically grounded arrogance about our theories of the nature of reality and human consciousness? Are we ready to acknowledge that the "historical Jesus" was a primary metaphor supporting the justification of Terror in the name of a virtually deified Science/Reason? These are compelling questions to which there are no simple answers. We must also ask our critics, "Can we honestly advocate the regression of consciousness as if one could undo the Revolution, Science, and Kant?" Can we reassemble the pieces of a Humpty-Dumpty Jesus? While we ponder these questions, the examples of revolutionary violence justified by both the religious and humanistic versions of the mimetic hermeneutic during the Revolution should encourage all parties to resist the archetypal pull of the conservative force of the unconscious that mediates a longing to go back to a pre–Modern Golden Age.

The answers to our dilemma cannot be found in any call for a return to Paradise, but that is, according to Whitmont (1997), the direction in which we currently seek our answers. Whitmont's analysis of contemporary culture reveals that the contemporary myth has three key themes: (1) "the hope for liberation," (2) "the theme of research and discovery," and (3) the theme of "the restoration of a lost Golden Age of freedom, human dignity and fulfillment" (150). For Whitmont, a careful analysis of our cultural artifacts reveals that the "Utopian myth of our day is a slightly disguised secularized version of various redemption and messianic myths of paradise lost and found again" (152). The quest for the Holy Grail, the archetypal Feminine, has replaced the Christian messianic message (153). For the heirs of the Revolution, the Quest appears to be our version of the quest for the Holy Grail—the quest for the symbol of Self, for "integration and fulfillment" (Whitmont, 1997, 152) that will assure our liberation. If Whitmont is to any degree close to the mark, as I believe he is, then it is time that we turn our critical skills to the task of detecting the unconscious forces driving our scholarship.

Conclusion

We can no longer rationally justify the claim that Science is independent of mythology. Abundant evidence points to the reemergence of the Goddess myth intertwined with Reason as the driving force for the Revolution and its continuing justification of Terror. To the extent that we remain unconscious of the archetypal basis of the Quest, we are in danger of expressing the destructive aspects of this new mythology. Above all, we need to ask, "What image of Self replaces the King and the Christ in the wake of the Revolution? Is the Quest for the historical Jesus possibly a dead-end road in an unacknowledged search for the secular equivalent of the Holy Grail?"

References

Ahlstrom, S. E. (Ed.). (1967). *Theology in America: The major Protestant voices from Puritanism to Neo-orthodoxy.* New York: Bobbs-Merrill.

Aulard, A. (1966). *Christianity and the French Revolution* (Lady Frazer, Trans.). New York: H. Fertig.

Baring, A., & Cashford, J. (1993). *The myth of the goddess: Evolution of an image.* New York: Penguin.

Barrett, W. (1987). *The death of the soul: From Descartes to the computer.* New York: Anchor/Doubleday.

Beik, P. H. (Ed.). (1970). *The documentary history of Western civilization: The French Revolution.* New York: Walker.

Camus, A. (1956). *The rebel* (A. Bower, Trans.). New York: Vintage.

Chadbourne, R. M. (1968). *Ernest Renan.* New York: Tayne Publishers.

Collingwood, R. G. (1956). *The idea of history.* London: Oxford University Press.

Cooper, B. T. (1995). *Rewriting the revolutionary past in* Les Prussiens en Lorraine. In G. M. Schwab & J. R. Jeanneney (Eds.), In *The French revolution of 1789 and its impact.* Westport: Greenwood Press.

Cumont, F. (1956). *The mysteries of Mithra* (T. J. McCormack, Trans.). New York: Dover Publications.

Daniel-Rops, H. (1965). *The church in an age of revolution, 1789–1870* (J. Warrington, Trans.). New York: Dutton.

Dansette, A. (1961). *Religious history of modern France* (Vol. 1–2). London: Nelson.

Dowd, D. L. (1948). *Pageantmaster of the republic.* New York: Books for Libraries.

Eliade, M. (1964). *Myth and reality.* London: Allen and Unwin Ltd.

Ferrero, G. (1968). *The two French revolutions, 1789–1796* (S. J. Hurwitz, Trans.). New York: Basic Books.

Gaigalas, V. V. (1972). *Ernest Renan and his French Catholic critics.* North Quincy: Christopher Publishing House.

Gay, P. (1966). *The enlightenment: An interpretation, the rise of modern paganism.* New York: Knopf.

Harding, V. (1983). *There is a river: The black struggle for freedom in America.* New York: Vintage.

Herberg, W. (1960). *Protestant, Catholic, Jew: An essay in American religious sociology.* Garden City: Anchor Books.

Jeremias, J. (1964). *The problem of the historical Jesus.* Philadelphia: Fortress.

Jung, C. G. (1959). *Aion: Researches into the phenomenology of the self* (R. F. C. Hull, Trans). Princeton: Princeton University Press.

Kley, D. K. (1996). *The religious origins of the French revolution.* New Haven: Yale University Press.

Maududi, A. A. (1971). *Come let us change this world.* Karachi: Bashir Art Press.

McManners, J. (1970). *The French revolution and the church.* New York: Harper.

Mommsen, T. E. (1959). *Medieval and Renaissance studies.* Ithaca: Cornell University Press.

Neumann, E. (1973). *The origins and history of consciousness* (R.F.C. Hull, Trans.). Princeton: Princeton University Press.

Qutb, M. (1964). *Islam: The misunderstood religion.* Kuwait: Darul Bayan Bookshop.

Renan, E. (1936). *The life of Jesus* (Trans. unspecified). New York: Albert and Charles Boni.

Rosenstock-Huessy, E. (1969). *Out of revolution.* Norwich: Argo.

Rousseau, J.-J. (1953). *The confessions.* New York: Penguin.

Schama, S. (1990). *Citizens: A chronicle of the French revolution.* New York: Vintage.

Schweitzer, A. (1961). *The quest for the historical Jesus* (W. Montgomery, Trans.). New York: Macmillan.

Solzhenitsyn, A. (1980). "A world split apart." (*Imprimis,* vol. 9, no. 3) http://www.columbia.edu/cu/augustine/arch/solzhenitsyn/harvard1978. html.

Thompson, J. M. (1976). *Robespierre and the French revolution.* New York: Collier Books.

Van Kley, D. K. (1996). *The religious origins of the French revolution.* New Haven: Yale University Press.

Whitmont, E. C. (1997). *The return of the goddess.* New York: Continuum.

Wink, W. (1973). *The Bible in human transformation.* Philadelphia: Fortress.

CHAPTER 7

Revenge and Religion

Zenon Lotufo Jr. and J. Cássio Martins

In 1938, one ministerial candidate of the Independent Presbyterian Church of Brazil—a "nationalistic" dissidence of the Presbyterian Church of Brazil—answered one of his exam questions before the Presbytery, saying that "he had not made up his mind as to the doctrine of eternal damnation and to the fate of the souls of the wicked, being himself sympathetic to the theory of annihilation." Such a response provoked so much havoc that the exam had to be suspended. The question was taken to the higher courts of the Church and argued until 1942, culminating with the withdrawal of the conservatives, who left the meeting for not accepting the position of the Synod (the highest court at the time). Although the Synod approved a motion that began with the words: "Considering that the Independent Presbyterian Church of Brazil is conservative and that it desires to uphold the Symbols of Faith . . . "; it also included the following resolution: "To recognize in equality of rights the ministers and believers who have difficulties as to the interpretation of some doctrinal points stated in the Confession of Faith."[1]

The episode is only an example, relatively recent, of the attitudes of Christians who not only believe in a terribly vengeful God, prone to submit His creatures to unspeakable horrors, eternal and devoid of any meaning, but who also want to make sure that such beliefs be disseminated as much as possible.

The problem is not new: Henri Strohl in his "O Pensamento da Reforma" [The Reformation Thinking][2] tells that "Calvin did not admit that a pastor refused to preach on predestination. His friendship with Toussain, the reformer of Montbéliard, was affected because this reformer affirmed he did not see what gain the pastoral ministry could have by preaching on this doctrine." In fact, what consequence, except the dissemination of the image of a notably cruel God, could result from a belief that maintains that the sufferings of the lost not only are eternal but also inescapable, since their condemnation was determined before the creation of the world?

It must be stressed that, although taken from the span of Reformation, which is familiar to us, examples like this are not the privilege of any particular religion or church. But they sound even odder within Christianity, to the extent to which they come as a herald of a message of unconditional forgiveness and love on behalf of a God who is both Father and Pastor.

Consider: first, that persons who hold these ideas not only uphold them as more or less nuisance appendixes of their confessions of faith, but place them in position of relief and cling to them in a compulsive manner; second, that these beliefs can pervade a culture and justify, as J. H. Ellens denounces, the resort to "gross violence."[3] It is worth pondering the factors that are at the root of the need to believe such doctrines based on revenge.

Vengefulness: An Artificial Emotion

First, it is good to define vengefulness, and we will try to do it within the scope of the Cognitive Systemic Analysis.[4] Let us distinguish at the outset two types of emotions: spontaneous emotions and artificial emotions. Spontaneous emotions are those that we share, grossly speaking, with irrational animals. They have as their main characteristics the fact of lasting only as long as the stimulus that produces them and of being of proportional intensity to the stimulus. As to artificial emotions, peculiar to human beings, they may last indefinitely, while they are fed back by the subject himself or someone else. On the other hand, once the individual accumulates them, they may result in reactions disproportionate to the stimulus.

Every day by late afternoon, Argos, our (Zenon's) Great Dane, wants someone to take him for a stroll in the neighborhood. Passing by the houses that also have their dogs, we see the animals become infuriated, seeming to want to destroy themselves, and being prevented from doing so only by the fences that separate them. Nevertheless, a few yards ahead, Argos seems totally tranquil, as if nothing had happened. It is not difficult to imagine how it would be if one of us rational humans, on a stroll of 20 minutes, had to go through half a dozen such violent quarrels! Argos does, however, have his enemies—that is, dogs against which he demonstrates a special hostility. But he is upset only when one of these foes is within the reach of his senses; he does not carry with him, we may infer from his behavior, the memories of the conflicts that might allow, even instill or feed, vengeful feelings.

Apparently, biblical authors had this distinction in mind as they recommended, "Be angry, but do not sin; do not let the sun go down on your anger" (Ps. 4:4; Eph. 4:26). We may conclude from these passages that those wise men were already aware that one thing is spontaneous aggressiveness, which leads to what we call assertiveness, and another is swollen anger, kept for days, weeks, months, or even years, which changes to rancor, vengefulness, resentment. Vengefulness is, therefore, the product of continued stimuli, produced by the person himself and/or the group to which he belongs. Without these stimuli, it may be presumed that violence among humans would be limited, more frequently, to reactions that are adequate to the solutions of the problems that inevitably loom as effects of our imperfections.

However, is vengefulness really an emotion? Authors that have dedicated themselves to the theme, amazingly few though they are, do not leave room for doubt. "Of course, vengeance is an emotion," writes, for instance, Nico Frijda, one of the most eminent researchers on the theme. "But the desire for revenge, the urge to retaliate, most certainly is."[5]

Speculation on the Origin of Vengefulness

Upon seeing that irrational animals may be highly aggressive, even though they do not have instruments, individual or collective, that would allow them to feed vengeful feelings,[6] we may also conclude that in the process of hominization there was a moment in which the capacity to create mental images and symbols, probably associated with the acquisition of spoken language,[7] made possible the keeping of the enemy and his offenses symbolically present. The advantage of stimulating aggressive emotions, even in the absence of the rival, is evident. If we imagine two primitive and rival groups of hominids competing for territory, it is not difficult to conclude that the one that could prepare for combat, for it can stimulate such emotions, would have greater possibilities of victory. The maintenance of hostile sentiments, which we may presume would be possible in the beginning only through external objects that symbolized the enemy and his offenses—with time and due to the competitive advantages that they yield—becomes internalized, inciting the ability to feed through mental images these hostile feelings. The enemy now may be "present" in the mental vision of each individual.

On the other hand, individuals for whom this possibility of sustaining mental images first occurred could count on this very useful instrument in the intra-group competition. This would allow them to hold positions of supremacy, even if they were not endowed with physical superiority. At the same time they would play the role of instigators of rancorous feelings in their peers. This characteristic can also be felt by the others as an asset to the group, and this would be one more factor to elevate the rancorous persons to positions of distinction.

Another point, among the most important to stress, is: Hostile feelings can be, and normally are, intensified by the very mechanism that feeds them. There are abundant and sad instances in all of human history of the intensity that vengeful feelings can reach between groups and nations. These feelings grow in a vicious circle: individuals who are hit by them, not being aware that they themselves and/or their own peers and/or elements of their own culture are the cause of most of the uneasiness that they experience, blame their enemies for their disturbance, which thus increases the rancor, the unease.

The Old Testament offers us a good example of the survival of the more vengeful. It is found in the story narrated in Genesis 34. One of the daughters of Jacob, Dinah, meeting all by herself in the field with Shechem, a son of Hamor, the Prince of a neighboring people, has sexual intercourse with the lad. The text is not clear as to whether there was any violence by him. The fact is that Shechem fell strongly in love with the girl, and he asked his father, according to the customs of the time, to go to Jacob and ask for her in marriage on his behalf. After being informed of the incident between Shechem and their sister, Jacob's sons were very angry and conceived a cruel revenge. When Hamor asks for the girl in marriage to his son, agreeing to give any dowry that would be asked, Jacob's sons simulate acceptance in goodwill, upon one condition: all men in the other group should be circumcised. In good faith Hamor agrees with the demand; but when all the men are in the peak of the pain caused by the operation, unable to defend themselves, they are attacked and slaughtered by Dinah's brothers, who, to complete the vengeance, ransack the city, despoiling it of everything of value, besides taking women and children as captives.

Another important report of how the more vindictive survive is that presented by the *Iliad*, Homer's story of the vengeance by the Greeks against the Trojans for having kidnapped Helen. Because of an odd love story, the whole city is destroyed.

Looking at things from the side of biology, we may suspect by what we have seen, that we are heirs of genes that induce us to vengeance; the more vengeful may have left a greater inheritance. That is possible; but what attracts our attention most of all, because it is where we can intervene, is our cultural heritage, in which we find factors that generate humanization side by side with factors that produce barbarism, which among other evils, arouses vengeance. Among these factors, probably the most mystifying and destructive are to be found in some of the great religions, which constitute notable instances of how concepts of great beauty and moral elevation live together with ideas that instigate hatred and vengeance.

Culture and Vengeance

Some elements of our cultures, which are often interrelated, may feed vengefulness:

History and Heroes—historical records, both formal and those of a more literary and mythical character that were transmitted initially orally and afterward in written form—often constitute instruments that transmit vengeful ideas from generation to generation. They are not often incorporated into the sacred canon, as has happened with the historical books of the Bible. They define the enemies and prevent old wounds from healing. These texts quite commonly tell of heroes noted for their vengefulness, such as Samson, David, Orestes, or Ulysses. "History," writes William James,[8] "is a bath of blood. The *Iliad* is a long recital of how Diomedes and Ajax, Sarpedon and Hector killed. No detail of the wounds they made is spared us, and the Greek mind fed upon the story."

In modern times these figures are embodied, for instance, in sportsmen of fame, whose aggressive and vengeful attitude is their hallmark. The heroes, as many authors point out, become models of great influence, especially for the young. Examples of vengefulness are found in many areas of culture:

Arts—As it could only be, these reports of vengeful acts and heroes are echoed in various artistic expressions, such as painting, music, drama, literature, and the like, especially those that have a popular character.

Judicial Systems—These reflect, naturally, the concepts of justice peculiar to a given society, particularly of penal codes; penalties may aim at satisfying mainly the need for vengeance of those who have been hurt, rather than, as a more humanistic and forward-looking penal system proposes, to impose sanctions that aim at that which is more adequate to society as a whole.[9]

Religion—As we shall see below, religion plays a most important role, whether it be in the direction of peace and forgiveness, or in furthering rancor and vengefulness.

Religion and Revenge

Perhaps the first question that we must tackle is, In what measure are religious ideas a cause, or consequence, of vengefulness? If we set aside the practically insoluble problem of what precedes what, which is irrelevant for our aim here, we may observe that there is a circular relationship between certain elements of religion and vengefulness. Both in cultural and individual terms they constitute a vicious circle. As to the individual, one may enter this circle through any of its phases; that is, persons with vengeful tendencies are attracted to vengeful forms of religiosity, while vengeful forms of religiosity may stimulate vengeful attitudes in the individual.

The religious forms that are most contaminated by ideas of a vengeful character have some common characteristics: Their leadership is autocratic and, consequently, demands blind obedience from believers to a leader or to a hierarchy. Obedience may be required directly to the leader, who presents himself as a herald of divinity, or as a delegate of a higher power; or it may be mediated by a sacred text and/or some "confession of faith." An authoritarian leadership generally needs external enemies against whom the rancor of the people is raised and nourished. This has the aim of keeping the cohesion and the control of the group. In a stimulating book, Elaine Pagels[10] describes the process and the use of demonizing the enemy so as to justify the hate toward it:

> Conflict between groups is, of course, nothing new. What may be new
> in Western Christian tradition . . . is how the use of Satan to represent

one's enemies lends to conflict a specific kind of moral and religious interpretation, in which "we" are God's people and "they" are God's enemies, and ours as well. . . . Such moral interpretation of the conflict has proven extraordinarily effective throughout Western history in consolidating the identity of Christian groups; the same history also shows that it can justify hatred, even mass slaughter.

That this is a strong tendency, even in our day, is demonstrated in the many publications on "spiritual warfare" lavishly spread in the Christian Fundamentalist milieu. One instance is *The Bondage Breaker*,[11] in which the author establishes, in an appendix, a list of satanic practices that would make those who had contact with them vulnerable to demonic blows. Among such practices are the most-known non-Christian religions: besides yoga, Silva Mind Control, Ecumenism (!), parapsychology (listed as occultism), and the like. No wonder, therefore, that this same author considers certain inadequate behaviors of little children as results of satanic blows. The great danger of a position such as this is that its internal logic leads to the consideration of the doers of these supposedly satanic practices, especially if they are insensible to appeals to repent their ways, as enemies of God and subject to the punishment of which these Fundamentalists might be the instruments.[12]

While the vindictive feeling is being fed, it can become so connected to the identity of the group that vengeance becomes a project that gives meaning to the existence of this group.

As it could not be otherwise, doctrines about God occupy a central position in the determination of the presence or absence of vindictive elements in religion. It must be emphasized once more that, because we focus mainly on the Protestant perspective, particularly its Calvinistic side, readers should not conclude that we think that terrifying and vindictive ideas of God are a privilege of these currents of thought. We use them as examples because they are more familiar to us and because they affect more closely our Western culture.

In this area, one of the factors more closely related to the question of vengeance is that of divine justice. The following passage of Calvin's *Institutes of the Christian Religion* well represents an idea about this justice that has exerted and still exerts great influence:

> To this question, I insist, we must apply our mind if we would profitably inquire concerning true righteousness: How shall we reply to the Heavenly Judge when he calls us to account? Let us envisage for ourselves that Judge, not as our minds naturally imagine him, but as he is

depicted for us in Scripture: by whose brightness the stars are darkened [Job 3:9]; by whose strength the mountains are melted; by *whose wrath the earth is shaken* [cf. Job 9:5–6]; whose wisdom catches the wise in their craftiness [Job 5:13]; beside whose purity all things are defiled [Job 25:5]; whose righteousness not even angels can bear [cf. Job 4:18]; who makes not the guilty man innocent [Job 9:20]; *whose vengeance when once kindled penetrates to the depths of hell* [Deut. 32:22; cf. Job 26:6]. Let us behold him, I say, sitting in judgment to examine the deeds of men: Who will stand confident before his throne?[13]

Calvin clings to the same idea of justice that centuries earlier induced Anselm in elaborating his theory of atonement, probably the most known in Christian churches both Catholic and Protestant, and whose nature Ellens sums up, saying that Anselm " . . . represented God as sufficiently disturbed by the sinfulness of humanity that he had only two options: destroy us or substitute a sacrifice to pay for our sins. He did the latter. He killed Christ."[14]

Still in relation to Anselm's concept of justice and its negative influence, another theologian, Hinkelammert, writes:

Therefore redemption for Anselm is not a mutual forgiveness of debts, but their collection. Nevertheless by being man unable to pay his debt, God—that is God's love—grants him access to the only imaginable means of payment. Instead of forgiving the debt, God sacrifices his Son in order that this blood may serve as a means of man's payment to fulfill his obligation to pay the debt. Therefore, man pays it with Christ's blood and saves justice's face.

With Anselm comes this type of justice that already doesn't have anything to do with justice as it is in the Bible. It is a justice of payment of what is due, a justice of conformity to norms, a justice that kills its own son to obtain the collection of debts and the fulfillment of norms.[15]

But this conception of justice collides head-on with what Jesus declares about God the Father. God's justice, seen through Jesus belongs to or is subordinate to love. This is very clear in various parables, especially that of the prodigal son; which many suggest, quite reasonably, should be named "The Forgiving Father," or "The Loving Father," or the "Waiting Father," because the father is the central figure, not the son. Let us consider the parable of the workers and the diverse hours of labor (Matt. 20:1–16): the landowner hires several groups of laborers, at different hours, in such a way that the first group works all day long and the last works only one hour. At the moment of payment, as agreed upon previously with the first ones, all received the equal amount, which aroused dissatisfaction for those

A Portrait of Jean Calvin by an unknown artist, 1536. The Art Archive/Bibliothèque Universitaire Geneva/Dagli Orti.

who had worked the greater amount of hours. The landowner did not act fairly, if we take as a criterion a merely equitable justice. Let us suppose, nevertheless, that those who worked for only one hour were sons or brothers of those who worked all day. How would they see the situation? Would they be unhappy with the "injustice" or be glad of knowing that those persons dear to them would be better off to support themselves and their own?[16] Another point that has caused dispute among Christian theologians is the question of whether the biblical references to God's wrath, and therefore his desire for vengeance, have to do simply with an anthropomorphization of the Supreme Being: Could he in fact be taken by such passion? The question is debated by Mackintosh in his classic *The Christian Experience of Forgiveness*. Against those who believe that the expression "Wrath of God" connotes mere caprice and willful passion, he argues that " . . . every philosophical argument used to deny this, on the ground that it implies excessive anthropomorphism, is an equally good argument for denying even His love." And he proceeds to recall also that " . . . the wrath of Jesus is made incontestably plain in the Synoptic Gospels."[17]

Nevertheless, if we keep in mind the distinction presented above between spontaneous and artificial emotions, it will be evident that, first, the wrath that Jesus manifests in some moments is spontaneous and useful. It aims at solving a question that arouses in him just, that is adequate and proportionate, indignation; we are facing assertive emotions. Second, vengeful wrath attributed to God is an artificial emotion, it is back-fed and self-aggressive. As it is not permitted to cool off, it keeps growing at each new stimulus in a process of accumulation that leads to reactions disproportionate to the causes; it is incompatible with the ideal figure of a mature and wise human being, all the more so with God.[18]

The Sacralization of Conflicts

An extremely common use of religion is to ascribe religious motivations to conflicts whose origin has nothing to do with religious factors. Such motivations, in turn, need to be linked to religious elements that would justify the aggression and that kindle vengeance. No soldier would engage for a long time in a fight for a cause in which he does not believe. On the other hand, once the conflict is broken out there come losses and sacrifices that lead to an automatic sacralization: these sufferings need to be linked to a higher, transcendent cause; they cannot be considered useless, pointless. Moreover, because of this they must be avenged and to get it done becomes a sacred duty.[19]

The Question of Resentment—Nietzsche and the "Genealogy of Morals"

Probably the most corrosive criticism ever crafted against the Judeo-Christian morals has come from the pen of Friedrich Nietzsche. In his *On the Genealogy of Morals*, published in 1887, the German philosopher argues that both Jews and Christians, in a subtle manner, subverted the true values that should guide superior men. For him, Christians mainly have dressed despicable qualities, characteristics of inferior beings, with virtuous clothing. So,

... impotence ... does not equate with "goodness of heart"; anxious lowliness with "humility"; subjection to those one hates with "obedience," ... one whom they say commands this subjection, they call God. The inoffensiveness of the weak man, even cowardice of which he has so much, his lingering at the door, his being ineluctably impelled to wait, here acquire flattering names, such as "patience," and is even called virtue itself; his inability for revenge is called unwillingness to revenge, perhaps even forgiveness. ... [20]

What is the "genealogy" of that transformation? It begins with the Jewish people, who, when enslaved in Egypt and prevented from reacting or giving way to their hatred in the face of mistreatment and suffering at the hands of their masters, are impelled to adopt a morality that is nothing but a gross rationalization, in the psychoanalytic sense of the term. It is the desire for revenge and its by-product, resentment, that are at the root of this morality. Christianity, in turn, is a branch from this trunk:

That, however, is what has happened: from the trunk of that tree of vengefulness and hatred, Jewish hatred—the profoundest and most sublime kind of hatred, capable of creating ideals and reversing values, the like of which has never existed on earth before, thence there grew something equally incomparable, a *new love*, the profoundest and most sublime kind of love, and from what other trunk could it have grown?

One should not imagine it grew up as the denial of that thirst for revenge, as the opposite of Jewish hatred! No, the reverse is true! That love grew out of it as its crown, as its triumphant crown spreading itself farther and farther into the purest brightness and sunlight, driven as it were to the domain of light and the heights in pursuit of the goals of that hatred: victory, spoil, and seduction, by the same impulse that drove the roots of that hatred deeper and deeper and more and more covetously into all that was profound and evil. This Jesus of Nazareth, the incarnate gospel of love, this "Redeemer" who brought blessedness and victory to the poor, the sick and the sinners—was he not this seduction in its most uncanny and irresistible form, a seduction and bypath to precisely those *Jewish* values and new ideals? Did Israel not attain the ultimate goal of its sublime vengefulness precisely through the bypath of the "Redeemer," this ostensible opponent and disintegrator of Israel? Was it not part of the secret black art of truly *grand* politics of revenge, of a farseeing, subterranean, slowly advancing, and premeditated revenge, that Israel must itself deny the real instrument of its revenge before all the world as a mortal enemy and nail it to the cross, so that all the world, namely all the opponents of Israel, could unhesitatingly swallow just this bait?[21]

In order to demonstrate how much Christian morals were contaminated by the desire for vengeance and resentment, Nietzsche cites two great names of Christian theology, foreseeing with joy the vision they will have from heaven of the wicked suffering in the flames of hell. Thomas Aquinas says: "The blessed in the kingdom of heaven will see the punishments of the damned *in order that their bliss be more delightful for them.*"[22]

And prior to him Tertulian, one of the Church Fathers says:

> However there are other spectacles—that last eternal day of judgment, ignored by nations, derided by them, when the accumulation of the years and all the many things which they produced will be burned in a single fire. *What a broad spectacle then appears! How I will be lost in admiration! How I will laugh! How I will rejoice! I'll be full of exaltation* then as I see so many great kings who by public report were accepted into heaven groaning in the deepest darkness.[23] (italics in the original)

The questions that arise from reading passages such as these are of two kinds: First, would it not be that Nietzsche's thesis could be applied, unfortunately, to a great number of Christians whose perspective that God will severely punish his enemies is one of the main motivations in religious life? Second, would it be that Nietzsche's criticism applies to the essence of the Christian message?

Factors of various origin lead us with sadness to answer affirmatively to the first question. The vengeful attitude averse to forgiveness, ignoring the unconditional love and grace so nuclear to the message of the Gospel, is very frequent among Christians, especially those of a Fundamentalist tendency. In that they do not differ from the Fundamentalist terrorists of Islam or of any other ideology.

The second question is more complex. Max Scheler tackled it in a more detailed form. In his essay "Resentment in the Construction of Morals"[24] Scheler aims at reaching two objectives: the first is to purify the soul of readers from the poison represented by resentment; the second is to refute Nietzsche's thesis about Christian morals, above all in the reference to love.

For Scheler, resentment is in fact "... a psychic *self-poisoning,* whose causes and consequences are well defined."[25] The main emotions and feelings related to it are a feeling and impulse to vengeance; hate, wickedness, envy, covetousness, and malice being the desire for vengeance "the most important of the sources of resentment"[26] (Scheler's italics). Desire for vengeance and resentment, though kin to one another, differ in that the second is the result of the first, and it comes up when vengeance becomes impossible and is repressed. In individual terms, repression of vengeful impulses is associated with a "sensation of impotence," and "a strong and painful feeling of depression."[27] But, while resentment acts in the mind of the individual " . . . impulses of hate and vengeance against strong, rich and beautiful men, etc., disappear completely and the resented person escapes, thanks to resentment, from the inner torment of these passions."[28] Others, by an unconscious process of self-deceit " . . . are not any longer worthy of a revenge, but, otherwise, of pity and compassion. . . ."[29]

From the standpoint of the repercussion in a culture, resentment can "dominate a whole 'morality' and pervert a whole hierarchy (of values) to the point of considering 'good' what passed as 'evil.' A quick look over the history of Europe convinces us that the role of resentment in the genesis of morals is here considerable."[30]

As to the application of such ideas on Christian morals, Scheler disagrees with Nietzsche: "We believe that Christian values are all too easily susceptible of becoming values of resentment and were too frequently considered so, but Christian ethics, in its essence, has not grown in the soil of resentment. We believe, on the other hand, that the core of the bourgeois morality that began to displace the Christian moral since the thirteenth century, and of which the French Revolution was the apogee has its root in resentment."[31] Recognizing that the Nietzschean explanation of the genesis of the Christian morality has great depth, Scheler observes that Nietzsche " . . . on the one hand knows nothing of the essence of the Christian morals, especially the Christian notion of love, that he measures with a false set of values, making a mistake that is more properly philosophical than historical or religious."[32] But he stresses: "On the other hand it is necessary to take into account that the Christian morality was distorted for being contaminated with values of a very different origin that exerted a considerable action on its latter development."[33]

De-Paganization

The keen and courageous vision of theologians such as J. H. Ellens,[34] corroborated by what we have seen above, suggests that Christianity was highly contaminated along its history by essentially pagan ideas that have disqualified the profound and redemptive message of Jesus Christ. All that points to the dire and urgent need of a movement for the de-paganization of Christianity. In the sense in which we use the word *pagan*, we allude to the distortion of all that which affects a direct, intimate, loving, and unconditional encounter with God. Therefore, any idea is pagan that implies some kind of mediation, exchange, or negotiation with God; or any suggestion that God's disposition toward humankind and the material world in general is in any way conditional, threatening, or a danger of some kind. The idea of a God that demands expiatory sacrifices, of a wrathful God that avenges his creatures with horrible and pointless penalties, is pagan.

A de-paganized perspective of the Christian message involves what we may call:

Obedience In-Depth

To obey God in-depth means, first, attention to what God speaks directly to our conscience every time this comes into conflict with what supposedly is his manifest will through external sources. Probably this is how Abraham became the "Father of Faith." Thus, the well-known passage in which the Patriarch agrees to sacrifice his own son may be interpreted in a manner different from the usual explanation, pointing to that which we call "obedience in-depth." The traditional form of reading the passage takes it for granted that Abraham demonstrates obedience to God when he obeys the divine order to sacrifice Isaac, his son. But such a reading does not take into account some points that seem to us of utter importance: (1) the sacrifice of children was something common among the Canaanites in whose midst Abraham lived. That is, by sacrificing Isaac he would not be doing anything different from that which pagans around him did, and so there wouldn't be any reason to see his act as exceptional; (2) child sacrifice is considered in the Bible as an abomination; (3) God is called Elohim, a generic name, also used by the Canaanites, in all passages where the sacrifice is claimed from Abraham. God is called Yahweh when the sacrifice is blocked. Elohim requires the sacrifice, and Yahweh impedes it. Abraham, according to our interpretation, believes as those who surround him, that to sacrifice his son is a proof of faith and that God (Elohim, the "outer" God) asks that from him. But the true God, the "inner" God, Yahweh, speaking to his conscience, seeks to talk him out of it. For the anguished Patriarch, harkening to God's voice in his conscience means to disobey the externalized God, and he proceeds with the preparation until courageously he—probably unaware at the moment—follows the inner voice of Yahweh. Then it is that he obeys the true God and becomes the "Father of Faith."[35]

The apostle Paul and Luther are good instances of people dedicated to take seriously obedience in-depth, people who in critical moments knew how to hear God's voice speaking to their conscience and whose courage led them to face down the "Outer God." We cannot fathom how great was the inner conflict of these men until we note the dramatic changes that occurred in their lives. Obeying in-depth involves intimate and personal communion with God; it requires such a unity that human will becomes one with the divine will, and that is impossible in the presence of intermediaries, whoever they are. Jesus brings to us God as Father, and no one needs any kind of mediation to come close to his own Father. Jesus always presents himself as God Himself: "He who has seen me has seen the Father" (John 14:9); "I and the Father are one" (John 10:30). But theological tradition has presented him as a "mediator," someone who needs to make intercession for us because otherwise we would be the targets of the wrath of God the Father. It is one more factor to produce fear of God; we will obey then, if that is the case, out of fear, but never by virtue of the love and trust that integrate wills and thoughts.

Each epoch, and every current of thought, has sought to impose its mediators, for through them and only through them, it is possible to control minds, hearts, and behaviors, preventing obedience to be done directly and profoundly to the Father himself. The mediator may be an ecclesiastical hierarchy, as it is among Roman Catholics and in Islamists, or it may be the Bible and/or the confession of faith, as for Protestants, indicated, for instance, by Troeltsch[36] and Brandt.[37] The aim is always the same: by means of the intermediary, to exert authority and to hinder direct contact with God.

Referring to how, in the function of the personality of his own father, he learned to see God as "the epitome of grace, patience, and decency," Ellens declares, "I could never know or believe any other kind of God."[38] To which we might add, no one can obey in depth any other kind of God, and only such an intimate relationship to a loving and forgiving God can set us free from hate and vengefulness.

Shepherding

Another aspect of the de-paganized Christian faith could be seen as that of *shepherding*. If the God of the Bible is a Shepherd to all of humanity then he is not a wrathful God, even less the inspirer either of aggression or of vengefulness. This is important because besides that of God-the-Father, the metaphor of the shepherd looms as dominant in the Bible, being found in the Torah, the Prophets, and in the Writings. Even centuries before the Bible was written, this image was typical and prevailing in the whole Fertile Crescent, from Egypt to Mesopotamia, obviously including Palestine, as a reference to kings and then to God, in every region.[39] In the Bible this metaphor is ascribed to God himself, or the Father, the Twenty-third Psalm being the leading example of it, plus Ezekiel 34, among other texts.

Jesus presents himself as the Good Shepherd in John 10. The personality and the ministry of this Son of God have to be understood in terms of this image. This was his style, very different from a wrathful divinity, which again might foster vengefulness. Even though we may not find a direct, literal reference to a pastoral function of the Holy Spirit, it seems hard to deny that his action is profoundly pastoral in its quality. This is seen both in the Old and New Testaments in so many instances. We take John 14 and 17 as an anchor for this contention.

Another reason why the shepherd image is important as a de-paganized aspect of the Christian faith is that, as Fabris teaches us, "it helps us to understand [that] the archetype of the shepherd [is] an image that has profound resonances in the unconscious, in the human psyche, above the nomad, Bedouin experience, or other. Also in the urban culture God is called shepherd."[40]

This means that in the whole Bible the systemic, basic need of the human being for support, help, protection, guidance, and meaning is to be fulfilled by the God who is able to perform this sublime task through his sovereignty, grace, and providence. It is the "holding the father's hand" (Ellens, 1982, op. cit.). This is what evokes, on behalf of humans, faith, confidence, joy, peace, meaning, and again, has nothing to do with vengefulness. And it means also that Nietszche, in his criticism, seems to have known nothing of all this. Because after all, this is very different from any "despicable quality," as he says; it is not "characteristic of inferior beings"; and it does not describe a "weak man," nor any "cowardice."

Also he did not consider that the Hebrew-Semitic mind has a very distinctive way to approach life and its meaning. It is most regrettable that much of the theology that has been produced in the last 20 centuries also fell into this same trap, that is, *literalism*, or reading the Bible too quickly, like one who glances through the morning paper and hurries away. This path leads the church surely into the situation of *irrelevance*, lacking the spiritual authority that was the hallmark of the great prophets. This makes people and countries unable to listen to the message the church claims to have.

Still another reason is that God's covenant is conceived of and held in terms of the *"agapē"* love, which is clearly held in the Bible as *the* main characteristic of God's being (I John 4:7–21). This *"agapē"* love is not only God's characteristic, but is meant to be a *commandment*, that is, golden principle for the life of God's people. Within the Christian faith, people are not left to decide whether or not to love (*"agapē"* love), as if it were an optional question on a school test. Thus, any use of religion to support aggression or vengefulness in this context must be a great mistake! Not only because *agape*, self-giving and unconditionally forgiving and accepting love, is a commandment, an external and formal principle, but really because of the *character* of the One who gives the commandment and because of his *image* (Genesis 1:26) in us.

Whenever people forget this and let themselves be carried away by their whims, fears, or obscure intentions, nothing can prevent them from using religion to support all kinds of witch-hunting. This is, in and of itself, the very opposite of *shepherding*. Even when in Ezekiel 34, God shows the stern face of the Shepherd-God in separating one kind of sheep from the other, he does not do it out of any humanlike feeling of revenge, irritation, or hatred, but as an act of pastoral discipline, pointing the way ahead, not closing it.

From all this we may say that the role of a de-paganized Christianity, which claims to be faithful to the Bible as Hebrew-Semitic literature, is to withstand any use of its content as a launching pad for vengefulness, first within the church itself and then in society. It is the precious mission of the church to help clarify the issues involved, so that creative ways may be found. This must be one purpose of this series of publications. For this to be accomplished, the church needs to seek *relevance*, that is, to speak out in terms that are understandable and meaningful for the world, both to common people and to authorities, in any country or the world at large. The church must address people's individual, national, and universal needs, including that of living in peace, respect, and understanding.

In this sense, much of theology throughout Christendom must review its labors, to produce a *theology of the world*, that is, an interpretation of the world of people, of nature, of nations, and of issues; plus a *soteriology*, which is in accordance with the character of the loving God; an *ecclesiology*, in which the church is capable of mirroring in its life God's character as a loving Shepherd-God; and a *homiletics*, which is capable of voicing that adequately. The same must happen to *Christian education*, to *evangelism*, to *ethics*, to *eschatology*, and finally to *pastoral theology*: one that will produce pastors and leaders whose understanding and ministry may teach who Yahweh, the Shepherd-God, really is. This will contribute to stopping the tidal wave of religious validation of sheer aggression on one side and sheer vengefulness on the other! This would be what we can call a *Christian ministry of peace, respect, and understanding* in a world of hate, disrespect, and vengefulness.

Notes

1. Lacerda, G. C. (2002). In *A questão doutrinária* [*The doctrinal question*] (Vol. 1, 5–20). São Paulo: Cadernos de O Estandarte.

2. Strohl, H. (1963). *O pensamento da reforma* [*The reformation thinking*] (150). São Paulo: ASTE.

3. Ellens, J. H. (2002). Psychological legitimization of violence by religious archetypes. In Chris Stout (Ed.), *The psychology of terrorism*. Westport: Praeger.

4. The main tenets of CSA have been expounded in the article "A teleological theory of emotion applied to Psychotherapy," by Zenon Lotufo Jr. and Francisco Lotufo Neto, published by the *Revista de Psiquiatria Clínica da Faculdade de Medicina da Universidade de São Paulo* [*Journal of Clinical Psychiatry of the Medical School of the São Paulo University*], Vol. 28, No. 5, 340–346. English copies may be secured through the e-mail zenonjr@uol.com.br.

5. Frijda, N. H. (1994). The Lex Talionis: on vengeance. In S. H. M. Van Goozen, N. E. Van de Poll, and J. A. Sergeant, *Essays on emotion theory* (265). Hillsdale: Lawrence Erlbaum.

6. Richard Wrangham and Dale Peterson, for example, in *Demonic males, apes and the origins of human violence* (New York: Houghton Mifflin, 1996), report violent incursions of chimpanzees in alien territories, in which they apparently organize themselves in order to assail/attack chimpanzees of other groups, attitudes which, prior to these reports, were believed to be absent in these animals. Nevertheless, it is not reported behavior that could be configured as revenge.

7. Jonathan Turner insists with well-grounded reasoning that

> . . . verbal language could increase fitness by adding new dimensions to communication and, hence, social organization—*given* selection pressures to get better organized. This happened, perhaps, during a period when species of hominids began to compete intensely with

each other. Under these conditions, the more organized hominids would be the most fit to survive.

Yet I cannot stress enough my point that verbal language came latter, and that therefore it is less primal than visually based communication. Language adds much to interaction, but by itself is not particularly effective in generating solidarities. (*On the origins of human emotions—a sociological inquiry into the evolution of human affect* [Stanford: Stanford University Press, 2000], 25.)

Our thesis runs parallel to that of Turner, except that he leaves aside the factors that bear upon the upsurge of one of the most important emotions for the survival of the group, vengefulness, that cannot be conceived of in the absence of symbols.

8. James, W. (1962/1896). *Essays on faith and morals*. Cleveland: Meridian.

9. This position is masterfully represented by the jurist and philosopher E. N. Cahn, in *The predicament of democratic man* (Westport: Greenwood, 1979). Opposed to him are S. Jacoby, in *Wild justice: the evolution of revenge* (New York: Harper & Row, 1983), and R. C. Solomon, in "Sympathy and vengeance: the role of emotions in justice" (in *Essays on emotion theory*, edited by S. H. M. Van Goozen, N. E. Van de Poll, and J. A. Sergeant [Hillsdale: Lawrence Erlbaum, 1994, 291–311]). Their contention is that punishment makes no sense without the satisfaction of the need for vengeance. Frijda seems to suggest, without getting into detail, an intermediary solution. He says, "One conclusion is specific to vengeance: When offense is real and unacceptable, desire for vengeance is acceptable. Society would do well to recognize this, and should find ways to deal with desire for revenge beyond denying or condemning its existence" (see Frijda, The Lex Talionis: on vengeance, 286). If we understood Frijda's position, those ways do not necessarily have to do with a penal system; they have to do mainly with social attitudes toward vengefulness of victims.

10. Pagels, E. (1995). *The origin of satan*. New York: Random House, xix.

11. Anderson, N. T. (1990). *The bondage breaker*. Eugene: Harvest House.

12. The attitude of collaboration with God in the chastisement of the wicked is a constant in the history of Christianity. Roger Bastide in his essay "Calvinisme et Racisme," included in the book *Le Prochain et le Lontain* (J. A. Ortega y Medina, and R. Bastide [Paris: Cujas, 1970]), quotes Ortega y Medina, saying:

The Calvinist Puritans, in the beginning of the colonization of the United States, by force of their own doctrines, saw Indians as their equals. But not much later they perceived that the natives " . . . made little progress in the way of their salvation . . . which constituted for Puritans an infallible indication of negative predestination, i.e., an inescapable condemnation. What else could they do, saints and Puritans, but help God in the task of cleaning these lands of "such beings"? (95)

13. Calvin, J. (1961). Institutes of the Christian religion. (III, XII, 1). In John T. McNeill (Ed.), *Library of christian classics* (Vol. XX). London: S. C. M., 755.

14. Ellens, J. H. (2002). Psychological legitimization of violence by religious archetypes. In Chris Stout (Ed.), *The psychology of terrorism*. Westport: Praeger.

15. Hinkelammert, F. J. (1990). Economia e teologia: as leis do mercado e a fé [Economy and theology: the laws of market and faith]. *Boletim da fraternidade teológica latinoamericana americana,* 4(11), 46.

16. This aspect of the parable was suggested to me by the reading of Henri Nouwen's *The return of the prodigal son* (1992 [New York: Doubleday]) commenting on the parable of the "loving father": "In the light of God I can finally see my neighbor as my brother, as one who belongs to God just as I myself. But out of God's household, brothers and sisters, husbands and wives, lovers and friends, become rivals, even enemies, each one permanently contaminated with jealousy, suspicion and resentments." That is, looking at things through the standpoint of the father and his love, the older son should not consider himself hurt; rather, he would be glad with the return of the prodigal brother (89).

17. Mackintosh, E. M. (1961). *The Christian experience of forgiveness.* London: Fontana, 143.

18. Writing about this brings to memory the keen observation by Rabbi Harold Kushner (1981) in *When bad things happen to good people* (New York: Schoken) related to beliefs that imply the vision of an evil God: "Some years ago, when the 'God-is-dead bit' was at its peak, I remember seeing a car bumper where one could read: 'My God isn't dead; sorry for yours.' I think my bumper sticker would be: 'My God isn't cruel; sorry for yours'" (135).

19. About this see the interesting publications of the Centre de Recherche sur la Paix, of the Université Catholique de Louvain, especially the article by Paul Levy in a brochure entitled "Les Religions Facteurs de Paix, Facteurs de Guerre" ["Religions: Factors of Peace, Factors of War"]. See "Quelques conclusions" ["Some conclusions"] by P. M. G. Levy (1979), in "Les Cahiers du CRESUP" (n. 2), Louvain-la-Neuve, Centre de Recherche sur la Paix of the Université Catholique de Louvain.

20. Nietzsche, F. W. (1887). *On the genealogy of morals* (I, No. 14). Compiled from translations by Walter Kaufman, R. J. Hoollingdale, and Ian C. Johnston. Text amended in part by The Nietzsche Channel.

21. Ibid., I, No. 8.

22. Ibid., I, No. 15.

23. Ibid., I, No. 15.

24. Scheler, M. (1970/1915). *L'homme du ressentiment* [*The man of resentment*]. Paris: Gallimard.

25. Ibid., 16.

26. Ibid., 16.

27. Ibid., 49.

28. Ibid., 60.

29. Ibid., 60.

30. Ibid., 66.

31. Ibid., 66.

32. Ibid., 97.

33. Ibid., 97.

34. In the case of Ellens, expounded mainly in his *God's grace and human health* (Nashville: Abingdon, 1982), and in his "Psychological legitimization of violence by religious archetypes" in *The psychology of terrorism*, edited by Chris Stout (Westport: Praeger, 2002).

35. An analogy of this situation is presented by Mark Twain in *The adventures of Huckleberry Finn*. Twain tells through the words of the character himself the adventures of a motherless boy raised in the streets, whose father was a drunkard. The boy finds a treasure and is entrusted to the tutorship of two old ladies. Unhappy for loosing his freedom, Huck runs away. Living on the banks of the Mississippi, he goes down the river on a raft in the company of Jim, a runaway slave, whom he meets on his way. Jim, who was the property of Mrs. Watson, an old lady, runs away because he was about to be sold to a farmer who badly mistreated his slaves. As the days go by, a solid friendship is born between the two; but Huck feels more and more tormented by guilt and fear. He knows, with certainty, that he is committing a grave sin, a theft, in collaborating with the escape of a slave.

At a certain point, two crooks they met during the trip betray Jim and denounce him for a few dollars. Feeling divided between his love for Jim and the guilt of transgressing the divine law, Huck doesn't know what to do. It is worth reading the whole passage:

> Well, I tried the best I could to kinder soften it up somehow for myself by saying I was brung up wicked, and so I warn't so much to blame; but something inside of me kept saying, "There was the Sunday-school, you could a gone to it; and if you'd a done it they'd a learnt you there that people that acts as I'd been acting about that nigger goes to everlasting fire."
>
> It made me shiver. And I about made up my mind to pray, and see if I couldn't try to quit being the kind of a boy I was and be better. So I kneeled down. But the words wouldn't come. Why wouldn't they? It warn't no use to try and hide it from Him. Nor from *me*, neither. I knowed very well why they wouldn't come. It was because my heart warn't right; it was because I warn't square; it was because I was playing double. I was letting *on* to give up sin, but away inside of me I was holding on to the biggest one of all. I was trying to make my mouth *say* I would do the right thing and the clean thing, and go and write to that

nigger's owner and tell where he was; but deep down in me I knowed it was a lie, and He knowed it. You can't pray a lie—I found that out.

So I was full of trouble, full as I could be; and didn't know what to do. At last I had an idea; and I says, I'll go and write the letter—and *then* see if I can pray. Why, it was astonishing, the way I felt as light as a feather right straight off, and my troubles all gone. So I got a piece of paper and a pencil, all glad and excited, and set down and wrote:

> Miss Watson, your runaway nigger Jim is down here two mile below Pikesville, and Mr. Phelps has got him and he will give him up for the reward if you send.

> HUCK FINN.

I felt good and all washed clean of sin for the first time I had ever felt so in my life, and I knowed I could pray now. But I didn't do it straight off, but laid the paper down and set there thinking—thinking how good it was all this happened so, and how near I come to being lost and going to hell. And went on thinking. And got to thinking over our trip down the river; and I see Jim before me all the time: in the day and in the night-time, sometimes moonlight, sometimes storms, and we a-floating along, talking and singing and laughing. But somehow I couldn't seem to strike no places to harden me against him, but only the other kind. I'd see him standing my watch on top of his'n, 'stead of calling me, so I could go on sleeping; and see him how glad he was when I come back out of the fog; and when I come to him again in the swamp, up there where the feud was; and such-like times; and would always call me honey, and pet me and do everything he could think of for me, and how good he always was; and at last I struck the time I saved him by telling the men we had small-pox aboard, and he was so grateful, and said I was the best friend old Jim ever had in the world, and the *only* one he's got now; and then I happened to look around and see that paper.

It was a close place. I took it up, and held it in my hand. I was a-trembling, because I'd got to decide, forever, betwixt two things, and I knowed it. I studied a minute, sort of holding my breath, and then says to myself:

"All right, then, I'll *go* to hell"—and tore it up.

It was awful thoughts and awful words, but they was said. And I let them stay said; and never thought no more about reforming. I shoved the whole thing out of my head, and said I would take up wickedness again, which was in my line, being brung up to it, and the other warn't. And for a starter I would go to work and steal Jim out of slavery again; and if I could think up anything worse, I would do that, too; because as long as I was in, and in for good, I might as well go the whole hog. (Ch. 31)

Very far from being, on the surface at least, a "Father of Faith" figure, Huck demonstrates how one can, by obeying the conscience, believe one is disobeying God, but in fact be obeying God in-depth.

36. Troeltsch argues that the Reformers, upon emphasizing the doctrine of the priesthood of all believers, found themselves destitute of support to exert authority upon believers and to control the proliferation of movements that claimed total freedom to interpret the Bible and to organize their form of worship. As they could no longer count on the ecclesiastical hierarchy, they laid hold of a vision of the Bible that makes it into a sacrosanct object, infallible and indisputable, creating with that what Troeltsch calls "bibliocracy," in fact, what is the present-day use made of the dogmas of Fundamentalism and much of conservative Christianity. Moreover, it leads inevitably to the exercise of power in the form of domination of men over other men. See *El protestantismo y el mundo moderno* [*Protestantism and the modern world*] by E. Troeltsch (Mexico City: Fondo de Cultura Económica, 1958/1911).

37. The dogma of verbal inspiration has subordinated the Bible to the law of doctrine. The Spirit of God himself has been subordinated to this law. The insistence with which even today one calls to faith in the Scripture as an untouchable doctrinal foundation reveals clearly that one is conscious of what follows: The living Spirit of God represents a threat to any law of faith. He threatens even the Bible to the extent to which its authority does not derive from its content, the Gospel of Jesus Christ, but is enforced by ecclesiastical and doctrinal laws. See *O risco do Espírito* [*The risk of the Spirit*] by H. Brandt (São Leopoldo: Sinodal, 1977, 14).

38. Ellens, J. H. (2002). Psychological legitimization of violence by religious archetypes, in Chris Stout (Ed.), *The psychology of terrorism*. Westport: Praeger.

39. Bosetti, E., and Panimolle, S. A. (1986). *Deus pastor na bíblia* [*The shepherd god in the bible*]. São Paulo: Paulinas.

40. Fabris, R. (1983). *Corso Biblico pastorale su Gesù buon Pastore* [*Biblical course on Jesus the Good Shepherd*]. Sao Paulo: Paulinas, unpublished manuscript. Bosetti & Panimolle, op. cit., 31.

CHAPTER 8

HELL HATH NO FURY: GOD, LANGUAGE, AND LACAN

Ilona N. Rashkow

Introduction

The Hebrew Bible relates three primeval episodes in which humankind tries to transcend mortal limits: the famous God-Adam-Eve tree of life saga (Gen. 1:26–3:24); the bizarre story of the Nephilim (Gen. 6:1–4); and the Tower of Babel narrative, the first task-oriented group activity (Gen. 11:1–9). In all three, humans are punished for attempting to be too godlike. Like any good story, all of these narratives combine exciting elements—in these cases, fantasies of omnipotence and persecution anxieties. On a less titillating level, they also highlight the basic problem of humankind's desire for knowledge and the limits of human curiosity. This paper examines two of the narratives, the story of the Nephilim and that of the Tower of Babel, in light of two major elements of Jacques Lacan's work: first, the Phallus as the symbol of power; and second, language as the pivotal concept linking self and society. What ties the Nephilim and the builders of the Tower together is words. Just as the fame of the Nephilim is a threat to monotheistic principles, the unified language of Babel is a threat to monotheistic power.

As background, it might be useful to explain, Why Phallus? Briefly, where Freud views the mechanisms of the unconscious as generated by libido, sexual energy, Lacan centers the theory of the unconscious on the sense within us of something being *absent*. Lacan describes two "levels" of absence: the less intense awareness of absence, which can take the form of mere lack, *manque*, or of need, *besoin*. Both of the lesser levels of absence force the psyche to make demands. An even deeper feeling of absence takes the higher form of desire, *désir*. Lacan defines *désir* as two-fold: first, it is a feeling toward an object that is unconscious; second, this object can and does desire us in return. Lacan's terms for the universal symbol or signifier of *désir* is the *Phallus*. It is important not to confuse the Phallus in this sense with the male sexual organ, the penis. According to Lacanian theory, *both* sexes experience the absence of and desire for the Phallus, which may be one reason Lacan's restructuring of Freud has appealed to feminists such as Hélène Cixous and Luce Irigaray. Indeed, the sexually critical and liberatory potential of Lacan is that although one sex has an anatomical penis, neither sex can possess the Phallus. As a result, sexuality is incomplete and fractured for *both* sexes. Moreover, although men and women must line themselves up on one or another side of the linguistic/sexual divide, they need not align themselves with the side with which they are anatomically identified. Thus, as I have discussed elsewhere,[1] for humans, the Phallus comprises an answer to two riddles, one of "having" and one of "being." Do I *have* the Phallus or not? *Am* I the Phallus? Of course no one "has" the Phallus and no one "is" the Phallus; yet these are categories of experience within which humans represent themselves *to* themselves. This is the register through which differences are experienced. It is also the concept which permeates and unites the Nephilim and Tower stories because these are the questions that the deity, who would presumably both *have* and *be* the Phallus, seems to ponder in both texts.

Lacan's theory of psychosexual development is also a revision of Freud's in that Lacan shifts the description of mental processes from a purely biological model to a semiotic one. For example, Freud discusses the first phase of childhood as the oral phase, in which the child's pleasure comes largely from suckling; the anal phase follows, when the child learns to control and to enjoy controlling the elimination of feces. For Lacan, the analogue of the oral phase is the "Mirror-Stage," from 6 to 18 months, in which the child's image of its bodily self changes from mere formlessness and fragmentation to an identification with a unified shape it can see in the mirror. During this development, the child experiences itself as *"le désir de la Mère,"* the desire of the mother, in both senses—as an object that is itself unconscious and one which can desire us in return. That is, the baby not only knows that it needs its mother but also feels itself to be what completes and fulfills the mother's desires, in other words, the child feels *itself* to be "the Phallus." From this phase Lacan derives the psychic field of the "Imaginary," the state in which a person's sense of reality is grasped purely as images and fantasies of the fulfillment of his or her desires. This stage, begun during the child's second year of life, continues into adulthood.

In Lacanian thought, repression and the unconscious occur, together with the acquisition of language, at around 18 months, when Freud's anal stage begins. Lacan derives his ideas of language and the unconscious from the semiotician Ferdinand de Saussure, as he was interpreted by the structuralist anthropologist Claude Lévi-Strauss. Briefly, Lévi-Strauss considered the unconscious as "reducible to a function—the symbolic function," which in turn was merely "the aggregate of the laws" of language (Lévi-Strauss, 1967, 198). The primary laws of language in structural linguistics are those of the selection and combination of primary basic elements. *Metaphor* is a mode of symbolization in which one thing is signified by another that is like it, that is part of the same paradigmatic class, for example, "a sea of troubles" or "All the world's a stage." Lacan sees metaphor as equivalent to the Freudian defense of "condensation," in which one symbol becomes the substitute for a whole series of associations. *Metonymy*, on the other hand, is a mode of symbolization in which one thing is signified by another that is associated with it but *not* of the same class, for example, the use of "Washington" for "the United States government" or of "the sword" for "military power,"—a syntagmatic relationship that Lacan regards as equivalent to Freudian "displacement."

As the child learns the names of things, his or her desires are no longer met automatically; now the child must ask for what he or she wants and cannot request things that do not have names. As the child learns to ask for a signified object by pronouncing a signifier, he or she learns that one thing can symbolize another and has entered what Lacan calls the "field of the Symbolic." As Muller and Richardson describe:

> From this point on the child's desire, like an endless quest for a lost paradise, must be channeled like an underground river through the subterranean passageways of the symbolic order, which make it possible that things be present in their absence in some ways through words. (Muller & Richardson, 1982, 23)

At this stage, desires can be repressed, and the child is able to ask for something that metaphorically or metonymically replaces the desired object. Lacan punningly calls this stage of development "*le*

Nom-du-Père"—"the Name-of-the-Father"—because language is only the first of the negations and subjections to law that now will begin to affect the child. In French the phrase *"le Nom-du-Père"*—"the Name-of-the-Father"—is pronounced exactly the same as *"le Non-du-Père"*—"the no-of-the-Father"—hence its connection to negation and subjection to law.

This paper will apply these Lacanian principles to the Tower of Babel and Nephilim narratives and attempt to show that in the Hebrew Bible words can represent a challenge to the deity. As discussed in the next section, all the deity had to do was speak and the world was created. In effect, by his use of language he was able to dominate the heavens, the earth, and all that inhabited both spheres. He both *had* and *was* the Phallus. However, in both of these stories, human discourse is seen as threatening to the deity and causes God to question "Do I *still* have the Phallus? Am I *still* the Phallus?" And as a result of his self-questioning, he acts to eliminate those threats.

Incident: The Towering Tower (Genesis 11:1–9)

According to Sigmund Freud, " . . . Words were originally magic and to this day words have retained much of their ancient magical power. By words one person can make another blissfully happy or drive him to despair, by words the teacher conveys his knowledge to his pupils, by words the orator carries his audience with him and determines their judgments and decisions. Words provoke effects and are in general the means of mutual influence among men" (Freud, 1926, 183). Freud's statement seems particularly applicable to the Hebrew Bible where words are paramount. Indeed, it is the deity's words "There will be light" in Genesis 1:3 which shatter the primal cosmic silence and signal the beginning of a new cosmic order. Divine words signify that the deity is wholly independent of his creation and imply effortlessness and absolute sovereignty over nature. As if to emphasize this concept, after citing the words of each of God's commands in the creation narrative, the narrator repeats the *ipsissima verba* of the directive when relating that it had been fulfilled. Significantly, from a Lacanian perspective, this idea is in contrast with Greek thought, where, as Hans-Georg Gadamer writes, "a word is only a name, i.e., that it does not represent true being" (1975, 366). In fact, while the Greek term for "word," *onoma*, is synonymous with *name*, by contrast, its Hebrew counterpart—*davar*—means not only *word* but also *thing*. Thus, the primary reality of the biblical deity is linguistic; this is a deity who *speaks* and *creates*, and it is language that is his ultimate tool.

Enter the builders of Babel who want to build a city with a huge Tower in its midst. Anything Freudian there, do you suppose? The story is quite brief:[2]

> The whole earth was of one language and one speech. As they journeyed from the east, they found a plain in the land of Shinar and settled and dwelt there. They said to one another, "Come, let us make bricks, and burn them thoroughly." They had brick for stone, and bitumen for mortar. They said, "Come, let us build ourselves a city, and a Tower with its top in the heavens, and let us make a name for ourselves, lest we be scattered on the face of the whole earth." YHWH came down to see the city and the Tower, which the sons of men had built. YHWH said, "Behold, they are one people, and they have all one language; and this is what they begin to do; and now nothing will be withheld from them that they have schemed to do. Come, let us go down, and there confuse their language, that they may not understand one another's speech." So YHWH scattered them abroad from there on the face of the whole earth, and they ceased to build the city. Therefore the name is called Babel, because there YHWH confused the language of the whole earth; and from there YHWH scattered them over the face of all the earth. (Gen. 11:1–9)

As can be seen, the narrative is divided almost equally between the doings of humankind (vv. 1–4) and the response of the deity (vv. 5–9). God's sudden intervention, precisely in the middle verse, signals an impending radical change in the situation. Pronouncements about the state of affairs on earth frame the entire episode, and the last verse describes the reversal of the circumstances portrayed in the first.

According to this brief tale, apparently humankind was nomadic after the Flood and migrated en masse to Babel from the east, that is, from the vantage point of Canaan. Having arrived, they wanted to build the infamous Tower. Why? According to the Rabbis,[3] the inhabitants of Babel said: "Once every one thousand six hundred and fifty-six years, the firmament topples. Come and let us make supports for it [under each of its four sides]" (Gen. R. 38:6), a seemingly benign enough reason. Josephus sees an equally harmless explanation. He suggests that the locals, inspired by Shem, the eldest son of Noah, understandably were afraid the mighty flood would recur and so they were building a Tower which would either support the heavens or split them so that waters would drain away slowly from the earth's surface:

Shem . . . descended from the mountains into the plains . . . and persuaded others who were greatly afraid of the lower grounds on account of the floods and so were very loath to come down from the higher place, to venture to follow their examples. (Josephus 1:3)

The biblical text is less specific. Their stated purpose was to avoid being "scattered abroad upon the face of the whole earth," indicating a level of insecurity which is representative of Lacan's description of the formlessness and fragmentation a child experiences prior to the "Mirror Stage." By building the Tower, the inhabitants of Babel replicate the child's development into the "Mirror Stage" in that they exhibit the attributes of the Imaginary. That is to say, their fantasy is that the Tower will lead to the fulfillment of their desire for permanency in Babel as a result of "making a name" for themselves. Finally, their attempt to maintain only one language replicates the Lacanian concept of language acquisition, described above, and its inherent power to "name" things, similar to that which the deity displayed when "naming" the various aspects of creation and thereby bringing them into existence. The syntagmatic relationship of the Tower as guarantor against dispersion, metonymy, and the Tower as fame metaphor, acts as a displacement of their anxiety of being scattered into a desire to "make a name" for themselves. At the same time, however, just as Lacan writes that desires and anxieties can be repressed and the child is able to ask for something that metaphorically or metonymically replaces the desired or feared object, *"le Nom-du-Père,"* for the inhabitants of Babel, the desire to build the Tower is, in effect, the desire to obtain the Phallus, the Lacanian universal symbol or signifier of *désir*. In other words, by building the Tower they will acquire fame; as a result of this fame, the deity will not scatter them "on the face of the whole earth"; and by preventing the deity from doing so, they obtain the Phallus, thereby usurping God's power.

The deity, apparently curious as to what was going on, "came down to look at the city" and investigated the scene. Of course, there is a certain irony here: the residents of Babel build a Tower "with its top in the sky," where God is thought to dwell. Almost as if to emphasize his incomparable super-eminence, God "goes down" to scrutinize their activities. Then, upon seeing what is taking place, the first thing he does is confuse their language. This dramatic act highlights the apparent insecurity of the deity, since the Bible offers no speculation about the origin of language.[4] God, during the creation narrative, uses language and his ability to create merely by uttering a word, an expression of himself as *the* Phallus. This creation narrative also reveals that the first human apparently was endowed with the faculty of speech, a level of intellect capable of differentiating between one creature and another, and with the linguistic ability to coin an appropriate name for each. However, despite the fact that Adam gave "names to all beasts, and to the fowl of the air, and to every living thing of the field" (Gen. 2:20), he was unable to *create* by fiat. Only God had this ability. The deity's action in the Tower narrative, on the other hand, seems to indicate that he perceives communication between human beings as a threat, a danger which can be avoided only by lexical confusion. In Lacanian terms, the Tower and all of its implications cause God to question "Do I *still* have the Phallus? Am I *still* the Phallus?"

The second thing God does is scatter the inhabitants of Babel over the face of the earth, the very thing they fear! Why confuse their language? Why scatter them? What possibly can be wrong with what the builders try to do? Certainly, their plan seems reasonable and innocent enough. Although it is clear from the story that the work on the city and Tower displeases God, the specific sin of the builders is never mentioned. Moreover, since no great offense is obvious, the deity's reaction to the project seems strange, to say the least. Indeed, this narrative has troubled many biblical exegetes and beginning with the ancients, interpreters have felt obliged to find something in these words that might justify the punishment that followed. The prevailing opinion of the Rabbis was that the Tower was designed to serve the purposes of idolatry and constituted an act of rebellion against God. "Said they [the builders]: ' . . . He has no right to choose the celestial spheres for Himself and assign us the terrestrial world! But come, let us build a Tower at the top of which we will set an idol holding a sword in its hand, which will thus appear to wage war against Him'" (Gen. R. 38:6).[5] According to this reading, what the builders wanted to do was supplant God. In effect, the Rabbis anachronistically seem to say that by building the Tower, establishing an idol, and waging war with God, they are attempting to wrest the Phallus away from him.

The Talmud goes a little deeper into the story and associates Nimrod, "the rebel," with its building (Hul. 89a), as does Josephus, who provides an intricate exegesis:

> Now it was Nimrod who excited them to such an affront and contempt of God. He was the grandson of Ham, the son of Noah,—a bold man,

and of great strength of hand. He persuaded them not to ascribe it to God as if it was through his means they were happy, but to believe that it was their own courage which procured that happiness. He also gradually changed the government into tyranny,—seeing no other way of turning men from the fear of God, but to bring them into a constant dependence upon his power. He also said he would be revenged on God, if he should have a mind to drown the world again; for that he would build a Tower too high for the waters to be able to reach! and that he would avenge himself on God for destroying their forefathers!

Now the multitude were very ready to follow the determination of Nimrod, and to esteem it a piece of cowardice to submit to God: and they built a Tower, neither sparing any pains nor being in any degree negligent about the work: and, by reason of the multitude of hands employed in it grew very high sooner than anyone could expect; but the thickness of it was so great, and it was so strongly built, that thereby its great height seemed, upon the view, to be less than it really was. . . . When God saw that they acted so madly . . . he caused a tumult among them, by producing in them diverse languages: and causing that, through the multitude of those languages, they should not be able to understand one another. . . . (*Josephus*, 1987)

In this reading, unlike in the biblical text, it appears that it is Nimrod rather than the builders who desire the Phallus. The builders are merely the conduit by which Nimrod hoped to displace God as the ultimate power. Yet even in Josephus's explication, the deity reacts violently against all of humankind rather than merely punishing Nimrod.

Milton blames Nimrod also: in *Paradise Lost* (Milton, Book XII, 11, 24–63), Nimrod appears as the lawless and impious tyrant whose ambition led to the disastrous episode of the building of the Tower of Babel. According to Milton's epic poem, Nimrod instructed his people to construct a tower to reach heaven. God punished Nimrod's arrogance and halted construction by condemning the human race to speak separate and mutually unintelligible languages and scattering it all over the world (454–55). Why God punished all of humankind so drastically because of Nimrod's actions Milton leaves unexplained as well.

Among modern commentators, Gerhardt Von Rad (Von Rad, 1961, 148–50) views the account as part of the sin-judgment-grace theme that he writes characterizes the Primeval History (Gen. 2–11), and David A. J. Clines reads the story from a similar perspective: the punishment inflicted in the Babel story is mitigated by God's renewal of the grace extended to humankind through Abraham, Sarah, and the other ancestors (Clines, 1978, 61–79).

Other exegetes explain the narrative as an explicit tenth-century criticism of Solomon, referring either to the hubris underlying the desire for a "name" (Brueggemann, 1968, 173–74) or to the failure to see that one's "house" and "name" consist of a people and not a temple (Lundbom, 1983, 203–9). By using Lacan's theories of language and power to examine the actions of the builders and God, I read the text differently.

As I stated earlier, the inhabitants of Babel had a plan that was quite specific: build a city with a tall Tower in it and make a name for themselves. Since building a city was not objectionable, it had to be the Tower, the "name," or both. While the text seems to outline a tripartite strategy, " . . . let us build ourselves a city, *and* a Tower with its top in the heavens, *and* let us make a name for ourselves," from a Lacanian perspective, the Tower and name are two aspects of the same act of rebellion against God—an act designed with only one purpose—to obtain the Phallus, God's power. Viewed from this perspective, making a name for oneself has connotations of fame and glory, the realization of a grandiose fantasy; but it also connotes a basic need for a name as a sign of collective identity. To achieve group identity via a common task means, in Wilfred Bion's terminology, that this is a "work group," the very first "self-help group" so to speak (Bion, 1963). As in the Garden of Eden narrative, the catalyst in this tale is what Lacan terms *"désir"* (discussed above).

In other words, in Lacanian terms, the builders of the Tower of Babel, the metaphorical children of the deity, want their Father's symbol of power, the ability to "make a name" for themselves, with a unified language as the means to accomplish their goal. Since the childhood fantasy that "big" and "tall" are related to "important," the Oedipal implications of architectural grandiosity are epitomized by this Tower. For both the builders and the deity, the Tower replaces God's power—his Phallus. In effect, the tale is almost paradigmatic of Lacan's theories: the Tower of Babel, with its top in the heavens, is emblematic of that which we want but cannot or do not have. It is a fabrication, a constructed model, an artifact that simulates what is missing and, simultaneously, renders it sacred and larger than life. In effect, the Tower, a unified language, and Phallus become synonymous to the builders since humans are always *inscribed* within language, but language does not constitute the ultimate reality. Since Lacan focuses on the use of *language* as an intermediary in the mutual interaction among society and the self, his approach seems particularly relevant to this narrative. Here *language* is the pivotal concept linking the individuals and their society to the deity. Certainly, verbal interaction would have been a necessary aspect of their labors since construction carried out on such a colossal scale and involving such large masses of people require a centralized tongue and a high degree of organization. The resultant monumental edifice would have been a great source of civic pride and thereby would have fostered an additional spirit of unity, power, and invincibility: just what the deity seems to fear.

Again, apropos of Lacanian thought, the story uses wordplay as its very means of narration, highlighting the irreducible multiplicity of language and the deep-seated linguistic confusion that marks the ultimate scene.[6] Beginning with the exact location of the Tower, virtually every word is essential to the story. For example, the fusion of words in the first part of the builders' plan, to "make bricks and burn them thoroughly" is in a literal translation of the Hebrew "brick bricks and burn for a burning": *xeimar*, "bitumen" becomes *xomer*, "mortar." And the Hebrew *sham*, "there," is repeated five times, directing our attention to the importance of the *particular* site chosen, yet, at the same time, its sound evokes an association with *shamayim*, "heavens," that with which the Tower's site is to be physically connected, and echoes *shem* "name," that which the builders hope to establish. Meaning in language, as the biblical writer seems to have recognized long before Saussure, is made possible through differences between terms in the linguistic system. Here difference is subverted in the very style of the story, with the blurring of lexical boundaries culminating in the deity's power to confuse tongues. The etymological conclusion, expressing in popular wordplay the origins of Babylon, gives the punning punch line for the whole narrative: God "babbles" the builders' language, a subtle satirizing of the Mesopotamian story of Enki, the Sumerian god of wisdom in the Ehuma Elish, who confounds the speech of the Sumerians. It is not the "gate of god," the Akkadian *Bab-ilu*, as the inhabitants of Babylon interpreted the name, or the navel of the earth, as they conceived their city to be, but a site of meaningless gibberish, the center from which humans were forced to flee because of the disastrous threat of language to God and his power.

Significantly, Lacan describes the child's desire for the Phallus as a normal part of maturation: the desire for that which is unattainable is part of psychosexual development. As such, the builders acted in a way that is typical of the developmental stage "*le Nom-du-Père*" (discussed above). In other words, they were not exhibiting deviant behavior. However, the deity reacted in a way which *does* seem abnormal since, according to Lacanian theory, all parents face the child's desire for the Phallus. Again, according to Lacanian thought, God's actions, as the parent, would cause regression and failure on the part of the child.

In this regard, the sixteenth-century Dutch painter Pieter Brueghel the Elder painted two versions of the Tower of Babel story that seem anachronistically psychoanalytic.

In both versions, the Tower begins to crumble, as if disintegrating from within. Although in the Genesis narrative the Tower is not destroyed, Brueghel's departure from the biblical text is significant and insightful, for his pictures are architectural metaphors of a psychological state, a pictorial parallel to Lacan's description of developmental regression and failure. They recapitulate the disintegration of the self, the realization on the part of the builders that a task of such grandiose proportions cannot succeed; and the

The Tower of Babel, Pieter Brueghel the Elder, 1563. The Art Archive/Kunsthistorisches Museum Vienna/The Art Archive.

manifest reason for inevitable failure is the deity's response. God, as is made explicitly clear in the text, regards the work as a threat to his own power and authority and he is compelled to prevent its completion. Instead of allowing this phallic edifice to storm his heavens and thereby have the people of Babel make a name for themselves through their use of language, God scatters them. "If this is what, as one people with one *language* common to all, have been able to do as a beginning, *nothing they may propose to do will be beyond their reach*" (emphasis mine).

Incident: Gods, Men, and Others of Renown (Genesis 6:1–4)

Significantly, the deity seems to have been similarly threatened previously in the book of Genesis, as narrated in this particularly bizarre story:

> When men began to increase on the face of the ground, and daughters were born to them, the sons of the gods saw that the daughters of the earth were fair and they took wives among those that they chose. Then YHWH said, "My breath shall not abide in man for ever, since he also is flesh, his days shall be a hundred and twenty years." The Nephilim were on earth in those days and also afterwards when sons of the gods came into the daughters of humankind and bore them offspring. They were the heroes of old, men of renown.

The account given in these few verses is surely one of the strangest in the Hebrew Bible. The first question that I see regarding this text is whether the Nephilim and the "sons of the gods" existed simultaneously, "the Nephilim were on earth *in those days*" (emphasis added), or whether the Nephilim were the *offspring* of the "sons of the gods" and the "daughters of the earth." I favor the second scenario. That is to say, I see the Nephilim as the progeny of the "sons of the gods" and the "daughters of the earth" rather than as co-inhabitants of the land. Indeed, legends about intercourse between gods and mortal women and between goddesses and mortal men, resulting in the generation of demigods, are widespread and familiar ingredients of pagan mythology, and this theme of celestial beings, the "sons of the gods," arriving on earth and intermarrying with humans, the "daughters of the earth," seems to belong to the same genre.

Read this way, the first group in this story which presents a threat to the deity is the mysterious "sons of the gods" who are the "fathers" of the Nephilim. Interestingly, despite the fact that they are called distinctly "the sons of the *gods*," some commentators, both ancient and modern, regard the "sons of the gods" as a distinct group of *human beings* (see, for example, Cassuto, 1978, 291). I disagree. Since the expression the "sons of the gods" is used here in contrast to the "daughters" of "men," referred to in the first part of verse 1, I see the *sons of the gods* as entities who exist *outside* the sphere of humankind, and thus they are more threatening to the deity and his absolute power than mere humans would be. Indeed, wherever the term "sons of (the) gods" occurs, the reference is to nonhumans. For example, in Psalm 29:1, most translations render "sons of gods" as "heavenly beings" and in Psalm 89:7, "sons of gods" is translated usually as "holy ones," (so Revised Standard Version and New Revised Standard Version). Significantly, for purposes of my argument, the reference in Job 1:6 to the "sons of the gods" seems to have precipitated the same feeling of vulnerability on the part of the deity: "Now there was a day when the sons of the gods came to present themselves before YHWH, and the adversary [often translated as Satan] also came among them." In this narrative, the deity feels so threatened that he allows his faithful servant Job to be violently persecuted. Thus, it appears that the "sons of the gods" are presented in the Hebrew Bible as superior to the average pre-diluvian man on the street and, hence, an even greater threat.

As additional support to my thesis that the "sons of the gods" are the fathers of the Nephilim, according to the biblical text, there exist "destroying angels" or "demons" who also are more powerful than humans (see, for example, Deut. 32:17, "They sacrificed to demons . . . to new gods that had come in of late . . . "; Psalm 106:37, "They sacrificed their sons and their daughters to the demons"). These demons are unlike the "angels," or literally "messengers of God," who represent the *glory* of God (see, for example, Psalm 103:20, "Bless YHWH, O you his angels [literally, "his messengers"], you mighty ones who *do his word, hearkening to the voice of his word!* [emphasis added]). The Talmudic sages held that the angels do not procreate but the demons do (B. Xagiga 16a), although there seems to be no biblical reference to support this claim. Thus, it seems logical that from the perspective of the deity, these "sons of the gods" who took human wives were of the demonic variety of "heavenly beings" and thus a clear and present danger.

Apparently, the major offense committed by the "sons of the gods," according to the traditional rabbinic interpretation, is the grave threat and opposition to the world order approved by the deity, and this was the reason for the punishment meted out to the generation of the flood: "[the sons of the gods] filled the world with abortions through their immorality" (Gen. R. 217). But this explanation does not seem to fit the language of the text, for example, "*And they took them wives.*" The only actions of the "sons of the gods" mentioned immediately prior to the deity's outburst in verse 3, "My breath shall not abide in man for ever, since he also is flesh, his days shall be a hundred and twenty years," is simply the usual expression for legal marriage! The passage does not contain a single word, either here or in the deity's speech alluding to rape or adultery or any act against God's will. According to the plain meaning of the text, it would seem that proper, honorable, "wedlock" is intended. And even if the "sons of the gods" *had* sinned, why should the "sons of men" suffer retribution?

So what is the reason the deity limits humankind's life span to a hundred and twenty years? Two major explanations of this decree have been suggested: (1) "until one hundred and twenty years I shall be forbearing with them; but if they do not repent, I shall bring a deluge upon them" (Cassuto, 1978, 296); (2) "the length of human life upon earth shall henceforth be a hundred and twenty years" (Cassuto, 1978, 297).

I disagree with both interpretations. First, not only has the wickedness of the generation of the flood not yet been discussed, but in the continuation of the passage there is no mention of the fact that the time limit had passed without the sinners repenting. As for Cassuto's second reading, I question the significance of human longevity as an issue here. Instead, I see this "punishment" as an enforcement of the need for control by the deity over humankind. Since the offspring, the Nephilim, are human on their maternal side, they will not enjoy immortality (see Gen. 1–3) and hence those who live the longest will *only* attain the age of a hundred and twenty years. In essence, the sense of the passage is this: the earliest, nonthreatening, generations, who were the strongest because of their nearness to the deity's verbal command that they exist ("Then God *said*, "Let us make humankind in our image, after our likeness . . . " [Gen. 1:26]), lived almost a thousand years, but the span of human life was diminishing from generation to generation, and now would be stabilized at the point where the healthiest person, if he or she did not suffer illness or any calamity, would be able to live only a little more than a hundred years, according to the round figure of biblical tradition. This would be the fate of all humanity, be they "ordinary" people or offspring of the mixed marriages of "sons of the gods" with the "daughters of men."[7]

In contrast, the second threatening group, the Nephilim, the descendants of the "sons of the gods" and the "daughters of the earth" who were "on earth in those days" were known as "mighty *men*."[8] It seems significant to highlight that the term *gibborim*—"mighty men"—is used relatively sparingly in the Hebrew Bible, usually referring to *honorable* humans, men of position and high status and with reputations beyond reproach, but more significantly as "men of *renown*." But who *were* these "Nephilim"? The etymology of Nephilim is uncertain. The obvious association with *n-f-l* yields the rendering "fallen ones," as Targum Jonathan translates, that is, "fallen angels." Indeed, echoes of this theme are found in other biblical passages. For example, the exclamation of Isaiah 14:12 ("How you are *fallen* from heaven, O shining one, son of dawn! How are you felled to earth") is the notion of heavenly beings in rebellion against God and thereby forgetting their "angelic" dignity. Job 4:18–19 similarly expresses the theme of the corruptibility of these beings: "If he cannot trust his own servants, and casts reproach on his angels [literally, "messengers"], how much less those who dwell in houses of clay?"

However, if the Nephilim are the *offspring* of the misalliances, the progeny of "sons of the gods" and the "daughters of the earth," as I read the text, they themselves continued to generate Nephilim in the course of their married lives. Indeed, the definite article describing them in verse 2, the "sons of *the* gods," points to a familiar and well-understood term, one which appears in Ugaritic and Phoenician sources in references to the gods of the pantheon. As *gibborim*—"mighty men," they approached the *size* and *power* of their fathers, the "sons of the gods," but as the children of the "daughters of the earth," they were still at least in part humans.

Because Numbers 13:33 ("And there we saw the Nephilim, the sons of Anak, who come from the Nephilim, and we seemed to ourselves like grasshoppers, and so we seemed to them") implies that these were people of extraordinary physical stature, the term seems to indicate that they were "giants." According to Midrash Genesis Rabbah, they were particularly mighty in size: "R. Abba said in R. Johanan's name: 'The marrow of each one's thigh bone was eighteen cubits long'" (Gen. R. 317).

Philo also assumes their mammoth proportions and provides an interesting reading:

> On what principle was it that giants were born of angels and women? The poets call those men who were born out of the earth giants, that is to say, sons of the earth. But Moses here uses this appellation improperly, and he uses it too very often merely to denote the vast personal size of the principal men, equal to that of Hajk or Hercules.

In addition, Philo sees these giants as having sprung from the combined procreation of two natures, namely, from the "sons of the gods" and mortal women:

> For the substance of angels is spiritual; but it occurs every now and then that on emergencies occurring they have imitated the appearance of men, and transformed themselves so as to assume the human shape; as they did on this occasion, when forming connections with women for the production of giants. . . . But sometimes Moses styles the angels the *sons of god*, inasmuch as they were not produced by any mortal, but are incorporeal, as being spirits destitute of any body; or rather that exhorter and teacher of virtue, namely Moses, calls those men who are very excellent and endowed with great virtue the sons of god; and the wicked and depraved men he calls bodies, or flesh. (Philo, *Questions and Answers*; emphasis added)

While it is not certain from the biblical text whether or not the Nephilim themselves procreated, it is clear that whoever they were, they were described as "heroes of old, men of renown" whose heroic exploits were the subject of many a popular tale. Based on Genesis 11:4, it is possible that they were guilty of some "vainglorious outrages," offencses that would certainly threaten the seemingly already-vulnerable deity. That "the Nephilim were on earth in those days and also afterwards that the sons of the gods came into the daughters of humankind and bore them offspring" involve quite a direct reference to the mechanics of the sexual act, one which yet again ties them to the gods in contemporaneous literature. The Hebrew idiom "come into" refers to the whole act of intercourse, not merely to vaginal penetration. As Alter points out, "the spatial imagery of the idiom 'coming into' appears to envisage entering concentric circles—the woman's private sphere, her bed, her body" (Alter, 1996, 27).

However, it also directs our attention to the more relevant fact that from a Lacanian perspective, the Nephilim have now "come into" God's sphere since "they were the heroes of old, men of renown." In effect, the Nephilim challenge God's supremacy. God's extremely negative reaction to the Tower of Babel incident calls attention not only to God's struggle to maintain the Phallus, but to the threat he perceives by these *renowned* men.

Interestingly, the fame of the Nephilim as a risk to God's power echoes similar incidents in other ancient narratives. For example, Hesiod recalls an unsavory stage in the history of the gods that involves the leading triad of the pantheon: Uranus, sky, wars against his children, but is defeated and emasculated by his son Chronus, who is vanquished in turn by his own son Zeus. The latter, however, must then do battle with a *renowned* group of *giants* known as the Titans, and subsequently with a particularly menacing monster named Typhon. Similarly, Hurrian myths parallel the Uranid cycle. Here, too, the sky god, Anu, is fought and emasculated by his son, Kumarbi, who in turn is vanquished by the storm god, Teshub. But before his victory is assured, Teshub must face a formidable, *renowned* stone *giant* Ullikummi. Any similarities there? As with the prospect that man and woman might eat from the tree of life in the Garden of Eden and be immortal ("Then YHWH said, 'See, humankind has become like one of us, knowing good and evil; and now, he might reach out his hand and take also from the tree of life, and eat, and live forever'" [Gen. 3:22]), God sees the sexual inter-mingling of human and divine as the damnable crossing of the line of human limitation. God is not about to confront a challenge to his authority similar to that which the Greek and Hurrian deities faced and lost. The biblical primeval Titans are perceived by God to be a danger and therefore must be destroyed. As a result, God sets a new, retracted limit to the human life span, including children of the "sons of the gods" and the "daughters of the earth": three times the formulaic forty.

Conclusion

It seems impossible to me *not* to hear the angst in God's voice in the Tower and Nephilim stories, his anxiety that humankind seeks to achieve equality with God or, even worse, to usurp God's authority, a fear that first manifests itself in Eden. In the Garden of Eden episode, God's motive for driving humans out of the Garden is to avoid having humankind "become like one of us"; to rid himself of "heroes . . . men of renown," the deity limits life spans further; and in order to prevent the builders of the Tower "making a name for themselves" as powerful as his own, God erects barriers of language and distance. The deity's dramatic reaction leaves no doubt in my mind that the construction of the Tower constitutes the breaking of a taboo, quite reminiscent of what Leo Stone describes as the father's jealous counterattack against a fraternal conspiracy of the primeval horde of his sons (Stone, 1979). It is hard to miss the sexual symbolism of the Phallic Tower culminating in a metaphorical castration. God's hand with the outstretched finger banishing the first humans from the Garden and then dispersing the builders of the Tower is a mirror image of Michelangelo's fresco of the Creation in the Sistine Chapel. In Michelangelo's fresco, God's finger is a *generative* Phallus, which creates Adam, the first man. In the Nephilim and Tower narratives, however, God's finger becomes a *punitive* Phallus directed against the hubris of his offspring who want to usurp his power. The common language of humankind signifies, from a Lacanian reading, the development of a symbolizing function, a capacity for *creating* links, just as God *created* the world and all that is in it. "Making a name" becomes the equivalent of the function of *the Word* ("and God said, 'Let there be . . . and there was . . . ' "), a capacity to rival God by combining disparate elements and binding them together.

Indeed, the quest for a concrete background to the theme of protecting YHWH's reputation leads one in the direction of so-called "holy war" ideology.[9] Battles between nations in the ancient Near East were construed as battles between their patron gods. Instigated perhaps by the deity's violence in these narratives, among others, this concept was shared later by the state of Israel.

While it is not my intent to discuss biblical holy wars in any great detail, it should be noted that much of Israel's earliest literature does describe divine activity primarily in terms of war. For example, Exodus 15, Deuteronomy 33, Judges 5, and Habakkuk 3 are hymns of victory recording Israel's early military successes. In these texts, God is described as fighting alongside Israel's tribal militia and the determinative factor in their victories. Israel's deity is depicted with explicit military language: "YHWH is a warrior, YHWH is his name. Pharaoh's chariots and army he cast into the sea" (Exod. 15:3–4). In addition, the "Book of the Wars of Yahweh," quoted briefly in Numbers 21: 14–15, and examples of other records of divine war (for example, Exod. 17:14–16), suggest that these texts are but a small sample of a larger literary corpus which once existed in early Israel describing God as a warrior defending his reputation. (Notable passages expressing this notion within the Hebrew Bible include Judg. 11:23–24 and 2 Kings 18:33–35.) Saul and David conduct their military campaigns according to the instructions provided by the Urim (a priestly device for obtaining oracles); holy wars resound with the blast of trumpets and horns (Josh. 6; Judg. 7:18); the priestly class participates in military expeditions (Josh. 6; Judg. 10:26–28; 1 Sam. 4); and the booty is brought to the house of God (Josh. 6:24; 2 Sam. 8:11; 2 Kings 12:19; Num. 31:50–54).

Thus, the theme of YHWH making his "name," in the sense of identity and power, known to and through Israel, appears to provide the conceptual underpinnings for many of the appeals to God to act for the sake of his "name," in the sense of reputation.[10] As Glatt-Gilad demonstrates, God's demonstration of power goes hand in hand with the enhancement or preservation of his reputation (Glatt-Gilad, 1998). It can be seen readily, therefore, to what extent this biblical model and divine warrior imagery have been a driving force behind the holy war ideology of all three of the major religions that have their roots in the Hebrew Bible: Judaism, Christianity, and Islam. Moreover, the medieval development of "Just War Theory," which still shapes the philosophy and psychology of the Western nations, can be traced to this violent biblical base.

In these two stories, the Tower of Babel and the Nephilim, prose turns language itself into a game of mirrors. Meaning in language, as Saussure and Lacan have made clear, is made possible through differences between terms in the linguistic system. In the Tower incident, difference is subverted in the very style of the story, with the blurring of lexical boundaries culminating in the limitations of mortality and the deity's confounding of tongues. Ironically, while the Tower incident centers around "naming" and "making a name" for oneself, the episode does not contain the "names" of any individuals. Instead, the key expression, repeated five times, is "all the earth"—the *entire* human race is presumed to have collaborated in the struggle for the Phallus. Both narratives conclude with a summary of God's actions, the nullification of human efforts to resist his will and the nullification of human efforts to obtain the Phallus. By the time we get to the book of Exodus, not only has humankind failed to "make a name for themselves," God won't even tell the people of Israel *his* name. Language is one thing. God's Phallus is another. Hell hath no fury like the deity threatened.

Notes

1. See Rashkow, 2000.

2. All translations are my own unless otherwise stated.

3. In this paper the word *Rabbis* refers to the particular group of Jewish religious leaders known technically as "the Rabbis." They flourished from the second until approximately the end of the sixth century in Palestine and Babylonia. Growing out of a sect of first-century Judaism, their cultural, social, and religious hegemony over the masses of Jews grew during this period, in which the major literary productions of rabbinic Judaism—the midrashim and Talmuds—were produced. Their closest historical cognates are the Fathers of the Church.

4. Belief in an original universal human language seems to have been current also in ancient Sumer. For example, a fragment of a myth "Enmerkar and the Lord of Aratta," relates that the speech of humankind was confounded as a result of strife and jealousy between two gods.

5. R. Leazar said: "Who is worse—the one who says to the king, 'Either you or I will dwell in the palace,' or the one who says, 'Neither you nor I will dwell in the palace'? Surely the one who says, 'Either you or I.' Similarly, the generation of the Flood said, 'What is the Almighty, that we should serve Him?', whereas the generation of Separation said: 'It does not rest with Him to choose the celestial spheres for Himself and assign the terrestrial world to us. Come, rather, and let us build a Tower at the top of which we will set an idol holding a sword, that it may appear to wage war with Him.' Yet of the former not a remnant was left, whereas of the latter a remnant was left! But because the generation of the Flood was steeped in robbery, as it is written, 'They remove the landmarks, they violently take away flocks and feed them,' therefore not a remnant of them was left. And since the latter, on the other hand, loved each other, as it is written, 'AND THE WHOLE EARTH WAS OF ONE LANGUAGE' [i.e., united], therefore a remnant of them was left" (Gen. R. 38:6).

6. Indeed, Fokkelman offers an ingenious and insightful analysis of the story that gives full recognition to the role of chiasm and paronomasia (1991: 11–45).

7. According to the Sumerian list of kings, the first postdiluvian monarch reigned precisely 1,200 years (Cassuto, 1978, 298).

8. According to Midrash Genesis Rabbah, they were called by seven names: *Nephilim, Emim, Refaim, Gibborim, Zamzumim, Anakim,* and *Awim.*

> *Emim:* their dread (*emah*) fell upon all; *Refaim:* all who saw them melted (*nirpeh*) like wax. *Gibborim:* the marrow of each one's thigh bone was eighteen cubits long. *Zamzumim:* they were the greatest of all masters of the arts of war [this does not actually explain the meaning of the word *zamzumim,* but is a comment on their might. R. Jose connects *zamzumim* with *zamam,* "to devise, intend," and it implies that owing to

their superior military power they could always carry out their schemes]. *Anakim:* they were loaded with chains upon chains [they increased the chains around the necks—they subjugated many people]. *Awim:* they cast the world into ruins, were themselves driven from the world in ruin, and caused the world to be ruined. *Nephilim:* they hurled (*hippilu*) the world down, themselves fell (*naflu*) from the world, and filled the world with abortions through their immorality.

9. I use the term *holy war* not to refer to a particular, historically conditioned institution, but to the whole array of concepts that shaped the biblical view of war.

10. See Gen. 11:4; 12:2; 2 Sam. 7:9, 23; Ezek. 16:14, and the use of *shem*— "name" in various biblical texts.

References

Alter, R. (1996). *Genesis.* New York: W.W. Norton.

Bion, W. R. (1962). *Learning from experience.* London: Heinemann.

Brueggemann, W. (1968). David and his theologian. *Catholic Biblical Quarterly, 30,* 156–81.

Cassuto, U. (1978). *A commentary on the Book of Genesis* (I. Abrahams, Trans.) (Vol. 1: *From Adam to Noah*). Jerusalem: The Magnes Press.

Clines, D. J. A. (1978). *The theme of the Pentateuch.* Sheffield: Journal for the Study of the Old Testament.

Fokkelman, J. (1991). *Narrative art in Genesis: specimens of stylistic and structural analysis.* Sheffield: Journal for the Study of the Old Testament.

Freud, S. (1926). The question of lay analysis: conversations with an impartial person. In J. Strachey (Ed.), *The standard works of Sigmund Freud* (Vol. 12, 183–250). London: The Hogarth Press and The Institute of Psychoanalysis.

Gadamer, H. G. (1975). *Truth and method.* New York: Seabury Press.

Glatt-Gilad, D. (2002). Yahweh's honor at stake: a divine conundrum. *Journal for the Study of the Old Testament, 98,* 63–74.

Josephus, F. (1987). *The antiquities of the Jews.* In *The works of Josephus* (W. Whiston, Trans.). Peabody: Hendrickson.

Lévi-Strauss, C. (1967). *Structural anthropology.* New York: Anchor Books.

Lundbom, J. R. (1983). Abraham and David in the theology of the Yahwist. In C. L. Meyers & M. O'Connor (Eds.), *The word of the Lord shall go forth: essays in honor of David Noel Freedman in celebration of his sixtieth birthday.* Winona Lake: Eisenbrauns.

Milton, J. (1957). Paradise lost. In M. Y. Hughes (Ed.), *Complete poems and major prose* (173–470). Indianapolis: The Odyssey Press.

Muller, J. P., & Richardson, W. J. (1982). *Lacan and language: A reader's guide to Écrits.* New York: International Universities Press.

Philo Judaeus (1997). *The works of Philo.* Oak Harbor: Logos Research Systems.

Rashkow, I. (2000). Lacan. In A. Adam (Ed.), *A handbook for postmodern biblical interpretation* (151–155). St. Louis: Chalice Press.

Sarna, N. (1989). *Genesis.* In N. Sarna (Ed.), *The JPS Torah commentary.* Philadelphia: The Jewish Publication Society.

Stone, L. (1979). Remarks on certain unique conditions of human aggression. *Journal of the American Psychoanalytic Association, 27,* 27–63.

Von Rad, G. (1961). *Genesis: A commentary* (J. H. Marks, Trans.). Philadelphia: Westminster Press.

CHAPTER 9

SPLITTING AND VIOLENCE IN THE NEW TESTAMENT: PSYCHOANALYTIC APPROACHES TO THE REVELATION OF JOHN AND THE LETTERS OF PAUL

Johan S. Vos

Introduction

In the New Testament the human world is split up into two groups, those who believe in Jesus Christ and those who do not. Mostly the world of the unbelievers is pictured in dark colors. Sometimes New Testament authors make differentiations in their picture of the unbelieving world, but often the whole outside world is pictured, without discrimination, as a *massa perditionis*. We see comparable differences in the descriptions of the eschatological judgment, the picture of how history will be brought to its end. All the authors of the New Testament expect an eschatological judgment in which the unbelieving world will be punished. In some books, however, judgment is only announced, while in others it is depicted in scenes of enormous violence and cruelty. In some passages there seems to be a relationship between the extent of the violence in the judgment scenes and the measure of differentiation in the picture, between the believing and unbelieving world. A comparison of the Revelation of John with the letters of the apostle Paul greatly clarifies this correlation. In this chapter I have chosen to examine the writings of these two authors in the light of various psychoanalytic theories that deal with the relationship between the phenomena of splitting and violence.

Undated engraving of St. John writing the Revelation. Library of Congress.

The Revelation of John

Splitting and Violence

A primary characteristic of the Revelation of John, the last book of the New Testament, is the fact that it contains an absolute dichotomy. In its visions of the eschatological events, the world of man is split into two groups. On the positive side, there are the saints, the righteous, the holy ones, the servants of God, those "who keep the commandments of God and hold fast to the faith of Jesus." They are pure and blameless, as symbolized by the white garments in which they are clothed. They are virgins because "they have not defiled themselves with women." They are the one hundred and forty-four thousand who have been redeemed from the earth. They are marked with a seal: the names of the Lamb and his Father have been written on their foreheads. Their own names have been written in the book of life from the foundation of the world.[1]

On the negative side stands the rest of humankind, those who did not give up worshiping demons and idols, the evildoers "who did not repent of the works of their hands," the dogs, the polluted, the sorcerers, the fornicators and the murderers, those who love and practice falsehood, those who have committed fornication with the great whore, Babylon. They are recognized by the mark of the beast and the name Babylon written on their foreheads. Their names are nowhere to be found in the book of life from the foundation of the world. In the perception of the author, the Jews who do not confess the name of Jesus belong to this part of the world. For him they are "the synagogue of Satan."[2]

In the visions of the prophet John the eschatological or eternal fate of both groups is described. Whereas those who are written in the Lamb's book of life will enter the heavenly Jerusalem, where they will live in eternal light and reign forever,[3] the other inhabitants of the earth will experience the wrath of God and the wrath of the Lamb in a most violent way. They will suffer every conceivable kind of torture: they will be subjected to darkness and smoke, to the fierce heat of the sun, to huge hailstones being dropped from heaven, to fire mixed with blood being hurled to the earth, and to waters that have turned to blood. They will be tortured by locusts that have the sting of a scorpion. They will be thrown alive into the lake of fire that burns with sulphur and will be tormented forever and ever. People will gnaw their tongues in agony and wish to die and yet they will be unable to. They will be killed by every kind of plague imaginable: earthquakes, fire coming from heaven, poisoned water, famine, pestilence, and foul and painful sores. Some of them will be killed by the sword of the rider who is sent by God to execute his judgment and who is clothed in a robe dipped in blood. Their flesh will be eaten by the birds.[4] It seems as if the author cannot get enough of describing the tortures of the unbelieving part of mankind. He even incites the believers to rejoice at the violent destruction of Babylon.[5]

The Book of Revelation and the Christian Communities in the Roman Empire

It is widely agreed that the author of the Book of Revelation, with his symbolic language, is referring to the expected destruction of the Roman Empire and the city of Rome. The intensity of the vengeance fantasies is often explained as a reaction to the situation of the Christians in the Roman Empire. It is assumed that Domitian regarded himself as a living god, that he demanded that sacrifices be offered to him, and that he launched a persecution of the Christians who refused to do so. Recent research, however, has argued plausibly that Domitian did not persecute Christians and that the Christians in the cities of Asia—to whom the author of the Book of Revelation addresses himself—led quiet lives. After a thorough investigation of all relevant sources, Leonard L. Thompson concludes:

> So far as one can tell, Domitian did not prosecute either Jews or Christians with exceptional vigor. In fact there is a provincial tradition that portrays Domitian as a benevolent emperor towards Jews and Christians alike . . . Jews in Asia were probably among the most integrated and assimilated of Jews living outside Palestine . . . Imperial officials did not seek out Christians to persecute them; in fact they preferred not to get involved with the sect. But if local residents opposed Christians and reported them through proper channels, they could force them to trial. For the most part, however, Christians lived peacefully with their neighbors in the Roman political order . . . John reports surprisingly few hostilities toward Christians by the non-Christian social world. He anticipates conflict, but conflicts stemming from his fundamental position that church and world belong to antithetical forces. In other words John *encourages* his audience to see themselves in conflict with society; such conflict is part of his vision of the world.[6]

According to this view, the radically antagonistic view of the relationship of church and world in the Book of Revelation is a construction of the author and is relatively independent of the social-political reality of the times in which he lived.

Psychoanalytic Interpretations of Splitting and Violence in the Revelation of John

Various interpreters have attempted to explain the apocalyptic visions of John by means of psychoanalytic theories. The outcomes of these interpretations differ widely, depending on the psychoanalytic school to which the interpreter adheres. In the following paragraphs I will give four examples of a psychoanalytic interpretation of the phenomena of splitting and violence in the Revelation to John. Two of them are based on the work of Carl Gustav Jung, while the other two rely mainly on the work of Melanie Klein.

Eugen Drewermann

In his interpretation of the Book of Revelation[7] the German theologian Eugen Drewermann is strongly influenced by Carl Gustav Jung. According to Drewermann, from a historical-critical point of view the visions of the Book of Revelation are totally superseded.

Judged from the outside, these revelations amount to nothing more than a collection of historical mistakes. The author of this book predicts the fall of the Roman Empire and the beginning of the messianic kingdom in the near future, but none of this happened in the way he foretold. On the contrary, a few centuries later, the church would be married to "the whore Babylon," the Roman Empire, a union that would last more than 1,500 years. Only from the perspective of depth psychology does the divine and universally valid dimension of these visions become clear: they are projections of the human psyche onto the sphere of world history. The visions actually represent conflicts in the human psyche. The cruelly avenging God, for example, represents the superego, Satan and the animals represent energies of the id or "es." The visions represent an inner voyage that leads to the discovery of the Self and healing. The visions in 8:2–22:5 have the structure of a spiral: in various stages the process of individuation is represented, that is, the way in which a human being returns from anxiety and alienation to himself and the origin of his being.

According to Drewermann, apocalyptic literature has a lot of characteristics in common with schizophrenic experience. Both are dominated by an absolute dualism between two opposite worlds. In the Revelation of John the struggle between the opposing mythological powers represents the struggle between opposite aspects of the psyche, between the unconscious and the conscious, instinct and soul, id and superego, sensuality and morality. In the view of Drewermann, however, the message of the Revelation of John is that the situation of being split is not the final word. Visions like that of the heavenly woman and the birth of the child,[8] the marriage of the Lamb and the bride,[9] and the New Jerusalem[10] are all phases in the process in which opposing elements become integrated.

Violence is an essential part of the various stages a human being has to go through on his way from anxiety to trust. To give but a few examples, according to Drewermann: the vision of the first six trumpets[11] represents the hopeless situation of the human being at the beginning of the process of individuation. The vision that hail and fire mixed with blood would be hurled to the earth represents a bombardment of the superego, or severe feelings of guilt. God himself plays the role of the internal father who punishes harshly. The plague of locusts represents oral insatiability, the excessive longing for happiness that in the long run stings one's own flesh and ends in desperation. The plagues of fire, smoke, and sulphur represent a disruption at the three levels of the psyche: the ego, the superego, and the id. Every torture is interpreted by Drewermann in a similar way, as a step in the process of individuation and integration.

Edward F. Edinger

The interpretation of the Revelation of John by the Jungian analyst Edward F. Edinger,[12] although it differs in many details, has much in common with that of Drewermann. For Edinger "the 'Apocalypse' means the momentous event of the coming of the Self into conscious realization." Whether this occurs in the individual psyche or in the collective life of a group, it is experienced as a world-shattering event. The content of the Apocalypse archetype presents "the shattering of the world as it has been, followed by its reconstitution."[13] According to Edinger, there is evidence all around us that this earth-shaking archetypal event in terms of collective phenomena is taking place right here and now in the political and social world, for example in the breakdown of the social structures of Western civilization and in political, ethnic, and religious groupings.

In the individual manifestation, four aspects which also occur in Apocalyptic literature are relevant: First, *Revelation* has the psychological correlate of a shattering new insight accompanied by the flow of transpersonal images into consciousness. Second, *Judgment* is experienced in the form of an abrupt, profound awareness of the shadow, the negative side of things, which at times can be so overpowering that it can threaten complete demoralization. Third, the theme of *Destruction or Punishment* is manifested as the individual's anxiety in the midst of this transformation ordeal. Fourth, the coming of a *New World* corresponds to the emergence of mandala and quaternity images within the psyche as the possibility of a conscious relation to the Self and its wholeness begins to appear.[14]

In the view of Edinger, the Book of Revelation is a *separatio* document. The contents of the book mainly involve a decisive, radical separation between heaven and earth, all things upper and lower, between spirit and matter or nature. The book contains a whole series of very violent *separatio* images. This *separatio* has to be understood as a necessary psychological process required at a stage of the development of the collective psyche. It is a crucial feature of the Western psyche as a whole. This state of affairs, however, is due to change in the new aeon that aims toward the union of what has been split apart.[15] The New Jerusalem coming down from heaven symbolizes this reconciliation of opposites and a new state of wholeness.

Violence is an essential part of the way toward union of the opposites. In the same way as Drewermann, Edinger interprets the plagues as stages in the development of the psychic process. For example, the image of stars falling from heaven represents an invasion of consciousness by the collective unconsciousness. The invasion of locusts has a parallel in the Old Testament plagues upon Egypt. We can understand these plagues as responses from the unconscious against ego tyranny, as represented by "Pharaoh" in the story of the Egyptian plagues. When the seven golden bowls of plagues are emptied over the earth, heaven is being cleansed of a lot of disagreeable stuff. This is an image of highly negative contents of the collective unconscious. A psychological "overflow" can arise after a prolonged neglect of the unconscious, allowing the buildup of problematic libido, which the ego has tried to cope with by way of repression.[16]

"Apocalypse" imagery for the *individual* signifies disaster only if the ego is alienated and antagonistic toward the realities that the Self is bringing into consciousness; but if the ego is open and cooperates with the "coming of the Self," the very same imagery can signify a "broadening out of man to the whole man."[17] In the *collective* psyche the Apocalypse is now living itself out in an unconscious and destructive way. According to Edinger the extent of the destructive collective process will depend on how many individuals can achieve Jung's "level of consciousness."[18]

Hartmut Raguse

A totally different interpretation of the relationship between splitting and violence in the Revelation of John is given by Hartmut Raguse.[19] For his interpretation of the phenomenon of splitting in that text, he relies mainly on the work of Melanie Klein. For that of violence he draws upon the work of Béla Grunberger.

The mechanism of splitting is a central element in Klein's work.[20] Klein distinguishes two basic configurations in the psychic history of the child. The first one is the *paranoid-schizoid position*. There are two aspects that typify this configuration: splitting and projective identification. The infant deals with both his innate destructive impulses and his frustrating experiences by splitting both his ego and his object representations—primarily the mental representation of his mothering parent—into good and bad parts, in such a way that no link exists between the two domains. At the same time the infant projects his destructive impulses onto the bad object. His fear of this threatening object takes the form of fantasies of persecution. By splitting the early mother into two mothers the child wants to preserve as exclusively good the one mother whom he experiences as being good, while it creates a second mother, upon whom he projects all that he experiences as frustrating and life-threatening.

The second configuration is the *depressive position*. This is not a disease, but a developmental stage. The main characteristic of this position is that the child can tolerate ambiguity and recognize that his mother as well as he himself contains both good and bad aspects. In this position there is no need to project destructive fantasies onto the external world. The awareness of the infant, however, that both his love and hate are directed toward the same object causes an inner conflict and feelings of guilt. The "I" fears damaging or having damaged the loved opponent, and fears the accusation of the conscience. That is the reason why Klein terms this configuration the "depressive position." In the opposite case, when the world is split into good and bad, feelings of guilt are impossible. Raguse adds: "Everywhere in the world, where religious or political systems have a dualistic character, all bad opponents can be destroyed without scruples."[21] Not only in the earliest stages of life, but during the whole life cycle people constantly move between these positions.

To explain the element of violence and cruelty in the Book of Revelation, Raguse introduces Grunberger's theory of an original narcissism.[22] According to this theory the human fetus in the womb has the feeling of cosmic unity. Its birth represents an expulsion from paradise, comparable with an apocalyptic catastrophe, and results in the desire to return. All pictures of a lost paradise, the golden era, or the heavenly Jerusalem can be traced back to this experience. The other side of this desire is a hostility toward every form of reality that opposes this illusory unity: the father who stands between the mother and the child, the instincts which destroy the purity of the original narcissistic situation, and every factor that differentiates, for example, between genders and generations, because it causes tension and conflict. For the narcissist the world is split up into a good and a bad part. Often this position is combined with the fantasy that the mere fact of the destruction of the bad world will bring the ideal narcissistic world into existence. According to Grunberger, all kinds of religions and ideologies promise the shortcut of illusory satisfaction or the pleasure principle instead of the long hard road of maturing through confrontation with reality. In his view, faith is a flight into a narcissistic regression. Grunberger finds an expression of this in the words of Jesus: "Take courage; I have conquered the world."[23] Of necessity, these religions and ideologies have a violent character. In all kinds of religions we find militancy and fanaticism. Religions preach peace, fraternity, and love, but time and again they cause cruel conflicts. The believer cannot live without his enemy, the heretic, the ungodly, on whom he projects everything he denies in himself.

In the Book of Revelation, Raguse finds many elements of the paranoid-schizoid position described by Melanie Klein and of narcissism as understood by Béla Grunberger. According to Raguse, the Book of Revelation is characterized by an absolute dichotomy in which only "either-or" exists and that precludes any form of mediation. The narrator wants the readers to take a position that is characterized by a radical split between good and bad. He does not want them to be "lukewarm" but either "hot" or "cold."[24] When they accept the words of the prophet and show obedience, they will belong to the community of the chosen ones. This is an egalitarian community that turns its mind only to God, a community in which sexuality is denied. They all are clothed in the same white garments. The New Jerusalem is a city from which all shadows have been banished and in which all kinds of differences have been neutralized. It is a symbol of the mother's womb.

Considered from a psychoanalytic point of view this purity and uniformity are possible only because every opposing element is projected onto the enemy. Sensuality as a whole is projected onto the whore of Babylon. In the Book of Revelation, sexuality exists only in the form of perversion. It is split off, perverted, and destroyed. The same applies to all elements that threaten the purity of the saints. Those who perish will be burned in a lake of sulphur. According to Grunberger, the archaic aggression is symbolized by the metabolic process. In the Book of Revelation the model of hell is that of the digestive tract, with the elements of heat, gas, and sulphurous smell. All elements that threaten the purity of the chosen ones are projected onto the outside world and presented as feces.

In the visions of the Book of Revelation the ideal situation in the New Jerusalem has been made possible only by a previous judgment in which everything different has been destroyed. According to Raguse, the light in the New Jerusalem is a light that can shine only from a violent destruction of everything that stands in the way of one's own ideal. The radical splitting up of the world allows the narrator to indulge in sadistic fantasies to an extreme degree without feelings of guilt. The chosen ones sing a new song while the smoke of a burning world simultaneously ascends. While the world, complete with all its economic and cultural life, is destroyed by fire and sulphur, the Christians, who carry palm leaves in their hands, will be exempted.

In contrast to Drewermann and Edinger, for Raguse the Book of Revelation does not symbolize a way to integrate the opposing elements or an inner voyage that leads to the discovery of the Self and healing in a Jungian sense. Instead it symbolizes the paranoid-schizoid position described by Melanie Klein and the violent narcissism analysed by Béla Grunberger. According to Raguse, Drewermann gives an allegorical interpretation of the Book of Revelation that actually functions as an anti-text and has the function of disarming the original text. Drewermann, for example, regards the readers as victims of the violence symbolized in the visions. According to Raguse, however, the author of the Book of Revelation incites the readers to side with the heavenly beings who cause the cruelties on earth and to rejoice at the violent destruction of the unbelievers. In his view, both parts of the world as described in the visions of the Book of Revelation, the pure community and the sulphurous, burning masses, are two parts of one perverse universe. It is characteristic of perverse systems that they project their own perversion upon others. In the Book of Revelation all pictures of peace and harmony stand within a sadistic context.

An important factor in Raguse's view is the reception history of the Book of Revelation. In later periods the author did have readers who possessed the power, with the available ideas, to actually set a target for their violence. Wherever the vision of a thousand-year reign in combination with the ideal of purity and the heavenly Jerusalem became a political program, the text had a terribly destructive effect. Raguse refers not only to the medieval apocalyptic movements described in the work of Norman Cohn,[25] but also to German history between 1933 and 1945.[26] In these cases it seems cogent to discern the catalytic effect such religious visions as those of the Book of Revelation had in facilitating the worst horrors of violence and abuse in Western history. This should have been anticipated, in light of the contribution the Christian movement made to the subversion of the political structures of the Western Roman Empire already in ancient times, as a result of its inherent apocalyptic and eschatological antipathy to culture, political structures, and the status quo of the first to the third centuries in the Mediterranean basin. Within the canon of biblical writings, Raguse finds a counterbalance to the Book of Revelation in the message of Jesus and the apostle Paul.

P. E. Jongsma-Tieleman

Like Raguse, P. E. Jongsma-Tieleman[27] takes the psychoanalytic developmental psychology of Melanie Klein as her starting point. She compares our earliest ways of handling good and evil with mature behavior and applies this to religious texts. On the whole, however, her evaluation of the phenomena of splitting and violence in the Book of Revelation differs from that of Raguse. This has to do with the fact that, in addition to the work of Melanie Klein, she uses the work of W. R. Bion and D. W. Winnicott as well as drawing upon her experiences as a Pesso (Boyden System Psychomotor) therapist.

She shares Klein's belief that splitting and projective identification are the earliest mechanisms of defense an infant uses against evil. Everything perceived internally as harmful and dangerous is segregated off and projected onto the outside world. According to W. R. Bion, however, splitting and projective identification have a communicative function and not just a defensive function in normal emotional development. The infant makes the empathizing, mothering parent feel the unbearable experience. The parent functions as a container of the infant's projective identification.[28] This kind of projective imagination is a step in a process in which the infant learns bit by bit that intensely distressing experiences are not deadly, but bearable and by which he gradually learns not to evacuate bad experiences at once, but to keep them inside. Whereas in normal development a child uses projective identification in the hope of communication and containment, the pathological form of projective identification is characterized by the great violence with which it is carried out. The unconscious motive behind pathological projective identification is evacuation of bad feelings without any hope that the object can be good.

In normal development the paranoid-schizoid position is not permanent, but there is development toward the depressive position, in which the child learns to take distance from his own feelings and to discriminate between feeling and reality. Distance toward one's own feelings in the depressive position offers the possibility of discriminating between "acting as if" in a play of the imagination and "acting in reality." The depressive position makes expression of aggression at a symbolic level possible, for example, with the help of fairy tales, play and play therapy, or Pesso psychotherapy. Here the splitting of good and evil is used as a play of the imagination, discriminated from reality. Ideal images are used as an aid to discriminating between good and bad aspects of reality. In this sense they are signs of hope. At this point Jongsma-Tieleman refers to D. W. Winnicott's concept of the "transitional sphere."[29] Winnicott regards transitional objects, for example, a teddy bear or a blanket, on which love and hate can be projected, as helping the infant to make the transition from the world of projection to that of reality.

Jongsma-Tieleman views religious texts as instruments of the transitional sphere.[30] For her an essential point on which to question religious texts concerns their function: "Is the text written/can it be read from an attitude of hope, or does it reinforce an attitude of mistrust and despair?" Does the text put us into the world of the paranoid-schizoid position or the depressive position? Is the discrimination of good and evil used as splitting up of outer reality and ego in a *literal sense*, or is discrimination between good and evil used in the play of the imagination *at a symbolic level* while retaining reality testing. The same question can be posed concerning the handling of aggression. The discriminating point between the paranoid-schizoid and the depressive position does not lie in the expression of aggression in itself or in the amount and vehemence of the aggression. The key questions are rather: Is the depiction of violence in the text an imitation at a symbolic level, or does it stimulate the imitation and acting out of aggression? Is the solution experienced as evacuation of aggression, or is there a longing for containment of aggression, someone who sees it and is able to hold it?

With reference to the Revelation of Saint John, Jongsma-Tieleman notes that the symbols of good and evil used do not necessarily lead the reader of the text to a splitting up of reality. The whole struggle between good and evil is described with the help of symbols. It is not directly clear who or what is meant by symbols of evil, such as the monstrous dragon and the great whore. Probably the first Christians recognized in these images the demonic power of the Roman Empire; but later readers had different views. For Jongsma-Tieleman the enormous amount of violent aggression depicted in the Revelation of Saint John is comparable with a Pesso session. In a therapy session of this type, aggression is experienced and expressed, and is directed at negative figures by means of shouting, swearing, hitting, and kicking of cushions in a role play situation. This can give a feeling of relief, on condition that there is room for the good, that the handling of aggression takes place in the service of restoring ideal images and hope. Reading the Apocalypse and comparing it with Pesso sessions, Jongsma-Tieleman sees the violent scenes as symbolic expressions of aggression by a suppressed and distressed people. The hosts standing up for them are heavenly hosts; they cannot be identification figures to imitate, but should instead be seen as ideal parents, protecting and defending their children. The reader, in Jongsma-Tieleman's opinion, is invited to trust God and patiently endure oppression. To use Bion's terminology, the violent scenes in the book can have the function of a container of the aggression of the oppressed believers, thereby offering a transition from the paranoid-schizoid position to the depressive position: an attitude of acceptance of reality, of waiting while holding onto hope and trust.

From her knowledge of reception history, Jongsma-Tieleman is unable to conclude that the first Christians identified with the heavenly hosts destroying evil. During the first centuries of Christianity, chiliastic expectations were vivid, but what was at stake in their chiliasm was the anticipation of a millennial empire on earth, not an identification with the heavenly *militia christi*. In Jongsma-Tieleman's opinion, the handling of aggression in the text of the Revelation of John does not necessarily lead toward splitting and projective identification. However, she admits that it is possible to use the text in that way; and she gives some examples from the reception history of the book. Like Raguse, Jongsma-Tieleman refers among others to the millenarians who regarded themselves as executors of God's wrath. In the chiliastic movements as described by Norman Cohn,[31] she sees the primitive defense mechanisms of splitting and projective identification at work, but this is a special case because Cohn describes one special form of millenarianism, namely, the revolutionary form. This form of millenarianism held a particular appeal for people without roots and without basic trust. In her view, the symbols of good and evil in the Book of Revelation do have a destructive potential, but this depends on the use readers make of them.

Jongsma-Tieleman shares with Raguse the Kleinian presuppositions concerning developmental psychology and their application to religious texts. Both reject the Jungian conception of archetypes.[32] Her conclusions concerning the interpretation of the phenomena of splitting and violence in the Book of Revelation, however, are more akin to those of Drewermann and Edinger than to those of Raguse. For her, it is not the destructive but the healing function of the visions of judgment and wrath that predominate.

My own perception is more in agreement with Raguse's interpretation. I have the following critical remarks to make on the point of view of Jongsma-Tieleman:

First, according to Jongsma-Tieleman, the discrimination of good and evil in the Book of Revelation occurs at a symbolic level; and the symbols of good and evil used in the book do not necessarily lead the reader of the text to a splitting of reality. In my opinion, however, the Book of Revelation identifies clearly defined elements of reality with either good or evil. The real world is split into those who believe in Jesus Christ in the way the author advocates and those who do not. To the world of evil belong all the inhabitants of the earth who do not have the seal of the Lamb and his Father inscribed on their foreheads. When the author speaks about the execution of the judgment, the catastrophes hit the real earth and its inhabitants, namely, all the inhabitants who are not among those who hold fast to the faith of Jesus. In addition to this, a symbolic name does not always give room to all kinds of interpretation. For the contemporary reader of the Book of Daniel, for example, the symbol of "the abomination of desolation"[33] was unambiguous: It referred to the altar in honor of Zeus erected in the Temple of Jerusalem by Antiochus IV Epiphanes; but in the Gospel of Mark[34] the same symbol gives room for various interpretations. With regard to a symbol like the "Whore of Babylon" the author of the Book of Revelation gives so many hints to his contemporary readers that it would be hard for them not to think of the city of Rome.[35]

Second, contrary to what Jongsma-Tieleman suggests, I do not find a single trace of what Melanie Klein terms the "depressive position" in the Book of Revelation. The readers are exhorted without any discrimination to regard all inhabitants of the earth who are not Christians as a *massa perditionis*, as people who did not give up worshiping demons and idols, as evildoers who did not repent of the works of their hands, and who are fated to burn in the lake of fire and sulphur. In no way is the reader of the Book of Revelation taught to tolerate ambiguity and recognize that the world as well as he himself normally contains both good and bad aspects.

Third, according to Jongsma-Tieleman the violent scenes are symbolic expressions of the aggression of a suppressed and distressed people. She compares the Christians of the Book of Revelation with the people in distress who participate in a Pesso therapy session, people who have often been physically and/or emotionally traumatized in their early childhood. The question, however, is whether the intended readers of the Book of Revelation actually belonged to this category. As mentioned earlier, the radically antagonistic view of the relationship between church and world in this book is probably a construction of the author and one that is relatively independent of the social-political reality of his day.

Fourth, in her account of the depiction of violence in the Book of Revelation, Jongsma-Tieleman is right in saying that the hosts, which are executors of the wrath, are heavenly hosts and cannot therefore serve as identification figures to imitate. She may also be correct in her view that the occasions in the history of the church in which the Book of Revelation was used to legitimate physical violence should be judged in relation to the specific conditions prevailing at those times. From my own experience in orthodox Protestant churches, however, I would like to add that the spiritual violence evoked by the pictures of the Book of Revelation can have devastating effects. From this perspective it is hard for me to regard the visions in which the eschatological judgment is executed on the earth, as the handling of aggression at a symbolic level, in the service of restoring ideal images and hope. On the contrary, to this very day the violent visions of this book function more as a source of anxiety and distress for many people than as a spring of hope.

The Letters of the Apostle Paul

In the letters of Paul we find elements that remind us of the paranoid-schizoid position as well as elements that are characteristic of the depressive position as described by Melanie Klein. In these writings the world is split into a good and a bad part, into those who believe in Jesus Christ and those who do not, those who are to be saved and those who will perish, the objects of God's mercy and the objects of his wrath, the saints and the wrongdoers.[36] The apostle himself, as the messenger of the gospel, functions as a splitting force: "For we are the aroma of Christ to God among those who are being saved and among those who are perishing; to the one a fragrance from death to death, to the other a fragrance from life to life."[37]

According to Paul, everyone who does not believe in Christ belongs, without any discrimination, to the world of sin and death. The pagan world is a world full of ungodliness, impurity, and unnatural sexuality. Pagan minds are darkened so as not to see the revelation of God in the Creation. The Jews, although they boast that their righteousness is in their honoring the law, dishonor God by breaking it. Their minds are hardened so as not to see and hear the truth.[38] We can speak here of projection because Paul is in no way interested in reality testing. Without any discrimination or differentiation he seems to project every bad quality he can imagine onto the pagans and the Jews.

At the same time, however, there are passages in the letters of Paul in which he gives a more differentiated picture. As opposed to the picture of the Jews who possess the law but actually break it, the apostle puts forward a picture of Gentiles, who do not possess the law but do by nature what the law requires.[39] Along the same lines, he can discern between the Jew who is Jewish outwardly and the Jew who is one inwardly, between those who are only circumcised physically and those who are "circumcised" in the heart.[40] These passages may be hypothetical and may only have a rhetorical function as part of an indictment. A clearly differentiated judgment about the Jews can be found, however, in Romans 9–11. Paul terms the Jews "my brethren, my kindred according to the flesh," and he acknowledges not only that they have a share in the gifts of the covenant, but also that they have "a zeal for God." Instead of a radical separation of the Jews who do not believe in Christ, as found in the Book of Revelation, the apostle expresses his kinship with them. The ambivalence is clearly expressed in the words: "As regards the gospel they are enemies of God for your sake, but as regards election they are beloved for the sake of their ancestors."[41]

According to Melanie Klein's theory, the confluence of hatred and love toward the object gives rise to a particularly poignant sadness she termed "depressive anxiety."[42] The apostle Paul utters comparable feelings as soon as he deals with his ambivalent feelings toward the Jews: "I have great sorrow and unceasing anguish in my heart, for I could wish that I myself were accursed and cut off from Christ for the sake of my brethren, my kinsmen according to the flesh. . . ." His explicit wish to be accursed for their sake can be interpreted as an expression of feelings of guilt. Characteristic of the depressive position is the need for reparation: efforts are undertaken to maximize the loving aspect of the ambivalent relationship with the damaged whole object. Parts of Romans 9–11[43] can be seen as just such an effort.

A similar recognition of the fact that the non-Christian world contains both good and bad aspects can be found in Romans 7 where the apostle pictures the pre-Christian "I," be he a Jew or a Gentile. This person contains an "I" who delights in the law of God and wants to do good and another "I" who is in fact incapable of doing what is right. The feeling Paul arouses in his readers with regard to this pre-

Christian "I" is that of depressive anxiety: "Wretched man that I am! Who will rescue me from this body of death?" The feelings of the readers of these passages cannot be ones of hatred, because Paul has chosen a literary form by which the reader cannot but identify himself with this ambivalent person.[44]

Like the author of the Book of Revelation, Paul expects the "day of wrath" on which God's righteous judgment will be revealed and those who are not obedient to the truth will be punished while those who believe in Christ will be saved.[45] Unlike the prophet John, however, Paul never pictures the punishment of the unbelievers in his passages about the eschatological events. In 1 Corinthians 15, where he describes the eschatological events from the resurrection of Christ until the end of the world, he mentions only the coming of Christ, the resurrection of the believers, and the establishment of the kingdom of God. The reader is even given the impression that the apostle expects salvation for everybody: "For as all die in Adam, so all will be made alive in Christ."[46] Even if this "all" refers only to the believers, a controversial point among New Testament scholars, it has to be noted that Paul is in no way interested in the fate of the unbelievers. To be sure, the enemies of God will be destroyed, but these enemies are not human beings, but the personified powers of sin and death. Paul is even more specific in Romans 11: As soon as "the full number of the Gentiles" has come in, "all Israel" will be saved.[47] Whereas the words "all Israel" are unambiguous, "the full number" of the Gentiles does not necessarily mean "all Gentiles." It is possible that Paul is thinking of the predestined number. However, at the end of the passage he uses a similar universalistic formulation to 1 Corinthians 15:22: "God has imprisoned all in disobedience so that he may be merciful to all."[48] As in 1 Corinthians 15, in Romans 11 the apostle places no emphasis on the punishment of unbelievers. The same can be said of 1 Thessalonians 4:13–18, a passage in which the apostle also gives a detailed picture of the eschatological events. Whereas in the Revelation of John the destruction wreaked by the violent judgment extends not only to mankind but also to the earth and the sea, Paul expects that the whole of Creation itself will share in the salvation of the children of God.[49] It seems as if Paul is interested only in the wrath of God insofar as he can use it to encourage his hearers to believe his gospel. When he sees the wrath of God already at work in the present, he is thinking more in terms of the accumulation of sins than the destruction of the unbelievers.[50] Nowhere in his letters do we find the sadistic pleasure in the eschatological judgment of the unbelievers that is so prevalent in the Book of Revelation. P. E. Jongsma-Tieleman identifies an essential point on which to question a religious text, one that concerns its function: "Is it written/can it be read from an attitude of hope, or does it reinforce an attitude of mistrust and despair?" In the letters of Paul, I can see much more of this attitude of hope than in the Book of Revelation.

Of course, the fact that Paul does not maintain such a radical stance as the prophet John in his attitude toward the unbelieving world, and especially toward the Jews, does not mean that the reception history of the apostle Paul produced an entirely different effect from the Book of Revelation in this respect. From the fourth century right up to Germany's Third Reich, the words of Paul were used to legitimate the suppression of the Jews. It does not take a great leap of the imagination to picture the reception history of Paul's words about the Jews as a history of death and destruction. At the same time, however, it can be demonstrated that Paul's positive judgments about the Jewish people often functioned as an antidote against anti-Semitism. In the Third Reich, for example, his words functioned as a bone of contention for many anti-Semites, and among theologians the struggle against anti-Semitism was undertaken in the name of the apostle Paul.[51] In the end, the decision as to the positive or negative effects of a text lies with the reader.

Notes

1. 7:3–4, 9, 13; 8:3; 12:17; 14:1, 3–4, 12; 21:27; 22:11.

2. 2:9; 3:9; 9:4, 20–21; 13:8, 16–17; 14:9; 17:1–2, 8; 18:2–3; 19:20; 20:15; 21:8; 22:10, 15.

3. 21:1–22:7.

4. 6:1–9:21; 14:6–19:21.

5. 18:20.

6. *The Book of Revelations. Apocalypse and empire* by Leonard L. Thompson (New York and Oxford: Oxford University Press, 1990, 171–172, 174); cf. also Adela Yarbro Collins, *Crisis and catharsis: The power of the apocalypse* (Philadelphia: Westminster Press, 1984, 69–73); Norman Cohn, *Cosmos, chaos and the world to come. The ancient roots of apocalyptic faith* (New Haven and London: Yale University Press, 1993, 214–216).

7. Eugen Drewermann, *Tiefenpsychologie und exegese*, 5th ed., vol. II (Olten and Freiburg im Breisgau: Walter-Verlag, 1989, 436–591).

8. 12:1–18.

9. 19:1–10.

10. 21:1–22:5.

11. 8:2–11:19.

12. Edward F. Edinger, *Archetype of the apocalypse: A Jungian study of the Book of Revelation*, edited by George R. Elder (Chicago: Open Court, 1990).

13. Ibid., 5.

14. Ibid., 7.

15. Ibid., 122.

16. Ibid., 67; 89–91; 125–127.

17. Ibid., 182.

18. Ibid., 177.

19. Hartmut Raguse, *Psychoanalyse und biblische interpretation: Eine auseinandersetzung mit eugen drewermanns auslegung der Johannes-Apokalypse* (Stuttgart: Kohlhammer, 1993); Anxiety and Splitting in the Psychoanalysis of Melanie Klein, Erasmus Intensive Program: *Psychoanalysis and interpretation of religious texts*, 1998. http://www.theol.rug.nl/~vanderme/erasmus/texts/klein_uk.htm, consulted on October 21, 2002.

20. Melanie Klein, Notes on Some Schizoid Mechanisms (1946), in *Envy and gratitude, and other works* (1946–1963), with a new introduction by Hanna Segal (London: Hogarth, repr. 1993, 1–24). Cf. R. D. Hinshelwood, *A dictionary of Kleinian thought* (London: Free Association Books, 1991, 138–166).

21. Raguse, *Anxiety*, § 2.

22. Béla Grunberger, Über den Glauben, in *Narziss und anubis: Die psychoanalyse jenseits der Triebtheorie*, Aus dem Französischen von Eva Moldenhauer, vol. 1 (München and Wien: Verlag Internationale Psychoanalyse, 1988, 215–236). Cf. also Béla Grunberger and Pierre Dessuant, *Narzissmus, Christentum, Antisemitismus: Eine psychoanalytische Untersuchung*, Aus dem Französischen übersetzt von Max Looser (Stuttgart: Klett-Cotta, 2000).

23. John 16:33.

24. 3:16.

25. Norman Cohn, *The pursuit of the millennium. Revolutionary messianism in medieval and reformation Europe and its bearing on modern totalitarian movements* (London: Mercury Books, 1962).

26. Raguse, *Psychoanalyse*, 154.

27. P. E. Jongsma-Tieleman, "Splitting and projective identification: a primitive discrimination between good and evil" (Erasmus Intensive Program); *Psychoanalysis and interpretation of religious texts*, 1998. http://www.theol.rug.nl/~vanderme/erasmus/texts/split_uk.htm, consulted on October 21, 2002.

28. For Bion's concept of the "container" and the "contained," see Ronald Britton, "Keeping things in mind," in Robin Anderson (ed.), *Clinical lectures on Klein and Bion* (The New Library of Psychoanalysis 14, London and New York: Tavistock/Routledge, 1992, 102–113).

29. Cf. D. W. Winnicott, *Playing and reality* (New York: Penguin, repr. 1982).

30. Cf. also her book, *Godsdienst als speelruimte voor verbeelding. Een godsdienstpsychologische studie* (Kampen: Kok, 1996), and her lecture "The

Importance of Winnicott's Theory for the Interpretation of Religious Imagination" (Erasmus Intensive Program. *Psychoanalysis and interpretation of religious texts*, 1998). http://www.theol.rug.nl/~vanderme/erasmus/texts/split_uk.htm, consulted on October 21, 2002.

31. Cohn, *The Pursuit of the Millennium*.

32. Jongsma-Tieleman, *Godsdienst*, 199.

33. 9:27; 12:11.

34. 13:14.

35. Cf. David E. Aune, *Revelation 17–22*, Word Biblical Commentary 52c (Nashville: Thomas Nelson, 905–961).

36. Rom. 9:21–23; 1 Cor. 1:18; 2 Cor. 6:14–7:1.

37. 2 Cor. 2:15–16.

38. Rom. 1–18; 3:21; Rom. 11:7–11; 2 Cor. 3:12–16.

39. Rom. 2:14–16.

40. Rom. 2:25–29.

41. Rom. 11:28.

42. Hinshelwood, *Dictionary*, 138.

43. Esp. 9:1–5; 11:11–32.

44. Cf. also Raguse, *Anxiety*, § 3.

45. Rom. 2:5; 1 Thess. 1:10.

46. V. 22.

47. V. 25.

48. V. 32.

49. Rom. 8:19–25.

50. Rom. 1:18–32; 1 Thess. 2:14–16.

51. For positive and negative examples from the history of reception see J. S. Vos, De Letter Doodt, Maar de Geest Maakt Levend, in T. Baarda et al. (eds.), *Paulus en de Andere Joden* (Delft: Meinema, 1984, 146–170, esp. 164–167).

References

Aune, D. E. (1997). *Revelation 17–22*. Word Biblical Commentary 52c. Nashville: Thomas Nelson.

Britton, R. (1992). Keeping things in mind. In R. Anderson (Ed.), *Clinical lectures on Klein and Bion*. The New Library of Psychoanalysis 14. London and New York: Tavistock/Routledge.

Cohn, N. (1962). *The pursuit of the millennium. Revolutionary messianism in medieval and reformation Europe and its bearing on modern totalitarian movements*. London: Mercury Books.

Cohn, N. (1993). *Cosmos, chaos and the world to come. The ancient roots of apocalyptic faith*. New Haven and London: Yale University Press.

Collins, A. Y. (1984). *Crisis and catharsis: the power of the apocalypse*. Philadelphia: Westminster.

Drewermann, E. (1989). *Tiefenpsychologie und exegese* [Depth psychology and exegesis] (Vol. 2; 5th ed.). Olten Freiburg im Breisgau: Walter-Verlag.

Edinger, E. F. (1990). *Archetype of the apocalypse: A Jungian study of the Book of Revelation* (George R. Elder, Ed.). Chicago: Open Court.

Grunberger, B. (1988). Über den glauben [About faith]. In *Narziss und Anubis* [Narcissus and Anubis] (E. Moldenhauer, Trans., Vol. 1). München and Wien: Verlag Internationale Psychoanalyse.

Grunberger, B., & Dessuant, P. (2000). *Narzissmus, Christentum, Antisemitismus: eine psychoanalytische untersuchung* [Narcissism, Christianity, and anti-Semitism: a psychoanalytic study] (M. Looser, Trans.). Stuttgart: Klett-Cotta.

Hinshelwood, R. D. (1991). *A dictionary of Kleinian thought.* London: Free Association Books.

Jongsma-Tieleman, P. E. (1996). *Godsdienst als speelruimte voor verbeelding* [Religion as play area for imagination]. Kampen: Kok.

Jongsma-Tieleman, P. E. (1998a). Splitting and projective identification: a primitive discrimination between good and evil. Erasmus Intensive Program: *Psychoanalysis and Interpretation of Religious Texts.* http://www.theol.rug.nl/~vanderme/erasmus/texts/split_uk.htm.

Jongsma-Tieleman, P. E. (1998b). The importance of Winnicott's theory for the interpretation of religious imagination. Erasmus Intensive Program: *Psychoanalysis and Interpretation of Religious Texts.* http://www.theol.rug.nl/~vanderme/erasmus/texts/split_uk.htm.

Klein, M. (1993). Notes on some schizoid mechanisms. In *Envy and gratitude, and other works (1946–1963),* with a new introduction by Hanna Segal (Repr.). London: Hogarth.

Raguse, H. (1993). *Psychoanalyse und biblische interpretation* [Psychoanalysis and biblical interpretation]. Stuttgart: Kohlhammer.

Raguse, H. (1998). Anxiety and splitting in the psychoanalysis of Melanie Klein. Erasmus Intensive Program: *Psychoanalysis and Interpretation of Religious Texts.* http://www.theol.rug.nl/~vanderme/erasmus/texts/klein_uk.htm.

Thompson, L. L. (1990). *The Book of Revelations. Apocalypse and empire.* New York and Oxford: Oxford University Press.

Vos, J. S. (1984). De letter doodt, maar de geest maakt levend [The letter kills, but the Spirit gives life]. In T. Baarda et al., *Paulus en de andere joden* [Paul and the other Jews]. Delft: Meinema.

Winnicott, D. W. (1982). *Playing and reality* (Repr.). New York: Penguin.

CHAPTER 10

LEGION: A VIOLENT SOUL IN A VIOLENT SOCIETY (MARK 5:1–20)

Michael Willett Newheart

Introduction

For some years I have been attracted, one might even say "possessed," by the Gerasene of Mark 5:1–20, the man whose legion of demons, according to the story, was cast out by Jesus. In my first teaching post in a small Baptist college 20 years ago, I often performed in class dramatic monologues of biblical characters, and the Gerasene was one of my favorites. I occasionally took him "on the road" when I was asked to preach. He was always a hit! In 1991 the American Bible Society produced a nine-minute video of this passage, which turned out to be sort of an "MTV" version. When I first saw it I was transfixed and I have often used it in class.

I have begun to work on a book on this passage, tentatively titled, *"My Name Is Legion": The Story and Soul of the Gerasene Demoniac*, forthcoming from the Liturgical Press Interfaces series on biblical personalities. The Gerasene, with a legion of demons, has more personalities than anybody in the Bible!

Exposition

Why does the Gerasene intrigue me so? He is the wild man. Through him I live my wildness, my shadow, to use a Jungian term. But I also long for the healing he experienced. I have my own demons, though I usually do not name them as such. I suffer from generalized anxiety disorder (GAD) and depression, for which I am medicated and participate in psychotherapy. As I read of his exorcism, I experience vicariously being "in my right mind" (Mark 5:15).

I am also compelled by the violence of the passage. The Gerasene is someone who had to carry the violence of his people, yet Jesus delivered him from the violence. For over two decades, I have been active in the peace movement, culminating in my recently becoming a Quaker, a member of the Religious Society of Friends, which has stood against violence since its inception in seventeenth-century England. My interpretation of the passage, then, is shaped by my commitment to nonviolence.

In this chapter I wish to read soulfully the story of the Gerasene.[1] But first, what does it mean to read a passage soulfully? I have discussed my soul-hermeneutic in detail elsewhere, and I will only summarize here (Newheart, 2000, 1–8; Newheart, 2001, xiii–xxi).[2] It is composed of three elements: analytical and archetypal psychology, African American cultural experience, and reader-response criticism. First, analytical and archetypal psychology, as developed, respectively, by Carl Jung and James Hillman, attempts to bring soul back into psychology through focusing on images in dreams, literature, and society at large. Hillman, for example, contends that one must "love the image," which means sticking with it, twisting it by doing wordplays,[3] and making analogies, or likenesses, for the images (Hillman, 1978, 81–82, 86–87).[4] I therefore attempt to find the soul of the biblical passage in the images and with what Hillman calls "a poetic basis of mind" (1975, xi) I open up these images, and my own soul, by twisting them and doing wordplays with them. Furthermore, I also open up the images by finding contemporary analogies, or likenesses, for them.

Second, African American cultural experience is often referred to as soul, as African Americans have given us soul music and soul food, and they often refer to one another as soul brother and soul sister. Psychologists Alfred Pasteur and Ivory Toldson identify soul with "black expressiveness, which is based in rhythm" (Pasteur & Toldson, 1982, 4). Such rhythm or soul can be seen especially clearly in African American poetry. If poetry is the voice of the soul, so African American poetry might be considered the soul of soul. My poetic readings of the biblical images reflect the rhythms of this poetry, and I find the likenesses to these images in this body of literature.

Third, reader-response criticism focuses on the reader's role in shaping the meaning of a text (cf. Tompkins, 1980). A reader-dominant, as opposed to text-dominant, mode of reader-response criticism highlights the reader as an individual subject, influenced by one's personal narrative, or as a member of an interpretative community, shaped by a certain social location, including race, gender, class, sexual orientation, and religious affiliation. In my soul-hermeneutic I attempt to do justice to both individual and community, considering the reader's soul-state, which encompasses both psychological and social dynamics. For example, I am a European American, heterosexual, Christian, intellectual male working in a predominantly African American institution.

In treating this passage psychologically, in a soul-word way, I first translate Mark 5:1–20 and poetically play with its images. Second, I find likenesses to these images by exploring images of violence in contemporary African American poetry. Third, and finally, I briefly discuss the likenesses to the images in my own soul.

A Soul Reading of Mark 5:1–20

Translation[5]

And they came to the other side of the sea,
To the region of the Gerasenes.
And when Jesus got out of the boat,
Suddenly there met him out of the tombs
A man with an unclean spirit,
Who was living among the tombs,
And no one could restrain him,
Even with a chain,

For he'd been fettered and chained many times,
But he had torn apart the chains
And smashed the fetters,
And no one was strong enough to tame him.
And every night and day
In the tombs and on the mountains
He was screaming
And cutting himself with stones.

And when he saw Jesus at a distance,
He ran and kneeled before him,
And he screamed terribly,
    "WHAT'VE YOU GOT TO DO WITH ME,
    JESUS SON OF THE HIGHEST GOD?
    I SWEAR TO YOU BY GOD,

DON'T TORTURE ME!"
For Jesus kept saying to him,
"Come out of the man, you unclean spirit!"

And Jesus asked him,
    "What's your name?"
And he said to him,
    "My name is Legion,
    For we are many."
And he begged Jesus earnestly
Not to send them
Out of the region.

Now on the mountainside
Was a large herd of pigs grazing.
And the spirits begged him,
    "Send us into the pigs,
    So we can enter them."
And he let them.
And the unclean spirits
Went out of the man and into the pigs.

And the herd,
About two thousand strong,
Rushed off a cliff into the sea,
And they were drowned in the sea.
And the ones grazing the pigs fled
And told what had happened
In the city and the country,
And people came to see.

And they came to Jesus,
And they saw the demonized one,
The man who had had the legion,
Seated, dressed and sane,
And they were afraid.
And those who had seen
What had happened to the demonized one
Also told them about the pigs.

And they began begging Jesus
To get out of their country.
And as he got into the boat,
The ex-demonized one
Begged Jesus to be with him,
And Jesus did not let him, but said,

"Go home to your people,
Tell them what the master has done
How he's had compassion on you."

And the man left
And began to preach
In the Decapolis
What Jesus had done for him.
Everyone was amazed.

Playing with the Images of the Story

Following is a playful, poetic commentary on the passage. Yes, playful and poetic . . . and possessed! A story about a man possessed by a legion of unclean spirits and a man possessed by the holy spirit calls for a possessed commentary! So you will encounter misspellings, poor syntax, ungrammatical expressions, inconsistent capitalization and punctuation . . . and plenty of puns, puns, puns. And what is this playful, poetic, possessed commentary possessed by? An unclean spirit or the holy spirit? Good question. We'll see.

So our story begins, though Mark has begun a long time ago: "The beginning of the good news of Jesus Christ, son of God" (Mark 1:1). Because we're beginning in the middle, we have a lot of catching up to do. Mark begins his Gerasene story: "And they came to the other side of the sea." Mark's a storyteller, and he's always saying that this happened, and this happened, and this happened, and . . . Polysyndeton, the grammarians say. Huh? Polly sinned a ton!? No, polysyndeton, lots of connectives. Mark it well.

"And they came . . ." They? Who "they"? Hoo dey? Jesus and the disciples. Jee-zus and de ddddisciples. Jesus? Yes, Jesus, that messianic sonagod (1:1), baptized-holyspirit-into-him (1:9–10), disciple-calling (1:16–20; 2:13–14), uncleanspiritanddemon-outcasting (1:21–28, 34, 39, etc.), diseased-healing (1:34, 40–45, etc.), scribesandPharisees-roiling (2:1–12, 15–17, etc.), parable-speaking (4:1–34), windandsea-peace-be-stilling (4:35–41) Jesus. Yes, him.

But not just Jesus (though Jesus is certainly just), also his disciples. Duh ddddisciples. And it seems that they are always saying, "Duh!" After the windsea calming, they say, "Duh! Hoo den is dis dat—who then is this—that even wind&sea obey him?" (4:41) You knuckleheads! Don't you listen to the narrator (1:1), to the voice from heaven (1:10), to the unclean spirits (3:11) dat say dat dis iz de sonagod, that say that this is the son of God!? Man, that Gentile Roman centurion knows more than you (15:39). He knows, he nose, has the nose for news, the good news, that Jesus was sonagod. But da disciples don't get it, not in this sea crossing or any of the others (hearts hardened at water-walking, 6:47–52; misunderstanding Jesus's yeasty-words, 8:14–21). Things don't get any better for them. Sure, they cross the sea . . . but they don't see the cross. Each time Jesus passion-predicts, disciples misunderstand (8:31–33; 9:30–32; 10:32–40). In this passionate section blind men seeing (8:22–26; 10:45–52) frames seeing folks (i.e., disciples) blinded. What's wrong with them? They have been given the secret of the kingdom of God (4:11); they've been called to be with Jesus and preach and cast out demons (3:13–19a), which they do (6:7–13); but they don't quite get it. Don't quite, so they quit. They forsake Jesus—in the garden, which is not paradise for them (14:50). Indeed, they disappear from the scene in this story: no mention of them after the first line. Where are they? Have they drowned in the sea?

So Jesus and his disciples go to the other side of the sea, that is, the other side of the sea of Galilee (1:16). On this side, he's been fishing for folk who are Jews. Now he goes to other side to fish for folk who are Gentiles. Gentle Gentiles? Not according to Jesus, who chauvinistically calls them "dogs" (7:27). So Jesus' fishing for dogs here on the other side.

Jesus and disciples go to other side of the sea, to the region of the Gerasenes (garish scene?). Gerasenes, where people of Gerasa live. But hey, get out your map: Gerasa's not within hollerin' distance a de sea a galilee. (Matthew moves the story to Gadara, 8:28, which is closer to the sea. Some manuscripts of Mark also have that.) Hmm. Mark has moved Gerasa next to the sea. Things are already gettin' eery. But stay tuned!

So Jesusanddisciples come to the sea's other side, to the Gerasene region. And . . . and . . . and Jesus gets outa de boat. (Do da da disciples stay in de boat?) So Jesus get outa de boat, de boat dats been his lectern as well as bunk (Mark 4:1, 38). When Jesus get outa d boat— wham! suddenly immediately straightway (I like dat ol' KJV term.) Things always happenin' in Mark immediately straightway *euthus* (Greek) wham! It's a fast-paced book (huff-puff) Jesus in a hurry for example chapter 1 comeup outa water Wham! heavenrip spiritcomedown voice Wham! spirit throws him out into wilderness (1:10–12), Capernaumsynagogue teaching Wham! uncleanspirited man (1:21–23), leave synagogue Wham! enter SimonAndrewshouse

(1:29–31), beggingkneeling skin-diseased man "Be clean" Wham! skin disease go bye-bye and he clean (1:40–42).

Now, Jesus outa d boat Wham! met by dis coming-outa-d-tombs-with-unclean-spirit-man. A man amen a man a hu-man who-man with (in?) an unclean (profane, not-profound) spidit—spirited uncleanness, outta-place spirit, uncleansed breath, impure wind. Spirit, spit it out! Not first unclean Jesus seen. Began Galilee gig (his Jewish jaunt) by exorcising (exercising? hit de deck & gimme five!) an unclean spirit, cleanly showing his new authoritative teaching (1:21–28). Now begins Gentile juggernaut by exorcising unclean spirit. And dis spirit was quite unclean cuz it put dis guy in de tombs, an unclean place for Jewish sensibilities. Three times Mark associates him with the tombs (5:2, 3, 5). Not only is this man's spirit unclean, but he's also dead! And folks try to chain and fetter him. To keep him from going to the tombs? To keep him from leaving the tombs? Whatever their reasons, the unclean spirited (U.S.?) man rips de chains and smashes de fetters. Rip (like de heavens, 1:10?) and smash! But binding and freeing happens "manytimes." It seems that the people are chained and fettered to the U.S.man. René Girard, in his chapter on this passage in his book *The Scapegoat*, talks about the "cyclical pathology" of the townspeople and the U.S.man and about the violent and ritualistic character of the people's actions toward him (Girard, 1986, 168–69). Walter Wink, building on Girard, says that the demons are the spirituality of the people (Wink, 1986, 48). So the man and the people are chained and fettered together! But while the people are bound, the U.S.man is free: he breaks his bonds. He is the satanically strong man who can't be bound (3:26–27). He is the wild animal, whom no one NO ONE can tame. (Down boy, down!) (Jesus will soon be with this diabolically wild beast, 1:13.)

This wildly strong, beasty boy would roam among the tombs and on the mountains (go tell it on the mountain!) SCREAMING, and no wonder he was doing that because he was also self-stone-cutting. (Simon's not the only Rocky in dis story, 3:16.) Taking on de punishment de peeple wanna give him? Chaining and stoning. Girard: "an example of the reciprocal relationship of mimetic rivalry" (Girard 1986, 171). People with (unclean?) spirits in Mark often engage in self-mutilation: see the case of boy with mute spirit who throws himself into fire water to kill himself (9:22). Maybe they are taking on society's violent condemnation of them by trying to destroy their spirits by destroying themselves. (Indeed, Jesus' spirit leads him to the cross!)

Once the U.S.man had had enough tomb-dwelling, chain-smashing, night&day-screaming, self-stoning, he sees distant Jesus shoring up and he runrunrunrunruns to him and kneels before him (like the U.S.s usually do, 3:11). He realizes that Jesus is a holy spirited man— H.S.man—much more powerful than U.S.man. This strong man knows that this one can bind him and plunder his house (3:27). So he screams even more terribly: "WHAT'VE YOU GOT TO DO WITH ME, JESUS SON OF THE HIGHEST GOD? I SWEAR TO YOU BY GOD, DON'T TORTURE ME!" Much like the Capernaum U.S.man, who screamed too (though not terribly), "WHAT'VE YOU GOT TO DO WITH US, JESUS OF NAZARETH? DID YOU COME TO DESTROY US? I KNOW WHO YOU ARE: GOD'S HOLY ONE!" (1:24). U.S.men must have a set speech they learn in training when they meet H.S.men: first, they ask what the H.S.man has to do with me/us (interesting that the man with only one U.S. says "us," while the man who later says that he has "many demons" initially says "me." Perhaps the first man is representative, speaking for the whole demonic force of Satan.); then, they call the H.S.man by name and title (Capernaum U.S.man gives Jesus' hometown, which is also in the Galilee, and says that he's God's holy one, while the Gerasene calls Jesus sonofGod, like the seeing, kneeling, shouting U.S.s, 3:11, like the narrator, 1:1, God, 1:11, and like the executing centurion, 15:39; does the centurion have the spirit now? the disciples most certainly don't); then, they talk about destruction or torment. The Gerasene swears by God, Jesus' father, not to be tortured. If he doesn't want to be tortured, then why did he run to Jesus anyway? Jesus does tell the U.S.man to exit, but he doesn't silence the Gerasene as he did the Capernaum U.S.man and the usual U.S.s. (Ssshhh! It's a secret, a messianic secret.)

Instead, he asks the Gerasene his name. Presumably, Jesus already knows his name, but the reader doesn't, so Jesus has him introduce himself. He says that his name's Legion, for "we're many." Legion, huh? Oh! Now that explains a lot. "Legion" is a military term for a division of Roman soldiers, numbering 4,000–6,000. Yes, yes, things are starting to fall into place. This man, possessed by a legion of demons, is representative of his people, who themselves are possessed by a legion of Roman soldiers. He acts out what they are living. No wonder they want to chain him, just as they are chained. But he breaks free. Indeed, he's the freest man in the region, for he "acts out" rather than submit to imperial conquest. So he's liberated from, yet bound to, their projection. He becomes their scapegoat, and he does it so well that they don't even have to stone him (which they would like to do to the blasphemous Romans), for he stones himself! He internalizes their self-hatred.

Enter here Frantz Fanon, Algerian psychiatrist, who wrote in his classic 1963 work *The Wretched of the Earth* about the "Manicheism" of colonialism, in which the colonized world is sliced in two: between the colonizers, who have everything, and the colonized, who have nothing. This "Manicheism" maintained through violence, both the physical violence of armaments and the psychological and emotional violence of identifying the colonized as absolute evil. The colonized work inside this framework either by accepting it or flipping it so as to identify the colonizers as absolute evil (Fanon, 1963, 33–42). The colonized conceptualize crisis through mystifying it: fate or god or devil or demons are responsible for the plight of the colonized (43). The colonizers are let off the hook, which is a good thing because oftentimes when the colonized take up arms it results in widespread violence and further repression by the colonizers. Yet it's only a partially good thing because it prevents the colonized from coming to consciousness about their political situation.

Fanon notes the prevalence in the colonial situation of demon possession and exorcism, which "allow the accumulated libido, the hampered aggressivity to dissolve as in a volcanic eruption" (Fanon, 1963, 46). He also documents the mental illnesses that arose during French colonialism and the Algerian revolution: psychoses, neuroses, depression, and delirium, often leading to suicidal or homicidal tendencies (203–251). Paul Hollenbach, depending upon Fanon for his interpretation of the Gerasene, writes, "The colonial situation of domination and rebellion nourishes mental illness in extraordinary numbers of the population. . . . Mental illness can be seen as a socially acceptable form of oblique protest against, or escape from, oppressions" (Hollenbach, 1981, 575–576). Richard Horsley, who also uses Fanon in understanding this passage, writes, "Demon possession . . . can be understood as a combination of the effect of Roman imperial violence, a displaced protest against it, and a self-protection against a suicidal counterattack against the Romans. . . . The demoniac became the repository of the community's resentment of the violent effects of Roman domination" (Horsley, 2001, 145).

So much for the serious, sane prosaic excursis; let's return to the playful, possessed poetic commentary. His name is Legion We're Many. Manymanymany. In 21st century shrinkspeak, he has Multiple Personality Disorder. Rome's New World Order has brought him

Disorder! So dis disordered demoniac then begs Jesus not to send the many outa de region a de Gerasenes. They're unclean spirits, and they wanna live in this uncleen place. The Roman legions don't wanna leave the territory they're occupying.

Mark then widens his narrative lens and shows the reader a herda pigs on the mountainside. It's a great herda pigs. Had ya hearda da herda pigs? The spirits see it too. They (not the spirited man but the spirits themselves) negotiate with Jesus concerning their being cast out. They urge him to send them into the pigs (oink oink). Pigs after all are unclean animals according to the Jews, and that would be a good place for uncleen spirits, in uncleen animals. Also they're often used as symbols for Romans in literature of the day (Carter, 2000, 212–213). So Jesus grants the U.S. request. And the unclean spirits leave the man and enter the pigs (oink OINK oink OINK OINK). Then they rush off a cliff into the sea (OINKOINKOINKOINK OINKOINKOINK—KERSPLASH!). And there are about 2,000 of them. (Does that mean that there were 2–3 unclean spirits per pig?) They become the "scapepigs" (Wink 1986, 47); they, rather than the man, go off the cliff (Girard, 1986, 182–183). And dey're drowned in the sea (oink . . . oink . . . glub . . . glub . . . glub), drowned like the Egyptians, who drowned in the Re(e)d Sea (cf. Horsley, 2001, 141). I'm sure that the U.S. didn't plan on that! So the U.S. legion drowns in the sea, pointing toward what the folks of that region long for: the Roman legions drowning in the sea, thus initiating a new Exodus. The violent Roman oppressors will meet a violent end! By God![6]

The piggrazers hightail it outa there and tell what had happened and cityandcountryfolk come to see. They see not only Jesus but also de demonized dude, de former legionaire, seated, shirted and sane. Seated, shirted and sane—oh my! Oh my! they say, cuz they were SCARED, like de ddddisciples n de boat (4:41). In Mark fear and faith don't go together. These folk are fearful, faithless ones. Perhaps they even asked, "Who then is this, that even a legion of demons obey him?" (cf. 4:41) And the witnesses of the pigpossessionanddrowning tell their story, and so they beg Jesus (people and spirits always begging Jesus to do something, 5:10, 12) to get out out out. Outa their region, the region of the Gerasenes. This is an unclean region; how dare you clean it up for us! Besides, we had a nice little sick relationship with this guy and the Roman demonic legions, and you messed it up. So get the hell, er, heaven, outa here!

Jesus is pretty compliant in this passage when conscious beings "beg" him to do something, so he leaves. He gets into the boat . . . but there's one more request. The ex-demonized one wants to be with Jesus, to be like one of the 12, who've been appointed (on the mountain!) to be with him and to be sent out to preach and to cast out demons (3:13–15). Now that would be pretty cool, wouldn't it? He had a legion a demons, Jesus cast them out, and then he could cast out demons from others. But Jesus doesn't agree to beggar's request this time. Perhaps he doesn't want this Gentile among his Jewish followers. They are fearful and faithless; they don't know that he's the sonof God, which this guy does. In many ways he, like other Markan minor characters (e.g., woman with a hemorrhage, 5:25–34; Bartimaeus, 10:46–52), replaces the disciples. Jesus tells him to go back home (Jesus doesn't want to send him out of the region) and tell folks (like the pigfarmers have dun) what the master, the lord, Yahweh God, the highest God, the Jewish God, has done for him, and how he's mercied him, had compassion on him, suffered with him (literal meaning of "com-passion") and healed him of his sufferings. So it is the compassion of God flowing through Jesus that has de-demonized this man (just as it will sight blind Bartimaeus, 10:47–48). No need now to keep it a secret (unlike the ex-skin-diseased man, 1:44).

So the man (and he is the Man now . . . but what's his name?) goes away. Is he disappointed? sad? excited? Dunno. Neverthless, he begins preaching, proclaiming the gospel (John, Jesus, and apostle-like, 1:4, 14; 3:14) in the Ten Cities of de Decapolis, of which Gerasa is one. (Through his efforts and that of others, the gospel is preached to all the Gentiles, 13:10). This man's gospel is about what the masterlord Jesus has done for him. (Is he obedient to his commission? He doesn't go home, or does he? If so, he defines home in a large way, as all of that region. and he doesn't proclaim what God has done compassionately but what *Jesus* has done.) And all de Decapolitans who heard him are amazed (like Pilate is amazed later on, 15:5; will they too crucify Jesus?). They're amazed into silence. What do they say? What do they do?

And what happens to de Man? Mark leaves him in de Decapolis. Does he become an itinerant? Does he go back to the Gerasene region? Does he form, wherever he is, a community of Jesus-followers that are fulla clean spirits, the holy spirit. I like to think that he begins living by Jesus' teachings and he becomes again a man possessed, this time not by a violent legion of demons but by a spirit of peace.

And the Gerasene people? Oh, they probably just get new pigs, maybe even a new demoniac. Things probably just stay the same. . . . Or maybe, just maybe . . .

Looking for Likenesses in Contemporary African American Poetry

After playing (both poetically and possessively) with the images in the story, we now go looking for likenesses to those images in contemporary African American poetry. African Americans have historically been and remain the U.S. (unitedstates/uncleanspirits) scapegoats. They have experienced the violence of slavery, segregation, lynching, and discrimination. In these poems we hear the scapegoat dealing with violence. We hear images of pain, death, and hope.

I begin with a poem on the passage. Veronica Williams's "Haiku(s)" gives voice to the Gerasene: "Pain is all I feel / Ow! I just want to be healed / So, I ran and kneeled" The verb tenses are interesting here: the man has come to Jesus, but he's still feeling pain. Is he speaking to Jesus, hoping that Jesus can alleviate his pain and heal him? And exactly what pain is he talking about? The pain of the cuts that he's inflicted on himself? The pain of isolation and depersonalization from the people? Williams seems to feel some of that pain herself. "Ow!" Is it the pain of being an African American woman in this racist and sexist society? The poem is typewritten in a font that makes it appear like a child's handwriting. The Gerasene has regressed to a "wild child," giving vent to all the region's rage over Roman imperialism. Yet he is also the "identified child," the one deemed possessed when it is the entire region that is possessed by Rome.

Ruth-Miriam Garnett deals with the possession of contemporary violence, in her poem "Concerning Violence," which is dedicated to Frantz Fanon. She says that "this war" gives "reasons for our madness." Dogma and mask take her people "noiselessly to burial." So they kill with bare hands. The poet concludes by saying that she has "two minds," one of which is the warden for the other (Miller, 2002, 251). The Roman imperial oppression, which eventually gave way to war, gave reason for the Gerasene's madness. He was delivered "noiselessly to burial," and he cut himself with his own bare hands. He had many more than two minds—a whole legion of them, and maybe one was the warden and others were guards (the pigs!).

Like the Gerasene, many poems by African Americans come "out of the tombs." Baba Lukata saw three young African American men lying in a cemetery, and he wonders if it is a "Rehearsal" (Miller, 2002, 252). The poet is aware that young African American men are an endangered species, and indeed, one or more of the three may be on the underside of that graveyard now. Also set in a cemetery, Ira B.

Three African American men are on the ground after being shot by armed men on horseback in the background. Sketch by W. Webb Metz, 1874. Library of Congress.

Jones's poem "Alley Games 6 / The Ascension" hauntingly describes the funeral of a young man who was a victim of "an alley war game." His mother's eyes were "Dreary with the pain of prayers hung on a broken cross" (253). Indeed, it is the Markan Jesus that tells his disciples to deny themselves, take up their cross and follow him (8:34). What might that mean in the 'hood?

A "funeral grief song" also begins Mbali Umoja's anthem-like poem "Say Something: A Change Is Gonna Come," which speaks of "zombied hunters armed with self hatred and a gun," who "murder for fun." The poet asks how many more funerals, bodies, and dead boys there will be, for people are cracking under the emotional weight. But the change that's gonna come involves love, that is, self-love, which will lead to healing and freedom (Miller, 2002, 277–79). Yes, the Gerasene cracked under the magnitude of it all. Crrracked. But his healing, his liberation, involved compassion that the master had upon him (Mark 5:19), which doubtlessly enabled him to have compassion upon himself.

Looking for Likenesses in My Own Soul

Where are the likenesses to the story's images in my own soul? I am most taken with the Gerasene U.S.man s's self-inflicted violence: screaming and stone-cutting himself. SCREAMing and CUTting. I scream (inwardly) and I cut myself with stony words: "I hate myself." "I'm no good." "I want to die." It's the depression and anxiety speaking. They are the unclean spirits that invade my soul. Can I, however, harness clean, holy spirits to proclaim the good news: "I love myself"? ("And a voice came out of the heavens, 'You are my beloved child, in which I'm pleased,'" Mark 1:11.) "I am good." "I want to live."

I identify in this passage with the victim. In what ways am I the victimizer: the townspeople who scapegoat the man, and even the Romans, represented by the demonic legions, who maintain their privilege through violence? I am a white, male intellectual. How much more privileged can I be in our society? In what ways do I participate in the violence of this U.S. imperialistic society that scapegoats the poor, ethnic and racial minorities, and homosexuals? And how is this scapegoating violence in society at large reflected in the scapegoating violence that I perpetrate in my own psyche? And in what ways do I resist both social and psychological scapegoating violence?

Soon after I agreed to write this chapter, I participated in a 24-hour advanced Alternatives to Violence Project workshop at the Maryland Correctional Institution at Jessup, Maryland. I had done the beginning workshop the previous year.[7] The day following the workshop I read Mark 5:1–20 and wrote this poem:

they r
they r
da scapegoats
uv r society

da prisnrs
our demons
dey got

our penalties
r sins
dey got

stone m
humiliate dm
d / humnz m

strip awa dere manhood   persnhood
dis iz dere hood   now
dere hood
dere hood

r scapegoats
da prisnrs

kil m

n we kill   n imprisn   n d   humnz   r   selvs

da chaind 1s

2 wich we r chaind

i dunno if i can evr reed da story   da same way   agn

he iz leejun
they r leejun
i m leejun

we all   ALL   r   leejn

Yes, yes. All of us. As long as we tolerate the dehumanization of the criminal (in)justice system, we are in a sick relationship with the state and with these prisoners, and we as a society and individuals are demon-possessed.

So how are we healed? How might we all come to a place in which we're, like the Gerasene, "seated, shirted, and sane"? Diagnosis is much easier than cure. I am tempted to list off a bunch of things, but I see on my office wall here my mission statement, and I think that it will be healing, at least for me, to include it here:

I believe
in humanity,
in the human individual in human community
in humanization, that is,

      nurturing all people
      so that they might become more and more human.

I believe
in my own humanity,
    which I nurture
    through meditation, through writing, through reading,
    through exercise, through creative expression such as poetry and
        art,
    and through living in community with my nuclear family:
    Joy, Anastasia and Miranda Newheart.

I believe, then,
in my family's humanity,
    which is so bound up with mine.
    They humanize me as I humanize them,
    loving them, listening to them, supporting them, and encouraging
        them.
    My first priority is to Joy
    as we join together in raising this family as a witness to human
        community.

I believe, finally,
in the humanity of all persons,
    which I serve professionally at Howard University School of
        Divinity
    and ecclesiastically at Adelphi Friends Meeting,
    joining with these groups to humanize the world,
    promoting peace and justice, building community,
    so that all people might be free.

So that all people might be free . . . of U.S. imperialism, both in this country and abroad. As I write (December 30, 2002), that means challenging the threatened "Iraq Attaq," in which the New World Order attempts to create further disorder in the Middle East through scapegoating Saddam Hussein.[8]

Before I conclude, I would like to comment about a troubling aspect of the story of the Gerasene: Violence is finally resolved through violence, indeed, divine violence. Yes, it is pigs that die, but they are stand-ins for people, Romans specifically. Just as God drowned the Egyptians in the sea, so will God terminate the Romans and their oppressive rule. We can be nonviolent because God is ultimately violent. He (and this image of God is certainly male) does our dirty work for us. He accepts our rage . . . and vents it on our scapegoats. How

healthy is that? Not for the victims and not for us the "victors."
Actually, it sounds pretty passive-aggressive to me: we're passive,
God's aggressive. We never accept our rage; we just pass it on to our
suffering servant, who sends suffering on those making us servants.
Is there an Alternative to divine Violence? If so, that's my Project.
Will you join me in a workshop?

Conclusion

Upon waking one morning a few days ago, I felt anxious about fin-
ishing this chapter (I won't get it done on time; it won't be good enough,
yada yada yada), so I wrote two poems (entitled "breeth" and "fear here:
haiku," respectively), then I drew a picture on the computer (entitled
"gerasene terror"), then I read the following passage in a book I've been
reading on artistic inspiration, entitled *The Demon and the Angel*:

> [Federico Garcia] Lorca rejoiced in the impulsive fluidity of drawing,
> the sheer pleasure of making "senseless black strokes with the
> pen." . . . Drawing was for him a calmer haven, less imperiled than writ-
> ing, more grounded and harmonious. . . . Lorca felt that in making
> graphic art he had his feet planted firmly on the ground, which was not
> the case with writing, where he moved through fiercer and more
> abysmal ground and was sometimes lifted into stranger and more
> unknown dimensions. . . . The demons Lorca tended to keep at bay in
> his exuberant graphic art were released into his poems and plays,
> which are more desperately shadowed by death, and more fully become
> rites of exorcism. (Hirsch, 2002, 23)

Has this poetic playful exegesis been an exorcism for me? Has it been
right? rite? write? Am I seated, shirted and sane. Sane? Such a relative term, isn't it? Seated and shirted here, am I saner than before? I
hope so. At least, more in touch with my (our?) insanity, which is
surely a symptom of sanity.

I am certainly like the Decapolitans at the end of the story: I am
amazed.

Notes

1. I will treat the parallels Matt. 8:28–34, Luke 8:26–39 only in passing.

2. The introduction to Newheart 2001, in which the cited pages are
found, can be read online at the Liturgical Press website, http://www.
catalog.litpress.org.

3. In this way Hillman is similar to the psychoanalytic literary critic Jacques Lacan, who through his various puns and witticisms attempts to express unconscious discourse. For a brief summary of Lacan's work and his relevance to biblical studies, cf. The Bible and Culture Collective 1995, 196–211.

4. Cf. Hillman 1978, 1979, where he develops his approach to image further.

5. I have preserved Mark's mixing present- and past-tense verbs.

6. If Mark was written during the first revolt against Rome (66–70), as usually thought, then this image of legions being drowned in the sea would have been particularly relevant for the first readers of the Gospel.

7. For information about the Alternatives to Violence Project (AVP), see the website of AVP-USA, http://www.avpusa.org.

8. I particularly like the "Pledge of Resistance" of the anti-Iraqi-war organization Not In Our Name. The pledge begins, "We believe that as people living in the United States it is our responsibility to resist the injustices done by our government, in our name." Cf. its website http://www.notinourname.net.

References

Bible and Culture Collective, The. (1995). *The postmodern Bible*. New Haven: Yale University Press.

Carter, W. (2000). *Matthew and the margins: A socio-political and religious reading*. Maryknoll: Maryknoll.

Fanon, F. (1963). *The wretched of the earth* (Constance Farrington, Trans.). New York: Grove.

Girard, R. (1986). *The scapegoat* (Yvonne Freccero, Trans.). Baltimore: Johns Hopkins University Press.

Hillman, J. (1975). *Revisioning psychology*. New York: Harper & Row.

Hillman, J. (1978). Further notes on images. *Spring, 40*, 152–182.

Hillman, J. (1979). Image-sense. *Spring, 41*, 130–143.

Hirsch, E. (2002). *The demon and the angel: Searching for the source of artistic inspiration*. New York: Harcourt.

Hollenbach, P. W. (1981). Jesus, demoniacs, and public authorities: A socio-historical study. *JAAR, 99*, 567–588.

Horsley, R. A. (2001). *Hearing the whole story: The politics of plot in Mark's gospel*. Louisville: Westminster John Knox.

Miller, E. E. (Ed.). (2002). *Beyond the frontier: African American poetry for the 21st century*. Baltimore: Black Classic Press.

Newheart, M. W. (2000). Soul 2 soul: A post-modern exegete in search of (New Testament) soul. *Journal of Religious Thought 55*(2)–*56*(1), 1–17.

Newheart, M. W. (2001). *Word and soul: A psychological, literary, and cultural reading of the fourth gospel*. Collegeville: The Liturgical Press.

Pasteur, A. B., & Toldson, I. L. (1982). *Roots of soul: The psychology of black expressiveness.* Garden City: Doubleday.

Tompkins, J. P. (Ed.). (1980). *Reader-response criticism: From formalism to post-structuralism.* Baltimore: Johns Hopkins University Press.

Wink, W. (1986). *Unmasking the powers: The invisible forces that determine human existence.* Philadelphia: Fortress.

CHAPTER 11

Reflections of a Psychoanalyst on the Dynamic Bond Between Religion and Violence

Cassandra M. Klyman

Personal

I am a psychiatrist and psychoanalyst, a professor, a grandmother of a dozen grandchildren. Religion has always been of significance to me, and I welcome this opportunity to explore how and why I understand it personally and professionally. In the beginning, I must acknowledge that I would not be who I am without the compassion and goodness of religion in its organization and in its spirit. Perhaps, my little Jewish grandson would not be so fit if his eight-year-old sister had not decided to "accept Jesus into my life so I won't hit him so hard." Let me begin, at the beginning I know of, with an event in 1876. There was a smallpox outbreak in the West Indies. My great-grandmother, a silk merchant, was infected while she was a passenger on the United Fruit Steamer between clients in Panama and Jamaica. The captain put her on land and the benevolent nuns took her into their convent, which they had converted into an infirmary. Miraculously, they nursed her back to health, and when she went into labor they delivered her baby daughter, whom they christened Marie. When they were ready to leave, my grandmother wanted to open her steamer trunk and put on her finery to return to her Jewish plantation-owner husband, who would probably see her before he could even read her letters. She wanted to see herself as he would see her. All the reflecting surfaces had been covered in the convent with black buntings to keep the smallpox victims from seeing themselves. But

my great-grandmother pulled down the bunting in her cell, saw her
disfigured skin, and had a sudden cardiac arrest, a vaso-vagal synco-
pal attack, that was fatal. Little Marie was subsequently raised and
educated by the Sisters. In her late teens, as was the Spanish custom,
she and other young, unmarried proper girls would go Sunday after-
noons to the parade grounds and walk counter-clockwise while the
young British Officers walked clockwise looking into their eyes.
Thus, she met my grandfather, who later left her much of the time
while his battalion fought in India. He was later awarded posthumously the Cross of Victoria. My father, the second child of that marriage, was an altar boy who learned deception from his manservant
who would bilk him out of smaller shillings for bigger copper pen-
nies. He was sent to New York to study dentistry and continued to
tell his mother that he was going to school while he took a position
as secretary to Enrico Caruso. He moved into the social world of
Italian Americans. He lived in an eastside brownstone in Manhattan,
where he was often disturbed by phone calls in the lobby for a young
redheaded nursing student named Dolores who lived on the top
floor. He invited her to skating parties that he would arrange in
Central Park, cooked meals for her and his skating group, and wooed
her away from other men. The community phone in the lobby
stopped ringing and they married.

Dolores had been raised in a small mining town in Pennsylvania.
Like my English grandfather's family, my Polish grandparents were
scandalized. Marie was a "girl from the Islands." Frank was a "man
from the Islands" and neither matched in the eyes of the established
family in the 1890s or those of the new immigrants pre–World War II.
Both families rejected the young couples. Neither also had been married in the right church. Marie and her captain were married in a
Catholic Church, not the appropriate Anglican one; and a Justice of
the Peace married Dolores and Frank. The latter was hastily done
because Dolores suspected she was pregnant and Frank had divorced
his first wife and had, therefore, been excommunicated from the
church. Unbeknownst until later was his concurrent marriage with
Annie and the fact that they had a son together named Ronnie.
Frankie divided his time between both families.

I went to a public school but entered catechism in the Roman
Catholic Church for preparation for my First Holy Communion. How
I loved the Church of the Ascension. It was white and gray concrete
on the outside in Gothic architectural style and inside the white mar-
ble altar, the stations of the cross, the stained-glass windows, and the

smell of incense were beautiful and mysterious. The Latin Mass added to the sacred sounds. Going into the confessional was thrilling, and when I came out after saying my five Hail Marys and one Our Father, I felt my ankles were winged and I skipped the mile home. The thrill of the confession began to lead to conflicted feelings. My venial sins were always the same. I lied to my mother, mostly to stop her intrusive questions about whether or not I had a bowel movement that day. Her repeated questions were as bad as the suppositories she had used to "train" me when I was nine months old. I resisted her questions but I knew she was wrong to be so intrusive. So how sincere could my confession be? Furthermore, while I resented her being away working long twelve-hour shifts to support us, I also appreciated how dedicated she was to me. I wanted God to appreciate it too and let her into heaven when she got very, very old. That seemed unlikely because she never went to confession or received Holy Communion.

It was wartime, World War II, when dentists were called to serve in the armed services, and my father, with partial dental training, worked not only as a dental mechanic but also as a sub-rosa dentist. I loved his black "doctor's bag" and would go with him on his "rounds" in the Bronx, "house calls," where he would pull teeth, make dentures, and be adored by his patients. He would come to see us with pockets filled with candy and occasionally a puppy or kitten, the runt of the litter that often did not survive very long. Being with him was always a thrill followed by a sour disappointment.

This arrangement contrasted with what I learned should be in a Catholic home. I worried that my parents were sinners who would not go to heaven, that they would burn in hell. I worried for them, cried for them, begged them to go to confession so they could receive communion, to no avail. They knew they were excommunicated for having married following a divorce. They told me they put their belief in a personal God who punished them enough on earth but who would welcome them in heaven. The admission would be based on their good intentions and good deeds to their patients, who did adore them for their skill and their conscientiousness. Still I was expected to go to Mass regularly, often alone or with my mother suffering her Sunday migraine headache for lack of caffeine-rich hospital java. The other Catholic kids I knew were Irish, and they went to a Catholic school and special early services on Sundays. I envied their camaraderie but little else. Here were kids of families where the dad came

home roaring drunk on payday and beat their mothers, who were usually pregnant. Their toddlers would sit or stand in dirty front-room
windows with their gray, wet diapers, pulling their stringy hair, yel-
low-green mucus draining from their noses all winter. Although this
was Manhattan in the 1940s, it bears resemblance to what later I
would read with shocked recognition in Courts's *Angela's Ashes*. Billy,
John, and Andrew were my playmates, except they often smelled
badly of urine and just plain accumulated dirt. I played barber and cut
their hair regularly. Occasionally, they had baths in my apartment,
but that stopped when they went home once wearing my flower-
print, lace underwear, and their mother finally showed some interest
in their whereabouts. By the time I was 14, I had distanced myself
from my neighborhood element and met the West End girls in my
"rapid advanced" class in middle school. Two sisters suggested that I
go with them to their youth prayer group at the Presbyterian Church.
It was a welcoming and supportive community. They had potluck
dinners, all kinds of outreach to the community, pool tables, dart-
boards, Friday-night dances, Bible study, and field trips. The pastor
and his wife were involved and interested in what was going on.
When the Bible was read, we were asked to think about what was in
the writing. This was certainly meatier than just the gospel portion
delivered at Mass.

One afternoon after school, I walked to the Ascension rectory,
opened the nine-foot-high black grill gate, and lifted the ornate brass
knocker. The housekeeper told me to wait on the steps until she
called Father. He came; I introduced myself. I told him that I was a
member of the parish; that my Presbyterian girlfriends had youth
activities on weekends that kept gangs from forming and brought
families together. "Couldn't something like that get started for
Catholics?" The Puerto Ricans who were immigrating by that time
and were in dire need of something as an alternative to their rumbles
at the edge of Harlem, where I lived, cowered and ran for safety when
they wore their "colors" and let out their distinctive whistle calls. He
looked at me sternly and asked if I went to the Catholic school. "Only
catechism, father. My mother can't afford more than that and tuition
at your school is high." "Well," he commented, "then you don't have a
voice here," and he turned and shut the door. I thought at that time,
I remember, that I would not belong to such a church, which passed
the collection plate for the poor outside the United States but would
not feed its very own.

I began "church shopping." I learned that I could get robbed in the most affluent of church cloakrooms, that those who looked to that afterlife could be corrupt in this one.

I was now in college taking comparative religion, chemistry, biology, and government. My mother, who worked at a Jewish hospital, had always talked about the skill and fame of the surgeons, the loving care of many Jewish men toward their sick wives, the philanthropic foundations that their charities endowed. I liked reading that Jews felt God moved through history. That good deeds on earth rather than faith had priority in one's being judged as good or bad. That God would forgive no sin if there were not reconciliation with the person sinned against. At age 19, I walked into Temple Emanuel, up Fifth Avenue from St. Patrick's, where as a little girl I had dreamt of getting married. There, I completed my conversion to Reform Judaism and got a certificate of graduation.

That summer, waitressing at Grossingers in the Catskills to subsidize my scholarship to college, I met Howard, a rabbinical student at the Union Theological Seminary, who became my mentor and lover for the next three years. As a medical student, I anticipated I could never be a rabbitzin and a doctor along with being a wife and mother. I could juggle, but juggling those several roles would be an extraordinary feat. Anyway, Howard was not ready for the responsibility of marriage and so our relationship ended.

Cal entered my life as a guest in the Adirondacks hotel where I was working the following summer. He came from a Canadian immigrant family who were conservative Jews. My reformed Judaism was "inadequate," but my future father-in-law warned me, "Are you sure you want to be really Jewish? You know they throw stones at Jews." But I took more religious instruction because I was in love with that tall, brilliant lawyer who challenged every part of me. I wanted to marry him and have my future family, his parents, and our children worship together.

When I went under the water at this second conversion at the ritual mikvah, I laughed, thinking this was a greater baptism than I had at the Saints' Fount. I loved the instructions my Rabbi gave my husband-to-be . . . that he was to please me emotionally and sexually, the latter was specifically prescribed for the fulfillment of the Sabbath.

As I entered my psychoanalytic training some years later, I was impressed that Sigmund Freud, a Jew, also benefited from both great religions. His patrimony was Jewish, but he had the experience of going to church with his nursemaid. I think it helped him understand guilt, shame, and the inhibition of desire as well as to understand the universality of human themes. Some of the most significant religious themes have to do with a violent event.

The Bible, Freud, and Other Literary Masterpieces

In Genesis, God looked at His creation and declared it good. He had set man in dominion over all, setting up a hierarchical rather than any equalitarian utopia. Then, rather than create or clone a companion for Adam, He cut into his already perfect creature and removed a rib to create a woman, whom He later curses to suffer in the act of her pro-creation. Adam and Eve begot Cain and Abel, and the violence continued and incest must have occurred for these four to multiply. The narrative of Abraham and Isaac foreshadows the story of the Crucifixion. In both Old and New Testaments, God seems to promote sacrifice (infanticide), only to stop it with elaborate rationalizations—circumcision and crucifixion leading to a redemptive covenant in the Old Testament and an opportunity through faith in the Resurrection for possible admission into the Kingdom of Heaven in the New. In the centuries in-between, what happened to all those good people? How were they rewarded for their faith, for their good deeds? Where they floating around in some kind of Purgatory?

Sigmund Freud relied upon Sophocles's *Oedipus Rex* to help illustrate his understanding of our contemporary unconscious conflicts about parricide, infanticide, and incest—the three violent themes also found in Genesis. In the play and in the myth it is based upon, King Laius and his queen, Jocasta, conspire to send Oedipus away so the curse of the Gods will not be fulfilled, namely, that Laius will be killed by his son. The king instructs the shepherd to pin the child's feet onto a mountainside and let him die. The reader and listener are left uncertain as to the extent of the biblical Sarah's and Jocasta's knowledge about what is to befall their sons. But certainly Sarah was instrumental in sending away Ishmael with Hagar. Jocasta's hanging of herself seems to implicate her acknowledgment of guilt in what was done to her son and husband, as well as her incestuous relationship with Oedipus (swollen feet). Death to the first-born was Moses' curse for the pharaoh and is applauded as a necessary means to freedom and reenacted every Passover seder in the twenty-first century.

Sophocles, a Roman copy of a Greek work from 45
B.C. Library of Congress.

These are dramatic, violent sins exalted in our Western religious and
cultural myths.

Religion is often thought of as an aspect of our superego—the
interjected prescriptions and prohibitions. However, the Ten
Commandments of the Judeo-Christian tradition really reveal that
these evils of murder, adultery, idolatry, deceit, false witness, and covetousness were rampant always and need to be condemned in every
country and every culture and within every man and woman who
struggles with competitive and narcissistic impulses. We were
endowed with those by our Creator who did not set up a "one person,
one vote" universe, but one where might prevails. Might prevails
when there is a struggle over sexual prerogatives, property rights,
and freedom of belief and expression.

In Freud's *Future of an Illusion*, he states that there are two wide-spread human characteristics that are responsible for the fact that the regulation of civilization can be sustained only by a certain degree of coercion, namely, "that men are not spontaneously fond of work and that arguments are [to] no avail against their passion" (Freud, 1968/1927, vol. 21, 8). And that "these instinctual wishes are born afresh with each child . . . incest, cannibalism and a lust for killing" (9). "Cannibalism alone seems to be universally proscribed [though transubstantiation avers that Catholics are truly taking in the body and blood of Christ]. . . . the strength of incestuous wishes can still be detected by the prohibition against them . . . under certain conditions killing is still practiced and indeed commanded by our civilization" (11). He went on, "As external coercions gradually become internalized, man's superego takes over and includes it among [his personal] commandments . . . when [legalized murder] takes place . . . opponents of civilization become it victims" (11). Rhetorically he asked, "Who does not hesitate to injure other peoples by his fraud so long as they remain unpunished for it?" While we may shrink from murder or incest, we do not deny ourselves the satisfaction of avarice, aggressive urges, or sexual lust, despite vows to the contrary. The sexual scandal in the Catholic Church that bridges this millennium has been foreshadowed by the Crusades and the Inquisition and the moral morass that led Luther to legitimize the Reformation. And al Qaeda's latest manifesto that promises greater terrorist attacks unless America converts to Islam is among other perverse expressions that warp religious ideas of a peaceful brotherhood.

In an essay on "Dostoyevsky and Parricide," Freud gives his definition of a moral man: "one who reacts to temptation as soon as he feels it in his heart without yielding to it. The essence of morality is . . . renunciation" (Freud, 1968/1927, vol. 21, 183). He states, "Parricide . . . is the principal primal crime of humanity as well as of the individual" (183). "It can scarcely be owing to chance that three of the masterpieces of literature of all times, Sophocles's *Oedipus Rex*, Shakespeare's *Hamlet* and Dostoyevsky's *The Brothers Karamazov* should all deal with the same subject, parricide. In all three, moreover, the motive of sexual rivalry for a woman is laid bare. The most faithful one is in the Greek legend. In the English play, the presentation is more indirect. The hero [Hamlet] does not commit the crime himself. It is carried out by someone else for whom it is not parricide—[but fratricide—shades of Cain and Abel] . . . forbidden motive of sexual rivalry for a woman does not need therefore to be disguised . . . he [procrastinates and ruminates over whether and when] he ought to avenge the crime . . . it is his sense of guilt that is paralyzing him; but in the matter of keeping with neurotic processes the sense of guilt is displaced onto his projection of his inadequacy for fulfilling his task . . . [Hamlet] despises others no less than himself" (188). "Be every man after his dessert and who should 'scape living."

Freud goes on to quote Theodore Reik (*Imago*, 1929, Vol. 15): "The Russian novel . . . is a step further in the same direction. There also someone else commits the murder. The other person stands to the murdered man in the same filial direction as the hero Dimitri. In the other person's case, the motive of sexual rivalry is openly admitted; he is a brother of the hero. It is a remarkable fact that Dostoyevsky has attributed to him his own illness, the alleged epilepsy . . . It is a matter of indifference who actually committed the crime; psychology is only concerned to know who decided it emotionally and who welcomed it when it was done. A criminal is to [Dostoyevsky] almost a Redeemer who has taken on himself the guilt which must have been borne by others" (Reik, 196). "Renunciation was once the criterion of morality, today it is only one of many. If it were the only one, then the excellent citizen and the Philistine, who, with his dull sensibility submits to the authorities and from whom renunciation is made much easier by his lack of imagination, would be far superior to Dostoyevsky in morality (Freud, 1968, vol. 21, 190, 196).

Return to the Personal

Well, my father died in my late twenties and my husband died in my early fifties. Both deaths were sudden and the grief devastating. However, after Cal's death, I dated men of various backgrounds and faiths, feeling each one was unique and special. I knew I could never duplicate the husband whom I had lost, and I would need a new type of partner.

Hancock was the son of a state senator and a born-again Christian. I sympathized with his feelings as he prayed over me hoping that the Spirit of the Holy Ghost would enter me so that I could be reborn in Christ and then accept his pledge of marriage so we could be together now and at the Day of Judgment. He gave me tapes of his minister's sermon at the Zion Tabernacle Church and asked me to come hear him sing in the choir. I went with him to tent-revival meetings to see relatives of his become ministers. As a psychiatrist, I had a stereotyped impression of those who "spoke in tongues"; they were psychotic, hysterical, and in an altered state of consciousness, with multiple personalities perhaps and vertical-splits in their experience. But Hancock seemed steady, loving, gentle, kind, and his best friend was an American Indian Evangelical who was a big brother to underprivileged Indian youths. However, I discovered both to do unthinking, cruel things. They had gone on a camping trip in the fall, Hancock with his son and Joe with his "little brother." The latter developed a cold and a cough that kept the others up in the shared tent. Joe evicted his "little brother" and made him sleep in the car. When they returned, the boy had developed pneumonia and Joe underwent an investigation for child neglect and was kicked out of the Big Brother Organization. Food from the camping trip had been left over; Hancock put a package of the deli meat in the suitcase and when he got home put it in the refrigerator. His son made a sandwich of it that next day and developed food poisoning. There I found God-fearing men who almost killed two young boys. Ignorance, arrogance, and a kind of blind optimistic faith that everything will work out if you are a believer, that was not for me.

Then Gabe came into my life. He had been born in Jordan, a Christian in a country with a large Muslim population. Religious prejudice had created a glass ceiling beyond which he could not rise regardless of ambition or talent, either in the military or in industry. He left his job with British Petroleum and came to Detroit in the fifties. He and his large family were lapsed Christians who relied on an aunt who was a Mother Superior of Rosary College and Convent to pray for them. She had been distressed over his two previous divorces, but when she met me she told him, "No matter what the Holy Father says, you will be blessed now and deserve blessings." This was an opportunity for me to go back to my Christian Catholic roots, and I asked myself again, "Why did I give up Jesus?" I always prayed to God the Father. I never felt the need for intercessories. I did not feel that it was necessary for a priest or for a saint to help me feel that I was having my heartfelt messages heard. Jesus didn't do any miracles that impressed me. They seemed to either relate to hysterical experiences and/or insubstantiated magic tricks; they hardly touched the world's problems of hunger, disease, poverty, and enmity.

Some of the parables that I have been exposed to strained my credulity and logic. Why were the first last and the last first in the vineyards? Why were Martha's efforts put down and Mary's exalted? Why was the prodigal son lavished upon when the faithful one was treated "business as usual"? If this "unfairness" was what the faith affirmed, I didn't like it. Furthermore, I had always abhorred, from adolescence, the Catholic Church's rules about divorce and abortion. As I mentioned earlier, the inability of the Church to accept my parents' divorces caused me tremendous grief, distress, worry, and fear. Recently I saw a rerun of *Father Knows Best*, a play that ran for an enormously long time on Broadway after World War II. And in that play (and the movie version) the wife and the children, too, were sickened by their discovery of the fact that the "upstanding" idealized father had never been baptized. The arrogant husband-father deserved to be humbled, but it was unlikely that a formal ritual would do it. The demand that the church has for certain rituals to be followed often seems not to create joy or help one live responsibly.

I had some first-hand experience, or perhaps it is better to say third-hand experience, with abortion as I was growing up. Though it was illegal in the state of New York, my father often would be a conduit or broker between young, unwed girls and his first mother-in-law, my adopted grandmother Balardi, who was willing to do clean and safe abortions in her sterile kitchen, rather than the alternative back-alley abortions that left so many young girls infertile or terribly ill. Even if I agree now to stipulate that the fetus has legal rights, we are dealing with two competing individuals: one so dependent, the other with equal rights and so often a woman knowing she is unprepared to be a mother and who responsibly decides to postpone or defer parenthood, one of life's biggest responsibilities. The church's belief that sexual pleasure should be subordinate to physiological reproduction seems hardly a divine way to live one's life. It is dismaying that in a 2002 conference sponsored by the University of Michigan, entitled "Understanding the Gift of Sexuality," a quote by John Paul II is chosen for the cover, "A nuptial means the body is the fundamental element of human existence in the world. If man lives according to it, he fulfills the very meaning of his being and existence." Sex for procreation is instinctually motivated sex, similar to the intercourse of animals, rather than a human way of praising God for this blessing of pleasure, release, and union. Institutional religion, Roman Catholic, Protestant Fundamentalist, and Jewish Orthodox, that is pro-life in the twenty-first century, can be rational only if it also promotes birth control and abortion in cases of rape, incest, and contraceptive failure.

Our technology for control of reproduction is so varied, advanced, but not perfect, that the general failure to provide this rational choice is destructive to women with unwanted, unintended pregnancies.

It is disheartening that the Republican House Majority Whip in the 2002–2003 United States Congress can claim that only Christianity offers a comprehensive worldview that covers all areas of life and thought and offers a way to live in response to the realities that we find in this world. Moreover, he apparently thinks he is called by God to promote this idea.

The church is also supposed to speak for peace, but where was Pope Pius XII in World War II? Rationalizing, he was protecting German Catholics by silence; he allowed Catholics, Jews, and Gypsies to go to concentration camps. What did he do to prevent their being turned away from God-fearing nations, like the United States, which were reluctant to take them in but might have had he prevailed? Where was Pope John during the Bosnia-Herzegovina conflict? Where were the Imams and the Greek Orthodox Patriarchs? Definitely not in the public media. Roman Catholicism can be politically correct in the South American and Central American continent. There, the thought is to be against godless communism, not necessarily to help create opportunities directly for the indigent nations, who must grow drug crops to make a subsistence living. Is Islam as a religion any different? Or is it filled with its own contradictions and inequalities and perfidies to its female worshipers? Though Muhammad's first wife was an accomplished older woman who supported him and made possible the spread of Islam, the interpretation of organized religion in Saudi Arabia, Iran, Iraq, Pakistan, Afghanistan, and Malaysia makes women second-class citizens.

Writers like Hannah Arendt, novelists like Henrich Böll and Gunter Grass, tell us of the banality of evil in the physical decimation and moral decline in post–World War II Germany. Alan Stone, M.D., in a guest editorial, writes about "Psychiatry, Good and Evil, and Bosnia." He discusses traits (individual psychopathology) and states (situational factors), believing that the trait/state differences are highly relevant to wartime atrocities. When we want to condemn the Nazis or Karadzic, they are evil, sick, or both. However, when we want to explain atrocities on our side, we emphasize the traumatic stresses at the time.

There is of course a big difference between leaders and those forced to carry out the order to kill or be killed. Drazen Erdemovic was an ordinary soldier who first revealed the assassinations of Muslims to the international media during the Bosnian-Serb war. But his story tells of his expedient self-interest where he went from one side to the other, first the Bosnia Muslim government, and when the Serbs were winning, he deserted to Croatia and helped (for money, of course) Serbs escape. Then arrested as a criminal in Croatia, he went back to Bosnia; and only because of his pregnant girlfriend, joined the Serbian forces. Stone states terrible crimes, even crimes against humanity, can come not from primitive depths of rage and prejudice but from expediency and self-interest (*Clinical Psychiatric News*, 10/02/02, 45). Erdamovic, it seems, is but another example of this banality of evil that Arendt talked about in her study of Adolph Eichmann.

Conclusions

Freud, in his three great psycho-sociological monographs, *The Future of an Illusion, Totem and Taboo*, and *Civilization and Its Discontents*, concluded that religion was both a consoler and a controller. He felt it encouraged a welcome regression back to the infantile state of oceanic bliss. It plays an important role in enforcing our superego/conscience to prescribe cultural ideals and prohibit their transgressions. He did not go so far as Marx to call religion the opiate of the people. He did dispute that he had what he called the necessary genetic predisposition to even feel that oceanic feeling of spirituality, that which allows some to feel religious even if they have no religion.

Freud believed that it was necessary to have control over an innate, aggressive instinct that came from a variety of sources: (1) self-survival when angry destructive feelings are displaced outward rather than left to turn on the self—a necessary step for distinguishing the self from the other; (2) the violent feelings that result when our needs are not met because our caregivers are never constantly and consistently available; (3) a need for mastery over the environment that treats us as irrelevant; (4) the failure of sublimation; and (5) "the narcissism of minor differences" (Freud, 1968/1930, 114).

Those phenomena in which conflict inevitably arises between communities with adjoining territories are similar in relation to one another in many ways. They, like siblings, get engaged in constant feuds and in ridiculing each other. Freud gives examples like Spain and Portugal, North and South Germany, the English and the Scots, and we can readily add the Irish and English, the various communities of Semites, the Kurds, Iraqis, and Turks, and Iran and Iraq. He concludes in *The Future of an Illusion*, "it is this battle of giants that our nursemaids try to appease with their lullabies about heaven." At the end of the book, Freud states that this "inclination to aggression . . . constitutes the greatest impediment to civilization . . . that is the battle of the giants that the nursemaids above are trying to appease" (Freud, 1968, 122).

If we look to religion, we find that its first and primary commandment is "love thy neighbor as ourselves." But this is so unrealistic, it is an aim so high and it cannot be achieved, for we do not love ourselves in an unambiguous way. If we try to solve the ambivalence, we do it at the expense of making ourselves falsely superior by projecting our negative characteristics to others. This is what leads to racial stigmatization and prejudices such as "the black man is a sexual beast," "the Asian is wily and untrustworthy," "the Russians are drunks," "the hippies are all substance abusers." Unfortunately, if one does not externalize, he will interject and internalize his aggression into his superego, and that results in a conscience that can be overharsh. The consequence of that can give us a sense of guilt, which expresses itself in a need for punishment—"decent people would say sinful and deserving of punishment"—and it makes us act, therefore, in self-destructive ways. A current illustration is the situation of the Maryland sniper, who in 2002 left clues for the police and in a letter complained that the clues were not followed up on more expediently. If they had been, then he would have been caught sooner and more lives would have been saved.

Freud (1968, 136) goes on to say that religion claims to redeem mankind for its sins of guilt. In Christianity, this redemption is achieved by the sacrificial death of a single person, Jesus Christ, who in this manner Himself takes on guilt common to everyone. Earlier on in history, the primal father, he hypothesized, did not attain divinity until long after he met death by violence after a lifetime of being mocked and maltreated brothers and sons.

"Love thy neighbor" is the strongest defense against human aggression, but it is an excellent example of the nonpsychological underpinnings of a cultural superego that religion creates. It is impossible to fulfill; the inflation of love lowers its value (Freud, 1968, 143). All it can offer is a smugness of being able to think oneself better than others and a promised ticket to heaven; but as long as virtue is not rewarded upon earth, ethics will preach in vain.

Why is man unable to love his neighbor? In *The Future of an Illusion* Freud disputes the communist claim that the institution of private property has corrupted man's essentially good nature. He calls it an illusion based on another illusion that man was originally good. It is interesting that for a Jew, Freud was a believer in man's inevitable "badness," if not original sin. What was at issue before private property to fight over? Before material property, he stated there was envy and jealousy over sexual prerogatives. And I would add knowledge, carnal and otherwise, which takes us right back to the Garden of Eden and the expulsion from it.

Although Freud was not able to experience the oceanic bliss of spirituality, it seems he was able to appreciate the powerful, pleasurable passion of sex; and he returns again and again to talk about the fact that the Christian doctrine puts low esteem on earthly love and devalues and dilutes love when it commands "Love Thy Neighbor As Thyself." It takes away that bliss of loving unambivalently and feeling you are in a merged relationship. It offers affection, not passion, which is the true motivator. Freud recognizes communal life is disturbed by the instinct of aggression and self-destructiveness. His prescient and pessimistic words are: " . . . men have gained control over the forces of nature to such an extent that with their help they would have no difficulty in exterminating one another to the last man. They know this and this becomes part of their current unrest, their unhappiness and mood of anxiety" (Freud, 1968/1927, 145).

And religion, our constant cultural illusion, seems not to have the effective answers. While Freud believes that religion offers us the consolation from the disillusionment of our inevitably failing parents and gives us some measure of control over our instinctual aggression, he sees the negative side of institutionalized religion when he observes that "it is always possible . . . to bond together a considerable number of people in love so long as there are other people left over to receive the manifestations of their aggressiveness . . . in this respect the Jewish people, scattered everywhere, have rendered the most useful service to the civilization of those countries that have been their hosts" (Freud, 1968/1930, 114). Freud believes that inevitably there will be a neighboring entity that will receive all the hatred. A nation founded in love will inevitably have enemies of their own making.

Conclusion

In my conclusion, I would remind us that history repeats itself, yet the futility of war remains. Our religions represent the several illusions that Freud and psychoanalysts consider. Several of them are that "men are inherently good," that "all men are created equal," that "property corrupts," and that it is a realistic and attainable commandment to love thy neighbor as oneself. Religion is an overarching, though illusory, attempt, to console, because what science cannot prove or give us, we cannot expect religion to provide. Religion remains an illusion, but is a necessary one, and the best that man has yet to invent to indoctrinate children, says Freud. He does not hold out the hope that children so exposed will easily attain the desired primacy of intelligence over the push of instincts. The dynamic bond between violence and religion exists because violence is always with us and religion is its most trusted palliative measure. Mankind experiences them as yoked together and so he plods along behind.

References

Freud, S. (1913). Totem and taboo. In J. Strachey (Ed. and Trans.), *The standard edition of the complete psychological works of Sigmund Freud* (Vol. 13, 1–162).Toronto: Hogarth Press, 1968.

Freud, S. (1927). The future of an illusion. In J. Strachey (Ed. and Trans.), *The standard edition of the complete psychological works of Sigmund Freud* (Vol. 21, 3–58).Toronto: Hogarth Press, 1968.

Freud, S. (1930). Civilization and its discontents. In J. Strachey (Ed. and Trans.), *The standard edition of the complete psychological works of Sigmund Freud* (Vol. 21, 59–148).Toronto: Hogarth Press, 1968.

John Paul II. (2002, December 7). Quoted in *Understanding the gift of sexuality*. Symposium presented by the Lansing Guild of the Catholic Medical Association in joint sponsorship with the Michigan State Medical Society.

Stone, A. A. (2002, October). Psychiatry, good and evil in Bosnia. *Clinical Psychiatry News*, 45.

CHAPTER 12

DESTRUCTIVE AND CONSTRUCTIVE RELIGION IN RELATION TO SHAME AND TERROR

Jack T. Hanford

Throughout our history, religion has been interpreted to justify the most moral and the most immoral actions. Its justification of the immoral in the form of terror was taken to incredible extremes by the cruel deed of September 11, 2001. This action destroyed about 3,000 persons, was the most destructive violent act of terror on American soil in our history, and was motivated by a religion. Was the hit also triggered by shame and humiliation? This chapter will offer distinctions between destructive and constructive religion in relation to shame and terror. It begins with the destructive and continues with the constructive.

Destructive Religion Produces and Legitimates Prejudicial Shame, Toxic Shame, and Shamelessness; Terror and Violence; and Anti-Intellectualism

James W. Fowler (1996) defines three dysfunctional expressions of shame. The first is often shame as blame that is racial, social class, and gender prejudice usually against minority groups. The second is toxic shame such as in the debilitated addict and co-dependent personality. The third, shamelessness, is the most unhealthy. This person or group feels no conscience and smiles while killing or doling out cruelty against innocent victims. This unhealthy shame is a major human condition from a theological perspective. In fact James Fowler

(1996, 135) uses dysfunctional shame to expound the biblical story, specifically Genesis 3, interpreting the fall of humans into sin as the original shame. Fowler and especially Stephen Pattison (2000) expose the destructive views of religion, which produce such dysfunctional shame. Did shame or shamelessness incite the terror attack of 9/11?

Americans are frequently asked, "Where were you on 9/11?" I was in my study reflecting on shame: personal and social, healthy and unhealthy. Another question became obvious. Could scholars, specifically, shame theorists, shed light on the terror and violence of that September morning? Four months later I asked such a scholar, Thomas Scheff, a sociologist emeritus of the University of California at Santa Barbara, "Dr. Scheff, do you think your basic theory of shame-anger and rage-producing violence applies to and illumines the 9/11 tragedy by bin Laden? How does religion fit in? Would you also apply the same theory to some expressions of Christianity?"

Professor Scheff had already written an answer to a part of my question in his "Sept. 11: Male Emotions and Violence" (Scheff, 2002). He begins by acknowledging shame, humiliation, fear, anger, rage, aggression, and potential violence in himself and in males generally. Men are socialized to deny shame and humiliation, and these powerful emotions erupt in rage, and often in a cycle of these feelings projected in violence. Scheff (1994) documents this cycle personally and in Hitler, and historically in Hitler's rise to power in Germany. He describes this cycle in Osama bin Laden and in the history of the Middle East and elsewhere. He challenges us and especially our national political leaders to become aware of the vicious cycle. But what about the role and function of religion?, I ask Scheff. He shows that humiliation-shame-rage-revenge motivate the violence of 9/11 and that Mark Juergensmeyer supports this claim. Juergensmeyer (2003) shows that religion incites violence in America and the world. We need to understand the relation between shame, religion, and terror.

Osama bin Laden's destructive religion approves killing Americans and Shiites because he believes that God is on his side. But mainstream Muslims believe bin Laden's violence is a heresy against Islam. Also, al Qaeda is trying to move beyond the Sunni versus Shiite division and animosity. They plan to unite all Muslims against the West, especially the United States. Helen Rose Ebaugh blames the Fundamentalism of bin Laden and of Muslims for inciting violence. Also, Karen Armstrong (2002) notes that they do not see God in the modern secular enlightenment in America. Rather, the Fundamentalists are rooted in fear, in terror, and therefore in defensiveness. Since their back is against the wall, they respond in violence and terror.

This Fundamentalism is intensely political. In fact, Muslim faith seems inevitably political since they consider their faith superior to the authority of the state, meaning that they tend toward a theocracy much more than a democracy. This foundation might mean that Fundamentalism will lead toward violence, that is, a battle for their God. On the other hand, Islamic thought might suggest democracy by its emphasis on equality, opposition to oppression, and a brotherhood of the poor.

What is the nature of religious violence? Is it caused by fanatical Muslims who feel a deep resentment regarding American success? Does this anger create violence? Tom Scheff would say yes because he believes the shame-rage dynamic triggers violence (Scheff & Retzinger, 1991). Does monotheism, that is, exclusive religion, produce fanatics whose literature and scripture incite violence, such as Mark Juergensmeyer's (2003) five religious groups? Their destructive religion incites terror, and their groups are marginal in relation to their mainstream traditions.

One of the most outrageous actions by the Taliban was when they destroyed the images of the Buddha in stone. The way they responded to widespread criticism was to charge that if critics really cared about life then they would oppose sanctions that starve children. The Taliban changed the issue and focused on an important issue; but, this certainly did not justify their destructive act, produced by their destructive view of their religion.

Thus, religion is destructive when inciting terror and violence, an unjust, abusive, damaging action of force. Violence might also be an emotional force, power. For example, an enraged, shameless person cannot control his violence. While destructive religion empowers violence and the punch of terrorism, the power of terror and violence in turn reciprocates by giving recognition, prestige, and importance to small groups of dissident terrorists. In this sense, violence and terror work; they achieve their political goal. Terrorism threatens our existence. It includes anxiety and fear and is similar to war, especially since we are confronted by state-sponsored terror such as by Iraq, Iran, and Syria. Israel projects terror but is the victim of almost constant terror and has been condemned for terrorism. The 9/11 attack on America traumatized much of the U.S. population, lingers on in its

Afghanistan's hardline Taliban rulers ordered the destruction of all statues as insulting Islam, including this, the world's tallest standing Buddha statue, which was already damaged in fighting. The Taliban said they began to destroy the statues Thursday, March 1, 2001. AP/Wide World Photos.

effects, and cannot be easily avoided. Many of those trying to avoid it nevertheless still experience stress.

The profiles of the 9/11 terrorists surprised and confounded Americans. Many of the hijackers attended our universities, projected sophisticated views of Islam, and nurtured powerful metaphorical visions of heaven and paradise. They were devoted to Osama bin Laden, who is well educated, willing to sacrifice his wealth and privileged position because of his religion and commitment to God. While this preparation of terrorists was going on for years on American campuses, most of our churches were unfortunately reducing their campus ministries. Terror from the outside was reinforced by feelings of terror from inside America. One of many examples, John Salvi III,

Uniformed and plain-clothes Kenyan police officers and investigators at the Paradise Hotel in Kikambala, Kenya, after a terrorist attack Thursday, November 28, 2002. In a twin attack, suicide bombers in Kenya killed 12 people at an Israeli-owned beach hotel and two missiles narrowly missed an airliner carrying home Israeli holidaymakers. AP/Wide World Photos.

a student considering the priesthood, a hairdresser, attacked three abortion clinics and murdered two people because of his opposition to abortion. When caught, he pled innocence. He said that if convicted, he wanted the death penalty. Otherwise, he planned to become a priest.

Terror is our crucial concern. My response to terror is that September 11, 2001, presents the strongest argument for the scientific, academic study of religion because of the violence linked with an interpretation of religion. What are the social-psychological dynamics of religion that might motivate such a tragedy? In the search for an answer, we will explore the power, yet neglect, of frustrating and unhealthy shame that motivates anger-rage, producing violence, wrapped up in interpretations of Christianity, Judaism, and Islamic religion, especially their radical and Fundamentalist renditions. For example, Thomas Scheff and S. M. Retzinger (1991) have written *Emotions and Violence: Shame and Rage in Destructive Conflicts.* Stephen

Pattison's (2000) *Shame* illuminates the entanglement of shame in Christianity and points to the work by the late Norbert Elias (2000/1939) to show the power of shame in "the civilizing process." Benjamin Barber's (1996) *Jihad vs. McWorld* asserts what must be done especially in higher education; and Kenneth Vaux (1992) suggests what must be done by the three Abrahamic faiths.

There is destructive religion in America. In America anti-intellectualism is from Fundamentalism and from our history in revivalism and popular religion, according to Mark A. Noll (1994) and Richard Hofstadter (1963). Moreover, the *Christian Century* reported recently that many church clergy search committees do not rank life of the mind as among the top credentials for being qualified. Another serious concern is expressed by Stanley Hauerwas (1994, 156), who described the contrast between the selection and attitude of students to the medical school and the divinity school at Duke University.

A problem from the side of the university: a significant book by George Marsden (1997) documents the bias of many academics against faith leading to learning. The university is a "virtual establishment of nonbelief," according to Marsden. Science is closer than religion to being an established religion, especially if we only consider funding. At the same time, Christian teaching has been privatized. Our culture is therefore hollow, and yet many university search committees are suspicious of degrees in theology and religion.

A problem from the mind: pluralism reinforces relativism and uncertainty, and America is the most pluralistic country. Ethics, along with religion, was removed from education in our history. Consequently, history shows religion being used to justify immorality and morality. Constructive religion must replace destructive Fundamentalism. Mark Noll (1994) is representative of the encouraging movement of Evangelicals who are not only exposing the illusions of Fundamentalism but also creating significant academic institutions, colleges, and seminaries to provide, nurture, and inspire constructive religion.

This first section suggests that shame-anger-rage produce violence and terror. Shame unrecognized tends to blame others including their view of religion and education. The religion of the Taliban was perfectionist to the extreme, "puritanical" superego sense, which correlates with perfectionist shame. Thus dysfunctional shame reinforced destructive religion, which reinforced judgmental shame. Education by the Taliban was used to impose their interpretation of their religion and they took over the state. Destructive shame, religion in the form of Fundamentalism, fanaticism, and anti-intellectualism became a vicious cycle in Afghanistan and perhaps in America.

Constructive Religion Provides Critical Analysis of Terror and Violence, Stimulates an Academic Study of Religion, and Develops Healthy Shame

Terror

Constructive religion must provide cultural norms that can be shown to terrorists to be superior; terrorists who have genuine humane grievances must be given voice and tactics beyond blind violence. Bin Laden and al Qaeda should be challenged in their views of the Qur'an, a major source of norms. They claim authority over all Muslims because they believe they are fulfilling the will of Allah. Therefore, they insist that jihad is the foreign policy for all Muslims. They claim universal authority that transcends nation-states. The West must unite and cooperate with Muslim scholars to win the theological battle. Military might alone will not succeed because al Qaeda is multidimensional, including movements of religious revival, social and political reform, and economic enhancement over widespread poverty. Al Qaeda is not only a recruitment agency, it is an educational and employment agency. Terrorist groups have historically survived a decade or two, but al Qaeda, especially with bin Laden and his leadership, is not a typical terrorist operation. He is presently the Muslim archetype.

Education

The need for education in relation to terror is clear in the following news poll. Andrea Stone (2002) reported that Muslims view the West through the perspective of anti-Americanism. Sixty-one percent of Muslims polled in nine countries—Indonesia, Iran, Jordan, Kuwait, Lebanon, Morocco, Pakistan, Saudi Arabia, and Turkey—denied that Arabs were involved in the 9/11 attacks; and just 9 percent said they thought U.S. military action in Afghanistan was morally justified. In Kuwait, a country liberated by the U.S. from Iraqi aggression in 1991, 36 percent said that the 9/11 attacks were justifiable. Just 7 percent said Western nations are fair in their perceptions of Muslim countries.

Americans must be educated about the recruitment of Americans within America to al Qaeda and the extensive presence of al Qaeda in America. Steven Emerson (2002) provides an informative though controversial book diagramming recent and current militant Muslim groups all around the outer edges of the United States, four cells of al Qaeda, many support groups for Hamas, 331 al Qaeda terrorists in America, and additional warning signs of danger and violence directed toward increasing terror by jihad in America.

CNN reported on November 12, 2002, that Saudi Arabia is reforming its educational content. They have acknowledged Zionist-related content contributing toward learning hatred and rejection of some people. They vowed to replace this content with the true message of Islam to accept people. They also stated their intent to teach English. These efforts should be reinforced by Christians and Jews, to show a common tradition from Abraham. Harold Koenig (1994, 105, in Chapter 7) claims that common faith of monotheism is "relevant" to Jews, Christians, and Muslims.

In a lecture to the American Academy of Religion (December 1983), Norman Brown announced that world unification is the only alternative to world destruction. I believe that world understanding is necessary to prevent world destruction, especially the importance of understanding religions of the world. Professors must become very competent communicating insights from the religious traditions into the college learning experience. Even the students from parochial high schools will deny much knowledge of religion. An academic study of religion sounds strange and even out of place. Some students will drop a course that even hints toward a critical study of religious insights. One particular student who was planning to transfer to a Baptist college was advised to drop a religion and ethics course because it referred to science. So, teaching in this area is a struggle and yet a necessary challenge.

Since religion is the substance of Islamic culture, gaining an understanding of the Islamic themes would enrich, broaden, and give significance to teaching religions of the world and would give greater concentration on the Muslim religion and its relation to Judaism and Christianity. The knowledge is crucial for comprehending the Middle East and world politics since at present we are especially concerned to know the relations between American and Muslim countries. We need to study their sophisticated view of a theocracy, prophecy, mysticism, eschatology, justice, permanent revolution, equality, messiah, terror, resurrections, and revelation. They also advocate victory in spite of the tragedy of death, women wearing veils, and men and women abstaining from alcohol. America is viewed as Satan, and there is Islamic hatred of the United States and the materialism of capitalism. Many Muslims view war as a glorious commitment sanctified by God, giving an opportunity for martyrdom and direct access to paradise, that is, salvation for the dead and redemption for the living. The above themes represent a fusion of religion, philosophy, politics, and ethics. Yet this powerful tradition is relatively unknown in America. We live in the peril of danger without such knowledge. On the positive side, we live without the potential for its enrichment.

Much authority and trust were lost because of the chaos of the 1960s, when religious traditions that supported professions were demeaned and cast aside. The prestige of the ministry also declined with the demise of the mainline denominations and the near-irrelevance of campus ministry. It was reported in the *Christian Century* (January 17, 1996, 39) that the rigor of academic performance was called into question because typically 80 percent of admissions of applicants had indicated a lack of quality selection, even at Yale Divinity. This criticism was asserted by the other graduate professors at Yale. If Yale Divinity is deficient, what does this mean for the other seminaries? The seminaries at major universities are supposed to be among the best. Such criticism is extremely damaging because America has given its universities the task of producing competent professionals who create and interpret constructive religion.

An academic (that is, clear and precise) study of religion is necessary for education. To begin, let us note the imperative for the development of the *mind* from the Old Testament to the New. In Deuteronomy 6:4–5 (223, RSV, Oxford Annotated Bible): "You shall love the Lord your God with all your heart, and with all your soul, and with all your might." This is a part of the meaning of the First Commandment in 6:1–25. Next, we note a significant addition, even a fulfillment in Jesus the Christ in Matthew 22:37. "You shall love the Lord your God with all your heart, and with all your soul, and with all your mind" (New American Standard Bible). We need to learn this wisdom and connect it with the functions of church and university, heart and mind, church and seminary, seminary and university. We also must show the difference that Christian convictions can make. Our one option is to make the university credible to the gospel of faith, hope, and love by dialogue, witness, *koinonia*, and the transformation that begins with me. In Romans 12:2: "Do not be conformed to this world but be transformed by the renewal of your mind, that you may prove what is the will of God." This is a transformation of the mind toward the *koinonia* calling us and the university to vocation, that is, the church in mission because the world is our parish.

This is an academic, rational, moral faith that is needed: "in the world but not of the world."

Many theologians claim that religion, if believed in strongly enough, can solve almost all human struggles. Religion is effective as a source of meaning, including insight into the meaning of illness, evil, suffering, shame, terror, and death. Religion, or more specifically, faith offers hope in spite of despair, and courage in the face of death, cancer, and other illnesses and tragedies. Education can evolve into experience. Experience can be a personal encounter with Jesus Christ, and with God. There can be the witness of God's Spirit within our spirit, which is true, constructive religion.

Shame

James W. Fowler (1996) defines the spectrum of universal shame that includes the three unhealthy, dysfunctional views of shame previously mentioned. Healthy and perfectionist shame round out his five distinctive definitions of shame. Perfectionist shame might be healthy or unhealthy depending on the psychological dynamics within and outside the person. We might use the terms of Sigmund Freud to explain this. Perfectionist shame is overly loaded with the superego structure of a personality that is rigidly inhibited, guilt ridden, and ignorant of the important distinctions between guilt and shame. We need to understand and master shame to gain control of anger, humiliation, aggression, violence, and decisions for war or peace.

Constructive religion needs to produce healthy shame not only to counter terror and violence but to enhance growth and maturity in all of life as well. There is a spiritual and social need that has not been given as much attention as the intensity of the need demands. That need is identified with the emotion of shame, which is universal. I will first identify shame and then offer appropriate ways to meet the need.

As long as humans have been alive, there have been suffering and pain, and currently, much of this misery has been caused by unidentified and untreated shame in its many unhealthy and toxic forms of expression. So much attention has been focused on guilt that shame has been overshadowed or assumed to be simply included in guilt. But guilt has been defined in terms of what we do, while shame emotion might be compared to the situation with depression some decades ago, when psychiatrists did not have effective medications for depression. Consequently, depression was known to be painful but rarely diagnosed. Why diagnose what cannot be treated effectively?

There is toxic and healthy shame. Healthy shame can easily be conflated with the feeling of guilt that triggers our conscience and usually keeps us out of trouble. By contrast, shame in the malady of shamelessness means no conscience is functioning, such as in the tragic experience of a sociopath and in politics. James Fowler has constructed a useful set of definitions ranging from this shamelessness to perfectionism in superego religion and personality, and finally to healthy shame in shyness (Fowler, 1996, 13, 113).

The crucial need in shame pertains to its impact on the self when shame basically leaves the person feeling unworthy, not good enough, even in rage against the self and others. A frequent defense is to create a false self to cope with the agony of an inadequate self. Suppose one is born "illegitimate"; how might one cope with constructing a robust sense of worth and dignity? One might feel shame and thereby envy the other person but not appreciate oneself. Constructive religion transforms this self-rejection into self-acceptance.

Shame is not simply feeling bad because of something we did wrong; more basically, shame is feeling bad because of who we are, especially when we are vulnerable, exposed, and wounded. Erik Erikson identified shame formation from one and a half to three years of age in his second of eight stages of personality development. Perhaps the twos are terrible because of the awful struggle between autonomy versus shame and doubt. If the most serious dysfunctions are rooted in the earliest years in our development, then we see why shame is very serious indeed and important in our journey toward growth and faith. Erikson insists that guilt originates in the third stage or transition and therefore not quite as crucial but closely associated with shame in the rudiments of our existence. We have researched guilt more than shame in spite of Erikson's discovery.

Bioethics has almost no research on shame, as shown by the single reference to "shame" in the Index for the five-volume *Encyclopedia of Bioethics* (1995). There is more shame than this in bioethics because shame pervades most, if not all, of our lives and existence; in fact, it is universal. Patients are extremely vulnerable to shame. They are ordered to remove their covering, their clothes. Their bodies and selves are exposed as they wait, frequently for a very long time. Old people are shamed for being old. Since seniors are often patients, they receive the shaming more intensely and more often than other patients.

Shamelessness can be illustrated by many of America's nursing home environments in which the pharmaceutical industries charge intolerably high prices of medications for seniors. At the same time, pharmaceutical and managed-care executives take huge salaries. Additional needy patients have been identified by John Bradshaw (1988a, 1988b) and others who have defined the dependent, addictive nature of toxic shame. Shame can also emerge from prejudice against minorities, which incites violence and war. Perfectionist, superego shame is widely available, contaminating those within the Christian church and beyond, according to Stephen Pattison (2000) in his personal, excellent book titled *Shame*. Our hope is to progress beyond these needs to healthy shame, in which we affirm what is good, righteous, and worthy of honor and respect in human personality and build communities of justice and peace.

People can recognize and validate feelings of shame in therapy and in life. Shame feelings range from not being felt at all, such as unconscious ones, to being felt all the time as dominant consciousness. Communication of these feelings of shame is helpful, specifically feelings of shame associated with sexuality such as in books by Gershen Kaufman (1991, 1992, 1996). Patients in therapy have to work on the mundane shame associated with coming to and leaving therapy sessions, wondering, What will people think?

Constructive religion is in many great Wesley hymns that give hope in spite of tragic shame and death. We can be nurtured and strengthened by these words. But is our faith bound to shame? Or, is our faith liberated to struggle for the needs of the poor, the oppressed, the victims of terror and violence?

Since shame is a complex emotion, what are the healthy forms of shame (Fowler, 1996, 92, 113)? Healthy shame enables us to become as good as we are through constructive religion in:

- education
- ministry from hospital chaplains
- teaching others
- parenting our families and our children, brothers and sisters
- being a wage earner
- being true to self from the scrutiny of our mythology, our story, our past, and present
- our attitude toward our work. Do we hide ideas in confused writing? Do we deny the self felt in shame?
- being a loving, compassionate agent for world peace through world law and justice

Pastors and practitioners need to educate about shame because it is unacknowledged in bioethics and elsewhere. Since stigma accompanies diseases, patients might associate shame with their perception of their diagnosis and conclude that they are defective or inadequate, all triggers for the pain and suffering of shame now added to the impact of their illness. But on the other hand, if our lifestyle did actually contribute to our illness, we might appropriately feel healthy shame and guilt. A discerning professional might help us make a discrete distinction between healthy and unhealthy shame.

Feelings of shame can lead to anger at the bedside. So, the patient might blame the physician for not being more attentive, or for talking about obesity at a time like this in the hospital. Unless the physician understands these dynamics, he or she might also feel shame because of being criticized. Nevertheless, the patient needs communication and support to counter irrational shame, such as being blamed for "heart failure" in cardiology, or shame in feeling "inadequate" because of diagnosis of infertility. The language varies, but the feelings of shame pervade through all the specialties and beyond. This unnecessary suffering from dysfunctional shame can be added to the work of various support groups that health-care personnel initiate, organize, and meet.

Since the patient is often, more or less, naked, shame associated with the body is often prevalent. While the practitioner knows that self and body are united, she might separate them in concern for the identity and nurturance of the self. Thus, the body will be appropriately covered and privacy maintained for dignity and honor (J. Hanford Web site, http://www.BioethicsAndFaith.com).

Helen Lewis (1971) showed that psychotherapy was not successful unless it dealt with shame, which is similar to the point that the confessional will not be effective unless it deals with shame in depth. This illustrates the parallel development through history of the priestly confessional and psychiatric psychotherapy. Here is a hypothesis: The church through the centuries had and still has a "treatment" for guilt but none for shame. The confessional could relieve guilt. But shame might not be relieved unless it would be the kind of shame integral to guilt or vice versa. So, the feelings of shame might in fact be increased by the confessional, just as therapy is a shame-inducing experience, and guilt with healthy shame is needed to maintain boundaries. In addition, the needs of priests embedded in shame would not be dealt with, and by removing guilt only, these priests might be tempted to act out their shame-based needs for affection. This predicament might have contributed to the scandals of recent decades.

Christian faith might cope with shame or be interpreted in ways to cause shame. This means that the practitioner might refer to the hospital chaplain for an appropriate way to deal with shame. The chaplain might come to the bedside with the health care person, meet the patient individually or in groups, or meet separately with the professionals at the hospital or church, synagogue, or mosque, or other religious community. Presently, we might learn that sexual abuse is a cause of shame and even humiliation, an intense spiritual and social need. Shame might be deep within the psyche, the soul. The Bible, prayer, and intelligent theology might provide constructive ways to minister, care, and heal. Shame might have to be treated effectively before the real conscience can function and authentic ethics begin. A psychiatrist might also be needed as an effective counter to toxic shame, which psychiatry appears to have an emerging interest in, along with additional mental health workers. We might need to get acquainted with these care professionals to discover which ones have interest, experience, and special knowledge to treat toxic shame and humiliation. Informed theologians such as James Fowler (1996), Stephen Pattison (*Shame*, 2000), Dietrich Bonhoeffer (*Ethics*, 1955), and John Bradshaw can be helpful with toxic shame and the church.

The way to meet the spiritual and social needs stemming from shame include: the practitioner's awareness of his or her own shame and understanding that if shame is projected and attributed to the patient, then the doctor will not be valuing and affirming the worth of the patient. The physician must be able to diagnose shame. For example, he or she can learn the facial signs of shame, such as the eyes turned down.

Unhealthy shame has not been given as much attention as its problems and suffering demand. The crucial need in shame pertains to its impact on the self when shame basically compels the patient to feel unworthy, not good enough. Unhealthy shame destroys trust in self and in the physician. Therapy, good treatment, and constructive religion can turn unhealthy shame into healthy shame and trust, such as trust in self, in relation to the caregiver, and even in relation to God. A person with this healthy sense of shame can control violence because this person understands the vicious cycle of shame, anger, rage, aggression, violence, and terror. This cycle has destroyed life and hope in the Middle East for millennia and seems to be spreading worldwide. But, destructive religion, shamelessness, and terror can be replaced by constructive religion, healthy shame, and peace with justice.

References

Armstrong, K. (2002). *Islam: A short history.* New York: Random House.

Barber, B. (1996). *Jihad vs. McWorld.* New York: Ballantine Books.

Bonhoeffer, D. (1955). *Ethics.* New York: Macmillan.

Bradshaw, J. (1988a). *Healing the shame that binds you.* Deerfield Beach: Health Communications.

Bradshaw, J. (1988b). *Bradshaw on the family.* Deerfield Beach: Health Communications.

Elias, N. (1939, 2000). *The civilizing process.* Malden: Blackwell.

Emerson, S. (2002). *American jihad.* New York: The Free Press.

Fowler, J. W. (1996). *Faithful change.* Nashville: Abingdon.

Gunaratna, R. (2002). *Inside al Qaeda.* New York: Columbia University Press.

Hauerwas, S. (1994). *Dispatches from the front.* Durham: Duke University Press.

Hofstadter, R. (1963). *Anti-intellectualism in American life.* New York: Knopf.

Juergensmeyer, M. (2003). *Terror in the mind of God* (3rd ed.). Berkeley: University of California Press.

Kaufman, G. (1991). *Dynamics of power.* Rochester: Schenkman Books.

Kaufman, G. (1992). *Shame.* Rochester: Schenkman Books.

Kaufman, G. (1996). *The psychology of shame.* New York: Springer.

Koenig, H. (1994). *Aging and God.* New York: Haworth.

Lewis, H. (1971). *Shame and guilt in neurosis.* New York: International Universities Press.

Mackey, S. (2002). *The reckoning.* New York: W. W. Norton.

Marsden, G. (1997). *The outrageous idea of Christian scholarship.* New York: Oxford.

Noll, M. A. (1994). *The scandal of the evangelical mind.* Grand Rapids: Eerdmans.

Pattison, S. (2000). *Shame.* New York: Cambridge University Press.

Scheff, T. (1994). *Bloody revenge.* Boulder: Westview.

Scheff, T. (2002, February 27). Sept. 11: Male emotions and violence. *Journal of Mundane Behavior.*

Scheff, T., & Retzinger, S. M. (1991). *Emotions and violence.* Lexington: Lexington Books.

Stone, A. (2002). Islamic world says Arabs not involved in 9/11. Poll in *USA Today*, 1.

Vaux, K. (1992). *Ethics and the Gulf war.* Boulder: Westview.

CHAPTER 13

THE ROLE OF SELF-JUSTIFICATION IN VIOLENCE

LeRoy H. Aden

Introduction

"Two men went up to the temple to pray, one a Pharisee and the other a tax collector" (Luke 18:10). The tax collector, a secular and dishonest grafter, stands a great distance from the altar, smites his breast, and with downcast eyes confesses, "I am a sinner. God, be merciful to me." The Pharisee, a very religious man, also stands apart from the crowd. His belief in himself as a righteous person fills him with contempt for those who do not match his goodness. "God, I thank you that I am not like other people." I am not a thief, a rogue, an adulterer, or "even like this tax collector." To sharpen the contrast, the Pharisee highlights his deeds of supererogation: "I fast twice a week. I give a tenth of all my income" (Luke 18:12).

Jesus was not impressed, and Christians can see why. We recall the oft-repeated statement that we are saved, not by good works but by faith in what God through Christ has done for us. St. Paul posits a radical distinction between these two ways of justification, of getting right with God. He is explicit about the absolute necessity of being justified by God's unearned grace, and every theological tradition that has followed in his wake has emphasized its importance. What has not been explored as intensely is how justification of the self by one's works, self-justification, operates in human relationships. What happens when humans try to make themselves the source of their own righteousness or, more to the point, how does self-justification relate, or even perpetuate, violence against others?

Exposition

I do not come at this question from an abstract theoretical concern as much as from a post–September 11, 2001, perspective. Osama bin Laden and his al Qaeda network struck at the heart of America's empire in the name of religious concerns. The Middle East hangs on the brink of chaos as two nations, Israel and Palestine, engage in self-righteous defense of their own aggressive acts of war. India and Pakistan justify their lust for Kashmir by self-proclaimed reasons why each must defend itself against the other.

In all of these cases, there seems to be a triadic link between religion, self-righteousness, and violence. The most ironic, and disturbing, link is that religion, instead of putting a rein on, or an end to, self-righteousness, can be used to support and advance it. Individuals, or even nations, can justify their aggressive acts in the name of God and with the blessing of their own self-proclaimed righteousness.

Justification of one's self, and therefore justification of what the self does or fails to do, is not an innocent and inconsequential activity. It goes to the heart of human evil, not only in our relationship with God but also in our relationship with each other. The depraved dynamics of self-justification are implicit in the parable of the Pharisee, but they need to be drawn out and related to the perpetration of violence. Violence, as we see it, is not limited to physical forms, though that is often its most blatant manifestation. It is any destructive desecration of the other person, or of the self, whether by physical or nonphysical means. An unkind word, made jagged by contempt, can be as destructive as a physical assault.

The Dynamics of Self-Justification

Self-justification is a multilayered illusion that has both personal and interpersonal dimensions to it. It is composed of at least four interrelated dynamics.

Self-Justification Is Blind

It is not interested in the whole truth about oneself. It lives in half-truths that reinforce, or seem to prove, one's status or particular point of view. In actuality, the Pharisee is more like the people he condemns than he would care to admit. Instead, he emphasizes the obvious ways in which he is not like them and tries to hide, from himself and others, the common bond he shares with all people—the need to reverse the direction of his life and to admit the many ways in which he is not righteous.

If self-justification is blind to the reality of the self, it is also blind to the reality of others. It sees others as it wants to see them, which usually means that it is convinced that they are aggressive and evil, far from being as trustworthy as he or she is. This negative perception of the other person need not terminate in violence, but it certainly sets the stage for the person to be violated, if there is any inclination or apparent reason to do so.

The blindness of the self-justified person precludes any possibility of genuine dialogue with the other person. In fact, it reduces the other person, as it did in the case of the tax collector, to someone who, at best, does not measure up and who, at worst, becomes the rightful object of anger and contempt. Where the unfortunate person falls on this continuum is determined by the vileness of the self-justified person's self-righteousness. Any actual conversation between the two parties is mono-logical rather than dialogical, is more concerned to parade "my side of the story" than it is to hear the other side. This in itself is a violation of the person, if not by overt desecration then by the reduction of the other person to an "It."

Self-justification, then, is at best a failure to see the other side or to take it seriously. At worst, it is an egocentric preoccupation with my "rights" or my "side" to the exclusion of genuine and open dialogue. The importance of dialogue in human relationships can be, and has been, portrayed in various ways.

The biblical corpus, especially the Old Testament, is clear and persistent in seeing us as creatures of address and response. The primary form of this dialogue is between Creator and creature. God calls and people respond, or, going in the other direction, the Psalmist pleads and God answers. There is also life-forming dialogue between persons. The prophet Nathan goes to David and tells him of a rich man who took a poor man's only lamb (2 Sam. 12:1–7). David is incensed and blurts out, "The man who has done this deserves to die." The dialogue becomes a piercing arrow when Nathan says, "You are the man!" In the New Testament, a different sort of dialogue is inherent in Paul's exhortation to the Galatians: "Bear one another's burdens and in this way you will fulfill the law of Christ" (Gal. 6:2).

In our time, the essential nature of human dialogue has been spelled out by theologians like Martin Buber. One of Buber's key concepts is "being fully present to" the other person. It means dwelling in the realm of the "in-between," the realm of reciprocal relationships in which "whole and active beings" (Friedman, 1960) possess "a concrete imagining of the other side" (Krasner & Joyce, 1995; the quotation is from Friedman, 1960) without losing sight of their own reality. It is entering into, and finding one's essential nature, in genuine dialogue.

Barbara Krasner, a family therapist, adopts Buber's philosophy of persons and makes honest dialogue or, to use Krasner's term "direct address," a key ingredient in the healing of estranged families. She uncovers the many ways in which the individual's capacity to be truly present is compromised by family-of-origin issues, but she also constructs a therapeutic approach that opens the way to dialogue, initially by having the therapist listen to, and give credence to, the counselee's story and then by encouraging the counselee to return to his or her family to invite genuine listening and sharing.

Over against honest dialogue, self-justification, with its blind and mono-logical preoccupation with the self, precludes even a preliminary step toward the dialogic healing of broken relationships. It is, in fact, an arrogant assertion of one's rights, even as it dismisses the rights of the other person.

Self-Justification Is Pompous and Prideful

Self-justification is the exact opposite of the tax collector who humbled himself and pleaded for mercy. Modern-day Pharisees may not be haughty in any outward way, but inwardly they are convinced of their absolute goodness and the rightness of their cause. Along the way they may even think of themselves as victims, which in their mind only goes to prove the rightness of their cause and the necessity of their contempt or violence. In any case, the whole point of self-justification is not only to be right but also to be the source of rightness.

In the last section, we said that the self-justified person hides certain truths about the self from the self. One of the truths that he or she hides is what lies unseen and unacknowledged underneath the facade of pride, namely, a sense of inadequacy and low self-esteem. The self-justified person does not have a solid sense of worthwhileness; otherwise, there would be no need for justification. Furthermore, the undertow of self-doubt is not extraneous to pride but a source of it. The show of pride is necessary to hide the unsureness of low self-esteem. Pride and self-doubt, then, are two sides of the same coin, the one feeding into the other.

Nevertheless, what shows is self-justification, even self-aggrandizement, in relation to tax collectors. Theologically, we are talking about hubris, the elevation of the self above the God who constituted it. "In being untrue to God, [humans beings] are even more profoundly untrue to themselves and so are shattered upon a rock of self-contradiction" (Jungel, 1974). The self gets caught in the feverish attempt to make itself good and acceptable, even as it labors against the violence it has done to itself. This violence is often projected onto others, who then become the innocent victims of righteous indignation.

There is a time-honored practice of working out our guilt or failure by putting it on someone or something who seems to have the potential power to heal us. This practice is epitomized in the Old Testament ritual of scapegoating. Once a year—on the Day of Atonement—Aaron, Moses' older brother, was to lay his hand on the head of a live goat and confess over the goat "all the iniquities of the people of Israel" (Lev. 16:21). The goat was then sent away into the wilderness, bearing all the transgressions of the people. This ritual was a conscious and community affair that bound the people together and released them from their guilt before God.

Today, the scapegoating that is practiced by individuals, families, or nations, is in many ways the exact opposite of the Old Testament ritual. It is often not a conscious act, either in terms of the perpetrators or the victims. It gives a dubious sense of fellowship to those who are aligned against the victims. It may involve the working out of guilt, but it can be used to address all kinds of individual or family or national problems. And, finally, it has little to do with God and everything to do with horizontal relationships.

Given the difference between the biblical ritual of scapegoating and the modern practice of scapegoating, we are led to ask, "What is the difference? Why is scapegoating in some instances healing and reconciling and in other instances destructive and divisive?" The difference seems to be that in the one case God does the justifying and in the other case the self does the justifying. In the New Testament, Christ as scapegoat is God's answer to our guilt, while in family scapegoating we take matters into our own hands and make someone else the bearer of, and the victim of, our guilt, failure, or some other problem. Our treachery is that we take God's salutary work as our own. We turn a sacrificial system that frees into a self-generated righteousness that justifies.

For the self-justified person, the name of the game is blame. It is not the appropriate recognition of wrongdoing on the part of the self and on the part of the other person. It is the projection of excessive and absolute culpability onto the other person, even though underneath the facade there may be a sense of one's own culpability. But the self-justified person is fixated on the other's guilt and culpability and uses this fixation to reinforce his or her own cause. Like the Pharisee, he or she is filled with contempt for the other person and despises the other person's lack of goodness and moral fiber.

This is a prelude to violence. It is not an automatic step into violence, but it certainly condones violence if the other person is seen at all as a provocateur. Actually, the spark that ignites violence need not come from the actions of the other person. It can come as well from the perception of the self-justified person who imagines that he or she has been slighted, insulted, or shamed. In either case, violence seems a logical, if not the only, response to the situation, and once started it tends to create its own cycle of justified retaliation.

Religion plays into this cycle, or is made to support it, if it does not stand in judgment of all attempts to live by one's own righteousness. More than most other forms of human endeavor, religion is subject to this distortion because it deals with ultimate things and carries an authority that is difficult to question. Anyone who "has religion" and who is inclined to use it for selfish purposes can use it as an effective means to justify the actions of the self. Actions attributed to the will of God, or deeds done in the service of God, take on an air of authority, even if they are really seeped in human self-righteousness. One of the few ways that religion can escape this misuse is by putting exclusive emphasis for our renewal on God rather than on any form of human endeavor (goodness). Paul is persistent in making the point: "For we hold that a person is justified by faith [in what Christ has done for us] apart from works prescribed by the law [and fulfilled by us]" (Rom. 3:28).

Self-Justification Is Resistant to Help and Healing

The Pharisee, standing apart from the "unrighteous" crowd, shows no sign of needing or wanting help. He went to the temple to pray, not because he was in need but because it offered him an opportunity to brag, maybe to demand. Actually, he stood in dire need of healing, but he did not know it and would not acknowledge it.

Saul of Tarsus offers a case in point. When he was brought low on the Damascus road, he could be counted among the righteous: He was brought up in the right family and was zealous to keep the law. In his zeal, he had obtained a letter from the high priests that allowed him to go to the synagogues in Damascus and persecute any Christian Jews who were found there. He had permission to vent his fury, and his fear, on the new sect in the name of rendering unto God the highest possible service. He had no need to be helped or healed, because on his own he was earning an enviable standing before God.

A voice from heaven brought Paul to his knees and stopped his violent behavior. "Saul, Saul, why do you persecute me?" Paul's righteousness turned into worthless ashes with this question. It was not his zeal for the law that was going to save him, but God's salutary work in and through Christ. It took a life-shattering experience to bring Paul to this realization. The experience did not change his obsession to work for the Lord. He endured "imprisonments, with countless beatings," often near death (2 Cor. 11:23). He received "forty lashes less one" five different times. He was shipwrecked three times and continued his missionary journeys "in toil and hardship, in hunger and thirst, often without food, in cold and exposure" (2 Cor. 11:27). But Paul was no longer a self-righteous bigot. He was a servant who stood in daily need of help, and because he received it he could also share it.

The self-justified person, believing himself or herself to be right and above reproach, has no exit out of his or her self-righteousness and no entrance into wholeness. The Christian faith also makes it clear that the self-justified person has no entrée to, or standing before, God. "I tell you [the tax collector], went down to his house justified rather than the [Pharisee]" (Luke 18:14). It takes what the tax collector had, and not the Pharisee, namely, humility and openness to self-examination, to turn life around and to establish a dialogic relationship with the tax collectors of the world.

In Scripture, humility stands over against arrogance and violence and opens up the possibility of peace and harmony, whether it is used to designate a class of people or to refer to a subjective trait. In the Old Testament, humility is often a social-economic term that refers to the poor and the afflicted, to the ones who "must acknowledge their own helplessness and utter dependency upon God." They were a special concern to Yahweh, and while Israel thought that Yahweh could act to humble a man, it did not think that Yahweh in any way upheld "a social system built on pride and wealth" (Buttrick, 1962). In the New Testament, humility becomes a character trait and a Christian virtue, leading to peace and nonviolence. Paul's equivalent

is "love in a spirit of gentleness" (1 Cor. 4:21), which emphasizes both
a concern for others rather than the self and a spirit of meekness that
eschews power and prestige. Humility, whether it refers to a social
class or a character trait, is the last thing that a Pharisee, a self-
justified person, would embrace and prize.

Self-Justification Is Morally Corrupt

Self-justification is oriented to the law, but it does not fulfill the law.
It dwells on and lives by the letter of the law and levies harsh judgment on the neighbor who does not measure up. In this sense alone, it
does not fulfill the law: "You shall love your neighbor as yourself"
(Matt. 22:39). And it certainly does not fulfill the spirit of the law:
"You have heard that it was said, 'You shall love your neighbor and
hate your enemy.' But I say to you, 'Love your enemies and pray for
those who persecute you'" (Matt. 5:43–44). The Pharisee is too quick
to assign blame and too filled with contempt to fulfill the law.

But the Pharisee, and self-justified people generally, are morally
corrupt for a deeper reason. It is not just the law that they fail to
obey. It is their God-given destiny, what they were created to be, that
they fail to fulfill. Or we can extend their failure in the direction of
Martin Buber's existential guilt. The self-justified person, by the
contempt and self-righteousness that he or she posits in the realm
between persons, ruptures and injures "the justice of the human
order" (Boszormenyi-Nagy & Krasner, 1986). Buber clarifies: "Each
man stands in an objective relationship to others; the totality of this
relationship constitutes his life as one that factually participates in the
being of the world . . . It is his share in the human order of being, the
share for which he bears responsibility . . . Injuring a relationship
means that at this place the human order of being is injured"
(Krasner, 1986; the quotation is from Martin Buber).

The Pharisee sincerely thought he was a moral and religious person. He even paraded some examples of his supposed goodness: "I
fast twice a week. I give a tenth of all my income." But, in fact, the
Pharisee was morally inept. He desecrated humanity both in himself
and in the neighbor, and he left the temple as he had come—self-
deceived and unjustified. In this state, he could resort to violence in
response to any number of provocations—if his righteousness was
questioned, if his status was eroded, if his pride was hurt, if his religion was attacked, if the tax collector came back at him, if his prayer
was not accepted and the tax collector's was. The ultimate concern of
self-justification is the self, and one of the logical endpoints of a hurt

and battered self is violence. This generally tends to be the policy and program of the Fundamentalist or Evangelical, whether Christian, Jewish, Islamic, or other.

The Antidote to Self-Justification

It is obvious why self-justification can end in violence. But Jesus and Paul stand firmly against self-justification and maintain that the only way to be justified before God is to be justified by God's unearned grace. We are to lay aside all our attempts to make ourselves righteous and are to depend solely on what God in Christ has done for us and has given to us. Out of this gift comes a life of love and humility, of justice and servanthood, instead of a life ruled by pride, prestige, and violence.

A cursory view of the history of the church quickly reveals that the followers of Jesus have not avoided violence. In fact, in many instances, like the Crusades, they have perpetuated and promoted it. Given this track record, the questioning becomes, "How can a life marked by humility and servanthood become oppressive, aggressive, and self-seeking? Is there something in being justified by grace, as there is in being justified by the self, that prompts or encourages violence?" Several possibilities suggest themselves, each containing an element of truth.

A first possible explanation is that being justified by God causes resentment in us. We want to be the source of our own justification and not depend on someone else. So while we may seem to accept God's gift of grace, we seethe underneath and may vent our anger when circumstances aggravate our resentment beyond a certain point. This psychological explanation of how divine justification may promote violence may tie into the theological understanding of sin, which says that we have a certain enmity toward God and do not want to acknowledge God as God.

A second explanation is a contrast to the first one. It maintains that once we are justified by God we tend to identify with God. Instead of resenting God, we tend to think that we are on God's side. Besides, we know the Lord's will, and we are engaged in the Lord's battles. This kind of thinking may be encouraged by Paul when he says to the Colossians, "I am now rejoicing in my sufferings for your sake, and in my flesh I am completing what is lacking in Christ's afflictions for the sake of his body, that is, the church" (Col. 1:24). And Jesus can be conscripted to add to the call to prepare for battle when he says,

"Because you do not belong to the world, but I have chosen you out of the world—therefore, the world hates you" (John 15:19).

In our day, evangelical Christians seem to illustrate this position. Once they have accepted Christ as their personal Savior, they seem to know what is God's will. They may even imply that they are closer to God and more righteous than the rest of us. The result can be alarming. Several years ago I received a publication from them that featured a "victory for the Lord." A college student, who was in contact with an evangelical group, declined to give up a sport to devote more time to the mission of the group. In conversation, he made the casual comment, "If I break a leg, I'll be available." Several weeks later in a freak accident in practice the student actually damaged his leg so severely that he had to quit the sport. The group marveled at the mysterious way in which the Lord had worked. To me the incident was an unfortunate and violent happenstance. To members of the group, the godly end seemed to justify the violent means.

A third explanation is more theological and is related to our first point. It maintains that while the individual may be declared righteous by God because of Christ, still the "old Adam" remains. Consequently, self-justification is still alive and can lead the individual to act out in violence. In a word, the individual is *simul justus et peccator.* This paradox, this dual standing before God, is played out in an "anthropological conflict" within the individual, as Paul indicates in his self-assessment: "I do not do the good I want, but the evil I do not want is what I do." Paul goes on to pinpoint the conflict—the sin that dwells within him versus the regenerated will to do good and avoid evil. But as Paul indicates, the battle is at best a constant tug of war, and the individual who still lives by the law and feels condemned by it will strike out in violence when his or her pride and self-esteem are at stake.

These three explanations of why followers of Christ can be violent have a good measure of truth in them, but we are still faced with the question "Is there something within justification by grace itself that encourages violence?" If there is, we are faced with the possibility that religion's so-called destructive power resides in the very heart of the Christian gospel. Given my commitment to the Christian faith I may not see what is evident to others, and in any case all the nuances of my understanding of God—a God who is for love and peace and fellowship—lead me to avoid such a blatant and treacherous contradiction within God.

My concern, however, does not stop humans from using God, or religion, for destructive purposes. But we should note that the destructiveness is first in *us* before it is in our *constructs*. Certain religious symbols or acts, like Christ dying on a cross, are multifaceted enough to invite people who are so inclined to interpret them in ways that support violence, but the violence is in the eye of the beholder, not in the drama of a gracious God paying the price for our sins in order to reestablish relationship with us. Sin requires a radical remedy, and the remedy is more of a sacrificial act than it is an act of violence. After all, God suffered as his son suffered.

We must also grant that not all violence is negative and destructive. The drilling of a dentist intends to get the bad out, not to destroy the good. If the Christian faith is destructive, it is most destructive, and most healing at the point that it destroys our righteousness, our feverish attempt to make it on our own. Unfortunately, its judgment may prompt us to be destructive, for we do not like its piercing light and its implied guilt. If then we can assign the destruction to God, or build it into our religion, we do not have to deal with our own unrighteousness. Meanwhile, we hate to see Christ on the cross, in fact we often cover up its gory details, not just because we do not like to see someone suffer but also because we know that our righteousness and violence sent him there. And if the cross does not remind us of our unrighteousness, maybe some of our daily events do. As we look out of the window of our "banquet halls" and see the hungry children below, we may not be able to deny our unrighteousness. And this violation of our complacency, this correction of our myopia, can serve a very positive purpose.

Religion can be destructive, yet positive, in another way. The Christian faith, for example, makes radical demands of us and expects a radical commitment. If faith in Christ does to us what it did to Paul, who wants it? Who wants to be imprisoned, shipwrecked, beaten, threatened with death, and made to survive without food, water, or shelter in the name of God? For that matter, who wants to be an unpretentious but faithful follower of Christ and be persecuted by those who do not agree with us? Do we back away because of the violence involved or because of the sacrifice that is required or because of both? In any case, the demands of the gospel can undermine the comfortableness of our status quo and can tear down our facade of assumed righteousness.

As we have seen, the antidote to self-justification is to be justified by God. Even that, however, does not end human violence. We humans seem to become violent wherever it is possible—in the marketplace, in the home, in the practice of our religion. Like Adam we are still covering up our acting out by saying, "God, remember the neighbors you gave me. They made me do it." Over against this denial of guilt, Christ on the cross faced his adversaries directly, acknowledged their guilt, and asked for their forgiveness: "Father, forgive them for they know not what they do." Even this exemplary act of mercy has not stopped us from trying to justify ourselves nor has it stopped us from striking out at the person who would question our righteousness.

The Road to Peace

The road to peace with our neighbor is through genuine dialogue. Genuine dialogue does not sanction violence nor can violence survive in its presence. It is a moment of harmony and unity in the midst of diversity where self speaks to self about things that matter. It is born of mutual respect and is as attentive to the reality of the other person as it is to one's own reality. It does not insist on its own way but is willing to arrive at a conclusion that is beneficial to both parties, even if that conclusion involves significant differences between them. It is the self in touch with itself and with the other self, and in that contact it finds itself by losing itself in the other person even as it fulfills the other person by giving itself to the other person. Genuine dialogue is the antithesis of self-righteousness and the end of self-justification. This is as true for communities and nations as for individuals and families.

The road to peace, or genuine dialogue, presupposes that one is empowered by the peace of God. The peace of God is a multifaceted reality if we take seriously both the Old and New Testaments. It is a state of wholeness or completeness or, if it is applied to groups or nations, it is the absence of hostilities and the presence of harmonious relationships of mutual benefit and goodwill. It is the enjoyment of good health or the blessing of prosperity. It is a serene state of mind, one that is devoid of fear or conflict while being filled with the fruits of the Spirit. Above all, it is to be reconciled with God by being justified by God's grace and accepted as God's own. The peace and generosity of God free us to enter into genuine dialogue with the other person and empower us to share our lives and our destiny with each other. It marks the end of violence and the beginning of a worldwide community.

References

Boszormenyi-Nagy, I., & Krasner, B. R. (1986). *Between give and take: A clinical guide to contextual therapy.* New York: Brunner/Mazel.

Buttrick, G. A. (1962). *The interpreter's dictionary of the Bible: An illustrated encyclopedia* (Vol. II). New York: Abingdon.

Friedman, M. S. (1960). *Martin Buber: The life of dialogue.* New York: Harper Torchbooks.

Jungel, E. (1974). *Death: The riddle and the mystery.* Philadelphia: Westminster.

Krasner, B. R., & Joyce, A. J. (1995). *Truth, trust, and relationships: Healing interventions in contextual therapy.* New York: Brunner/Mazel.

CHAPTER 14

RELIGION AND VIOLENCE: FROM PAWN TO SCAPEGOAT

Paul N. Anderson

Introduction

As I traveled through Europe several years ago, I was impressed that people there blamed religion for much of the violence in Western civilization. Historically, of course, the notion of the divine right of kings was used to certify national power and authority, whether just or despotic. Moreover, appeals to religion often got stronger the more questionable regal policies became. The Crusades pitted Christian against Islamic forces, as well as against other kinds of Christians, and the aftermath of those conflicts continues. Civil wars in England, continental Europe, and America, as well as the world wars on the European continent, during the twentieth century were bolstered by religious claims on all sides. Great atrocities were defended on religious grounds. Saddam Hussein, who was involved in the killing of hundreds of thousands of Iranians and other Muslims, called a challenge to his regime an attack against Islam. But is the assumption that religion itself is to blame for the violence in the world a valid assumption or a simplistic reduction?

Indeed, John Lennon's song "Imagine" captured the hearts of a generation by posing a utopian ideal wherein "nothing to kill or die for, and no religion too" promised a new messianic age wherein the world could finally live "as one" if religion were put in its deserved, marginal place. But is this an adequate hope, or even a sound analysis? Religion has great organizing potential, both for good and ill, and the attitudes of many people allow for the consideration of only the negative side of that reality. Furthermore, because religion has great power to motivate people, it is frequently and easily yoked to political plans and agendas. Religion is unlikely to disappear from the face of the earth. Thoughtful people must, therefore, come to terms with its uses and abuses.

The purpose of this chapter is to sketch a broad outline of reality we face here and attempt to discern where the truth lies in the matter of the role of religion in society. I wish to make some cogent observations about whether religion tends to be appropriately indicted or used as pawn and scapegoat within popular discourse. In so doing, Jesus' admonition for his followers to be as wary as serpents and harmless as doves seems worth some thoughtful reflection.

Exposition

Let me begin with an illustration. "For God and Country" is a slogan that has great organizing potential and effect. Throughout the world and its history the pitting of these religious and social values against an alien foe frequently marshaled the willing hearts of young men and women into the cause of war and violence. Appeals to these values seem to imply that they are threatened by a malevolent foe, at home or abroad. Has that usually really been the case, in practical fact? Probably not. And yet, these twin human loyalties sometimes are used as a myth for informing the conscience of our youth for violence and war. One could even argue that much killing has been done in the name of preserving such ideals, whether with culpability before God or honoring of God or country. The blame lies with none of the ideals. The fault lies with the posing of dilemmas wherein the contrived threat is not the real one.

This fact came to me vividly when as a young pastor in seminary, I stood in the doorway of a small Indiana Friends church greeting people on their way out after a Sunday morning service. As I greeted a young man only three years younger than myself, I asked him, "So what are you going to be doing next year?" He told me he was going to enlist in one of the armed services, whereupon I inquired how that squared with his Quaker upbringing. His response was interesting. He looked into my eyes and asked, "If the Russians were going to come and rape and kill your mother or grandmother, would you just stand there and let it happen; or would you use force to prevent it?" Well, as any red-blooded man who loves his family, I hoped such a plight would never happen and would have taken some sort of action to ensure alternative outcomes.

Rather than falling into the trap of a concocted dilemma, however, I found myself asking *why* one value was being pitted against another. As my eyes scanned the cornfields of the Indiana countryside, visible from the threshold of the meetinghouse, I really could not imagine Russian armies invading Hoosier territory seeking to do harm to mothers or grandmothers. The threat was absolutely nonexistent! But why, then, would a fine young man consider learning violence and the skills of warfare to do damage to other people's mothers and grandmothers, or at least their sons and grandsons, in response to such a contrived threat? The answer, of course, had to do with the simple matter of what was championed as of a high value. One of the highest of God-given values is the sanctity of beloved family relationships; and the mythical threat to this value was being used as a *pawn*, to erode principled Quaker commitments to peaceable ways of life.

Now is motherhood or grandmotherhood to blame for the violence resultant from even well-meaning desires to protect beloved family members? Should motherhood be marginalized along with religion? Should we add to Lennon's song "and no motherhood too"? Nonsense! God, Mom, and Apple Pie, icons of ultimate and beloved values, can be used as instrumental pawns to motivate moral compromise among the unwitting. Ironically, though, upon subsequent reflection it seems to be primarily God and religion that get scapegoated, not country, motherhood, or apple pie. Why?

The first question we should ask deals with what is meant by the term *religion*. We might define religion as an organized system of beliefs and practices designed to embrace and advance spiritual ideals and experiences and their applications in the world. Obviously, religious approaches to life's problems assume some sort of understanding of the divine—monotheistic, polytheistic, or atheistic. Religious aspirants organize themselves in a variety of models of faith and practice. While this analysis could be applied to any religious movement, I want to target the three great monotheistic and biblical religions: Judaism, Christianity, and Islam, with a primary focus on Christianity. My reasons for doing so are threefold: first, these three great religions encompass over half of the world's population and have contributed most extensively to the rise of progress and Western civilization. Indeed, their power and impact are an obvious fact to any student of world history and culture. Second, violence and good have also been extensively associated with these three religions, leading to a third factor; the rise of European Christendom has not been evaluated in this regard with adequate thoroughness. Devotees and opponents of any faith tradition often fail to realize the crucial importance of both a celebration of one's faith and the necessary critical analysis of it. What often results is either the exaltation or the denigration of religion, while adequate analysis will produce a more nuanced appraisal. Consider the following ways that religion contributes to the difficulties in this issue.

The Psychological Power of Religion

Religious faith and spirituality are a great source of personal empowerment and psychological sustenance. Humans have long derived personal strength from their religious practices and beliefs; people have always drawn personal strength from religious and spiritual resources. Historically, humans faced with impending challenges have sought divine assistance. That will likely always be so. Religion is powerful because it affects the human psyche and becomes one of the greatest sources of personal direction and strength.

Understandably humans create mental portraits of deity commensurate with their perceptions of need. From animism to monotheism, acute senses of human need form the lenses through which people construct appraisals of the Transcendent, and elements of projection will always inform theological constructs. This is not to reduce theology to psychology or to anthropomorphism, but it is to acknowledge the place and function of psychological need and projection within any theological or religious system. The point is to distinguish between religion as a culpable source of violence, and religion as a more benign resource empowering human endeavors, including managing inter-group and intra-group conflict.

On this score, God may get more credit for victory and defeat in warfare than deserved. Consider the fact that more Christians killed and were killed by other Christians during World War I than the total number of humans killed by other humans in the history of civilization altogether.[1] Unfortunately, this phenomenon was not limited to that conflict alone. Christians' killing of other Christians has been a tragic historic feature of Western civilization, including the Thirty Years War, English and American Civil Wars, Spanish and Dutch wars, both world wars, and many other conflicts. The point here is not to suggest naively that religion makes people more violent.[2]

Congolese families pray for peace and salvation at the Army of Victory
Church in Kinshasa, Congo, August 1998. AP/Wide World Photos.

Neither is it to suggest that killing Christians is worse than killing anyone else.

The point is to connect the constructive power of religion with the fact that warfare taxes all resources, physical, economic, industrial, and psychological. Humans are inclined, in extremity, to use their resources in evil ways. Like physical exercise, religious exercise will be accessed as a resource to the degree to which it is deemed beneficial. I suppose there might be less conflict if people would get less exercise and become less physically able to do harm to others, but blaming exercise and physical health for the devastating results of war misses the point. Food provides sustenance for doing violence or good, but depriving people of food is not the best way to avert conflict; they could then not do good either. Should food be blamed for damage done under the strength it affords, or should electricity be credited with fostering the death penalty, rather than crediting it with affording healthy light and useful power? Why blame religion when people use it monstrously to act unwisely or immorally, violently?

This relates to the theological problem that Islamic warriors on both sides prayed for victory to the same Allah in the Iranian-Iraqi war of the 1980s. What do we make of the fact that European Christians have prayed to the same God for victory against one another for the last 2,000 years, as did Christian Unionists and Confederates during the American Civil War? Do we ascribe victory to God's favoring one side over the other? Whatever the case, one's belief in God's sovereignty conflicts inevitably with the tragedy of the warfare. Inhumanity is done to persons beloved of God, and this poses a striking theological problem. Does God take sides? While claiming divine assistance is appreciated on personal levels, crediting a just and loving God with the devastating outcomes of warfare, where victimizing is the center of the enterprise, remains problematic. One must acknowledge that people will draw on religious and spiritual resources in facing the great ordeals of life, which include the throes of warfare, but crediting religious resources for the conflict and its outcomes is quite another matter.

On the other hand, religion can contribute to violence on personal and psychological levels, and this tendency should be factored into the equation. An important aspect of religious power is that it creates an "us." It solidifies group identity and appeals to religious certainty, eternal consequences, and principled loyalties. These shape individuals and groups. Indeed, Yahweh's warfare against tribal adversaries in

Hebrew Scripture, the dehumanization of infidels in the Qur'an, and the temporal and eternal warnings against the unfaithful in Christian Scripture function to create an us-versus-them mentality common to prejudice and violence. In that sense, the organizing power of religion to create intra-group solidarity becomes a devastating contributor to inter-group opposition. Religious ideology or motivation, thus, can contribute to the planning for and the carrying out of violence; but within Judaism, Christianity, and Islam, religion also makes claims for the humanity of "the other" and calls for loving regard and gracious behavior toward even the stranger and the enemy. So religion, while empowering the individual to meet obligations or needs, even if violence-producing ones, can also function to soften the hearts of combatants toward one another. This experience is attested to by many.[3]

It is also a fact that personal rage and hatred in the name of God's justice may emerge as one considers injustice and violence done against one's people, or even against other groups. The impulse to right particular wrongs can be a deeply religious one, and some may resort to violence as a remedy to perceived transgressions. The point here is to consider that while religion has a great capacity to strengthen and motivate people on personal psychological levels, this does not imply that it is to be blamed when those energies are misused, or implicate God with what is done in God's name. God, like Mom and Apple Pie, may provide strength for the day, psychologically and otherwise, but deeds performed in the name of religious aspirations can also transgress religious appeals for altruism and the humane treatment of others. The honest evaluator will see the difference.

Sociological Aspects of the Equation

Religion and appeals to God play significant organizational roles in society, and these factors are also worth considering here. Some may yoke the justice of God to the deserved treatment for perpetuators of violence and injustice. They would then be operating on what James Fowler calls the Stage Two level of Faith Development,[4] and the societal organization of its energies against such perceived threats illustrates Stage Three, Synthetic-Conventional Faith. On this level, persuasive leaders foster group solidarity to mobilize energy for a particular course of action. Obviously, the names of God and religion offer great organizing potential in such ventures, and few values are as deeply held as religious and patriotic ones.

Such appeals can instill a sense of group solidarity, mobilizing an us-versus-them mentality, deprecating the values, objectives, and religious distinctions of the "enemy" while elevating one's own. While there is much in the Bible and the Qur'an that speaks against this, the demonizing of other groups and their values energizes such destructive pathos and inspires a sense of superiority and hence self-justification in the spirit of the perpetrating group(s). When others become objectified and dehumanized, it becomes more tolerable to work for their demise. Ironically, however, the greatest oppositions against such devaluations are also religious ones. The anti-nationalistic rhetoric of Jonah and Ruth, for instance, call for Israel to consider God's working within and through even the pagan nations of Assyria and Moab. Jesus's dining with "sinners" and outsiders declared in the name of God an inclusive embrace of "the other" even *before* they offered any solidarity from their side.[5] Indeed, if one takes Jesus' actions and teachings on the love of enemies as representative of the divine will, one is struck by the fact that God does not regard any individual or group as "the other." So why do Christians allow themselves to do this when the God present in Jesus does not? The answer may be found in the employment of particular biblical themes and texts to legitimate violence.

One of the primary ways that religion contributes to violence is that sacred scriptures and religious motifs are used as legitimators of violence, a significant reason religion needs critical evaluation. Texts that warrant wars and violence in the Bible or Qur'an in the name of a just and loving God raise the question as to how he could command such atrocities as those mentioned in the Hebrew conquest narratives of the books of Joshua and Judges. These are juxtaposed to clear teachings of Jesus on nonviolence and love of enemies. This kind of text is a difficult theological problem in the sacred scriptures of Judaism, Christianity, and Islam. Surely such narratives in any sacred scripture represent a confusion of the will of God with the foreign policy ambitions of the nation involved.[6] It is useful to notice several features of Israel's "Holy War" theology that we easily lose sight of when we appropriate the violence of the conquest narratives to justify our behavior today.

Israel's view of Holy War stood in contrast to the plundering and subjugation practiced by surrounding nations. A second feature of biblical Holy War was that combatants were to be chaste in their dedication to God. Even relations with one's wife were forbidden (see Uriah's example in 2 Sam. 11), and the holy warrior was to be dedicated to fighting for Yahweh alone in the course of battle. Quite conveniently, modern appeals to the conquest narratives omit these aspects of the biblical "precedent" for engaging in violence today. A third feature is the emphasis that Yahweh was doing the fighting. An explicit contrast was drawn between Yahweh's deliverance by means of powers of nature and other exceptional media (see Exod. 15) and the standing armies of Pharaoh, or even Saul.[7] Indeed, Israel's Holy War hinges more upon trust in Yahweh than in its own ingenuity or military might.[8]

Appeals to the wars of the Bible rarely take these features into account when these texts are appropriated for the purpose of legitimating violence. The mention of an event or topical development in the Bible does not imply its appropriateness for ethical practice today. Indeed, many times a sequence of events is narrated simply to emphasize the story, complete with its tragic outcomes, and many times narrations of violent events serve the function of warning against such in the future. Instructive asides emerge sometimes indirectly, and their adequate inference always requires a discerning interpretation.

A second biblical theme used to legitimate violence and force may be found in a narrower text, Romans 13:1–7. Here the Apostle Paul appears to be sanctioning the divine right of kings, advocating force and violence as divinely ordained if commanded by a magistrate. On one hand, Paul calls upon his readers to submit to the magistrates, arguing that their appointment as leaders is divinely ordained and that God has even granted some the "ministry of the sword." From such a passage, one might construe a theocratic model of governance by which God is thought to endorse whatever directives and laws a monarch commands, whether or not they are in keeping with God's ways as revealed in Scripture and represented by Christ.

Upon closer analysis, however, such is not the case. Within the larger context, the passage fits into the broader interest of Paul's seeking to win Gentiles to the faith by means of a loving and nonviolent witness. In the verses preceding Romans 13:1–7, Paul introduces the passage by calling readers to live at peace with all persons, as much as it is possible to do so, in order that by one's loving example "coals" of convicting fire will stir the conscience of others toward the Gospel of Jesus Christ (Romans 12:9–21). In the passage following verses 1–7, Paul advocates the way of love as the means by which to fulfill the entirety of the law (Romans 13:8–10). The point to be noted here is that submission to authorities in Romans 13:1–7 is called for as a means of distinguishing the Jesus movement as one characterized by nonviolence and love.

Where followers of the Galilean Jesus might be confused with followers of "the Samaritan," or Theudas, or "the Egyptian,"[9] or even Jewish zealotry, Paul calls for intentional distancing from such associations. This may have been called for owing to the fact that Jesus had been put to death on a Roman cross, the standard penalty for sedition and criminality in the Roman provinces. The point here is that extracting from Romans 13:1–7 a theological platform of the divine right of kings, where even the violent or idolatrous mandates of the magistrate are to be obeyed as the directive of God, misinterprets Paul's content entirely. His primary concern was calling for upstanding living as Christians so as to be good witnesses to others.

A third example of how biblical content gets distorted involves the manipulation of Jesus's teachings and deeds in order to support violence. Consider these misappropriations of Jesus' presentation in the Gospels: "Jesus drove the money changers out of the Temple with a whip; we'll drive the Viet Cong out of South Viet Nam with napalm." "Jesus said, 'He who lives by the sword will die by the sword,' and those Yankees/Rebels will pay for what they've done!"[10] Notice how the first distortion infers that it is people rather than animals that are driven out? The text of John 2:15 says nothing about violence used against people, and the action was a dramatic prophetic action rather than a forcible program staking out territory and bringing injury to others.

The second example distorts a passage in which Jesus has just commanded his disciple to put away his sword (Matt. 26:52), stating clearly that the way of violence is not his way. The passage cited is a wisdom-saying emphasizing the futility of violence, *not* a command to violent action. If you kill you will be killed, especially by those wishing to dominate you. Does Jesus ever condone or command violence? No. He calls for the love of enemies, and he outlines the way of the Kingdom in Matthew's Sermon on the Mount (Matt. 5–7). Here the *ethos* of God's active reign is contrasted to the ways of the world. In contrast to conventional approaches to injustice and violence, *Jesus* called for his followers to love others unconditionally, to love even one's enemies, to renounce the right to vengeance and to demonstrate a spirit of exceeding generosity, to seek first the Kingdom of God and its righteousness, to turn the values of the world upside down, to embrace the cross, and be peacemakers in the world.[11]

In each of the above examples, the Bible does not advocate violence as our way of life. It advocates against it. Alongside these themes and passages appearing to support violence, most of the biblical witness calls for people to be more loving toward one another and to trust in God's provision and protection rather than relying on forcible means. The Minor Prophets especially exhort Judah and Israel *not* to trust in Egypt and its chariots for defense, and from a political standpoint, they were right. Pacts with Egypt in the eighth through the sixth centuries B.C.E. ironically evoked retaliatory responses from the Assyrians, and later the Babylonians, and one wonders how history might have been different if Israel and Judah had trusted in Yahweh rather than chariots. What might have happened in Western civilization if Paul's exhortation in Romans 13 would have been interpreted appropriately as an appeal for the advancement of the gospel rather than the institutionalizing of the divine right of kings?

Genuine theocracy has not been the problem in the violent history of Europe. Rather, equating any human regime with the transcendent reign of God was the error. Much evil and violence have been carried out in the name of a religious certification of abusive human leadership. Paul was calling believers to live within the law in order that by their loving and upright examples others might be won to Christ. Even the good name of Jesus has been used to justify violence, though his example and teaching are the greatest source of nonviolent social action in human history. How can these things be? Religious authority and, in particular, distorted biblical interpretations are often used to create social toleration of violence when such would otherwise be unconscionable. This feature is especially vulnerable to manipulation by propagators of violence within and outside of religious communities.

Religious Equity and Its Political Manipulations

A corollary feature of sociological factors in these matters is the fact that entire societies get yoked into conflicts, and members of those societies are often forced into structured dilemmas that have no good options. Like psychological power, sociological power can be harnessed and manipulated politically, so a critical analysis of our subject must distinguish between intrinsic and extrinsic appeals to religion. When religion or any other asset is perceived as political equity, to be exploited and harnessed for some questionable scheme or program, it invariably becomes subject to corruption and misrepresentation. Indeed, religious power at times gets yoked to political campaigns or objectives; and one of the prime means of eroding principled opposition to violence is to pit another principle, often a religious concern, against it, forcing the choice of one value over another. This is one of the most common ways in which religious objection to violence is subverted by political manipulation. People who might otherwise object to violence are often maneuvered into situations in which they must fight lest another value be threatened. One might comply with the national call to a questionable war lest one contribute to national disunity at a critical or precarious moment in a nation's destiny, when the issues at stake are nonetheless quite ambiguous. If he or she does not go along with the prescribed actions a cherished value or commitment is jeopardized, and then that person becomes subject to villainization as a traitor or coward. This is how structural evil gets leverage. Good persons are forced into situations in which they must carry out harmful deeds, and moral persons become trapped in immoral societal structures.

This is also one of the reasons religion then gets interpreted as the source of the problem. Where political powers are the ones marshaling loyalty to a cause, using religion as a pawn, they will rarely construe the inevitable blame as being theirs in the aftermath of violent campaigns. Scapegoats will be concocted, and within the age of secularism, religion becomes an easy target. Is this a fair representation of the root cause of violence? Is this an honest critique? Moral persons within immoral societies will indeed draw upon all available resources for their sustenance and support, and notions of the good are often defined in provincial rather than universal terms. God's name will be invoked and thanked for victory in the struggles of life, especially ultimate ones, and good and moral individuals and groups will connect the victory of God with their own. From a more transcendent perspective, however, victory at the expense of others whom God also loves must be considered highly problematic.[12]

The temptation to subvert and use religious authority for ulterior motives will always be a real one. Political powers cannot but see religion (or even irreligion) as a resource to be tapped in their campaigns, especially military ones, or those in which morally questionable economic or social policies are employed. For instance, in the hope of preserving a terribly unjust societal structure such as slavery, the Epistle to Philemon was employed by advocates of slavery. There Paul encouraged Onesimus, a fugitive slave, to return home to his master; and passages in Matthew and John portraying *hoi Ioudaioi* (either "the

Jews" or "the Judeans") as those who rejected Jesus as the Messiah have been yoked to anti-Semitic campaigns in the Third Reich and elsewhere. Blaming the Bible or religion as the sole culprit in these grievous matters, however, is wrongheaded. Paul calls for Philemon also to treat Onesimus as a brother in Christ and declares elsewhere that in Christ there is neither Jew nor Greek, slave person nor free, male nor female (Gal. 3:28). John and Matthew are the most Jewish of New Testament writings. They were written by Jewish authors, and they both argue centrally that Jesus was indeed the Jewish Messiah. Nonetheless, the irreligious and even the marginally religious cannot but regard biblical and religious authority as societal equity to be yoked and leveraged, and such should be distinguished from more authentic and intrinsically motivated approaches to religion.

The fact that such subversion continues to be possible requires consideration, though, in and of itself. Why is it that programs of violence and injustice, when propounded with religious associations, also dupe the unwitting? A likely guess is that this is at least partially due to the uncritical character of religion. As the heart of religious experience centers in faith-related perspective and praxis, the faithful within any movement may be ill equipped to distinguish legitimate appeals to biblical and religious authority from their alternatives. As a step forward, religious appeals and all such claims should be subjected to the spotlight of critical scrutiny. Considering the implications and bases of religious appeals is an important step in considering effectively their authenticity. Here, Mark Twain's short story "The War Prayer" illustrates this approach dramatically. After a pastor prays a great and moving prayer for the victory of sons and loved ones being sent off to battle, a mysterious stranger interprets the prayer before the group and asks if people really want to have their prayer answered. Any prayer for victory is also a prayer for defeat, and such will always involve devastating human costs. This mysterious stranger asked, as a messenger from the throne on high, whether indeed people had considered the other side of their requests. He humanized the reality of war and its effects and asked if people still desired such. The point here is clear. Even sincere and morally upstanding people can become engaged in conflicts, applying religious resources to a cause, without considering the devastating consequences of success, even if they are diametrically opposed to the central values of that religion. So religion gets used sincerely from the inside, as a pawn, often distortedly, especially when people do not consider the global and long-term consequences of their aspirations.

Twain concludes the story with a provocative, ironic twist. After showing the devastating carnage of what victory would bring, he described the congregation as not understanding a single thing the messenger from on high had communicated, for they thought he was a lunatic!

Because religion is powerful and authoritative, the temptation to subvert it by those with political motives will be irresistible. The Bible and religion may be used by the religious, but their yoking will also be attempted by the irreligious, even those who have no religious commitment or who are anti-religious. The latter may also be tempted to blame religious factors as scapegoats, either in motivating adherence to a program of violence or in failing to support it adequately. It may also be used for diverting blame for unsavory outcomes. The discernment of such ploys is central to a critical and adequate appraisal of the appropriate role, function, and claims of religion. Unfortunately, even religious people have at times accepted such blame uncritically rather than considering them from a more accurate perspective. Jesus' admonition for his disciples to be wary as serpents and harmless as doves deserves consideration.

Harmless as Doves and Wary as Serpents

It may be that authentic, truth-seeking religion leads individuals or groups into violent conflicts in the world, but the majority of religious impulses evoke empathy for humankind. Self-sacrifice and commitments to justice and peace in the world are universal religious values. This being the case, a world with "no religion too" might not be a safer or a more humane one after all. While religion has indeed contributed extensively to violence against others, that has historically been the result of religious distortions; either a narcissistic religious focus, a misguided use of the Bible or Qur'an, or manipulation that yokes the personal and social power of religion to a particular political cause.[13]

Jesus, however, called his followers to love their neighbors (Matt. 22:39) and even to love their enemies, refusing to return harm for harm sustained (Matt. 5:38–48). Why is it that these clear admonitions have gone unheeded? Many explanations may be posed, but a central factor in Christians' sidestepping the clear commandment of Christ on nonviolence is the failure to distinguish authentic religious experiences and directions from false and manipulated ones. From the inside, religious adherents too easily fail to recognize their religious loyalties being used as pawns designed to legitimate violence. On this matter, another commandment of Jesus is especially relevant, within Christianity and beyond: his calling to be *wise as serpents* as well as harmless as doves (Matt. 10:16).

At a major consultation of the National Council of Churches of Christ in 1995, Eric Gritch called for a recovery of "serpentine wisdom" among the faithful.[14] Too readily, well-meaning Christians take the "harmless as doves" part of Jesus' dictum as an injunction to doormat passivity, when it is not. The goodness of God cannot be furthered by evil means, and active engagement is indeed called for, but not in unwary directions or counterproductive methods. Here furthering the active reign of God in the world involves challenging the *cosmos* not by imitating its evil ways of manipulation and force, but by providing a third alternative.[15] Elements of this wiser approach include the following:

- Challenge and expose concocted dilemmas that erode moral commitments against the use of violence and force. Ask why only two negative alternatives are being posed and assess critically whether there might be a third alternative providing a way forward.

- Examine critically appeals to the Bible or religion in which religious authority is leveraged toward the use of force or violence. Demand sound exegetical approaches to biblical citations, considering also alternative passages and interpretations, and ask whether appeals to religion represent the authentic teaching of that faith or a distortion of it.

- Expose the yoking of religious authority to politically motivated programs and platforms. Challenge the harnessing of religion as a pawn in a way that threatens to distort religious values at the expense of intrinsic religious loyalties. Consider whether there might be other parts of that religion's ethos that militate against such actions.

- Challenge the use of personal and sociological religious power in support of programs of destruction. Find ways of preserving the value of the sustaining power of religion without blaming religious factors for the ways it may be used by others.

- Join together within and across faith community boundaries, refusing to dehumanize other faiths or persons in the name of God's transcendent love, calling for authentic adherence to the highest of one's religious values. Especially within one's religious tradition, leaders and others should be willing to criticize and correct those religious spokespersons who yoke religious authority and the legitimation of violence or irreligious values and actions. Denounce quickly and loudly attempts to subvert the faithful in any direction unbecoming of the central ethos of that religious tradition and clarify who speaks for whom.

Conclusion

In sum, religion shares a great deal of blame for violence in the world, but it also deserves greater credit for good and redemption in the world, and these features should be included in any balanced appraisal of the subject. Of particular interest is the question of why religion gets used so deceptively as a pawn, functioning to legitimate violence, especially when those same religions tend to teach and work extensively against violence. Especially the faithful may tend to be unwitting in their failure to detect the manipulation and co-opting of religious power and equity, and on these matters religious people of all faiths need to be wary as serpents and harmless as doves. In so doing, incisive questions need to be asked, and tendencies to use religion as a pawn must be radically diminished. In all of this it is important to bear in mind that much of the yoking of religious political equity to one program or another might *not* be conducted by the authentically religious, and the same should be considered when evaluating claims that religion is the culpable cause of tragic outcomes. In both cases religion is used as a pawn and a scapegoat when neither is entirely deserved.

Notes

1. It is estimated that as many as 60 million people lost their lives in the First World War, including noncombatants, and most of these would have considered themselves "Christian." Further, casualties on all sides were inflicted by persons of Christian background, and it is the tragic irony of these facts that led Karl Barth and other Neo-Orthodox theologians to abandon the doctrine of modern liberalism that enlightened humanity had transcended Adam's fall. Indeed, in the Christian involvement in both world wars, the depravity of humanity was exposed as never before, precisely because of the fact that Christians were so adept at lethal warfare, even at the expense of killing other Christians! It was this stark reality that led in 1948 to discussions for forming the World Council of Churches (WCC) in hopes of minimizing the likelihood of persons of faith being subverted into the massive lethal ventures of modern warfare.

2. Indeed, Christianity has contributed greatly to the endeavor to make the world less violent. One of the reasons the World Council of Churches was organized was to see if Christianity could contribute to world peace and justice more than it had the first half of the twentieth century. At the first Assembly of the WCC in Amsterdam (1948), the report of Section IV (on "The Church and International Disorder") began with the following point: "War is contrary to the will of God." (See *Man's Disorder and God's Design: The Amsterdam Assembly Series* [New York: Harper & Brothers, Volume IV, 217–228].) See also the following statement signed by 78 Christian leaders entitled "The Church, the Christian and War," first produced in *Fellowship* XIV, No. 8 (1948, 17–24) but reprinted in *A Declaration of Peace*, edited by Douglas Gwyn, George Hunsinger, Eugene F. Roop, and John Howard Yoder (Scottsdale: Herald Press, 1991, 79–91). In these and many other statements, Christian leaders have been the most insistent on nonviolent responses to correcting injustice.

3. See, for instance, the argument of Cleo Buxton, who argues that Christians serving in the military contribute to its humane treatment of adversaries and civilians ("Moral Conduct in Combat," in *Command* 38, No. 1, 1998, 20–22).

4. See James W. Fowler, *Stages of Faith: The Psychology of Human Development and the Quest for Meaning* (San Francisco: Harper & Row, 1981). On the Mythic-Literal stage of faith development, people are especially concerned with fairness and justice, giving people what they deserve.

5. See especially the treatment of Jesus' challenging of ritual purity in John K. Riches, *Jesus and the Transformation of Judaism* (London: Darton, Longman & Todd, 1980).

6. See the companion essay within this collection: "From Conquest to the Teachings of Jesus: How Can the Same God Command Both Genocide and the Love of Enemies?"

7. In 1 Samuel 8, Israel's lust for a king like other nations is presented not as the abandonment of Samuel and the prophetic system of leadership (even though it was); it is portrayed as the abandonment of God and theocracy proper (see Paul N. Anderson, *The Christology of the Fourth Gospel: Its Unity and Disunity in the Light of John 6* [Valley Forge: Trinity Press International, 1997, 178, 229, 239]). Moralizing paragraphs punctuate the rest of the Samuel's narration of Israel's history with the following laments: This is why the kingdom eventually fell apart—Israel lusted for a king (envying the other nations), and God gave them their desire, tragic though it was. Along with standing armies, chariots, and royal entourage, Israel lost its sons and daughters to the king's service and became encumbered with burdensome taxation.

8. See Gideon's example, for instance, in Judges 7. Gideon reduced his army from 32,000 to 300, and the enemy was successfully routed, owing to

an ingenious surprise attack at night—an indication of Yahweh's fighting for Israel rather than its fighting on its own.

9. These were three messianic pretenders who arose in Palestine within two and a half decades after the death of Jesus. Josephus mentions their movements but also distinguishes John the Baptist as an authentic prophet. For more on Jesus' contradistinction from these first-century figures, see Paul N. Anderson, "Jesus and Peace," in *The Churches Peace Witness*, edited by Barbara Gingerich and Marlin Miller (Grand Rapids: Eerdmans, 1994, 104–130, especially 105–109).

10. Consider the gripping Broadway musical *Civil War*, where all sides of the conflict are portrayed graphically. For the appropriation of biblical themes in the conflict, consider the songs "By the Sword" and "Judgment Day."

11. See the fuller treatment of this theme in "Jesus and Peace" by Paul N. Anderson, especially 109–120.

12. See Ulrich Mauser, *The Gospel of Peace: A Scriptural Message for Today's World* (Louisville: Westminster/John Knox, 1991), where the Good News of Christ is contrasted to the conducting of violence, especially where weapons of mass destruction are involved.

13. A classic example of the contrast between using religion as a pawn and adhering to the heart of one's religious core is the contrast between the ordinary German Christians, on the one hand, and the Confessing Christians, on the other, in Germany of the 1930s and 1940s. Hitler's motivations cannot be construed adequately as authentic religious concerns; rather, he used Christianity as a tool in his nationalistic expansion, distorting the religion he co-opted. On the other hand, the Barmen Declaration of 1934 sought to recover the center of Christian faith and practice, the teaching and example of Christ; and its adherents were willing to suffer for their adherence to the truth as they understood it. One thing that is inexcusable about the subversion of Christian Germany during the rise and fall of the Third Reich is the way that even academics and biblical theologians did not oppose the misappropriation of texts and theological authority. This fact stands as a dark enigma in the history of biblical interpretation and theology.

14. The NCCC-USA Faith and Order Consultation, called "The Fragmentation of the Church and its Unity in Peacemaking" was held at the Notre Dame Joan B. Kroc Institute for International Peace Studies on June 13–17, 1995. The "Learnings" in the final report include this paragraph under point 8:

> As Christians, many of us would endorse—instead of "fight or flight"—Jesus's way of creative nonviolence which confronts enemies by unmasking sin and injustice. But we need to know just how to do this. Formation or training in peacemaking, then, is important on an ongoing basis, not just in times of crisis or war. Some consultation participants recalled the missionary injunction of Jesus to "be wise as ser-

pents and innocent as doves" (Matt. 10:16) as a call for healing and a summons to sharp discernment and vigilance against the sin of playing God (Gen. 3:5). Others recalled means and instruments of spiritual formation which can be drawn from Christian history—monastic discipline, penitential discipline for those who have killed as soldiers or guardians of the peace, or critical involvement in the affairs of the world.

15. On this matter, see the Powers Trilogy by Walter Wink, especially the award-winning *Engaging the Powers: Discernment and Resistance in a World of Domination* (Minneapolis: Fortress, 1992).

Afterword

Chris E. Stout

Series Editor
Contemporary Psychology

Religion and politics. Lightning rods and powder kegs. Such are the thoughts and images that may be conjured up reviewing this dynamic collection of works. Few topics can stir more opinion, bring more varied viewpoints, stimulate more debate and contention, or spark more potentially volatile reactions than discussions of religion as a motivator for murder, terrorism, and even war. Dr. Ellens has successfully assembled some of the best and the brightest contemporary scholars to expound on this most controversial, yet classically delicate, relationship.

So it is fitting that this set of volumes launches the new Praeger Series in Contemporary Psychology. In this series of books, experts from various disciplines will peer through the lens of psychology to examine human behavior as this new millennium dawns. Including modern behaviors rooted back through history, the topics will include positive subjects like creativity and resilience, as well as examinations of humanity's current psychological ills, with abuse, suicide, murder, and terrorism among those. At all times, the goal of the series remains constant—to offer innovative ideas, provocative considerations, and useful beginnings to better understand human behavior.

Developing a collection of the size, substance, and quality shown in *The Destructive Power of Religion* is no easy task. Indeed, I first met Dr. Ellens when he contributed to my earlier, similar four-volume set,

The Psychology of Terrorism (Westport: Praeger, 2002). The goal was to organize well-researched content and weave it into a fabric appealing to readers of differing backgrounds and interests. Certainly, this goal was achieved in Dr. Ellens' volumes.

While no editor of such a work wishes for homogenization of the content, it becomes a fine balance between maintaining thematic consistency among chapters with a healthy tension between differing perspectives. Therein again, this collection succeeds.

The first time I had the honor and the pleasure of meeting Dr. Ellens, he struck me as a virtual Roman candle of intellectual enthusiasm. Therefore, it comes as no surprise that he has been successful in gathering some of the greatest thinkers on the topic from around the world, including a Pulitzer Prize–winning author.

There is potential for these volumes to unleash a Niagara of discussion and debate.

Ideally, there is potential for these volumes to spark understanding that will trigger solutions to the problem of destructive powers unleashed in the name of religion.

This is to Dr. Ellens' credit, and it is to us readers' marked benefit.

INDEX

ABOUT THE SERIES

As this new millennium dawns, humankind has evolved—some would argue has devolved—exhibiting new and old behaviors that fascinate, infuriate, delight, or fully perplex those of us seeking answers to the question, "Why?" In this series, experts from various disciplines peer through the lens of psychology telling us answers they see for questions of human behavior. Their topics may range from humanity's psychological ills—addictions, abuse, suicide, murder, and terrorism among them—to works focused on positive subjects including intelligence, creativity, athleticism, and resilience. Regardless of the topic, the goal of this series remains constant—to offer innovative ideas, provocative considerations, and useful beginnings to better understand human behavior.

Chris E. Stout
Series Editor

About the Series Editor
and Advisory Board

CHRIS E. STOUT, Psy.D., MBA, holds a joint governmental and academic appointment in Northwestern University Medical School and serves as Illinois' first chief of psychological services. He served as an NGO special representative to the United Nations, was appointed by the U.S. Department of Commerce as a Baldridge examiner, and served as an adviser to the White House for both political parties. He was appointed to the World Economic Forum's Global Leaders of Tomorrow. He has published and presented more than 300 papers and 29 books. His works have been translated into six languages.

BRUCE E. BONECUTTER, Ph.D., is director of behavioral services at the Elgin Community Mental Health Center, the Illinois Department of Human Services state hospital, serving adults in greater Chicago. He is also a clinical assistant professor of psychology at the University of Illinois at Chicago. A clinical psychologist specializing in health, consulting, and forensic psychology, Bonecutter is also a longtime member of the American Psychological Association Taskforce on Children and the Family.

JOSEPH A. FLAHERTY, M.D., is chief of psychiatry at the University of Illinois Hospital, a professor of psychiatry at the University of Illinois College of Medicine, and a professor of community health science at the University of Illinois College of Public Health. He is a founding member of the Society for the Study of Culture and Psychiatry. Dr. Flaherty has been a consultant to the World Health Organization, to the National Institutes of Mental Health, and also to the Falk Institute in Jerusalem.

MICHAEL HOROWITZ, Ph.D., is president and professor of clinical psychology at the Chicago School of Professional Psychology, one of the nation's leading not-for-profit graduate schools of psychology. Earlier, he served as dean and professor of the Arizona School of Professional Psychology. A clinical psychologist practicing independently since 1987, his work has focused on psychoanalysis, intensive individual therapy, and couples therapy. He has provided disaster mental health services to the American Red Cross. Dr. Horowitz's special interests include the study of fatherhood.

SHELDON I. MILLER, M.D., is a professor of psychiatry at Northwestern University and director of the Stone Institute of Psychiatry at Northwestern Memorial Hospital. He is also director of the American Board of Psychiatry and Neurology, director of the American Board of Emergency Medicine, and director of the Accreditation Council for Graduate Medical Education. Dr. Miller is also an examiner for the American Board of Psychiatry and Neurology. He is founding editor of the *American Journal of Addictions* and founding chairman of the American Psychiatric Association's Committee on Alcoholism.

DENNIS P. MORRISON, Ph.D., is chief executive officer at the Center for Behavioral Health in Indiana, the first behavioral health company ever to win the JCAHO Codman Award for excellence in the use of outcomes management to achieve health care quality improvement. He is president of the board of directors for the Community Healthcare Foundation in Bloomington and has been a member of the board of directors for the American College of Sports Psychology. He has served as a consultant to agencies including the Ohio Department of Mental Health, Tennessee Association of Mental Health Organizations, Oklahoma Psychological Association, the North Carolina Council of Community Mental Health Centers, and the National Center for Health Promotion in Michigan.

WILLIAM H. REID, M.D., MPH, is a clinical and forensic psychiatrist and consultant to attorneys and courts throughout the United States. He is clinical professor of psychiatry at the University of Texas Health Science Center. Dr. Miller is also an adjunct professor of psychiatry at Texas A&M College of Medicine and Texas Tech

University School of Medicine, as well as a clinical faculty member at the Austin Psychiatry Residency Program. He is chairman of the Scientific Advisory Board and medical adviser to the Texas Depressive & Manic-Depressive Association, as well as an examiner for the American Board of Psychiatry and Neurology. He has served as president of the American Academy of Psychiatry and the Law, as chairman of the Research Section for an International Conference on the Psychiatric Aspects of Terrorism, and as medical director for the Texas Department of Mental Health and Mental Retardation.

About the Editor and Advisers

J. HAROLD ELLENS is a Research Scholar at the University of Michigan, Department of Near Eastern Studies. He is a retired Presbyterian theologian and ordained minister, a retired U.S. Army Colonel, and a retired professor of philosophy, theology, and psychology. He has authored, coauthored, and/or edited 86 books and 165 professional journal articles. He served 15 years as Executive Director of the Christian Association for Psychological Studies and as founding editor and Editor-in-Chief of the *Journal of Psychology and Christianity*. He holds a Ph.D. from Wayne State University in the Psychology of Human Communication, a Ph.D.(Cand.) from the University of Michigan in biblical and Near Eastern studies, and master's degrees from Calvin Theological Seminary, Princeton Theological Seminary, and the University of Michigan. He was born in Michigan, grew up in a Dutch-German immigrant community, and determined at age seven to enter the Christian ministry as a means to help his people with the great amount of suffering he perceived all around him. His life's work has focused on the interface of psychology and religion. He is the founder and director of the New American Lyceum.

LeROY H. ADEN is Professor Emeritus of Pastoral Theology at the Lutheran Theological Seminary in Philadelphia, Pennsylvania. He taught full-time at the seminary from 1967 to 1994 and part-time from 1994 to 2001. He served as Visiting Lecturer at Princeton

Theological Seminary, Princeton, New Jersey on a regular basis. In 2002 he coauthored *Preaching God's Compassion: Comforting Those Who Suffer* with Robert G. Hughes. Previously, he edited four books in a Psychology and Christianity series with J. Harold Ellens and David G. Benner. He served on the Board of Directors of the Christian Association for Psychological Studies for six years.

ALFRED J. EPPENS was born and raised in Michigan. He attended Western Michigan University, studying history under Ernst A. Breisach, and receiving a B.A. (Summa cum Laude) and an M.A. He continued his studies at the University of Michigan, where he was awarded a J.D. in 1981. He is an Adjunct Professor at Oakland University and at Oakland Community College, as well as an active church musician and director. He is a director and officer of the Michigan Center for Early Christian Studies, as well as a founding member of the New American Lyceum.

EDMUND S. MELTZER was born in Brooklyn, New York. He attended the University of Chicago, where he received his B.A. in Near Eastern Languages and Civilizations. He pursued graduate studies at the University of Toronto, earning his M.A. and Ph.D. in Near Eastern Studies. He worked in Egypt as a member of the Akhenaten Temple Project/East Karnak Excavation and as a Fellow of the American Research Center. Returning to the United States, he taught at the University of North Carolina–Chapel Hill and at the Claremont Graduate School (now University), where he served as Associate Chair of the Department of Religion. Meltzer taught at Northeast Normal University in Changchun from 1990 to 1996. He has been teaching German and Spanish in the Wisconsin public school system and English as a Second Language in summer programs of the University of Wisconsin–Stevens Point. He has lectured extensively and published numerous articles and reviews in scholarly journals. He has contributed to and edited a number of books and has presented at many national and international conferences.

JACK MILES is the author of the 1995 Pulitzer Prize winner *God: A Biography.* After publishing *Christ: A Crisis in the Life of God* in 2001, Miles was named a MacArthur Fellow in 2002. Now Senior Adviser to the President at J. Paul Getty Trust, he earned a Ph.D. in Near Eastern languages from Harvard University in 1971 and has been a Regents Lecturer at the University of California, Director of the Humanities Center at Claremont Graduate University, and Visiting

Professor of Humanities at the California Institute of Technology. He has authored articles that have appeared in numerous national publications, including the *Atlantic Monthly*, the *New York Times*, the *Boston Globe*, the *Washington Post*, and the *Los Angeles Times*, where he served for 10 years as Literary Editor and as a member of the newspaper's editorial board.

WAYNE G. ROLLINS is Professor Emeritus of Biblical Studies at Assumption College, Worcester, Massachusetts, and Adjunct Professor of Scripture at Hartford Seminary, Hartford, Connecticut. His writings include *The Gospels: Portraits of Christ* (1964), *Jung and the Bible* (1983), and *Soul and Psyche: The Bible in Psychological Perspective* (1999). He received his Ph.D. in New Testament Studies from Yale University and is the founder and former chairman (1990–2000) of the Society of Biblical Literature Section on Psychology and Biblical Studies.

GRANT R. SHAFER was educated at Wayne State University, Harvard University, and the University of Michigan, where he received his doctorate in Early Christianity. A summary of his dissertation, "St. Stephen and the Samaritans," was published in the proceedings of the 1996 meeting of the *Societe d'Etudes Samaritaines*. He has taught at Washtenaw Community College, Siena Heights University, and Eastern Michigan University. He is presently a Visiting Scholar at the University of Michigan.

ABOUT THE CONTRIBUTORS

LeROY H. ADEN is Professor Emeritus of Pastoral Theology at the Lutheran Theological Seminary in Philadelphia, Pennsylvania. He taught full-time at the seminary from 1967 to 1994 and part-time from 1994 to 2001. He served as Visiting Lecturer at Princeton Theological Seminary, Princeton, New Jersey, on a regular basis. In 2002 he coauthored *Preaching God's Compassion: Comforting Those Who Suffer* with Robert G. Hughes. Previously, he edited four books in a Psychology and Christianity series with J. Harold Ellens and David G. Benner. He served on the Board of Directors of the Christian Association for Psychological Studies for six years.

PAUL N. ANDERSON is Professor of Biblical and Quaker Studies and Chair of the Department of Religious Studies at George Fox University, where he has served since 1989 except for a year as a visiting professor at Yale Divinity School (1998–99). He is author of *The Christology of the Fourth Gospel: Its Unity and Disunity in the Light of John 6* and *Navigating the Living Waters of the Gospel of John: On Wading with Children and Swimming with Elephants*. In addition, he has written many essays on biblical and Quaker themes and is editor of *Quaker Religious Thought*. He serves on the steering committee of the Psychology and Biblical Studies Section of the Society of Biblical Literature and teaches the New Testament Interpretation course in the Psy.D. program of George Fox University. His Ph.D. in the New Testament is from Glasgow University (1989), his M.Div. is from the

Earlham School of Religion (1981), and his B.A. in psychology and B.A. in Christian ministries are from Malone College (1978).

DONALD CAPPS, Psychologist of Religion, is William Hart Felmeth Professor of Pastoral Theology at Princeton Theological Seminary. In 1989 he was awarded an honorary doctorate from the University of Uppsala, Sweden, in recognition of the importance of his publications. He served as president of the Society for the Scientific Study of Religion from 1990 to 1992. Among his many significant books are *Men, Religion, and Melancholia: James, Otto, Jung, Erikson and Freud; The Freudians on Religion: A Reader; Social Phobia: Alleviating Anxiety in an Age of Self-Promotion*; and *Jesus: A Psychological Biography*. He also authored *The Child's Song: The Religious Abuse of Children*.

RAFAEL CHODOS has been a practicing business litigation attorney in the Los Angeles area for nearly 25 years. He holds a B.A. in philosophy from UC–Berkeley (1964). He earned his way through college teaching Hebrew, Latin, and Greek, intending to become a rabbi. But after graduating from Berkeley he entered the then-fledgling computer software field, where he worked for 15 years. He founded his own software company, which developed expert systems and sold them to most of the Fortune 500 companies. He then returned to law school and received his J.D. from Boston University in 1977. He is the author of several articles on legal topics as well as topics relating to computers, software design, operations research, and artificial intelligence. He has authored two books: *The Jewish Attitude Toward Justice and Law* (1984) and *The Law of Fiduciary Duties* (2000).

JOHN J. COLLINS is Holmes Professor of Old Testament Criticism and Interpretation at Yale University. He previously taught at the University of Chicago and at Notre Dame. He received his Ph.D. from Harvard (1972). His more recent books include a commentary on *The Book of Daniel* (1993), *The Scepter and the Star: The Messiahs of the Dead Sea Scrolls* (1995), *Jewish Wisdom in the Hellenistic Age* (1997), *Apocalypticism in the Dead Sea Scrolls* (1997), *Seers, Sibyls, and Sages* (1997), *The Apocalyptic Imagination* (revised ed., 1998), and *Between Athens and Jerusalem: Jewish Identity in the Hellenistic Diaspora* (revised ed., 2000). He has served as editor of the *Journal of Biblical Literature*, as president of the Catholic Biblical Association (1997), and as president of the Society of Biblical Literature (2002).

CHARLES T. DAVIS III studied at Emory University with Dr. Norman Perrin, graduating with the B.D. and Ph.D. degrees after special study at the University of Heidelberg. Although specializing in New Testament Studies, he has also published articles and book reviews in the fields of American religion, computers and the humanities, philosophy, and Buddhist studies. He is the author of the book *Speaking of Jesus* and currently serves as Professor of Philosophy and Religion at Appalachian State University, where he teaches biblical literature, Islam, and seminars on symbols and healing.

SIMON JOHN DE VRIES, an ordained minister in the Presbyterian Church, was born in Denver. He served in the U.S. Marines during World War II as a First Lieutenant, pastored three churches, and received his Th.D. from Union Theological Seminary in New York in Old Testament Studies before beginning seminary teaching in 1962. He is the author of numerous scholarly articles and reviews in the field of Old Testament exegesis and theology in addition to nine books, the latest of which is *Shining White Knight, A Spiritual Memoir.*

J. HAROLD ELLENS is a Research Scholar at the University of Michigan, Department of Near Eastern Studies. He is a retired Presbyterian theologian and ordained minister, a retired U.S. Army Colonel, and a retired professor of philosophy, theology, and psychology. He has authored, coauthored, and/or edited 86 books and 165 professional journal articles. He served 15 years as Executive Director of the Christian Association for Psychological Studies and as founding editor and Editor-in-Chief of the *Journal of Psychology and Christianity.* He holds a Ph.D. from Wayne State University in the Psychology of Human Communication, a Ph.D.(Cand.) from the University of Michigan in biblical and Near Eastern studies, and master's degrees from Calvin Theological Seminary, Princeton Theological Seminary, and the University of Michigan. His publications include *God's Grace and Human Health* and *Psychotheology: Key Issues,* as well as chapters in *Moral Obligation and the Military, Baker Encyclopedia of Psychology, Abingdon Dictionary of Pastoral Care, Jesus as Son of Man, The Literary Character: A Progression of Images,* and *God's Word for Our World* (2 vols.).

MARK ADAM ELLIOTT holds M.Div. and Th.M. degrees from the University of Toronto and a Ph.D. in New Testament from the University of Aberdeen, U.K. His area of concentration is Christian origins in Judaism. His first major publication was *Survivors of Israel:*

A Reconsideration of the Theology of Pre-Christian Judaism (2000). He has served as pastor in both the United Church of Canada and Baptist Convention of Ontario and Quebec, and taught biblical studies in two Ontario universities. Presently, he is executive director of the *Institute for Restorationist and Revisionist Studies* (www.irrstudies.org) and carries out research at the University of Toronto.

ALFRED J. EPPENS was born and raised in Michigan. He attended Western Michigan University, studying history under Ernst A. Breisach, and receiving a B.A. (Summa cum Laude) and an M.A. He continued his studies at the University of Michigan, where he was awarded a J.D. in 1981. He is an Adjunct Professor at Oakland University and at Oakland Community College, as well as an active church musician and director. He is a director and officer of the Michigan Center for Early Christian Studies, as well as a founding member of the New American Lyceum.

JACK T. HANFORD is a Professor Emeritus of Biomedical Ethics at Ferris State University in Michigan. He is a member of the American Philosophical Association, the American Academy of Religion, the Christian Association for Psychological Studies, and the Association of Moral Education. He is also an associate of the Hastings Center, the foremost center for biomedical ethics, the American Society of Bioethics and Humanities, the Center for Bioethics and Human Dignity, and the Kennedy Institute of Ethics, as well as several other societies. He has published many professional articles, including those in *Religious Education,* the *Journal for the Scientific Study of Religion,* the *Journal of Psychology and Christianity,* and the *Journal of Pastoral Psychology, Ethics, and Medicine.* His highest degree is a Th.D.

RONALD B. JOHNSON has worked as a clinical psychologist in private practice for 30 years. His academic background includes a B.S. at the University of Wisconsin, M.Div. at Denver Seminary, and M.A. and Ph.D. in psychology from the University of Iowa. He is currently working on a Post-Doctorate in Neuropsychology. He holds licenses in several states and in Canada. His interests are in therapy with men and children, the psychology of men, psychological evaluations, and forensic psychology. He writes in the areas of "friendly diagnosis," which includes personality type, intelligences, gender differences, personal development, and theological-psychological integration.

D. ANDREW KILLE received his Ph.D. from the Graduate Theological Union in Berkeley in Psychological Biblical Criticism.

He is the author of *Psychological Biblical Criticism: Genesis 3 as a Test Case* (Fortress Press, 2001). A former pastor, Dr. Kille teaches psychology and spirituality in the San Francisco Bay area and is principal consultant for Revdak Consulting. He has served as cochair of the Psychology and Biblical Studies Section of the Society of Biblical Literature and on the steering committee of the Person, Culture, and Religion Group of the American Academy of Religion.

CASSANDRA M. KLYMAN is Assistant Clinical Professor at Wayne State University College of Medicine, where she teaches Ethics, and the Psychology of Women to residents in psychiatry and supervises their clinical cases. Klyman is also a lecturer at the Michigan Psychoanalytic Institute and chairperson of the Michigan Psychoanalytic Society's Committee on Psychoanalysis in Medicine. She is a Life-Fellow of the American Medical Association, the American Psychiatric Association, and the College of Forensic Examiners. She is also Past-President of the Michigan Psychiatric Society. She has published papers nationally and internationally in peer-reviewed journals. Most of her time is spent in the private practice of psychoanalysis and psychoanalytically informed psychotherapy. She earned her M.D. at Wayne State University.

EDSON T. LEWIS is an ordained minister (emeritus) of the Christian Reformed Church. During 47 years of active ministry, he served a suburban New York City congregation for 8 years, an inner-city parish in Hoboken, New Jersey, for 12 years, and the campus of the Ohio State University, Columbus, Ohio, for 17 years. He is a graduate of Calvin Theological Seminary (B.D.), New York Theological Seminary (STM), and Trinity Lutheran Seminary (D.Min). During the 1990s, he played a key role in the revitalization of the church's higher education ministries in the United States and Canada. His participation in antipoverty and peacemaking ministries has been extensive.

ZENON LOTUFO JR. is a Presbyterian minister (Independent Presbyterian Church of Brazil), a philosopher, and a psychotherapist, specializing in Transactional Analysis. He has lectured for undergraduate and graduate courses at universities in São Paulo, Brazil. He coordinates the course of specialization in Pastoral Psychology of the Christian Association of Psychologists and Psychiatrists of Brazil. He is the author of the books *Relações Humanas* (Human Relations) and *Disfunções no Comportamento Organizacional* (Dysfunctions in

Organizational Behavior), and coauthor of *O Potencial Humano* (Human Potential). He has also authored numerous journal articles.

CHARLES MABEE is Full Professor and Director of the Masters of Divinity Program at the Ecumenical Theological Seminary in Detroit, Michigan. He is also a Visiting Lecturer and United Ministries in Higher Education Ecumenical Campus Minister at Oakland University, where he founded two subsidiary institutions, the Institute for the Third Millennium and the Detroit Parliament for World Religions. He is a founding member of the Colloquium on Violence and Religion, chairman of the American Biblical Hermeneutics Section of the Society of Biblical Literature/American Academy of Religion, southeast region, and has been Chair of the Department of Religious Studies at Marshall University in West Virginia. Early in his career, he was a Research Associate for the Institute for Antiquity and Christianity at Claremont Graduate University.

J. CÁSSIO MARTINS is a Presbyterian minister (Presbyterian Church of Brazil) and a clinical psychologist. As a minister, he held pastorates in São Paulo and Rio de Janeiro. As a psychologist, he runs his own clinic in São Paulo. He holds a Master of Theology degree from Union Theological Seminary, Richmond, Virginia. He is one of the coordinators of the course of specialization in Pastoral Psychology of the Christian Association of Psychologists and Psychiatrists of Brazil. He has taught psychology at the Methodist University in São Paulo, as well as courses and seminars to pastors and psychologists throughout Brazil, leading the creation of and exercising the Office of Pastoral Support of his denomination until July 2002. He has written numerous articles on psychology and theology.

MARTIN E. MARTY is the Fairfax M. Cone Distinguished Professor Emeritus at the University of Chicago Divinity School, where he taught for 35 years and where the Martin Marty center has since been founded to promote "public religion" endeavors. An ordained minister in the Evangelical Lutheran Church of America, he is well known in the popular media and has been called the nation's "most influential interpretor of religion." He is the author of 50 books, including *The One and the Many: America's Search for a Common God,* as well as a 3-volume work entitled *Modern American Religion.* He has written more than 4,300 articles, essays, reviews and papers. Among his many honors and awards are the National Humanities Medal, the National Book Award, the Medal of the American

Academy of Arts and Sciences, and the Distinguished Service Medal of the Association of Theological Schools. He has served as president of the American Academy of Religion, the American Society of Church History and the American Catholic Historical Association. Marty has received 67 honorary doctorates.

CHERYL McGUIRE is a member of the Colloquium on Violence and Religion, and her work was presented at Purdue University during the colloquium in 2002. She is a graduate of the University of Michigan master's program in Ancient Civilizations and Biblical Studies and is now involved with postgraduate work at the University of Detroit.

EDMUND S. MELTZER was born in Brooklyn, New York, and attended Erasmus Hall High School. He developed a passion for the ancient world, especially Egypt, and attended the University of Chicago, where he received his B.A. in Near Eastern Languages and Civilizations. He pursued graduate studies at the University of Toronto, earning his M.A. and Ph.D. in Near Eastern Studies and working in Egypt as a member of the Akhenaten Temple Project/East Karnak Excavation. He also worked as a Fellow of the American Research Center in Egypt. After returning to the United States, he taught at the University of North Carolina–Chapel Hill and at the Claremont Graduate School (now University), where he served as Associate Chair of the Department of Religion. In 1990, Meltzer and his family traveled to China, where he taught at Northeast Normal University in Changchun for six years. Subsequently he has been teaching German and Spanish in the Wisconsin public school system and English as a Second Language in the summer programs of the University of Wisconsin–Stevens Point. He has lectured extensively and published numerous articles and reviews in scholarly journals. He has contributed to and edited a number of books and has presented at many national and international conferences.

JACK MILES is the author of the 1996 Pulitzer Prize winner, *God: A Biography*. After publishing *Christ: A Crisis in the Life of God* in 2001, Miles was named a MacArthur Fellow in 2002. Now Senior Adviser to the President at J. Paul Getty Trust, he earned a Ph.D. in Near Eastern languages from Harvard University in 1971 and has been a Regents Lecturer at the University of California, Director of the Humanities Center at Claremont Graduate University, and Visiting Professor of Humanities at the California Institute of Technology. He has authored articles that have appeared in numerous national publications, including the *Atlantic Monthly*, the *New York Times*, the *Boston Globe*, the *Washington Post*, and the *Los Angeles Times*, where he served for 10 years as Literary Editor and as a member of the newspaper's editorial board.

MICHAEL WILLETT NEWHEART is Associate Professor of New Testament Language and Literature at Howard University School of Divinity, where he has taught since 1991. He holds a Ph.D. from Southern Baptist Theological Seminary and is the author of *Wisdom Christology in the Fourth Gospel; Word and Soul: A Psychological, Literary, and Cultural Reading of the Fourth Gospel*, and numerous articles on the psychological and literary interpretation of the New Testament.

DIRK H. ODENDAAL is South African and was born in what is now called the Province of the Eastern Cape. He spent much of his youth in the Transkei in the town of Umtata, where his parents were teachers at a seminary. He trained as a minister at the Stellenbosch Seminary for the Dutch Reformed Church and was ordained in 1983 in the Dutch Reformed Church in Southern Africa. He transferred to East London in 1988 to minister to members of the United Reformed Church in Southern Africa in one of the huge suburbs for Xhosa-speaking people. He received his doctorate (D.Litt.) in 1992 at the University of Port Elizabeth in Semitic Languages. At present, he is enrolled in a Master's Degree course in Counseling Psychology at Rhodes University.

RICARDO J. QUINONES is Professor Emeritus of Comparative Literature at Claremont McKenna College. He is author of *Renaissance Discovery of Time* (1972), *Mapping Literary Modernism* (1985), *The Changes of Cain: Violence and the Lost Brother in Cain and Abel Literature* (1991), and several volumes on Dante, including *Foundation Sacrifice in Dante's Commedia* (1996). He is also Founding Director of the Gould Center for the Humanities.

ILONA N. RASHKOW is Professor of Judaic Studies, Women's Studies, and Comparative Literature at the State University of New York, Stony Brook. She has also been the visiting chair in Judaic Studies at the University of Alabama. Among her publications are *Upon the Dark Places: Sexism and Anti-Semitism in English Renaissance Bible Translation* (1990), *The Phallacy of Genesis* (1993), and *Taboo or Not Taboo?: Human Sexuality and the Hebrew Bible* (2000). Her areas of interest include psychoanalytic literary theory as applied to the Hebrew Bible and, more generally, as applied to Judaic studies, religious studies, feminist literary criticism, and women's studies.

WAYNE G. ROLLINS is Professor Emeritus of Biblical Studies at Assumption College, Worcester, Massachusetts, and Adjunct Professor of Scripture at Hartford Seminary, Hartford, Connecticut. His writings include *The Gospels: Portraits of Christ* (1964), *Jung and the Bible* (1983), and *Soul and Psyche: The Bible in Psychological Perspective* (1999). He received his Ph.D. in New Testament Studies from Yale University and is the founder and former chairman (1990–2000) of the Society of Biblical Literature Section on Psychology and Biblical Studies.

GRANT R. SHAFER was educated at Wayne State University, Harvard University, and the University of Michigan, where he received his doctorate in Early Christianity. A summary of his dissertation, "St. Stephen and the Samaritans," was published in the proceedings of the 1996 meeting of the *Societe d'Etudes Samaritaines*. He has taught at Washtenaw Community College, Siena Heights University, and Eastern Michigan University. He is presently a Visiting Scholar at the University of Michigan.

DONALD E. SLOAT, is licensed as a psychologist in Arizona, California, and Michigan. His training includes a B.A from Bethel College (Indiana), an M.A. from Michigan State University, and a Ph.D. from the University of Southern Mississippi. Since 1963, he has devoted his professional life to helping damaged people find healing for their pain. He has worked most often with people who have been trauma victims, including those with post-traumatic stress disorder (PTSD) and other effects of physical, emotional, verbal, sexual, and spiritual abuse. He has worked with Detroit's Youth for Christ, with outpatient drug-treatment programs, a community health center, psychiatric hospitals, and in his current private practice. He authored two books detailing spiritual abuse, *The Dangers of Growing Up in a Christian Home* and *Growing Up Holy and Wholly*. In addition, he has presented workshops on spiritual abuse and shame at national conferences. His professional affiliations include the American Psychological Association, American Association of Christian Counselors, Christian Association for Psychological Studies, and the International Society for the Study of Dissociation. He has served on the advisory board of the National Association for Christian Recovery. His private practice is in Michigan.

MACK C. STIRLING was born in 1952 in St. George, Utah. He was a Mormon missionary in Norway from 1971 to 1973 and graduated from Brigham Young University studies in chemistry in 1975. He received the M.D. degree from Johns Hopkins University in 1979 and thereafter underwent specialty training at the University of Michigan, where he was Assistant Professor of Thoracic Surgery from 1987 to 1990. Since 1990, he has been Director of Cardiothoracic Surgery at Munson Medical Center in Traverse City, Michigan.

ARCHBISHOP DESMOND TUTU is best known for his contribution to the cause of racial justice in South Africa, a contribution for which he was recognized with the Nobel Peace Prize in 1984. Archbishop Tutu has been an ordained priest since 1961. Among his many accomplishments are being named the first black General Secretary of the South African Council of Churches and serving as archbishop of Cape Town. Once a high school teacher in South Africa, he has also taught theology in college and holds honorary degrees from universities including Harvard, Oxford, Columbia, and Kent State. In addition to the Nobel Peace Prize, he has been awarded the Order for Meritorious Service presented by President Nelson Mandela, the Archbishop of Canterbury's Award for outstanding service to the Anglican community, the Family of Man Gold Medal Award, and the Martin Luther King Jr. Non-Violent Peace Award. The many publications Archbishop Tutu has authored, coauthored, or made contributions to include *No Future without Forgiveness* (2000), *Crying in the Wilderness* (1986), and *Rainbow People of God: The Making of a Peaceful Revolution* (1996).

JOHAN S. VOS is Associate Professor of New Testament, Faculty of Theology, Vrije Universiteit te Amsterdam, The Netherlands. He was born in Gouda, The Netherlands. He studied theology at the University of Utrecht, the University of Tübingen, and Union Theological Seminary in New York. He received his Th.D. from the University of Utrecht in 1973 and was Assistant Professor of New Testament Studies at the University of Leiden in 1974 and 1975. From 1975 to 1981, he worked as a social therapist at a psychiatric clinic for delinquents in Nijmegen. He has been Associate Professor at Vrije Universiteit since 1981 and has published many articles on New Testament subjects. He recently authored *Die Kunst der Argumentation bei Paulus* (The Art of Reasoning in the Letters of Paul), WUNT 149, 2002.

WALTER WINK is Professor of Biblical Interpretation at Auburn Theological Seminary in New York City. Previously, he was a parish minister and taught at Union Theological Seminary in New York City. In 1989 and 1990, he was a Peace Fellow at the United States Institute of Peace. His most recent book is *The Human Being: The Enigma of the Son of the Man* (2001). He is author of a trilogy, *The Powers: Naming the Powers: The Language of Power in the New Testament* (1984), *Unmasking the Powers: The Invisible Forces That Determine Human Existence* (1986), and *Engaging the Powers: Discernment and Resistance in a World of Domination* (1992). *Engaging the Powers* received three Religious Book of the Year awards for 1993, from Pax Christi, the Academy of Parish Clergy, and the Midwestern Independent Publishers Association. His other works include *Jesus and Nonviolence* (2003), *The Powers That Be* (1998), and *When the Powers Fall: Reconciliation in the Healing of Nations* (1998). He has published more than 250 journal articles.